I0797823

Gratefully & Affectionately

For my parents, Éamonn and Mary

Gratefully & Affectionately

Mary Lavin & The New Yorker

Gráinne Hurley

NEW ISLAND

GRATEFULLY AND AFFECTIONATELY

First published in 2025 by
New Island Books
Glenshesk House
10 Richview Office Park
Clonskeagh
Dublin D14 V8C4
Republic of Ireland
newisland.ie

Print ISBN: 978-1-84840-929-3
eBook ISBN: 978-1-84840-930-9

British Library Cataloguing in Publication Data. A CIP catalogue record for this book is available from the British Library.

Product safety queries can be addressed to New Island Books at the above postal address or at info@newisland.ie.

Set in 11.5 on 14.25pt in Bembo
Typeset by JVR Creative India
Proofread by Susan McKeever
Cover design by Emer Brennan, emerbrennan.com
Cover images: (front) Mary Lavin by Evelyn Hofer © Estate of Evelyn Hofer; (back) Rachel MacKenzie in a Bread Loaf Writers' Conference staff photo, 1952, courtesy of Middlebury College Special Collections.
Index by Eileen O'Neill
Printed by L&C Printing Group, Poland, lcprinting.eu

The paper used in this book comes from the wood pulp of sustainably managed forests.

New Island received financial assistance from The Arts Council (An Chomhairle Ealaíon), Dublin, Ireland.

New Island Books is a member of Publishing Ireland.

10 9 8 7 6 5 4 3 2 1

Contents

Acknowledgements

I would like to express my sincere gratitude to Mary Lavin's family who have been incredibly generous, encouraging and supportive of my research, with special thanks to Kathleen MacMahon and James Ryan.

I am deeply grateful to The Ireland Funds and Princess Grace Irish Library in Monaco for appointing me as the writer-in-residence at the library in 2023, which afforded me valuable time to work on the book. I would especially like to thank Her Excellency Anne-Marie Boisbouvier, Paula Farquharson, Géraldine Lance, Mark Armstrong, Peter K. Murphy, Síle Jackson, Siobhán Gallagher, Nicki Lynch, Hannah Brogan, the Monaco Ireland Arts Society's talented trio Lynn Sharpe, Miranda Dawe and Nick O'Connor and Caroline B. Heafey at Glucksman Ireland House, NYU.

Sincere thanks to those who have promoted my research including Brian Donnelly, Professor Anne Fogarty, Professor Elke D'hoker, Professor Margaret Kelleher and Martin Doyle. I am very grateful to my colleagues at TU Dublin for all of their support.

I wish to express my appreciation to the following people who shared their memories of Mary Lavin with me: Charles McGrath, Cormac O'Malley, Claire T. Hartman, Seán Gilligan, Elmah Sweetman and the late Elizabeth Cullinan and Caroline Walsh.

I greatly appreciate the invaluable assistance of the librarians and archivists at the following institutions: Binghampton University Libraries Special Collections; Department of Special Collections, Princeton University Library; Howard Gotlieb Archival Research Center, Boston University Libraries, Massachusetts; James Hardiman Library, National University of Galway; Manuscripts and Archives Division; the New York Public Library, Astor, Lenox and Tilden Foundations; National Library of Ireland; University of Iowa Libraries, Iowa. In particular I want to thank Eugene Roche at the James Joyce Library, Special Collections, University College Dublin for being incredibly helpful and accommodating.

It has been an absolute pleasure to work with everyone at New Island Books. Huge thanks to Aoife K. Walsh and Djinn von Noorden for believing in the book from the get-go and for their expert guidance, patience and enthusiasm throughout.

My heartfelt gratitude to the inspiring ladies in my reading group for cheering me on, with special mention to the late Eileen Griffiths who was a huge admirer of Lavin's work.

I am immensely grateful to my family and friends, who have been so supportive of this book's journey with particular thanks to Dr Emer McManus, Nicole O'Neill and Valerie Sorohan. I am indebted to my parents, my brother, Éamonn, and my niece, Céleste. Above all, this book would not have been possible without the unwavering support and encouragement of my ever-patient husband Brian. Thank you.

I would like to extend my thanks to the literary executors, agents and estates for authorising quotations, extracts and images from copyrighted and unpublished material contained in the book with special recognition to Becky Brown, Bill Hamilton, Joan MacKenzie and Sophie Weiler. Mary Lavin's correspondence, some photographs and a stanza from her poem, 'Let Me Come Inland Always', have been reproduced with permission of Curtis Brown Ltd, London, on behalf of The Estate of Mary Lavin, copyright © Mary Lavin. Rachel MacKenzie's correspondence has been reproduced with permission of Joan MacKenzie, executor of Rachel MacKenzie's estate, copyright © Rachel MacKenzie. John McGahern's quotes have been reproduced by permission of the estate of John McGahern and Faber & Faber Ltd. William Maxwell quotes, copyright © William Maxwell, were used by permission of The Wylie Agency (UK) Limited. May Sarton's quotes have been reprinted by the permission of Russell & Volkening as agents for the author's estate, copyright © 2025 by May Sarton. Eudora Welty's quotes have been reprinted by the permission of Russell & Volkening as agents for the author's estate, copyright © 2025 by Eudora Welty, LLC. I would also like to thank Claire T. Hartman, executor of the estate of Elizabeth Cullinan; Maura Cregan and Sophia Hillan; literary executors of the Michael McLaverty Literary Estate; Sandra Spanier, Literary Estate of Sylvia Beach; and Andreas Pauly, executor of the Estate of Evelyn Hofer. The photograph of Rachel MacKenzie by Rollie McKenna (undated) © The Rosalie Thorne McKenna Foundation, courtesy Center for Creative Photography, The University of Arizona Foundation.

Mary Lavin's *New Yorker* Stories

'The Living', 22 November 1958

'Second-Hand', 18 April 1959

'The Great Wave', 13 June 1959

'The Bridal Sheets', 31 October 1959

'In a Café', 13 February 1960

'Loving Memory', 20 August 1960

'The Yellow Beret', 12 November 1960

'In the Middle of the Fields', 3 June 1961

'The Lucky Pair', 28 April 1962

'Heart of Gold', 27 June 1964

'The Cuckoo Spit', 3 October 1964

'One Summer', 11 September 1965

'Happiness', 14 December 1968

'Trastevere', 11 December 1971

'Tom', 20 January 1973

'Eterna', 8 March 1976

Introduction

> Your letters are like installments of the old Pearl White serials, each one ending with some unresolved happening that leaves the reader breathless.[1]

'I cannot tell you how cheered I was by your letter of November 27. I was so pleased, as well, to think that Mr Salinger should go to so much trouble on my behalf. Thank you very much for writing to me.' So Mary Lavin, the American-born Irish writer, wrote in response to *The New Yorker's* invitation for her to submit fiction for consideration.[2] The year was 1957 and the connection, initiated by J. D. Salinger, marked a new and important chapter in Lavin's life and career. She would go on to have a first-reading agreement with *The New Yorker* for twenty-nine years, during which time the magazine published sixteen of her stories. Lavin's first *New Yorker* story was published in November 1958 and her final one appeared in March 1976, although she continued to have a contract with the magazine until 1988.[3]

Getting published in *The New Yorker* was – and still is today – notoriously difficult, and the acceptance of a story a major accomplishment. Some of Lavin's most important and best-known work appeared within *The New Yorker's* pages, including 'The Great Wave', 'In a Café', 'In the Middle of the Fields' and 'Happiness'. Her fiction featured alongside stories by such *New Yorker* stalwarts as the Irish American writer John O'Hara, John Cheever and John Updike (also known as 'the three Johns') and other regular contributors.[4]

Lavin's association and success with the magazine, 'considered the best in the world', launched her onto a much larger international platform than she had previously encountered.[5] It also paid Lavin handsomely for her stories. The proceeds from her first published *New Yorker* story enabled her to purchase her much-celebrated Lad Lane mews, which became a gathering place for both well-known and aspiring writers and artists including fellow *New Yorker* authors Frank O'Connor, Benedict Kiely, Padraic Colum, Elizabeth Cullinan, John McGahern, and future contributors Colm Tóibín and Eavan Boland.[6]

The relationship with *The New Yorker* also produced extensive correspondence between Lavin and the publication, predominantly with her chief *New Yorker* editor of sixteen and a half years, Rachel MacKenzie, with whom she exchanged almost 400 letters. Drawing extensively from this two-sided correspondence, in addition to other *New Yorker*-related material, this book gives new perspectives and first-hand insights into Lavin's creative processes, the collaborative relationship between the writer and her editor, the inner workings and editing procedures of *The New Yorker* and the process of publishing a story from manuscript to print.

The correspondence casts light on MacKenzie, with whom Lavin enjoyed a very successful author–editor relationship. MacKenzie, one of the few women editors at the magazine, both discovered and handled some of *The New Yorker*'s most important writers, including Philip Roth, Saul Bellow and Muriel Spark. On MacKenzie's death in 1980, Nobel laureate Isaac Bashevis Singer, another of her *New Yorker* authors, remarked, 'I consider her the greatest editor who ever lived.'[7] And yet MacKenzie remains a much overlooked figure in the annals of *The New Yorker* and the writers she sponsored, especially when compared to her male counterparts. The neglect is somewhat understandable, as an editor's work is invisible as far as the reader is concerned. It is only after examining *The New Yorker* records that the instrumental role MacKenzie played in securing Lavin's success with the magazine comes to light.

Lavin and MacKenzie's correspondence dealt with the business at hand: the revision of drafts, news of acceptances and rejections and cheques in the post. They tended to write responses almost immediately after receiving each other's letters. Nevertheless, dealings moved at a slower pace due to the fact that letters, drafts, proofs and galleys had to travel back and forth across the Atlantic. They were sent either by surface mail or airmail, depending on urgency, as airmail could be quite costly, especially for longer manuscripts. Sometimes Lavin managed to get a friend to act as a courier. On one occasion she gave a manuscript to John Budlong, the director of Macmillan's trade book department in New York, 'hoping to get it over the Atlantic quickly and free. It is called IN A CAFÉ. Unfortunately Lemonade is not retyped, and very long for air-mail, but you should have it soon, for the more desperate I get financially the more reckless I get with such things as stamps and typing fees etc.'[8]

Waiting for the magazine's decisions on stories hampered Lavin's productivity. As she explained, 'I write now however to say that in the interval between posting a story to you, & getting your verdict it's hard to work on a completely new story & so I had a bash at one you rejected last year.'[9] Lavin preferred to get feedback on stories before she did further work on them. If a story was unsuitable, she would move on to a new one and return to the rejected work at a later opportunity. In order to speed up the process, Lavin would sometimes write her revisions on drafts and proofs, rather than getting them professionally retyped.

When Lavin travelled to Europe, letters and proofs were sent to various locations, including Rome, Florence and Provence. Communication was naturally much quicker when she was based in the United States during her twelve-week stint as writer-in-residence at the University of Connecticut at Storrs in 1967. Her temporary relocation also meant that she could meet with MacKenzie in person. Occasionally, cables, telegrams or telexes were sent for any urgent matters, such as when a concerned Lavin did not receive any feedback from MacKenzie with regard to her rough draft of 'The Mock Auction' and so she was hesitant to send her the final version. After unsuccessfully trying to reach MacKenzie by phone, Lavin grew increasingly concerned and so followed up with a telex, 'FEAR YOU MAY BE ILL'.[10] There is a note scribbled on the cable that reads 'answered by telephone'. While it is possible that MacKenzie was too busy to reply or that her response was mislaid or delayed in the post, it would not have been unusual for Lavin to be concerned that MacKenzie may have been unwell, due to the fact that she suffered from serious, ongoing health issues over the years.

Lavin's letters were either handwritten or typed or a mixture of both. They were not always formal in structure; often she returned to a signed-off letter and scribbled further thoughts on it. Sometimes she doodled on the letters. Lavin's letter-writing mirrored, to some extent, her approach to writing; she constantly revised her stories, even after publication. The job of deciphering Lavin's letters was at times a painstaking process because her handwriting was often illegible. It was an issue that MacKenzie encountered also and proved problematic when it came to revisions: 'I had trouble with them [the galleys of 'Heart of Gold'] only in one or two places, and they were where I had to guess at your handwriting! More accurately, where I wasn't at all sure of my guesses.'[11]

Lavin was aware that her letters could be unreadable at times and occasionally she tried to compensate by typing them instead:

> I must ask you to excuse the spaces between m y letters – like there now between the m and the y of 'my'. People are always asking me to get a new typewriter or get this one fixed, but alas it is not the machine, it's me, I strike the spacer it seems, almost without knowing it, and I never can detect myself doing it, or deter m y self. There it is again! But I think it is better than my handwriting.[12]

Lavin never learned to type, which she told Eavan Boland was 'one of the great regrets of my life'. She blamed her inability to type for the copious amount of drafts she produced, 'often written at such white heat that I couldn't read it when I went back to it'. But her method had its advantages because through the numerous drafts she grew to know her 'characters with an incredible intimacy'.[13] Sometimes Lavin employed the services of an amanuensis and on one such occasion she declared, 'It seems odd to be dictating a letter to you, but I am sure it's a relief to your eyesight!'[14] No doubt MacKenzie concurred. MacKenzie's letters, on the other hand, were always structured, typed and filed, reflecting perhaps that for her the letters were ultimately professional exchanges, despite any intimate content.

Lavin's letters, unlike her stories, were not written for posterity or with a greater audience in mind, and there is no sense that she censored them. On the contrary, they were conversational, open and at times searingly honest. As such, they are ephemeral snapshots capturing moments in time that place Lavin and her stories in their social and cultural context. The letters reference a broad sweep of current affairs encompassing John F. Kennedy's assassination in 1963, the deaths of both Frank O'Connor and Brian O'Nolan in 1966, and Bloody Sunday in Derry in 1972. They also offer an intimate glimpse into the various stages of Lavin's life and career and reveal the genesis and inspiration for some of her stories, many of which had semi-autobiographical dimensions.

The New Yorker editor Charles 'Chip' McGrath observed that MacKenzie had 'a way of becoming overly attached to her writers' and Martin Stannard, in his biography of Muriel Spark, wrote that MacKenzie 'prided herself on her closeness to her writers'.[15] It was not unusual for *New Yorker* editors to develop close relationships with their authors. William 'Bill' Maxwell, for example, formed very special lifelong friendships with many of his authors, most notably Frank O'Connor, Eudora Welty, John Cheever and Sylvia Townsend Warner.[16] On a professional level, the emotional investment tended to foster loyalty in their writers and aided the production of good work. However, this was not always the case and some contributors, among them Muriel Spark and Shirley Hazzard, took issue with MacKenzie's overfamiliar manner. As far as Spark was concerned, MacKenzie was 'a clinger and control freak' and she requested a different editor. Shirley Hazzard also found MacKenzie's excessive attention smothering especially when 'In the evenings, MacKenzie would telephone [Hazzard] with maternal inquiries.'[17]

MacKenzie likewise took a motherly approach to Lavin and her work. In early 1962 she was concerned for Lavin when she returned to writing after an unproductive winter due to a series of unfortunate events including illness and a burglary: 'But don't push yourself too hard, will you? I can see that you've had a really bad winter and should be looking after yourself a bit.'[18] Lavin did not appear to have any issues with MacKenzie's nurturing and intimate manner – rather, it was something she welcomed and reciprocated. The strong bond established early on, coupled with the production of valuable work, aided Lavin's advancement with the magazine.

The exchanges between Lavin and MacKenzie became increasingly intimate and affectionate, especially after they first met in person in New York in May 1963. Their meeting did not disappoint either woman; rather, it strengthened their connection and mutual admiration. Aside from the business at hand, Lavin and MacKenzie discussed other writers, their various ailments, family matters, financial concerns, holiday plans, living arrangements and day-to-day domestic activities.

The letters reveal how financial and family circumstances influenced Lavin's writing and productivity. She was reflective, anxious and philosophical about the struggles she experienced in combining her conflicting roles as a mother, daughter, professional writer, farm-holder and breadwinner. As a mother, Lavin was unconventional but completely committed to her daughters' well-being. She based her writing time around their schooling, although she did pull them out of school on occasion, such as when she took them on long trips to Europe and when she brought her daughter Caroline with her to the US when she took up her appointment as writer-in-residence at the University of Connecticut.

As an only child, Lavin had the added burden of having sole responsibility for her ailing widowed mother's welfare. MacKenzie identified with Lavin's difficulties in caring for her mother as she too had encountered similar experiences in looking after her own late mother. Managing both her family and literary life proved hectic and challenging at times for Lavin and in a letter to MacKenzie on 28 November 1960 she wrote that she was thinking of going to New York for a brief visit after Christmas to escape the pressures: 'it's a bit cracked but I must get away for a few days & the pressure of mother, children, farm, mews etc. is getting very bad – will talk about it again. I would not even do a reading – just a spree!'[19] The trip never materialised.

The correspondence reveals how Lavin was constantly concerned about providing adequately for her household and making a living from her writing. At times, she feared that her letters were a 'long, boring wail about money', but her lament is understandable because as a professional writer, apart from her annual retainer fee with *The New Yorker* (which fluctuated according to her sales), she had no idea where her next pay cheque was coming from.[20] As a result, she had to be practical and resourceful about marketing her work and extracting as many sales as possible from her stories.

The New Yorker kept Lavin financially afloat and one of Lavin's granddaughters, the novelist Kathleen MacMahon, noted that for many years her *New Yorker* income 'was her bread and butter'.[21] Hence, Lavin's overall compliance with *The New Yorker*'s editorial suggestions is understandable, but she also knew that she could always reinstate her original version of a story in any future publications. Despite

Lavin's financial insecurities, her daughter Caroline recalled that there was always great excitement whenever a cheque from *The New Yorker* arrived because her mother would splash out and buy her daughters new clothes and treat them to afternoon tea at Dublin's prestigious Shelbourne Hotel.[22]

Lavin and MacKenzie bonded over writers they mutually knew or admired including *New Yorker* writers Elizabeth Cullinan, Benedict Kiely, Frank O'Connor, Philip Roth, Muriel Spark, Jean Stafford, John Updike and Eudora Welty.[23] Both women also immersed themselves in their country gardens. For Lavin, gardening provided a form of release and distraction, while it was more of a leisurely pursuit for MacKenzie, who wrote of her Connecticut garden, 'I puttered around pruning and weeding and even planting a flower or two – coral bell, said to bring the humming birds.'[24] It is a wonderful glimpse of the off-duty MacKenzie, who tended to her garden as she did her writers.

Lavin and MacKenzie also shared a common interest in cars. Lavin had a penchant for sports cars, having driven one since her university days – an uncommon sight in 1930s Ireland. Lavin, who had a fear of flying, drove to Europe with her daughters in 1958 and 1959 in a self-declared 'ramshackle sports car' (a Morris Minor convertible), but she told MacKenzie of her plans to buy a new Triumph convertible in time for a trip to Italy in 1961.[25] MacKenzie may have been less adventurous in her car journeys, but she was equally adventurous when it came to her choice of car: in 1965 she purchased a 1957 pink Oldsmobile. Fellow *New Yorker* editor Derek Morgan recalled in his obituary of MacKenzie, 'When one day she was knocked down by a car, she proudly called in to the office to inform us that it was a Cadillac.'[26]

In 1975 MacKenzie took leave in order to concentrate on writing a novel, but ill health may have also been a factor. In the spring of 1970 she underwent open-heart surgery and in 1974, after being hospitalised again, she was placed on reduced working hours. Not long afterwards, MacKenzie took leave and the archives reveal a dramatic decline in Lavin's *New Yorker* correspondence and publications after MacKenzie's departure. The magazine published only one more story by Lavin, 'Eterna', on 8 March 1976.

MacKenzie died in March 1980 and her obituary in *The New Yorker* observed, 'Those who had the good fortune to be introduced to the editing process by Rachel MacKenzie were quickly enlightened and reassured. Her genius was a combination of absolute friendship and a shared love for the work in progress.'[27] Certainly, this reflects the relationship between Lavin and MacKenzie. Their fortunate union and collaboration produced some of Lavin's finest work. Lavin and MacKenzie emerge from the archives as pioneering, independent women who were successfully holding their own in the male-dominated publishing world. I hope that this account of their relationship will result in a renewed interest in these two neglected women of letters and will give them the attention they deserve. Ultimately, I hope that it will encourage readers to return to Lavin's *New Yorker* stories.

I
'The Fire Burned Slow'
1957–1958

> Our requirements are so peculiar that it's almost impossible for us to define them, but we're really hoping that we'll be able to say yes on one of your pieces some day.[1]

When *The New Yorker* first made overtures to Mary Lavin in November of 1957, she was a 45-year-old widow tasked with the sole responsibility of raising her three young daughters (the youngest of whom was aged four), caring for her elderly mother and managing the family farm in Bective, County Meath.[2] At this stage, Lavin was an internationally established writer, with six volumes of short stories, two novels and a children's book under her belt, but she had only resumed writing the previous year, following her husband's untimely death in May 1954.

Lavin's creative hiatus was not due to writer's block but because, as she later explained to *The New Yorker*, she 'didn't think life itself worth living'.[3] Her *Atlantic* editor, Edward 'Ted' Weeks, visited Lavin two weeks before her husband, William Walsh, died and witnessed first-hand the devastating effect his illness had upon her. He was doubtful 'that she would have either the time or the energy to write after her husband's death. Certainly, she did not have either now, but the difficulty ran deeper than that. She had lost faith in her ability to write.'[4]

As the family's breadwinner, Lavin relied heavily on writing for her livelihood. There was some income from the farm but the bills were beginning to rack up.[5] In the spring of 1956 she had written to her literary mentor, the Anglo-Irish writer Lord Dunsany, about lecturing opportunities in England but he recommended that Lavin consider reading in the US instead as it was more profitable and would be a better fit for her. Dunsany gave Lavin the address for his lecture agents in New York and let her know that Curtis Brown in London could put her in touch with lecture agents in London.[6] That summer Lavin consulted her friend Eudora Welty, the celebrated American writer from Jackson, Mississippi, about the possibility of giving readings in America.[7] Welty advised Lavin to contact Elizabeth Bowen ('you know how she esteems you') about potential opportunities, given that she had embarked on a series of lucrative literary lectures and readings in universities and colleges across the United States.[8] She also thought that Jean Stafford and the Anglo-Irish writer and critic James Stern would be able to give her good advice and she offered to write to the Poetry Center in New York.

Lavin was a great admirer of Bowen's work and Bowen was very pleased to have finally made Lavin's acquaintance and grateful to Welty for opening up the lines of communication between them. Bowen informed Lavin that the National Concert and Artists Corporation in New York managed her readings in the US and she had 'no doubt, knowing how your work is admired "over there", that you would have an enthusiastic reception'. Bowen suggested that Lavin contact the firm directly or get Edward Weeks, Eudora Welty, Jean Stafford or James Stern to do so on her behalf. She sympathised with Lavin on the death of William, having lost her own husband, Alan, four years earlier. Bowen invited Lavin to meet her for lunch upstairs in Jammet's, the famous Dublin restaurant, on 13 September: 'I could then tell you far more about America, besides the pleasure of seeing you and being able to talk.' The two women evidently met on this occasion because on 10 October Welty wrote to see how their meeting went and expressed how much she wished she could have been present also.[9]

Lavin also reached out to the American novelist and *New Yorker* contributor Nancy Wilson Ross, who likewise advised her to get in touch with Stern. She raised the possibility of Lavin reading, à la Dylan Thomas, at the Poetry Center where John Malcolm Brinnin was the director.[10]

Welty duly contacted the National Concert and Artists Corporation for Lavin but the agency was non-committal about the prospect of taking on Lavin on as a client because it felt that she was not very well known in the US, having had only one book published there.[11] In fact, the Boston publisher Little, Brown and Company had published two collections of Lavin's short stories: *Tales from Bective Bridge* in 1942, which won the James Tait Black Memorial Prize in 1943, and *At Sallygap and Other Stories* in 1947. It also reprinted her first novel, *The House in Clewe Street*, in 1945, which had been serialised in *The Atlantic Monthly* under the title 'Gabriel Galloway', and published her second novel, *Mary O'Grady*, in 1950.

In 1957 Lavin began corresponding with the renowned American writer J. D. Salinger, best known for his 1951 literary classic *The Catcher in the Rye*, about potential American markets and publishing opportunities.[12] Salinger and Lavin had never met but they had mutual friends in Eudora Welty, Jean Stafford and the theatre director and playwright John Beary, who likely initiated their communication.[13] Although Salinger revealed to Lavin that he only faintly knew Welty, he passed word to her through friends they had in common that he and Lavin were now acquainted.[14]

Lavin was on much more familiar terms with Welty. The two women greatly admired each other's work over the years and they finally met on Welty's first trip to Ireland in 1950, while she was extending her Guggenheim-funded tour of Europe.[15] Welty visited Lavin at her farm and the pair became lifelong friends, sending each other copies of their latest publications. Stafford was also a fan of Lavin's writing and in a letter expressed a desire to meet her on a planned visit to Dublin 'because I admire your work enormously'. She subsequently stayed with Lavin and William in Meath in 1949.[16] Incidentally, Salinger had also been hoping to visit Ireland, but he explained to Lavin that it was no longer possible due to illness in his wife's family and also because he had returned to work that he had begun a few years earlier.[17]

Salinger sympathised with Lavin on the precariousness of a literary career and her financial situation and encouraged her to contact *The New Yorker,* with which he had strong ties, because it paid well.[18] Welty and Stafford were among the many female authors, including Maeve Brennan, Mavis Gallant, Elizabeth Hardwick and Dorothy Parker, who were contributing fiction to *The New Yorker* at this time.[19] Holden Caulfield, the protagonist of *The Catcher in the Rye*, made his debut appearance in Salinger's first *New Yorker* short story, 'Slight Rebellion off Madison', published on 21 December 1946.

However, in 1951 *The New Yorker* had declined to publish an extract from the novel because 'the precocity of the four Caulfield children was not believable, and that the writing was showoffy – that it seemed designed to display the author's cleverness rather than to present the story'.[20] The rejection did not colour Salinger's opinion of the magazine and he continued to submit stories and encouraged Lavin to do likewise.[21] Lavin subscribed to *The New Yorker* and Salinger was grateful for her praise of his recent story 'Zooey', which featured in its 4 May 1957 issue.[22]

Salinger noted that *The New Yorker* was publishing work by fellow Irish writers Frank O'Connor and Maeve Brennan. O'Connor had a first-reading agreement with the magazine and was a prolific contributor (*The New Yorker* published forty-eight of his stories, two of which were published posthumously).[23] Lavin would go on to meet O'Connor for the first time in 1959 and the two remained firm friends until his death in 1966. Brennan was a *New Yorker* staffer and contributor of short stories, fashion pieces and the Long-Winded Lady vignettes for the 'Talk of the Town' section.[24] There is no evidence that Lavin and Brennan ever met or corresponded, although Elizabeth Cullinan vaguely remembered them meeting on one occasion.[25]

It had not always been the case that *The New Yorker* published fiction with an Irish setting. According to *New Yorker* staffer and writer Wolcott Gibbs, it was a 'virtual rule that we couldn't use them [stories] unless they were definitely set in New York City'.[26] This 'virtual rule' was set by *The New Yorker*'s founding editor, Harold Ross, who conceived of *The New Yorker* as a magazine that would be a reflection of New York City and its residents – vibrant, cultured, and sophisticated: '*The New Yorker* will be the magazine which is not edited for the old lady in Dubuque. It will not be concerned in what she is thinking about. This is not meant in disrespect, but *THE NEW YORKER* is a magazine avowedly published for a metropolitan audience and thereby will escape an influence which hampers most national publications.'[27] Exceptions were made and the directive had evidently relaxed when the magazine began publishing Sally Benson's St Louis stories in the 1940s.[28] By the mid-1940s fiction set in Ireland also appeared in its pages.

In 1957 James Thurber wrote to William Shawn, Ross's successor, asking if stories still had to be located in New York, recalling that this had been the case ten years previously. He described it as one of Ross's 'craziest obsessions, especially since by that time it was the Talk of the World and we were no longer provincial'.[29] O'Connor's and Brennan's stories paved the way for fiction by Irish writers including Lavin, Padraic Colum, Brian Friel, Benedict Kiely, John McGahern and Edna O'Brien.

Although Lavin's fiction had not yet been published in *The New Yorker,* her stories had featured in other prominent American publications in the 1940s and 50s, including *Harper's Bazaar, Cosmopolitan, Tomorrow* and *American Mercury*.[30] Lavin's work garnered recognition stateside: 'At Sallygap', originally published in *The Atlantic Monthly*, was selected for inclusion in *The Best American Short Stories 1942*; 'The Sand Castle', first printed in the *Yale Review* in June 1944, was included in the O. Henry annual collection of the year's best stories in 1945.[31]

The New Yorker reviewed some of Lavin's American publications, so she was not a complete stranger to its pages. In 1942 Clifton Fadiman's appraisal of *Tales from Bective Bridge* summed up its qualities as follows: 'I think any sensitive reader who chanced upon it should have recognised in Miss Lavin a modest oasis in the rather dreary waste of the contemporary short story.' He did not agree with Lord Dunsany's assessment of the stories, in his introduction to the volume, as the 'work of a master': 'They are hardly that, but they do have at times an intensity and a charm reminiscent of Synge. They have nothing to do with the war, or, indeed, with any aspect of the present. Peasants, fishermen, grocery clerks and priests are their men and women, glimpsed at brief but critical moments in their lives.'[32]

Edmund Wilson, in the 'Briefly Noted' fiction section of the magazine, reviewed *The House in Clewe Street* and despite his annoyance with Lavin's 'exasperating habit of making six words do the work of one', he concluded that she was 'a serious and talented writer and her novel, in spite of its wordiness, is a wholly integrated work'.[33] Wilson also later reviewed *At Sallygap and Other Stories* and described them as 'twelve distinguished short stories of Irish life, most of them pointed with an acceptable and delicate irony'.[34] Lavin's 1950 novel *Mary O'Grady* did not receive such a favourable review by one anonymous critic who remarked: 'One feels that the sorrows visited on her [Mary O'Grady] were less the will of God than the will of her talented but, in this case, ghoulishly capricious author.'[35]

Salinger had suggested to Lavin that she should consider writing a 'Letter from Dublin' for *The New Yorker*, similar to the magazine's series of letters from different cities by its foreign correspondents. At that time, the magazine was publishing Janet Flanner's 'Letter from Paris', written under the pseudonym 'Genêt', and the Anglo-Irish writer Mollie Panter-Downes's 'Letter from London'. Panter-Downes began her regular column in September 1939, corresponding on life in London during the Second World War.[36] *The New Yorker* editor Gardner Botsford credited her with being 'one of the most influential in the small band of journalists who, in the late thirties and early forties, transformed The New Yorker's absorption with the Dubuque-denying, lighthearted world of Manhattan into a recognition of the dark, dangerous world outside'.[37] By the time Salinger had written to Lavin, Panter-Downes had contributed letters from many other cities including two from Dublin in 1941 and 1946. On the same day that Salinger wrote to Lavin, he penned a letter to Bill Maxwell, his *New Yorker* editor, with the same proposition.[38] It was a generous and thoughtful gesture on Salinger's part, especially given the fact that he had never read any of Lavin's work, although he had informed her that he would be acquiring all of her fiction that spring.

Following Salinger's recommendation, Edith Oliver, a *New Yorker* editor and contributor, duly made contact with Lavin and invited her to submit fiction for consideration.[39] It is significant that the magazine solicited Lavin's work, albeit prompted by Salinger, at a time when it was busy rejecting writing from renowned writers. There is no doubt that Salinger carried a lot of clout, which sparked the magazine's initial contact with her, but Lavin was an established and successful author in her own right and already familiar to its pages. There were also other factors at play: in 1957 *The New Yorker* was experiencing somewhat of a crisis in terms of its short-story supply, as revealed when Katharine White, the magazine's chief fiction editor, wrote to Mary McCarthy: 'We are in the midst of a fiction shortage. Many of our best fiction writers, like you, are not writing short fiction now, and some few who are, are not writing very well.'[40] This was largely due to the fact that many of *The New Yorker's* regular contributors, including Sally Benson, Vladimir Nabokov, John O'Hara and Irwin Shaw discovered that penning novels or writing for the movies, theatre and for other magazines proved a more profitable endeavour.[41] The exodus of such veteran fiction writers opened the door for new ones such as Lavin, Shirley Hazzard, Philip Roth and Muriel Spark.

Oliver did not encourage Lavin to write anything regular like a 'Letter from Dublin' and she made it clear that the magazine could not guarantee any acceptance of work. Nevertheless, this contact from the prestigious *New Yorker* – a publication Lavin greatly admired – gave her a much-needed creative boost and sparked her to put pen to paper. She wrote over 30,000 words in ten days, resulting in drafts of two new stories, 'In a Café' and 'Lemonade'. Because *The New Yorker* operated a strict policy of only printing original unpublished work, Lavin could not capitalise on previously published stories.

Although Lavin was clearly delighted to be contacted by *The New Yorker* and flattered that Salinger should go to the trouble of writing to it on her behalf, it was over a month before she responded to the magazine's invitation. The delay, she explained, was due to her writing a brand-new story for the magazine, which she was then doubtful would suit *The New Yorker* as she believed it to be dreary and slow-moving. Nevertheless, she acknowledged, 'This, as you know, does not mean that it is a failure … but it does not make for easy sale.' She asked Cecil Scott, her editor at Macmillan New York, to send the magazine the story 'Assigh', which was due for inclusion in its forthcoming collection of Lavin's work, due to be published that year. Lavin thought the story would be 'a bit gloomy' for the magazine and she was also concerned in case the piece had already been sent for consideration, mindful of the fact that, 'If there is anything worse for an editor than having to read a bad or unsuitable story it must be to have it put upon his plate a second time.'

An ongoing issue Lavin had with her Dublin-born literary agent, Diarmuid Russell, son of the Irish writer George Russell (Æ), was whether he had already sent her stories to *The New Yorker* and the magazine considered them unsuitable, or whether he had not bothered submitting them at all: 'Like most authors with their agents, he and I live in a state of perpetual mutual misunderstanding and goodwill.' Whenever Lavin queried Russell on the matter he informed her that they would 'all go the usual rounds', which did little to enlighten her.[42] As a result, she did not want Scott to send more fiction to the magazine until she could ascertain which stories, if any, had been submitted.

The New Yorker editor Mary D. Rudd acknowledged that this issue sometimes arose, but she recognised that the situation was inevitable: 'I don't see how it can be avoided, unless author and agent choose to set up some sort of 1984 checking system, made entirely of red tape.'[43]

Russell informed Lavin that only one story, 'My Molly', which she deemed the poorest of the selection from the upcoming Macmillan collection, had been sent to *The New Yorker.*[44] Lavin was later to discover that 'The Mouse', which she subsequently sent to them, had previously been rejected by the magazine. A clearly exasperated and apologetic Lavin explained that Russell had furnished her with a list of where it had been sent but he had not included *The New Yorker*: 'He and I are at loggerheads for twenty years but the relationship still holds together! I tell him I haven't the temperament for dealing other than directly with people – but he doesn't agree.'[45]

On a list of Lavin's stories, dating circa late 1950s, which indicates the publications to which eighteen of her stories had been submitted, not one of them was sent to *The New Yorker.* The list, more than likely the one she received from Russell, is otherwise pretty exhaustive, with stories sent to numerous publications.[46] It does beg the question as to why Russell did not send Lavin's new stories, as a matter of course, to *The New Yorker* for consideration. It is possible that, based on his familiarity with the magazine, he did not think certain stories suitable, or it could have been the case that he was a little dubious of *The New Yorker* as a result of his experience in submitting certain work for consideration. Suzanne Marrs reveals: 'From 1940 to 1941, the magazine had rejected three [Eudora] Welty stories and an essay, and Russell chose not to send its editorial staff the two Welty stories he circulated in 1943 and 1944. Nor did he send them her novel *Delta Wedding*, which *The Atlantic Monthly* published in four instalments in 1946.'[47] Perhaps Russell encountered a similar situation with Lavin's fiction. Nevertheless, Lavin's frustration with him concerning the marketing of her stories is completely understandable, especially as she only had one opportunity, pre-publication, to make a sale to *The New Yorker.*

Salinger's suggestion of writing a factual piece for the magazine did not appeal to Lavin; as she explained to Oliver, she had not 'written anything but fiction since my student years. I do not think that I could write anything now unless it were under the saving cover of imagination.' However, she informed Oliver that she was embarking on a reading tour of Holland, Belgium, Germany, Italy and France and that both Macmillan and Michael Joseph had asked her to keep a journal of her travels in the hopes of publishing it, although Lavin suspected that their request was more to do with 'the idea of myself and the girls at large in Europe in our ramshackle sports car as a certain promise of breathtaking accidents and side splitting stupidities on my part'.[48]

We get a glimpse of Lavin's sense of adventure, or 'recklessness' as she perceived it, when she informed Oliver: 'Life here in our cottage in Meath, in the middle of the fields, with not a house in sight, is hectic enough at times without our faring forth into a wider world. But fare forth we do, at the end of February.'[49] The trip was also to be somewhat of a literary pilgrimage as Lavin planned to visit Bandol 'to explore every cranny of the Katherine Mansfield scenes', and Zurich to see James Joyce's grave, and possibly D. H. Lawrence's villa, presumably Villa Igea in Gargnano on Lake Garda.[50] She wondered if the material might also be of interest to *The New Yorker*.

Lavin was not surprised or discouraged when 'Assigh' was rejected. She was merely grateful to *The New Yorker* for inspiring her to write again, as she explained that 'the fire burned slow, until one day I got a letter from – why! from you, of course, haven't you guessed?' Industrious as ever, Lavin was working on another story, 'The Glass Hill', before she departed for Europe, 'directed straight at *The New Yorker* target too, even if it misses', which she planned to send from Italy.[51] Oliver was pleased to hear the role *The New Yorker* played in getting Lavin writing again. She encouraged Lavin to continue sending her stories but noted, rather ambiguously, that the magazine's 'requirements are so peculiar that it's almost impossible for us to define them, but we're really hoping that we'll be able to say yes on one of your pieces some day'.[52]

It was not until the end of March that Lavin and her daughters, Valentine 'Valdi', Elizabeth and Caroline, finally managed to embark upon their much-anticipated European vacation. Unfortunately, while abroad, Lavin got word in quick succession that 'What's Wrong with Aubretia', which Russell had subsequently submitted, 'Lemonade', and 'In a Café' were rejected. Maxwell gave Russell rather vague reasons for the rejection of 'What's Wrong with Aubretia': 'There is a lot about it that we like, including the story itself, but it isn't right for *The New*

Yorker, chiefly because the characterisations, for this particular story, did not seem to us clear and full enough, and the writing in general not quite all that is needed.'[53] 'Lemonade' was rejected because it was 'too sentimental'. Lavin had anticipated that the story would be too long for the magazine and offered to cut it when she returned from her travels, but Rachel MacKenzie informed her that shortening the text would not change their decision. However, she passed on Rudd's suggestion that 'with some changes at the beginning, "Lemonade" would make a fine children's book'.[54]

Although *The New Yorker* editors found that 'In a Café' contained 'remarkably good things', nevertheless they felt that the story needed to be severely cut: 'And after such major surgery', Rudd remarked, 'we aren't sure what would be left of <u>your</u> story.' They also took issue with the main protagonist being portrayed as a writer: '(By the way, I should tell you, for the future, that we prefer not to publish stories about writers or writing, although we do occasionally make exceptions. I put this in parentheses because it is not an important point in this instance.)'[55] Lavin agreed with the magazine's criticism of 'In a Café', and even though she was not especially keen on the story, she did not give up hope on it. Being away from Ireland gave Lavin a fresh perspective on her writing to the extent that she wanted to 'slash so many of the stories I wrote last winter'. Lavin ruminated: 'Really our beautiful luscious fields do make for mental indolence – richness yes – but the weeds grow well too.'[56] In this same frame of mind, she later informed MacKenzie that, time permitting, she would 'take a pruning shears' to 'In a Café' and resubmit it.[57]

Cecil Scott offered Rudd his own misgivings about 'In a Café', which he did not think was representative of Lavin's finest work, even though he knew the magazine thought the story had potential, 'Her best stories are great, or almost great; and interesting though this is, I don't believe it is up to the level of such stories as THE SMALL BEQUEST or THE WILL. In any case, it takes 46 pages to describe an incident which could easily have been told in 20 pages.' As a result, he was opposed to including the story in the forthcoming *Selected Stories*. While Scott recognised Lavin's great talent as a writer, he was of the opinion that she was a novelist and that she would 'write a novel which will give her genius the proper room in which to be felt'.[58] Although MacKenzie agreed with Scott's assessment of 'In a Café', she nevertheless appreciated the story's merits: 'it seemed to me to contain the raw stuff of grief and bereavement and I still regret that it wasn't disciplined into the first-rate story it might have been'.[59]

It seems rather unprofessional for Scott to have shared such views with a magazine to which his client was seeking to sell her stories, especially given the fact that the short story was Lavin's preferred genre and the form upon which her reputation was built. The composition and 'magazining' of stories suited Lavin's lifestyle as she did not have the luxury of time and needed to earn a regular income, whereas writing a novel was a more protracted endeavour. In addition, Lavin was able to capitalise on stories published in magazines and journals by subsequently getting them printed in collections and in other publications that considered previously published work. However, Scott did have a point in that the pressure to turn out stories, in order to make money quickly, discouraged Lavin from writing novels, as evidenced later that year when she informed MacKenzie: 'I have got five or six thousand words of the novel done, without waiting, as I wanted, for time and security.'[60]

The European trip on 'which [they] set out so recklessly' unsettled Lavin – money was tight and she felt that she ought to be writing. The receipt of a cheque while abroad eased the pressure somewhat and enabled the family to remain on holiday until the middle of May. It also freed Lavin 'from tension & anxiety for a few months' upon her return home. The income, combined with the holiday, re-energised Lavin and she declared: 'I feel so livened up by being away that I hope to yet make that high grade – a sale to The New Yorker.'[61] Lavin's anxieties were further eased when in May she got word that her story 'Second-Hand' had been accepted by *The New Yorker*.[62] It appears to have gone through with few changes. Scott approved of the magazine's decision to accept the story: 'I am delighted to know that you have taken one of Mary Lavin's stories because at her best she is absolutely first rate.'[63] Incidentally, Jean Stafford was in *The New Yorker* office when the decision was made to purchase the story and MacKenzie informed Lavin that she 'spoke of you warmly and asked me to remember her to you'.[64] Lavin was paid $840 for 'Second-Hand', from which Russell earned his 10 per cent fee. The payment was a sizeable amount, given that the average annual salary in the United States was $5,100 that year.[65] She was appreciative of both

The New Yorker's generous fees and its support: 'Apart from the money for that first sale, which I needed so badly, my gratitude to you all in *The New Yorker* was for your interest & encouragement.'[66]

'Second-Hand' was not published until the following year, in the 18 April 1959 issue. Ilonka Karasz's cover depicts a crowd of tourists queueing at a boat terminus for sightseeing tours of Manhattan.[67] Lavin's story about an unmarried daughter, Essy, who is left impoverished in Dublin after her mother's death, sits incongruously between the magazine's usual adverts for high-end department stores such as Brooks Brothers, Saks Fifth Avenue and Tiffany & Co., as well as promotions for cars and European vacations.[68] A Chevrolet advert bluntly boasts 'As fine a car as anyone (including wealthy people) could want', while a Pan American ad reads 'Halfway to Europe between cocktails and coffee'; its accompanying picture resembles more a stylish bar than an aeroplane cabin, with its promise of airborne cosmopolitanism.[69] The aspirational advertising could not be further from Essy's bleak situation in 'Second-Hand', where she lives hand to mouth in a rundown house on Clanbrassil Street: 'There was never any money at any time, and there was none now after the funeral, except the few pounds they found under poor Mother's own mattress.'[70]

The story's nine pages are shared with a poem, 'A Little Morning Music' by Delmore Schwartz, and several cartoons; the caption of one, by Charles Addams, reads: 'You'll never get me up in one of those things.' (One caterpillar to another as they look up at a flying butterfly.)[71] Addams, one of *The New Yorker's* regular cartoonists, was briefly romantically involved with Maeve Brennan. Drawings of his Addams Family first appeared in *The New Yorker* in 1938. Another cartoon carries the quote: 'My dear, I've been drinking to your very good health.' (Drunken man having returned home to his visibly angry wife who is propped up in bed reading a book.) The publication also carries posters for the latest Broadway theatre shows including Tennessee Williams's *Sweet Bird of Youth,* directed by Elia Kazan and starring Paul Newman and Geraldine Page.[72] Cinema postings include one for Billy Wilder's recently released *Some Like It Hot*, starring Marilyn Monroe, Tony Curtis and Jack Lemmon.[73]

MacKenzie took over as Lavin's chief *New Yorker* editor in June of 1958 and she explained the roles of the various staff members to

Lavin: 'And my sympathy to you in your confusion about the number of us here you've heard from. We are a rather large staff. Edith Oliver works chiefly with fact – books and fact pieces. Mary D. Rudd, William Maxwell, and I are in the fiction department – along with several others whom you haven't heard from. You and I will be working together on editing and proof, and I am delighted about it.'[74]

The New Yorker operated a notoriously scrupulous editorial system under Harold Ross, which continued under William Shawn's tenure.[75] New stories were read by a panel of readers, 'the editors concerned', and Maxwell later recalled: 'It was a peaceable kingdom under Shawn. All of us had our own authors, and we all consulted with one another. There was great freedom.'[76] Nevertheless, Shawn in his role as the magazine's gatekeeper had the final say on all acceptances. When a story was accepted and any necessary revisions made, it was set in regular galleys and sent to the fact-checking department, then to the query editor and finally, and once again, to Shawn.

Rachel MacKenzie, who was born in Shortsville, New York, shared a similar academic background with Lavin, who was awarded a bachelor's degree in English and French and a master's degree in English from University College Dublin in 1934 and 1936 respectively.[77] MacKenzie graduated with a bachelor's degree in English from Wells College in Aurora, New York in 1930, where she served two years as vice president of her class. Her 1930 college yearbook, *The Cardinal,* noted that her 'ingenuity won her fame her first year. MacKenzie's cleverness with stunts, committees and programs, her unfailing cheerfulness in such trials, and the way she can make people want to work for her have become her reputation' – qualities sure to serve her in her future role as a *New Yorker* editor. While at Wells, MacKenzie was a member of Kastalia, a society that promoted the fine arts: to be eligible to join the club, one needed 'a creative ability in two arts or a marked ability in one'. She was also a member of The Owls and the Nightingales debating society. After getting her master's degree from Radcliffe in 1931, MacKenzie taught English literature at Ginling College in Nanking, China from 1932 until 1933, as part of a missionary initiative to educate women. She then returned to Radcliffe to undertake some graduate work for a year. In 1936 MacKenzie joined the College of Wooster's Department of

English and was appointed its Dean of Women in 1937, a position she held for eight years. She also taught English at Wellesley College and Tufts College Writers' Workshop in Massachusetts and was a member of staff at the Bread Loaf Writer's Conference and School of English at Middlebury College in Vermont, where she had been a fellow in 1948.[78] At Bread Loaf, MacKenzie lectured on the short story, having had her fiction published in various magazines. Her story 'Pattern' was published in *Good Housekeeping* in April 1938, alongside illustrations by Mac Conner; 'The Thread' featured in *Harper's* 1 September 1947 issue and 'The Funeral of Sandra Cunningham' was published in *The New Yorker* on 6 March 1948.[79]

The editor and publisher John Farrar established the Bread Loaf Writers' conference in 1926 with support from the poet Robert Frost, who lived nearby. Truman Capote attended the convention as a contributor in 1944, when he was a *New Yorker* copy boy.[80] Reports of the ensuing incident vary, mainly due to Capote's embellishment of the story, but the gist is that Capote caused offence to Frost by attempting to leave during one of his recitations, prompting an irate Frost to allegedly throw his book at him and declare: 'Well, if that's what the representative of *The New Yorker* thinks of my reading, I shall stop!'[81] Capote was promptly fired after Frost wrote to Harold Ross to complain. At the 1954 conference, the year of Robert Frost's eightieth birthday, MacKenzie gave a short-story 'clinic' with Saul Bellow, during which 'work by contributing members will be read aloud in whole or in part for joint criticism by staff members and audience. Work is presented anonymously, unless a given writer chooses to acknowledge his wares voluntarily, or is persuaded to do so by public acclamation.'[82]

When MacKenzie joined *The New Yorker* in 1956, as an associate editor of fiction, she began to handle Bellow's work and for the next twenty-three years she nurtured some of the magazine's most important writers including Muriel Spark, Isaac Bashevis Singer, Bernard Malamud, Penelope Mortimer, Philip Roth and Noel Perrin.[83] Charles McGrath, noted her 'discerning eye for talent (she more or less discovered Isaac Bashevis Singer and was a supporter of the young Philip Roth)'.[84] MacKenzie's 'discerning eye' also recognised Lavin's talent and she cultivated her as a *New Yorker* writer. The two women worked closely and tirelessly on the stories and Lavin greatly appreciated her guidance and welcomed the opportunity to workshop her drafts.

MacKenzie informed Lavin that the fiction editors had 'a great enthusiasm' for 'The Living', but they were concerned that it featured the corpse of a boy who had had an intellectual disability – the magazine avoided such topics.[85] This was yet another one of *The New Yorker*'s idiosyncratic house rules. MacKenzie suggested that Lavin substitute the woman's child with a feeble-minded husband. Lavin understood the magazine's concerns and reworked the story, replacing the child with a husband, who 'was a class of delicate ever since he was hit by the train'. Although she made the necessary revisions for *The New Yorker*'s purposes, Lavin nevertheless thought she might retain her original concept of the story when collected in a book.

Lavin was somewhat disheartened to receive only a brief note from Russell to let her know that 'The Living' was accepted. In fairness to Russell, he had only received a cheque for the story confirming acceptance and simply passed on the news to Lavin. She was also disappointed that she did not receive any reaction from MacKenzie on her amendments: 'I was so eager to know if the changes "just did" or if you thought they made the story any better?'[86] For Lavin, it was not just simply a matter of making a sale – she also needed feedback as to whether her revisions improved upon the stories. MacKenzie acknowledged that the required changes did not necessarily enhance the story but they were necessary for *The New Yorker*: 'The scene with the corpse doesn't have for me the poignance it had before, and at the moment, I think that's a loss (I'm thinking of the version you may want to use for book publication; for us, this is a real improvement.)'[87]

Lavin received $935 for 'The Living', a substantial sum considering that the average American full-time wage the previous year, 1957, was approximately $4,800 for men and $3,000 for women. Lavin wrote to MacKenzie of her plans for the payment: 'Well I was going to put it down as a deposit on a mews (converted coach house) in Dublin to have a base there for work & sleep a few nights a week while the girls were at day school. But it was not "for" me, as we say in Ireland because although I went to the price asked (very high) it was withdrawn from sale!' She was making a bid on another property, 'a shambles of a stable which will go very cheap I hope, &

which I will be able probably, to buy outright without accommodation from the bank & do up slowly & cheaply'.[88]

As Lavin specified, she needed to have a base in Dublin because her daughters attended Loreto College, her alma mater, which was located on St Stephen's Green in Dublin city centre.[89] In the meantime, during school term, Lavin and her daughters had been living between Abbey Farm in Bective, County Meath, and hotels near the school. She gave MacKenzie an insight into their temporary living situation:

> I have moved out of the depressing little hotel in to one depressingly dearer but in every other way very very nice. My little girls jump up and dress for school, and run down stairs – and lo! there is a breakfast ready. They come home in the evening, and lo! again there is a supper on the table. It's a good supper too, its [*sic*] not as salady as our meals at home, but we don't cook it nor wash up after it, and that's not to be dismissed lightly by any of us for we are a decidedly co-operative family.[90]

Lavin was replicating her own school days somewhat as she had lived with her mother, Nora, at 48 Adelaide Road in Dublin during the week and spent the weekends at Bective, where her father was the estate manager.[91] Although Lavin's parents were not formally separated, her mother tended to remain in Dublin.

Even though 'Second-Hand' was the first story purchased by *The New Yorker*, 'The Living' was the first story that it published.[92] It did not always follow that stories were published in the chronological order of their purchase, due to varying factors including space restrictions, periodic last-minute changes in the content of the issue, or rescheduling. Space was an obvious concern for the magazine and as a result it was more difficult to find room for longer stories. This was another drawback for longer pieces, although in some cases exceptions were made.[93] Another *New Yorker* rule was that stories had to conform to the season in which they were published, which prompted John Updike to write to Maxwell requesting that a Christmas story he submitted in February not be held until December: 'there is something repellent about holiday stories that appear on the holiday; they have a quality of being trumped up for the event, like spectators on TV and decorations in department stores'.[94]

'The Living' appeared in the 22 November 1958 issue, which was priced at twenty-five cents.[95] Arthur Getz's cover depicts an evening crowd gathering under a theatre's marquee while a man on a ladder erects the latest 'smash hit' signage.[96] A nearby news stand is selling newspapers. Only one woman is discernible among the throng of men donning trilbies and overcoats with newspapers under their arms. Lavin's story appears alongside fiction by Susan Gillespie, a poem by Louis Simpson, Janet Flanner's 'Letter from Paris' and a theatre review by Kenneth Tynan. 'The Living' shares its five pages with four cartoons, one of which has the caption, 'No woman I marry is going to have to give up her career.' (Slouching man to sophisticated woman at a cocktail party.) Another reads: 'Here's one you'll understand.' (Wife to husband in an art gallery about an abstract sculpture that resembles a twisted golf club.) The magazine often picked up on typos and grammatical errors in other publications and reprinted them in the magazine. One such find appears beneath Lavin's story. It is an advertisement seeking a hostess for a restaurant in Oklahoma: 'Hostess over 25, neat & trim, must have good clothes off at 10pm. $200 mo. and food. Dolores Restaurant 33 NE. 23.' The unfortunate missing comma makes the job offer a whole different proposition from the one, presumably, intended.

Due to the close proximity to Thanksgiving, which fell on 27 November, the issue is jam-packed with an abundance of adverts for champagne and spirits (Irish Whiskey Distillers took out a full-page advertorial) and luxury goods including a 'fake-dyed black Alaska fur seal custom made in the fur workshop' from Bergdorf Goodman. Readers are tempted with pictures of jewellery by Van Cleef & Arpels, Rolex, Cartier and Audemars Piguet, and with trips to Europe and luxury cars. Cadillac's caption reads 'Brilliant acclaim ... from the men at the wheel!' and a Chrysler's ad copy trumpets 'Built for the 1 man in 4 who wants a little bit more' (the advert, however, does not depict this one man in four, rather it is a photograph of a glamorous woman posing in the passenger seat). The '59 Mercury advert refreshingly has a woman in the driver's seat. The magazine also carries posters for the latest Broadway shows including the musical *Goldilocks* written by Jean and Walter Kerr and starring Don Ameche and Elaine Stritch, and Eugene O'Neill's play *A Touch of the Poet*, directed by Harold Clurman and starring Helen Hayes, Eric Portman, Kim Stanley and Betty Field.[97]

Early on in her dealings with *The New Yorker* Lavin had been contemplating managing her own transactions, not only because she was unhappy with Russell's placement of her stories but also because she preferred to take a hands-on approach to her writing: 'I may be making a change in my affairs & handling my own work, as I do not write a lot and am particularly ignorant of market requirements which can only be learned, I think, by direct dealings.'[98] She asked if MacKenzie would carry on dealing with her directly, rather than go through Russell, although he would continue to deal with the financial side of things. MacKenzie was happy to do so: 'Of course I plan to continue writing to you. It matters very much to me, too, that we keep in touch, and I should be terribly disappointed if I weren't to hear from you directly.'[99]

In October Lavin decided to part ways with her English publisher, Michael Joseph, who had published many of her works over the years, including five volumes of short stories, *Tales from Bective Bridge* (1943), *The Long Ago and Other Stories* (1944), *The Becker Wives and Other Stories* (1946), *A Single Lady and Other Stories* (1951), *The Patriot Son and Other Stories* (1956) in addition to her two novels, *The House in Clewe Street* (1945) and *Mary O'Grady* (1950). Lavin did not specify her reason for leaving the company, but it was more than likely due to the death of its founder, Michael Joseph, in March, which plunged the publishing house into uncertain times, although his widow continued to run the business. Lavin had been considering leaving the publisher back in 1956 but her good friend, the Irish short-story writer Michael McLaverty, advised against it as he feared her work would end up out of print.[100] Lavin eventually decided on Macmillan of London. To mark their union the firm was going to publish a collection of her stories: 'It is such an affirmation of my past work that I am deeply touched, and great [*sic*] excited. And want to work harder and better.'

Despite not being too keen on 'In a Café', Lavin sent MacKenzie a revised version of the story, having torn it to shreds:

> I don't particularly like it myself except for the talk of the widows, but it's written, and one or two people who have seen it like it well. I wonder if anyone will really see what I was trying to do in it at all, to show how a ray, a small ray of human feeling,

> vague, perhaps vaguely lustful too, but above all a human feeling, broke through the aridity of [an] older woman's mental attitude?

Lavin greatly appreciated MacKenzie's feedback and was hopeful for the story: 'Naturally I will be glad if you do happen to think In a Café will work out – or if you have any other changes to suggest. A few occur to me, but after all you are not running a writers school I know, & for my part, time presses & there is I feel a limit to what you can give to a story specially looking over your shoulder – like this –?'[101] MacKenzie thought the story was 'greatly improved' but that it needed to be cut and edited before making a decision on it.[102]

Outwardly, 'In a Café' is closely autobiographical as it features a widow named Mary who has a farm in County Meath. Critics readily acknowledge the parallels between Lavin's own life and the story and Lavin also declared that it was a 'semi-autobiographical' story that she found difficult to write.[103] The fact that her namesake in the story was originally conceived as a writer strengthens this reading.[104] It is surprising therefore to learn that, according to Elizabeth Cullinan, it was in fact the younger widow, Maudie, with whom Lavin identified.[105]

On Christmas Eve Lavin was thrilled to get word that her bid on the mews was successful: 'It's so exciting.'[106] The next step was to apply for planning permission to renovate it and then move in as soon as possible. The mews was located at the back of a Georgian townhouse, 11 Fitzwilliam Place in Ballsbridge, close to Baggot Street, an area that attracted students, artists, poets and writers, notably Patrick Kavanagh, Lucien Freud, Brendan Behan, Liam O'Flaherty and Frank O'Connor among others. Benedict Kiely referred to them as the 'Grand Canal Gang': 'In Dublin in that last great year of Frank O'Connor, there was, of a certainty, the Grand Canal Gang: O'Connor, Liam O'Flaherty storming by, Mary Lavin, around the corner in Lad Lane, Patrick Kavanagh, equal but separate, asserting his right to his own territory in Baggot Street.'[107]

MacKenzie had her own accommodation news. On New Year's Eve she moved from a studio into a new apartment with two 'spacious white-walled rooms', which she described to Lavin: 'Kitchen and bath and dining area besides, and I pad about like the lord of the manor. Do you know New York? I'm in midtown Manhattan and from my windows you can see down to the Battery and a loop of the Brooklyn Bridge. I doubt that I can ever take it for granted.'[108] On the same day, Lavin sent MacKenzie the story 'Bridal Sheets', noting, 'It's only a very rough version but if you don't mind reading it like this, it helps me, as I can get on with a new story, & I always like to let a story settle as I write (like a frame!) before I go at it again.'[109] She also let MacKenzie know that she would be sending 'The Tidal Wave' in a couple of days and she offered to further revise 'In a Café'. Clearly, the close of 1958 saw Lavin motivated and working harder than ever, due in no small part to the fact that she had wrapped up the year with two lucrative sales to the illustrious *New Yorker* and had bought a mews to boot, all unthinkable at the time the magazine first made contact with her just over one year before.

2
'Direct Dealings'
1959

> Anyway I am certain that to give you good stories occasionally I would have to be in direct communication with you.[1]

The year 1959 was a significant one for Mary Lavin, both financially and professionally. In January she eventually made the difficult decision to part ways with Diarmuid Russell because she wished to handle her own affairs and deal directly with *The New Yorker*. She also felt that their 'misunderstandings are past mending'. Lavin had requested that, if accepted, the payment for the reworked 'In a Café' should be sent to Russell in order to 'balance any losses he must have had on me in the past'.[2]

Russell explained the importance of his role to Eudora Welty, with whom he enjoyed a very successful author–agent relationship: 'He [the literary agent] is rather a benevolent parasite because authors as a rule make more when they have an agent than they do without one.'[3] Lavin did not share Russell's view and was unconvinced that he was marketing her work appropriately. Her decision to terminate Russell's services does not appear to have been financially motivated – rather, it served to give Lavin greater control over the sale of her work. By cutting out the middleman, she gained first-hand knowledge of the magazine's inner workings and requirements. In addition, it gave Lavin more direct contact with staff, particularly with Rachel MacKenzie. Lavin's savvy move greatly aided her success, security and longevity with the magazine. Rather than receive information third-hand she could push for and negotiate the sale of stories herself.

MacKenzie was hopeful that the 'The Bridal Sheets' would be accepted, but she asked Lavin to revise and shorten the opening passage because 'it establishes the tone of a more tragic story than the one that emerges'. She also asked for more clarity in terms of the setting and characters. MacKenzie reminded Lavin that revision was always 'speculative' but let her know that they only recommended changes when they had confidence in a story.[4] Lavin was naturally glad that MacKenzie liked the story and was 'amazed at the kindness & patience of your reading of it'. She was pragmatic in her approach to her writing and did not see the point in spending time perfecting stories that *The New Yorker* would have no interest in publishing, as she explained to MacKenzie: 'I feel I should be able alone to see these things, but the strain of having so little time – & the pressure of money needs, makes it almost imperative that I get a word of hope at a certain stage before I do the final polishing. If there's no hope I am better to go on to a new story, & leave the other. I will always come back to it – but at greater leisure.'[5] Lavin duly revised the story and in February it was accepted and she received a 'nice fat check' for $1,455 for the work.[6]

'The Bridal Sheets' was published in the 31 October 1959 issue and its seasonal cover fittingly depicts an autumnal Halloween scene, illustrated by William Steig, who is probably best known for his picture book *Shrek!*[7] Lavin's story shares its six pages with Ogden Nash's poem *Brief Lives In Not So Brief–1* and several cartoons.[8] Again, the life depicted in 'The Bridal Sheets' is worlds away from the luxurious and indulgent lifestyles promoted in the magazine. Lavin's story features a young woman, Brede, from the Irish mainland, who moves to an island off the coast when she marries her fisherman husband, Éamonn Óg, who drowns while fishing, four months into their marriage.[9] However, she appears more upset by the fact that she never got to wear her finery or use her bridal sheets when he was alive because she felt her surroundings were not good enough. She agrees to let him be laid in the bridal sheets but then changes her mind. Ironically, the publication carries an advert for Wamsutta 'quality and luxury' bed sheets with the tagline, 'You'll wish you could wear them … for fashion never created anything more exciting!'

The issue also features John Updike's story 'Dear Alexandros' and articles by Edmund Wilson and E. B. White. There is a poster for the latest Broadway musical, *Gypsy*, starring Ethel Merman, based on burlesque dancer Gypsy Rose Lee's memoirs that were originally published in *Harper's Bazaar.*[10] A shockingly sexist Japan Airlines advertorial, reflective of the times, brandishes the caption, 'How to train an airline hostess.' It presumably targets the male business traveller in its gender typecasting of the subservient Japanese stewardesses, who will attend to their every need: 'When one [said hostess], elegantly clad in her brocade kimono, offers you an *o-shibori* hot towel to refresh you, or presents you with a delicate array of Japanese hors d'oeuvres, you feel her real desire to please *you,* and only you. For she satisfies herself only as she succeeds in making you happy.' There is a poster for *The Miracle Worker*, a play based on Helen Keller's autobiography, *The Story of My Life*, about an Irish woman, Annie Sullivan, who taught Helen Keller to communicate. Anne Bancroft played the role of Sullivan, and Patty Duke the part of Keller.[11]

In March of 1959 there was more good news in store for Lavin. MacKenzie let her know that she was both 'impressed and moved' by 'The Great Wave' and that she was confident that the story would pass muster: 'Personally and officially, it's exciting to have you writing so well.'[12] Her inkling was right and the story was accepted. Lavin was paid 'an even fatter' sum of $2,408 – this included a 'quantity bonus' as the fourth story purchased within the 'quantity bonus cycle' and also earned Lavin a 15 per cent additional sum on each of the previous three stories sold, which amounted to $484.50. MacKenzie remarked of the scheme: 'Isn't it just like "Cinderella?",' adding, rather frivolously, 'Money can be such fun, and we <u>love</u> having your stories.'

Lavin was enjoying quite a windfall with *The New Yorker.* In the same letter she was offered the much coveted and lucrative first-reading agreement. This contract gave the magazine a first look at work in return for an annual bonus and an additional 25 per cent on any stories purchased. Furthermore, a cost-of-living adjustment amount (effectively an increase in pay to offset inflation) was paid quarterly and MacKenzie observed that these 'checks (office jargon for them is COLA) have a wonderful way of popping up when you've forgotten all about them'. While she hoped that Lavin would sign the agreement – enclosing a cheque for $100 'that makes the bargain legal' – MacKenzie assured her that she was not obliged to write for the magazine: 'There is no pressure attached that you write for us, and we understand that there are occasions when a longer piece of work – or life – gets in the way of your writing any short pieces at all.'[13]

Lavin signed the contract but it took her almost a month to return it as she was so overwhelmed by the offer and 'a bit stunned still by the good fortune'. She explained that 'this money can put up so many bulwarks between us and the hardship and tension I endured for so long. The strange thing, that frightens me, is that it was only when [the] appalling burthen was lifted that I really was aware of its weight.'[14] The proposal also made Lavin anxious in case she could not continue to produce quality work for the magazine. MacKenzie identified and sympathised with Lavin's predicament and had suspected that this was why she had not responded sooner: 'Indeed, I do understand about the money and the shock of relief. I had a five-year illness a few years ago, before I came to *The New Yorker*, and I know quite well what it is to live with that particular anxiety and how relief almost undoes one.' MacKenzie did not elaborate any further on her medical complaint but she reassured Lavin that, 'The agreement is not intended to exert pressure of any sort. It is only meant to help you write.'[15]

Signing the first-reading agreement earned Lavin a further 25 per cent on both 'The Bridal Sheets' and 'The Great Wave', which totalled an amount of $793.75. The contract was seen as a financial incentive for writers, while at the same time it gave *The New Yorker* the opportunity to consider the best work without any commitment to purchasing it. It was also a way for the magazine to circumvent haggling with other interested parties. Contributors bought into a club-like arrangement, which instilled a certain loyalty in them. John Updike was also offered a first-reading agreement when he achieved his first quantity bonus: Katharine White informed Updike that the first-reading agreement was an arrangement formulated for the 'most valued and most constant contributors', and she included a cheque of $100 in order to 'bind the deal'.[16] Lavin, when sent her first-reading agreement renewals for the years 1962 and 1963, was sent a cheque 'to bind the bargain'.[17] However, Updike's biographer, Adam Begley, perceived that 'the purpose of the deal was to bind the young writer [Updike] to the magazine' and that ultimately he 'was writing with only *The New Yorker* in mind'.[18]

This was also the case, to an extent, for Lavin, who informed MacKenzie that Edward Weeks of *The Atlantic Monthly* had asked her to let him see any work that did not suit *The New Yorker*, but her preference was to revise her stories for possible inclusion in *The New*

Yorker rather than give them to another magazine.[19] As she explained, 'I need hardly say that I'd go to endless lengths to try and make it suitable for you if you had any interest in it at all.'[20] This illustrates not only how highly Lavin revered the magazine but also how flexible she was with regard to modifying her stories in order to comply with *The New Yorker*'s demands. The fact that Lavin viewed her stories as unfixed and malleable greatly aided this process. It is also understandable from a financial perspective why she poured all her efforts into writing for *The New Yorker.* Nevertheless, she was practical and knew that she could sell rejected pieces elsewhere.

The editing of 'The Great Wave' is a good example of Lavin and MacKenzie's textual negotiations. Importantly, while their collaboration on the story gives a glimpse into Lavin's openness to *The New Yorker*'s editorial intervention, it also reveals that Lavin was not wholly amenable to suggested changes if she felt they threatened a story's integrity. 'The Great Wave', originally titled 'The Tidal Wave', features an Irish Catholic bishop, once known as Jimeen, who travels every four years from the Irish mainland to the island where he grew up in order to administer the confirmation ceremony. He reminisces back to when he was a boy and went out fishing with a young seminarian, Seoineen. A storm approaches and destroys the island community, leaving the boy and Seoineen the only survivors. In sending Lavin an edited version of the story, MacKenzie let Lavin know that the changes were 'mostly cutting and trimming' and she hoped that Lavin would let her know if she was unhappy with any of the revisions. MacKenzie anticipated that there would 'probably be further changes suggested after Mr. Shawn and the proof reader have had their day, but we won't let them at it until we have your changes on this version'.

MacKenzie's queries included how Seoineen's two hands got severed to the wrists, 'Not just the horror of it, but whether, in fact, he could lose two hands without in the process bleeding to death or at any rate losing too much blood to be walking about like that – isn't there an artery at the wrist? Terrible to be so literal, but something's lost if, even for a second, the reader stops to wonder about it, don't you think? (I did.)' MacKenzie suggested that 'he keep his hands hugged tight under his arms' in order to allow the reader to discover that his hands had to be amputated; she wrote that he could still state 'It has cost me my two living hands' as the reader would be aware that they were mangled in the nets.[21]

Lavin agreed and explained that she had not meant to imply the wrists were severed, as she had only intended 'for him to have lost his fingers to the knuckles'. She did not want to use the word 'amputated' and instead proposed the phrase 'where he had to lose his hands to the wrists'. She wanted to keep the phrase 'lost my living hands', as she believed it was significant with its priestly undertones, but in order to compensate for her tardiness in responding to MacKenzie's suggestions, she gave MacKenzie permission to use 'amputated' if 'urgently necessary'.

Lavin was taken aback, however, at the magazine's recommendation that Jimeen's mother would own a shop as she believed that it would be 'all wrong' due to the fact that one never wonders at their livelihood but sees it as 'a mystery of survival, almost of spirit I think'. Also, she explained, the shopkeeper 'is always a figure apart – a big man – often an alein [*sic*] from the main land or a returned American!' Although Lavin did not believe that it was necessary to detail the mother's way of life, she offered two alternatives, first that she could have 'the support of a bit of garden' or that she could make an income by gathering dillisk seaweed.[22] While Lavin usually acquiesced to suggested changes, knowing that she could undo them in later publications if they were not to her liking, when a modification was not authentic she stood her ground and challenged it.

MacKenzie took on board Lavin's concerns and objections. There was no amputation and MacKenzie explained that she was being literal in her suggestion of the term: 'like you, I prefer it left to be inferred, but was trying to account for the "off to his wrists"'.[23] *The New Yorker* version reads: 'It has cost me my two living hands.'[24] Lavin wrote to MacKenzie that she was surprised at how few changes were made, given that she wrote the story in a few hours. She was 'amazed' at MacKenzie's attention to detail and greatly valued MacKenzie's 'editorial exactitude' given that she, too, was 'passionately interested in the smallest points, which makes me think the short story is like poetry, where every word tells, and yet I am always afraid of appearing vain about it – as if <u>a word</u> could matter so much, with its implication that the story is <u>worth</u> all that trouble'.[25] Their combined revisions of 'The Great Wave' demonstrates just how important each word was to them both.

'The Great Wave' was scheduled for the 9 May 1959 issue but was replaced by another story. It was subsequently published on 13 June 1959 and MacKenzie noted the irony of its 'calm-water cover', which depicts a flotilla of sailboats on a glassy blue sea.[26] The story shares its ten pages with the poems 'Sticks And Stones May Break My Bones, But Names Will Break My Heart' by Ogden Nash and 'Lying Awake' by W. D. Snodgrass, and several cartoons.[27] The issue also features Anne Sexton's poem 'Sunbathers' and John Updike's story 'Should Wizard Hit Mommy?' Among the live entertainment adverts are posters for Lorraine Hansberry's new Broadway play, *A Raisin in the Sun*, starring Sidney Poitier, which opened on 11 March at the Ethel Barrymore Theatre, and Ella Fitzgerald's concerts with Count Basie and his orchestra at the Waldorf Astoria.[28] The book section contains a glowing review of *Memento Mori* by future contributor Muriel Spark, 'a gifted Scotch writer who has a love for intellectual high jinks', and briefly mentions James Thurber's memoir *The Years with Ross* about his relationship with Harold Ross: 'Since much of the book necessarily revolves about *The New Yorker*, the editors feel that, for obvious reasons, it does not lend itself for review in these pages.'

Lavin informed MacKenzie about the genesis of 'The Great Wave' a few years after its publication in *The New Yorker* and shared an interesting reflection concerning the 'mystery of imaginative creation'.[29] Readers from the US had written to her enquiring if it was based on the Cape Cod Hurricane, as the story must have borne some resemblance to the tragedy.[30] While there have been several major hurricanes off Cape Cod, it is likely that they were referring to the 1938 New England hurricane, considered one of the deadliest tropical cyclones, in which over 600 people perished. However, Lavin revealed that it was based on the Cleggan disaster of October 1927, when a hurricane struck the coast of Connemara in County Galway and sank a fleet of fishing boats, resulting in the deaths of forty-five fishermen and leaving many families destitute.

Lavin told MacKenzie that she was inspired to write the story after Michael McLaverty, one summer at his cottage at Strangford Lough, told her of a man who had his fingers ripped off by the weight of the nets during the storm while fishing.[31] McLaverty heard of the storm when he was staying in a cottage near Cleggan in Connemara, and hoped that Lavin would write about it. However, Lavin thought that McLaverty should compose the story himself: 'I saw at once that no one could write it as beautifully as he told it, and I have been teasing him to write it ever since.' McLaverty did pen the story but Lavin was dismayed that he was going to send it to *The Sign* and wondered if *The New Yorker* would consider it: 'To think of it being wasted on all the pious readers of the Sign when it could perhaps be read by some of the impious readers of *The New Yorker*!'[32] MacKenzie had promised that she would give his piece due consideration, but it was never published in the magazine.

Lavin's version of the story began to form in her mind when she was working on 'The Living', and she sought McLaverty's permission to write it. She recalled that she wrote it in a day or two.[33] Lavin set the story on an island and invented the characters of the bishop and his secretary and imaginatively conjured up the storm. She had presumed the incident took place in the previous century until a friend subsequently contacted the parish priest of Cleggan, who confirmed that the tragedy occurred on 28 October 1927. The friend sourced a newspaper article detailing the tragedy and Lavin was astonished to discover later that her story corresponded so closely to the newspaper's report of the disaster, 'words & phrases here & there, used by eye-witnesses & survivors & saw that many of them were the same – or nearly the same, as many I had used'. It brought to her mind Keats's misquoted lines: '"I believe in the holiness of the hearts affections – & in the truth of the imagination" & I tried to say how much I believed in this.'[34] Lavin was also taken aback when she returned to Cleggan and saw Inishbofin Island, a small island off the village, which she had not remembered from a previous visit.[35] McLaverty wrote to Lavin shortly after the story appeared in *The New Yorker.* While he thought 'the journey to the island and the Bishop's robes and the water swilling around the hem of them is beautifully done', he felt upon first reading that it was unrealistic towards the end, 'where they are cast too far up on the land and the fairytale quality of the weed'.[36]

Lavin informed MacKenzie that she had already sold a couple of stories before she was offered the first-reading contract, one of which was due for publication in *Harper's Bazaar.* Also, *Vogue* had been in touch with her about doing a 'very brief and illustrated' piece about her home, and *Holiday* were proposing a travel article: 'What I had in mind for Holiday was that they send me on a trip like the one I took last year with the children, when I drove 7,000 miles in Europe, only this time, I was going to make it a purely literary tour.' Among the destinations she hoped to visit were 'the little white gate at Cuverville where Gide used to meet – in real life his wife – and in the Porte Etroite Alissa'. Lavin also wanted to return to Katherine Mansfield's Villa Pauline in Bandol and James Joyce's grave in Zurich. *Holiday* would cover the travel costs, which naturally appealed to Lavin as, she reasoned, 'otherwise you are using money to go that could be used otherwise'. She queried the protocol with regard to any potential commissions from other magazines: '(Unlikely except in so far as you people add such éclat to my name that it comes about through this.)'[37] MacKenzie let Lavin know that magazine was not concerned about stories that had been previously sold and that there was no conflict with the *Holiday* article: 'It sounds a wonderful idea, and if you can have a trip paid for, wouldn't it be wicked to use your own money!'[38] She asked Lavin to continue to check with them about such pieces, although she did not envisage that they would pose any problem.

The correspondence between Lavin and MacKenzie gradually became more intimate and they began to discuss personal as well as professional matters, prompted somewhat by MacKenzie's more familiar approach and Lavin's open and trusting nature. MacKenzie's opening salutation and closing of her letters to Lavin progressed from formal to more affectionate terminology, 'Dear Mary Lavin' became 'Dear Mary' and 'Yours' and 'Sincerely' developed into 'Affectionately' and 'Love'. MacKenzie's sentiment was not lost on Lavin, who remarked, 'And one last thing of all. I was so touched by the way your letter ended – affectionately. Indeed it is the way I felt like ending all my letters to *The New Yorker*, and specially to you since the first one I got from you.' Lavin followed suit and ended her letter, 'Gratefully and affectionately'.[39]

In May Lavin informed MacKenzie that she had received a letter from Ethan Ayer, who she believed was a friend of MacKenzie's.[40] In another letter, written from a deckchair in Stephen's Green, Lavin mentioned that Putnam was publishing her friend Robert Asprey's book *Panther's Feast*. Asprey had visited Lavin 'when he was very young on his first trip to Europe'.[41] The family were fond of him and he kept in constant contact with her. Lavin recalled seeing a story of his in *The New Yorker* the previous year. The story, 'Rough Shoot', was published in the magazine in 1957. Just as Salinger had promoted Lavin to *The New Yorker,* she in turn often recommended writers whose work she admired to the magazine. But later she also confessed to suggesting less impressive aspiring authors to MacKenzie: 'By the way sometimes I am too weak to refuse to write letters from young men, who are alas, often only eager, not gifted. Could we have an arrangement that I'll really SHOUT if ever I want to recommend anyone to you of my own volition.'[42] MacKenzie gladly conspired with Lavin: 'About letters for the young men – consider that we have an agreement; in future I shall go by tone rather than by words.'[43]

Lavin wanted to apply for the Guggenheim Fellowship, an annual competition that is open to citizens and permanent residents of the United States and Canada in one category, and of Latin America and the Caribbean in another. She held American citizenship, having been born in Massachusetts, but the fact that she resided in Ireland made her ineligible for the award. Edward Weeks had been unsuccessful in his attempts to get the John Simon Guggenheim Memorial Foundation to reconsider Lavin's case but ultimately an exception was made. Lavin dilly-dallied over making the application until her good friend from university Father Michael 'Mike' Scott wrote her a firm airgraph from Australia urging her to make to make the effort, while stressing that she had 'two great responsibilities – to look after the children – and to write'.[44]

Towards the end of April 1959 Lavin was awarded the prestigious fellowship, which commenced on 15 September 1959. Besides her hitherto impressive body of work, it must have helped her application to have had the eminent J. D. Salinger and two-time Guggenheim fellow Eudora Welty act as her sponsors.[45] Edwin Muir and Michael McLaverty also wrote letters of recommendation. McLaverty noted in his letter to the Foundation that he first met Lavin through their mutual friends Cyril and Maureen Cusack soon after William died: 'And this year two stories sold to *The New Yorker* helped to keep the fire in the grate and give a springing step to life.'[46] Having work accepted by *The New Yorker* may have been advantageous as it would appear that its contributors were favoured. MacKenzie let Lavin know that 'Philip Roth, a young writer I'm interested in (did you read 'Defender of the Faith'?) also has one [a Guggenheim] for this year.'[47] *The New Yorker* contributors Mary McCarthy, Wallace Stegner and John Updike were also awarded the Guggenheim Fellowship that year. Past *New Yorker* recipients of the Guggenheim Fellowship for fiction included Saul Bellow, John Cheever, Vladimir Nabokov and, as previously mentioned, Eudora Welty.[48] Receiving the Guggenheim grant was not the only thing that Lavin and Updike had in common that year: they both had stories published in *The New Yorker* on 13 June 1959 and 31 October 1959.

The Guggenheim Memorial Foundation sent Lavin a form that required her to estimate her expenses, which proved a difficult exercise. John Bietz, an officer at the American Cultural Centre in Dublin, suggested that a sum of $5,800 would be sufficient 'to maintain a family of my size in Europe for a year'. She put down an additional $300 for travel expenses. In the accompanying letter, Lavin explained to Henry Moe, the administrator of the Guggenheim Memorial Foundation, that her income for three years was approximately $300 but that she survived on 'security of the farm', and that while she had sold some stories to *The New Yorker*, which had also offered her a first-reading agreement, there was 'no guarantee that I will be able to satisfy their requirements, nor to what extent'. She could only rely on the income from her farm. Lavin stated that she wished to work on a novel during the fellowship and concluded her 'Statement of Project': 'This summer the idea for a novel became so imperative in my mind that I made a rough draft of it. It is to work on this draft and complete it that I make this application.'[49]

The foundation awarded Lavin a stipend of $4,500.[50] Recipients of the generous grant could spend the money however they pleased; its purpose was to give fellows the opportunity to devote a block of time to their work.[51] Many awardees chose to travel, as Welty had done previously, with Europe being a popular destination. Lavin was also going to travel to Europe with her daughters and she informed MacKenzie that they would 'take our old sports car with us, and so we are going to drive down slowly through France, taking two or three weeks (we will come back through Austria and Germany please God at the end, but <u>that</u> is not to be thought about at this stage'. She also invited 'all suggestions from the seasoned travellers in *The New Yorker*'.[52]

Lavin informed MacKenzie that Frank O'Connor brought his friend and colleague Wallace Stegner and his wife to visit her at Bective because the couple were in Ireland before they embarked on their journey to Florence, thanks to the Guggenheim grant: 'F.OC [Frank O'Connor] said he wanted to torture himself by the sight of two of us going off!'[53] Lavin had only met O'Connor for the first time in March 1959 and she informed MacKenzie that they had 'a great "goster" as he called it'.[54] Back in May O'Connor had brought Arnold Sundgaard and his family, who were holidaying in Ireland, to Bective on Whit Monday and Lavin told MacKenzie how much she liked them and that that they all spoke of her.[55] Lavin must have also met with them prior to their visit as MacKenzie had written to her the previous month to let her know how much Sundgaard enjoyed being in Lavin's company.[56] Sundgaard had received the Guggenheim Fellowship in 1951 in the field of music. His opera *Giants in the Earth*, which he co-wrote with Douglas Moore, won the Pulitzer Prize for Music that year.

MacKenzie was going to Nova Scotia for a fortnight in July but she had a lot of work to clear before the impending trip because, in addition to her own duties, she was filling in for the poetry editor, Howard Moss, who had taken a year's leave. Nevertheless, she remained calm and focused: 'I chug along in my highest gear.'[57] Sylvia Plath was one of the poets MacKenzie dealt with during Moss's absence and she accepted her poem 'The Net-Menders; Benidorm, Spain' on 23 November 1959.[58] Incidentally, Plath's rejection from Frank O'Connor's Harvard writing seminar is said to have prompted her first suicide attempt in 1953, which inspired her only novel, *The Bell Jar*.[59]

Lavin had intended to project-manage the work on the mews herself but with her recent change of fortune she instead hired a contractor. She also appointed the renowned and controversial architect Sam Stephenson, who had recently restored a similar coach house on Leeson Close, not too far from Lavin's new abode, for his first family home. The ensuing building work made it difficult for her to work, as she explained in her letter written from Buswell's Hotel, a short distance from the mews:

> the mews is started at last & the sledging and banging that is going there is such that I feel at any minute that the whole house, and the Georgian terraces in front may crack down & be my liability so I walk around with my hands over my ears.

> There is no question of my doing any work for a little while but, this, I think is good. The framework of society, as well as dear old Mother Nature seems to be able to set its own limits to over-production![60]

In their discussions about sharing photographs of their respective new living quarters, MacKenzie proposed, 'If you will send me pictures of your place, I'll send you pictures of mine. But the best trade I can offer for pictures of the girls is one of an engaging small dog – how about two poses of him for one each of the children?'[61] Lavin promised to return the photos and added, 'I'd like to see one of the occupant too if possible.'[62] She informed MacKenzie that a friend in Australia, presumably Father Michael Scott, would send photos of the mews and she asked if she would also show them to Cecil Scott, 'if New York is – as I am told – so small you can do that kind of thing from office to office as we do it here from half-door to half-door!!'[63]

Lavin was getting pulled in all directions and so she was relieved to know that the quantity bonus period had elapsed. While the bonus was a welcome financial incentive, it also put added pressure on her as she made every effort to earn it within the time frame. *The New Yorker*'s multi-faceted payment scheme understandably caused Lavin confusion at times.[64] MacKenzie clarified that Lavin's bonus period began on 13 May 1958 with the purchase of 'Second-Hand' and that it had ended on 13 May 1959. She also explained that the quantity bonus was separate from the first-reading agreement, which ran for a calendar year, from 6 March 1959 until 6 March 1960, resulting in 'a bonus of 25% on everything we buy; it doesn't depend on or vary with the number of stories'.[65]

Lavin continued working on 'In a Café' and she thought she might 'sharpen it up still more than I did, bring the outer circle of it nearer to the inner part where the widows talk, and yet that outer circle is the story'.[66] Her pragmatism and perseverance paid off. In July, 'In a Café' was accepted and MacKenzie let Lavin know that William Shawn believed it to be 'one of your best'.[67] Lavin was paid $1,856.25 for the story and $515.30 for the quarterly COLA payment.

Before Lavin and her daughters set off for Italy on 15 September on her Guggenheim grant, she informed MacKenzie that she was 'in a state of panic, hysteria & melancholy prior to departure – like all Irish emigrants I am now Public Emigrant No 1 (Frank O'Connor having gone up the gang-plank ahead)'.[68] Fergus Wright covered their departure in the Panorama section of the *Sunday Independent*, with the eye-catching headline 'Mary Lavin Sails Abroad With Three Daughters and a Baby Car'. The article announced:

> Distinguished Irish writer Mary Lavin sets out for Europe on Wednesday to spend her year's Guggenheim Award in foreign places. With her go her three daughters Valentine (15), Elizabeth (ten) and Caroline (six) and her faithful Morris Minor convertible. She will spend a while in France ('I'm rather nervous about driving in Paris' she told me over lunch in Dublin last week) and then move on to Italy.

Wright mentioned Lavin's home renovations: 'During the past few weeks the decorators have moved into the mews house she bought off Fitzwilliam Square. Though a country dweller, she is at last making sure that when she returns she will spend more time in the Dublin which she loves and where she was educated.' The article revealed that documentary- and film-makers Jim O'Connor and Tom Hayes were hoping to film one of Lavin's stories. Lavin had previously informed MacKenzie that they were also planning to film Frank O'Connor's 'First Confession', and that he had suggested 'The Young Girls' as Lavin's most suitable story for the project.[69] Lavin wrote to MacKenzie of the film, 'It is a small venture but I am so interested.'[70]

Wright noted in his article that Lavin's new collection received 'superb notices from US critics'. The book, *Selected Stories*, was published by Macmillan New York on 3 June 1959. Lavin had dreaded writing its 'wretched preface', in which she revealed that 'the actual writing down of stories has been done in snatches of time filched from other duties', something she reiterated in her letters to MacKenzie.[71] Only one new story, 'Asigh' (Lavin spelled the story 'Assigh' in her *New Yorker* correspondence), which *The New Yorker* had rejected the year before, features in the volume.[72] MacKenzie was pleased at how well the collection was received in the US and sent Lavin any reviews that came her way. MacKenzie often sent Lavin American reviews of her work and Lavin cut out and saved newspaper reviews, but it was not a subject she ever discussed in her communication with MacKenzie.

Reviews appeared in *The New York Times*, *The Washington Post & Times Herald*, *Chicago Tribune*, *San Francisco Bulletin* and the *New York Herald Tribune*.[73] Orville Prescott declared in his *New York Times* review, which also carried a photograph of Lavin, that, 'No one writing in Ireland can penetrate more unerringly to the very essence of individual Irish character than Lavin' and he observed that she 'has won herself a rank in Irish letters equal to that of Frank O'Connor and Sean O'Faolain'.[74]

Although 'In a Café' was accepted, it still required further revisions and Lavin continued to work on the story while abroad, which proved quite challenging for her between receiving the proofs at various locations and the frustration of trying to remember earlier versions without having them to hand. She had intended to work on new stories while overseas but things did not quite pan out that way. Understandably, it was difficult for her to take time to write, especially considering her youngest daughter Caroline was only six at the time. Also, the holiday proved somewhat of a disappointment, as she divulged to MacKenzie: 'In fact it's a bit of a mistake & I am plucking up my courage to ask Guggenheim if I can take the rest of it at home … It's very costly & the job of looking after the family is ten times harder in a foreign country. I made a bit of a mistake (bit of!! – 1500 miles drive from home!).'[75] Despite her unease, the family were still abroad in November when she wrote to MacKenzie from Aix-en-Provence.

In December Lavin's first-reading agreement was renewed and the customary cheque, 'to make the bargain legal', was \$600, due to the fact that both she and the magazine had had a successful year.[76] Lavin's *New Yorker* earnings in 1959 totalled an impressive \$7,032.14, a figure that exceeded the average American family's income that year. It was indeed a bit like Cinderella.

3
'Splitting Hairs'
1960

> I wanted to tighten it, and minimise it rather than lessen it. Is that splitting hairs? but you know I think that that is what short story-writing is – splitting hairs.[1]

The year 1960 got off to a good start for Mary Lavin. In January she signed her generous *New Yorker* contract with 'pleasure and gratitude', in the hope of doing 'good work for both our sakes'.[2] 'Asigh' was published in the January issue of *Cosmopolitan*.[3] The mews renovation works were finally complete and a cheery Lavin informed Rachel MacKenzie that their new Dublin abode was 'lovely, funny, gay, happy, comfortable (we put that last, so wear your coat when you come)'. This casual indirect invitation shows how familiar the two women had become. It also reveals how Lavin's spirits were buoyed up once again following the family's somewhat disastrous trip abroad. The Italian venture had evidently taken its toll on her, so much so that she needed time to recover and resolved to return only 'to rest and for fun'.[4]

The Poetry Center in New York invited Lavin to undertake a four-month reading tour across the United States from January to April of that year. Although open to the idea of giving a few readings, Lavin was disinclined to accept the offer as she was not prepared to lose precious writing time, 'give up three months of writing, and all the time before and after that I would be too excited to write'.[5] She clearly did not want any distractions or a repeat of the Guggenheim escapade, especially as she had only started writing again since she received the award back in April.[6] Lavin likened her sporadic approach to her writing to a snow globe: 'I have to take myself into a flurry, like those snowy paper weights, and then settle down again, just like I was before I can work.'[7] To illuminate her reasoning for passing on such a wonderful opportunity, Lavin recounted a childhood story of when she discovered an abundance of coins while on her way to school in East Walpole. The incident gave her 'a firm belief that you don't have to strive to make it, you go on doing what you set out to do … and!'[8] Presumably, the moral of the story is that if one focuses on the work at hand then things will right themselves in the end. Ultimately, Lavin turned down the offer but proposed going for a week or two instead.

'In a Café', which had been due to be published in December of the previous year, had to be pulled due to a 'scheduling emergency'.[9] The magazine wanted to publish it before late spring, which necessitated a slight change in the text in order to conform to the season in which it would appear. Lavin had reluctantly agreed to remove the reference in the story to birds nesting in order to conform to the magazine's seasonal scheduling: 'I feel bad about cutting out the birds, which really were put into my mind by the line of Yeats about Dublin and the linnet wings.'[10]

'In a Café' was published in *The New Yorker* on 13 February 1960, two weeks earlier than planned and almost two years after the story was initially submitted and rejected.[11] Due to the proximity to Valentine's Day, Leonard Dove's cover features four identically attired businessmen perusing heart-shaped boxes of chocolates in a candy store.[12] 'In a Café' shares its eight pages with several cartoons including one by Frank Modell of an advertising executive pitching a cigarette campaign with a tagline of 'Harmful? Probably but they taste fine' to a boardroom of disgruntled men, and a poem, 'The World and the Child', by James Merrill.[13] The issue features poetry by Robert Wallace, Charles Maitland Fair and, in keeping with the Valentine's Day theme, Marianne Moore's poem 'St. Valentine'. It also contains fiction by Phyllis Graham and Emily Hahn and carries an advertisement for the novel *Two Weeks in Another Town* by former *New Yorker* contributor Irwin Shaw.[14] A full-page advertorial for *Ladies' Home Journal* bears the caption 'Mommy, why can't daddy work like the man in the grocery store and come home every night at six?' The 'daddy' being discussed is Richard Nixon and 'The Nixons at Home' is the *Journal*'s February feature story because 'the personal lives of such public figures are of particular interest to women who may (as has been predicted) outnumber men at the polls in November'. The polls favoured the younger and more charismatic Senator John Fitzgerald Kennedy, who at forty-three was the youngest person elected president of the United States.

MacKenzie was pleased to announce that 'In a Café' was going to be included in *The New Yorker*'s third collection of stories, spanning from 1950 to 1960, due to be published in the autumn.[15] The illustrious list of forty-seven writers features eighteen women including frequent contributors Elizabeth Bishop, Maeve Brennan, Mavis Gallant, Nadine Gordimer, Elizabeth Hardwick, Dorothy Parker, Jean Stafford, Elizabeth Taylor, Sylvia Townsend Warner and Eudora Welty. The volume also contains works by Saul Bellow, John Cheever, Roald Dahl, Robert Henderson, Benedict Kiely, William Maxwell, Vladimir Nabokov, Frank O'Connor, V. S. Pritchett, Philip Roth, J. D. Salinger, John Updike and Tennessee Williams. The royalties were shared among the contributors.[16] Lavin was delighted to receive her two advance copies of the collection in November but she wondered why 'In a Café' was selected since 'surely it's not that good'.[17] MacKenzie explained their reasons: 'We all admire that story, and it's Mr. Shawn's favorite.'[18] She thought she had nominated 'Bridal Sheets' as her top choice but she also voted for 'In a Café'.

Despite Cecil Scott's earlier objections, 'In a Café' was going into the new Macmillan collection, *Twelve Stories*, that was being published the following year as part of a joint collaboration between Macmillan London and Macmillan New York.[19] Lavin explained that the volume was going to be released in advance of her *Collected Stories* because Macmillan thought the latter book would give the impression that she was older than her years. The yet-to-be-published 'Loving Memory' and 'The Lucky Pair' were also earmarked for the new collection, as well as the previously rejected 'Lemonade'. As a result, Lavin was under time pressure to 'magazine it soon' and she wondered whether *The New Yorker* would reconsider the story due to the 'drastic' changes she had made to it, which included cutting the text by fifty pages.[20] However, Lavin's major revisions did not change the magazine's original misgivings about the piece and she was unsuccessful in her attempts to get 'Lemonade' sold elsewhere prior to its publication in the collection.[21]

'The Yellow Beret', another story Lavin had been working on, was also due to go into the new book. Lavin loathed the story but she felt oddly compelled to finish the work: 'I hate it, it's not worth writing and yet it torments me, and I will have done incredible work on it when it is at last finished. But I cannot leave it. I must finish it before I can go on to another one.' She observed that the compulsion to improve upon such stories often gave them some worth and revealed her ease with MacKenzie when she confided, 'You will realise how much I trust you when I tell you of these difficulties because it is never wise to draw attention to the weakness in anything – even ourselves!'[22]

Lavin queried where she stood with regard to old stories that may or may not have been sent to *The New Yorker* for consideration, prior to her contract with the magazine. It was over a month before MacKenzie responded on the matter, having returned to the office after a bout of flu. She confirmed that once *The New Yorker* rejected a story, the author was free to sell it elsewhere, but that the magazine would always reconsider any revised rejected pieces.

Lavin continued to battle with the 'The Yellow Beret': 'It's like some breeds of dog, you wonder why?'[23] Towards the end of March, she finally sent the story to MacKenzie. Although Lavin believed it to be a 'dud', she recognised that she resented the story because she had worked so hard on it and she drew the analogy that it was 'like a hen hatching out a duck-egg when I write a story I can't recognise as mine'.[24] Lavin often employed maternal or biological metaphors when describing her creative processes. She felt a responsibility, almost akin to a parental duty, towards her stories and, as a result, was unable to abandon them.

Lavin remarked of her productivity at this particular point in time, 'It's really creepy the way I have done this rush of work almost exactly the same time as last year – when I did all those you took last year.'[25] She was referring to the previous year when she was equally industrious, resulting in 'a wonderful harvest' that saw her achieving her first four-story quantity bonus.[26] However, the apparent coincidence was not that unusual as Lavin's writing tended to be cyclical and she was more productive at certain times of the year, usually March and November, due to her children's academic timetable.

In April Lavin returned briefly to Italy in order to settle her sixteen-year-old daughter Valentine, who was going to be attending the University of Florence for the spring term. She wrote to MacKenzie from Gigli's Café in Florence (it is possible that Lavin misspelt the café's name and that it was in fact Caffè Gilli, one of Florence's oldest cafés near the Duomo), asking her to pull 'The Yellow Beret', 'if you have not already thrown it out the window'.[27] It was unusual for Lavin not to push for the sale of a story to the magazine, especially given that it was due to be included in the forthcoming Macmillan collection, but this reveals her genuine dislike for the work. Making a sale was not always her sole objective.

Despite Lavin's misgivings about 'The Yellow Beret', MacKenzie and William Maxwell were hopeful for the story but were awaiting William Shawn's verdict. MacKenzie reassured Lavin by letting her know that they 'wouldn't publish a story you were unhappy about, so there's no need to worry on that score'. MacKenzie asked Lavin for the publication date of the forthcoming book in order to get any stories due for inclusion that were held by the magazine published in advance. She also explained that 'clearance' was required for the republication of any *New Yorker* stories.[28]

William Shawn accepted 'The Yellow Beret', with the understanding that it required significant reworking. As MacKenzie explained, 'We all feel that the story gets under way rather clumsily and that it needs cutting throughout, but basically we like it, feeling that its real interest is not the surface action but the psychological play.'[29] Lavin agreed with their feedback, noting that the 'the beginning is rotten – it never got off the ground – it's like a plane with the propeller in the wind & its tail up'.[30] The magazine's approval of the story seemed to change Lavin's own opinion of it somewhat as she began to view it in a more positive light and admitted to MacKenzie, 'I really like it quite well now myself.'[31] Robert Henderson, a *New Yorker* editor and contributor, sent Lavin a cheque for $1,231.25 for 'The Yellow Beret' and ended his brief accompanying letter with great enthusiasm: 'Meanwhile, any new ones [stories] you have will be received with joy and eagerly read.'[32]

The trip to Italy greatly revived Lavin and she returned home in time to be with Elizabeth and Caroline for Easter, only to discover that her mother had taken ill, which meant that they would not manage to get to Bective over the holiday.[33] When her daughters returned to school on 27 April, Lavin found herself with a block of time to work until the school summer holidays on 10 June. The only looming event she had was Caroline's First Communion ceremony later that month, which Lavin described as being 'as bad as a wedding'.[34] She was finding it increasingly difficult to write due to the demands of her mother who she was in the process of rehoming in a convent nursing home. The situation had clearly taken its toll on Lavin, who found herself 'holding up her [mother's] heart all the time by the strength of my own'. She had the additional bother of trying to wangle out of the lease for the rented flat where her mother had previously resided. Lavin was again agonising over the 'wretched preface' for the new collection but the prospect of writing the stories that had formed in her head filled her with hope, 'they shine for me like a light ahead'.[35]

MacKenzie identified and sympathised with Lavin's filial duty and her 'heavy emotional burden'. She shared her similar experience of two years' anguish over her own mother, who had lived with her in New York for several months before going into a nursing home, where she died soon after. MacKenzie revealed that her beloved eighty-year-old father, who was a pastor, died of a heart attack in church after officiating a large wedding. She confided that she did not 'grieve for [him] at all though I loved him dearly, but my poor little mother still rests so heavy on my heart I can hardly speak of her without tears. It is never the personal burden, as you say, but an aspect of living that carries too much sorrow.' MacKenzie ended her letter with the comforting words, 'Remember that you are dear to us, and your stories, too, and if I could do anything for you, I would.'[36]

Lavin appreciated MacKenzie's 'kind and thoughtful' letter about her own mother and she let her know that things were alright; it was just difficult to write with the added responsibilities of looking after her mother as well as her daughters.[37] Despite all the pressures, Lavin remained upbeat and she asked MacKenzie if she had read Frank O'Connor's essay on her or if indeed she would like to read it. The essay in question was 'The Girl at the Gaol Gate', which was published in the *Review of English Literature* in April of that year. MacKenzie did not respond, presumably because she was on her three weeks' vacation.[38]

'The Girl at the Gaol Gate' was subsequently published in O'Connor's 1962 seminal book *The Lonely Voice: A Study of the Short Story*, which he wrote after Wallace Stegner encouraged him to record his thoughts on the short-story form. In the essay, O'Connor writes of Lavin, 'She fascinates me more than any other of the Irish writers of my generation because more than any of them her work reveals the fact that she has not said all she has to say.' He shares Cecil Scott's belief that Lavin's 'real achievements will all be done in the form of the nouvelle, in which she has done her finest work till now'. While Lavin would probably have concurred with O'Connor's remark about her still having more to say, she would unlikely have agreed with his thoughts on the nouvelle. In a 1968 letter to James (O'Shea) Wade, an editor at Macmillan New York, Lavin wrote, 'I am fifty six. And although I feel at times that my deepest work is yet to be written I know that it is on the whole body of my work that my reputation must be made.'[39] Lavin firmly considered that reputation to be built on her short stories. Other writers O'Connor deals with in *The Lonely Voice* include Anton Chekhov, Ernest Hemingway, James Joyce, Rudyard Kipling, D. H. Lawrence, Katherine Mansfield, Guy Maupassant and Ivan Turgenev. He had intended to devote a chapter to J. D. Salinger, which did not materialise, but he covers Salinger's influence on the short story in the introduction, in which he notes, 'But, at the time of writing, the most typical of modern American storytellers is J. D. Salinger. It is not only that he has developed the form itself as no one since Chekhov had done or that in his work it stands out as precisely what it is – the anti-novel.'[40]

The New Yorker was 'purely delighted' with 'Loving Memory': 'It's gone through with a whiz. A wonderful story, and such sure writing. Mr Shawn says, "Some of Mary Lavin's best writing, I think," and we all feel that.'[41] MacKenzie hoped Lavin enjoyed writing it after her struggle with 'The Yellow Beret'. Macmillan asked Lavin to 'coax for a not too distant date' for their publication in *The New Yorker* as the new collection was scheduled for the following March.[42] Lavin was paid $1,968.75 for the story, which was the third story accepted before the quantity bonus deadline of 7 July, her fiction bonus cycle having commenced on 7 July 1959.

Maxwell handled Lavin's work during MacKenzie's annual vacation and sent her the author's proof of 'Loving Memory' with several queries and fixes but reiterated how much they all liked the piece: 'We all found this an utterly delightful story.' He needed the corrections returned by 15 August as the work was 'tentatively scheduled' for the 27 August issue but assured Lavin that MacKenzie would be back in time for the galleys.[43] The story was subsequently rescheduled for the 20 August issue and MacKenzie sent Lavin a cable requesting the proof back that week.[44] Unfortunately, it arrived a day too late: 'We lost that race – did you guess it from the magazine?' MacKenzie explained that she removed any 'dummy fixes', where there was uncertainty, but ultimately she thought that the published version only varied from the author's proof in two spots where Lavin had made changes.[45] Lavin, who was apologetic for the delay in getting the proof to the magazine in time, had not realised that her more recent edits were not included in the magazine version, as she explained to MacKenzie that she never read her *New Yorker* stories when they appeared but simply filed the magazines away.[46]

The 20 August issue carries another Leonard Dove cover, this one features two smartly dressed young couples on a broken-down motorboat in the middle of the sea at night, within eyeshot of their party destination. Coincidentally, 'Loving Memory' shares its pages with Sylvia Plath's poem 'The Net-Menders; Benidorm, Spain', which MacKenzie had accepted and edited when she covered for Howard Moss. It also shares its pages with cartoons including one by David Langdon, which depicts a man on a beach painting the name 'Elizabeth' on a boat but when an attractive woman in a bathing suit sits down nearby he begins erasing the name.[47] The sentiment of the cartoon could not be further from that of 'Loving Memory', in which Mathias Grimes and his wife, Alicia, are so completely besotted with each other that they disregard all else, including their four children. The issue features poetry by Howard Nemerov and fiction by *New Yorker* staff writer Calvin Tomkins and Burton Bernstein, brother of Leonard.[48]

When Lavin asked to borrow the author's proof of 'Loving Memory', MacKenzie explained that authors' proofs formed 'part of the sacred record' and were archived, but she made an exception for Lavin as she had promised to loan it to her and Lavin promised to return it 'safely and immediately'. Lavin was unaware of the filing procedures in place: 'I had no idea it would still exist, much less be permanently filed, or would most certainly have hesitated to ask. I mean I thought that I might get it before it was scrapped.'[49]

Lavin welcomed the school reopening in early September after the summer break: 'It has been a very wearing & fretting time – this summer – & so wet – with all the girls so meddlesome – & such varied demands 16 – to 7!' Valentine was studying law at University College

Dublin and Elizabeth and Caroline were back at school. There was more order in the household and they had some help. MacKenzie had suggested to Lavin that if she had some spare time and wanted 'to combine a kindness with meeting a dear person', that she make contact with Elizabeth 'Betty' Cullinan, a *New Yorker* staffer and writer who had a taken a year to travel to Ireland.[50]

The New Yorker had published three of Cullinan's stories by this stage, namely, 'The Ablutions' on 6 February 1960, 'The Voices of the Dead' on 16 April 1960 and 'Le Petit Déjeuner' on 13 August 1960.[51] Cullinan, through the encouragement of her sister, Claire, began working at *The New Yorker* in 1955, initially as a typist. She then acted as Maxwell's secretary, whom she credited with teaching her how to write: 'I learned to write from William Maxwell – learned in the most simple, possible way.'[52] Cullinan had typed some drafts of his novel *The Château*, which she described as being 'kind of my senior thesis, invaluable for the close look at how a long manuscript changed, how things got moved around or replaced – all that sort of thing which I sat and soaked up'.[53] Maxwell was Cullinan's *New Yorker* editor and she found his revision of her work 'enlightening'.[54]

Cullinan was going to be staying at the Shelbourne Hotel from 23 September until she managed to find suitable accommodation: 'Her plan is to take a course at the University [Trinity College Dublin], and write. We are so fond of her and she is so very talented that I give you her name with gladness.'[55] A week later Lavin informed MacKenzie that she had left a letter at the hotel for Elizabeth to let her know that she and her girls would be 'only too glad to see & if possible help her'.[56] Cullinan was under the impression, or perhaps misremembered, that Maxwell instigated the introduction: 'he [Maxwell] was the one who gave me a letter of introduction to Mary Lavin and she, in turn, left a response at my hotel'.[57] In Cullinan's *New Yorker* story 'Nora's Friends', in which she based the character of Nora on Lavin and Cecilia Bell on herself, she wrote, 'She'd [Nora] take a chance on anyone, and surely Cecilia Bell had been worth taking a chance on – introduced by a letter from their American publisher and before that by a small book of poems.'[58]

At the end of August, MacKenzie sent Lavin a heavily cut working proof of 'The Yellow Beret' and advised her to review it and make any amendments, 'restorations where you may feel that the cutting is too much', before they set the author's proof. MacKenzie did not wish to repeat the 'run into the race with time' that they encountered with the author's proof of 'Loving Memory'.[59] Ultimately, Lavin agreed to the magazine's suggested cuts and gave her permission for it to be published, but hoped that she might have time to revise the beginning as she believed the story needed to be 'cut drastically'.[60] Lavin was 'grateful for the sharpening of both the story and the author! I always think – why couldn't I see that myself!' Although she substantially cut the stories as they went through different drafts, 'usually up to ten versions', she was always taken aback that even more could be expunged: 'You know I always am a bit sceptical of writers who claim to do fifty versions of a story etc, although I do about ten or fifteen sometimes, but I know that although a diabolic compulsion makes me often rewrite the entire story, the actual change is often a small one. And I do suffer from a need oftentimes to perfect the bit I am going to scrap. It's like a tailor – a crazy tailor sitting cross-legged hemming the bits of cloth he has cut away from the pattern.'[61] Colm Tóibín, who as a young teenager in Wexford 'read every word she [Lavin] wrote', recalled interviewing Lavin back in 1981 at her Bective home, when she discussed the subject of her revisions and numerous drafts. Tóibín 'realised that it had to do with harnessing her own voice, finding a mediating tone between the randomness of experience and the tight beauty of art'.[62]

The magazine wanted to indicate the location of 'The Yellow Beret' more overtly by incorporating Dublin into the title of the newspaper referred to within it. Lavin explained that there was no city newspaper and she did not want to concoct one. This chimed with *The New Yorker*'s ethos of being factual in its fiction, a principle which, perhaps, Lavin had subconsciously assimilated. She wondered if they would be content with the mention of *The Irish Times*, which would set the story in Ireland, and proposed that they 'leave it to the atmosphere of the paragraph, breakfast table, husband and wife, early morning paper etc to suggest a city?' Alternatively, she suggested that if they wanted a specific mention of Dublin they could say: 'After all murders are not two a penny in Dublin like they are in London' or 'are not all that plentiful in Dublin yet'.[63] MacKenzie informed Lavin that, 'The fixing of the place by using a Dublin paper was only a suggestion; if there isn't a paper that fits our needs, of course the suggestion's no good. You place it any way you like.'[64]

The editors had two queries concerning time in the galleys. The first was the reference to 'two murders in twenty-four hours', which conflicted with the later description of them, 'seeing they were both the same night'. William Shawn also queried how a murder that was committed in early morning could get published in that morning's paper. Lavin subsequently removed the time frame of twenty-four hours, which had been inspired by real-life events, but both murders, one of which occurred in 'the small hours', remained in the morning paper. The story printed in the magazine refers to *The Irish Times* and it includes the line, 'Dublin was a small city for two murders in one night' by way of context.

Lavin had written 'This headline gave me the idea for The Yellow Beret' next to an *Evening Press* article titled '2 Murders in 24 Hours', which was published in the paper on 20 July 1959.[65] This is curious because Lavin first mentioned 'The Yellow Beret' to MacKenzie in May of 1959. The newspaper report contains details about the discovery at 2 am that morning of a nineteen-year-old girl who was found strangled in London, which 'brought the toll of murders in London's mounting wave of violence to two in 24 hours': 'Miss Young was wearing a white blouse and red skirt. Detectives took away a pair of white sandals and a black and white check box-type handbag. She had been strangled with a rope.' The headline likely gave Lavin the idea to write about two murders in the story. In an RTÉ radio interview with Liam Nolan, Lavin confided that she had 'some quality of detection' in her and declared, 'I think I'd have liked to have been a detective.'[66] Certainly, Lavin's power of detection and discovery is cleverly employed in 'The Yellow Beret'.

The magazine had originally planned to publish 'The Yellow Beret' in the spring because 'Donny's examination and the walk rather suggest that season, but late fall would be appropriate, too, and the story is now slugged "late fall or spring".' The story was earmarked for the 5 November issue and MacKenzie let Lavin know that she needed the working proof back by 26 September to give them time to prepare the author's proof, as she explained the procedure: 'The preparation of the author's proof means that it has to be checked by the checkers and read by the proof department and by Mr. Shawn, and then it has to go and come from you again.'[67]

'The Yellow Beret' was published on 12 November 1960, a week later than planned. Arthur Getz's cover depicts exposed subway tracks running beneath Park Avenue with the Empire State Building centred in the background. Lavin's story shares its seven pages with a poem, 'Possibilities' by Peter Kane Dufault, and several cartoons, one of which is two men outside Joe's restaurant with a sign saying 'Out to Lunch' and the caption 'See what I mean? Nobody gives a damn any more!' The issue also contains a story by John Cheever, 'Some People, Places, and Things That Will Not Appear in My Novel', which was the title of his next volume of stories published in 1961.[68] The 'Goings on About Town Motion Pictures' section lists *The Battle of the Sexes,* a film adapted from James Thurber's *New Yorker* story 'The Catbird Seat', and it also promotes the Broadway show, *A Thurber Carnival,* adapted by the author from his stories, cartoons and casuals, which were mostly published in *The New Yorker.*[69] There are posters for the musical *Fiorello* based on *New Yorker* contributor and muckraker Samuel Hopkins Adams's novel *Tenderloin,* and for Brendan Behan's play *The Hostage* directed by Joan Littlewood, which premiered at the Cort Theatre in September. Movies advertised include *Butterfield 8*, which was based on the 1935 novel by John O'Hara, and starred Elizabeth Taylor, for which she won her first Academy Award.[70] The issue also carries a full-page advert for *The Stories from The New Yorker 1950 to 1960*, which lists and describes its contributors, one of whom was Lavin, as 'an honour roll of the decade's accomplished and adventurous writers'.

On 12 September MacKenzie informed Lavin that they were in the middle of Hurricane Donna, 'the wind making incredible sounds around our stacks of buildings (my office is on the 20th floor)'.[71] According to *The New York Times*, the hurricane, a category 3 storm, 'pounded New York City with winds gusting up to 90 miles per hour, dumped five inches of rain, and flooded lower Manhattan almost to waist level on West and Cortlandt Streets (at the southwest corner of what later became the site of the World Trade Center)'. Subways were closed and electricity and phone lines were down. It was the worst hurricane to hit the east coast at that time, causing thirty-six people to lose their lives and approximately $100 million in property damage.[72]

Lavin let MacKenzie know that they all loved Elizabeth Cullinan. MacKenzie was pleased that the two women were getting along so well and informed Lavin that she had received 'a very happy letter from Betty Cullinan, written after she had spent the evening with you. She liked you so much, but then I knew she would.'[73] The evening referred to was likely when Lavin invited Frank and Harriet O'Connor, who were back in Dublin, and Cullinan to supper. She only wished that MacKenzie could have been present also. Lavin received a letter from another young writer, Ralph Blum, informing her that *The New Yorker* had accepted one of his stories, 'The Day of the Lion', which appeared in the 14 January 1961 issue. She thought his stories were 'very sharp & clean' and she was particularly gladdened by the news because she had recommended that he contact the magazine.[74]

Although Lavin experienced great success with *The New Yorker* in 1960, she also suffered a number of rejections. 'The New Gardener', a story she wrote in a day, was rejected on 29 November 1960: 'Everything about it is so live and so endearing except the story, and that is just too much an old, familiar formula.'[75] Lavin was not surprised that the magazine did not like the piece and said that it was 'no good – not worth reworking' and 'If Vogue take it – well & good.'[76] *Vogue* did not take the story but it was published in *Cosmopolitan* in August 1962.[77] She sent MacKenzie a 'poeme' titled 'Neurosis': 'Oh that awful feeling that you don't belong/ When someone finishes your sentence,/ And finishes it WRONG.'[78] MacKenzie asked after Elizabeth Cullinan and told Lavin to let her know that she would be writing to her: 'I think of her so closely but as a correspondent I have no character, only intention and a long monologue going on in my head.' MacKenzie was busy organising Christmas presents, which included knitting her brother a pair of socks: 'Energies at the moment are all engaged in Christmas boxes. Every year the deadline seems to come earlier. One box, to go to Florida, is ready except for a pair of socks for my brother. I knit on them compulsively every evening. I think it must be a relic from kindergarten days to feel that at least one thing must be made each Christmas.'[79]

On 9 December MacKenzie sent Lavin her first-reading agreement cheque for $600 with the note, 'It's first-reading agreement time, and here is a check to seal the bargain – just in time for some Christmas extravagance. Are you a great Christmas celebrator? It's a season I love, in spite of the awful commercialization.' She hoped that Lavin would sign the agreement: 'We are so happy with the arrangement I hardly allow for your not being.' In Lavin's previous letter, Lavin had indicated that she might travel to New York on a jaunt. MacKenzie thought it 'a wonderful idea' and offered to help with reservations: 'Will you save some time for me? I so much want to know you.' She ended her letter 'a merry Christmas to you, and love. Please come see us.'[80]

Lavin divulged that she was working 'very hard – too hard – & feeling awfully low'. She felt bad for telling MacKenzie her woes, but she recognised that being able to write about them signified that she was over the worst, 'up over the edge again out into the light at least'. Lavin had been 'working harder than ever' but she was not managing to finish many stories. However, it was not all in vain as she reckoned that she had amassed at least two years' worth of work and 'need only polish & re-arrange which I could do on a bus'. Lavin was going to send in two stories, 'The Kiss' and 'The Bog Light' and she had three more 'forming' in her mind. She ended her letter reflecting that a trip to New York after Christmas 'might be the very thing to lift me up'.[81]

4
'A Moral Obligation'
1961–1962

> It's so comforting to feel that the New Yorker continues to exist even if I doubt at times that I do myself.[1]

Rachel MacKenzie's first letter to Mary Lavin in January of 1961 contained two cost-of-living adjustments (COLA) payments with the accompanying, comforting words: 'However things are, know that we love you and always welcome a new story.'[2] The cheques amounted to the sizeable sum of $648.87. *The New Yorker* had also erroneously sent Lavin a letter about its annuity plan, for which she was not yet eligible as it required the fulfilment of three first-reading contracts.[3] Lavin did, however, satisfy the other stipulation that subscribers must hold American citizenship.[4]

In early March, Margaret Messud from Houghton Mifflin wrote to Milton Greenstein to inform him that Martha Foley had again chosen three *New Yorker* stories for *The Best American Short Stories*.[5] The stories selected were Lavin's 'The Yellow Beret', St. Clair McKelway's 'First Marriage' and Peter Taylor's 'Miss Leonora When Last Seen'.[6] Foley had previously selected Lavin's story 'At Sallygap' for inclusion in *The Best American Short Stories 1942*. MacKenzie was amused by the fact that 'The Yellow Beret' was chosen, given Lavin's fraught relationship with the story: 'I wished we'd been within telephoning distance so we could laugh together about their choosing this step-story of yours. First Macmillan, then The New Yorker., and now Foley-Burnett.'

Lavin was 'disgusted' that 'The Yellow Beret' was selected for the O. Henry collection and wished it had been any of her other stories: 'It is a bit baffling, even disturbing the way stories I hate are always chosen for anthologies – like the awful Widow's Son that is now a text book story in USA, England & Germany – in every anthology – &

constantly being translated!'[7] It would appear that Lavin was confusing the O. Henry collection with Martha Foley's anthology. Lavin embraced MacKenzie's coining of the term 'step-stories' and it would crop up again in their future correspondence when discussing stories that Lavin grappled with.

Boston College had invited Lavin to join a team of writers including fellow *New Yorker* contributor Lionel Trilling and André Maurois for its humanities series that was taking place at the end of April.[8] Although Lavin longed to meet Trilling, she was reluctant to accept the offer because she had so little spare time for writing, as she explained to MacKenzie: 'For anyone like me who has only an odd hour an odd day – it seems madness to do anything else just these days with so many stories jostling each other in my mind.'[9] Lavin had also been invited to read at 'some place in Pennsylvania', but she wanted to postpone the visits until the autumn as the family were due to return to Italy in June and she wished 'to keep my powder dry for then'.[10]

Lavin was still struggling to find suitable accommodation for her 79-year-old mother, who had not settled in the mews that she had purchased for her. As a result, Lavin found herself having to sell the mews and rent her an expensive apartment.[11] Despite the demands made of her, she still managed to find time to entertain guests at her homes. Elizabeth Cullinan had become such a frequent visitor that Lavin declared in a letter to MacKenzie: 'Elizabeth is absolutely one of the Walshes now!'[12]

Given her financial responsibilities, it was not surprising that Lavin was anxious to make the quantity bonus again that year, which ran from 30 June 1960 until 30 June 1961. She already had two stories accepted in the cycle thus far, namely 'The Yellow Beret' and 'Loving Memory'.[13] Lavin spent February working 'tooth & nail' on 'Lucky Pair' and 'The Kiss'.[14] She was putting pressure on herself to get as much work done before Easter, which fell on 2 April, when her daughters would be on their school holidays.

On 20 March MacKenzie let Lavin her know that 'The Kiss' was accepted: 'And such a beautiful story. Of course we want it. We're all delighted with it, and moved by it, too.' MacKenzie thought the piece just needed some cutting. On the same day, Lavin, unaware of the successful outcome, wrote to MacKenzie for feedback on the story and stated that she had 'no feelings' for the work.[15] *The New Yorker* retitled the story 'In the Middle of the Fields'. MacKenzie explained the change in title when she sent Lavin the author's proof and payment for the piece, 'Here's the check for what came in as "The Kiss" but is going out to you as "In the Middle of the Fields" – and don't you think that's a lovely title? If by some miserable chance you don't, would you suggest another one? I've forgotten just why everyone felt that "The Kiss" doesn't do the story justice, but everyone did, and I do remember that I agreed with them.'[16]

Lavin must have been happy with the title change as she kept it for all future publications of the story and for the title of one of her collections.[17] The new title appears in the story itself: 'And, for that matter, where could you be safer than in the middle of the fields, with the innocent beasts asleep around you?'[18] Incidentally, one of MacKenzie's queries about the 'darling story' was regarding the repetition of this question by two different characters in the story.[19] MacKenzie retained the first utterance of the sentence by Ned the farmhand but reworded neighbouring farmer Bartley Crossen's line to read, 'What safer place could you be under the sky than right here, with your own fields all about you!'[20]

Lavin described Abbey Farm in very similar terms in her early correspondence with the magazine when she wrote, 'Life here in our cottage in Meath, in the middle of the fields, with not a house in sight.'[21] She later acknowledged that 'In the Middle of the Fields', which features a lonely young widow living on an isolated farm with her three young daughters, was semi-autobiographical.[22] In the story, Lavin explores the burdens of being widowed young, such as the responsibility of rearing children, besetting financial pressures and dependency on men for routine chores.

Lavin was paid an impressive fee of $1,325 for 'In the Middle of the Fields', which was her third story accepted within the quantity bonus cycle.[23] MacKenzie reminded Lavin that if she sold a fourth story before the end of the bonus period, she would earn an additional 15 per cent bonus on each of the four pieces and with the purchase of another two stories, the bonus would increase by 20 per cent resulting in a 35 per cent additional payment per story, A new cycle began upon the purchase of a sixth story or after the fourth 'if it becomes impossible to manage six within the bonus period'.[24]

'In the Middle of the Fields' was Lavin's only story to appear in *The New Yorker* in 1961. It was scheduled for publication on 10 June 1961 but appeared a week earlier in the 3 June issue, the cover of which is fittingly that of a giant vase of flowers in the middle of a field being tended by a gardener.[25] Lavin's story is spread across nine pages shared with a poem, 'The Life of Service' by Donald Davie, and several cartoons.[26] One of these depicts two university professors in the company of a young attractive graduate and her parents on her graduation day, the tagline of which reads: 'We're sure going to miss your little girl around here, Mr. Wilkins.' The sleazy implication is amplified by the fact that the mother and young woman are excluded from the man talk. The issue also contains poetry by Richard Wilbur and John Updike and fiction by S. J. Perelman.

Lavin was working on a new story, 'The Bog Light', after which she intended to work on 'The Faithful Heart', which she described as 'a real beauty' – she was sure that MacKenzie would like it. Lavin had in fact begun writing 'The Bog Light' the previous year and intended to send it to the magazine back in November. She had also almost finished 'They Call Us Children', a story she began in 1958 under the title 'The Glass Hill'.[27]

Lavin's persistence with stories she disliked was ongoing and she continued to misjudge stories she thought *The New Yorker* would reject. She had worked intermittently on 'The Lucky Pair' for six months, but she said it was 'another unsatisfactory story for a very different reason'. She believed it to be 'a very dull story' that could only be improved with 'incredible luck & dexterity' and she suspected that it would be refused.[28] In early May, MacKenzie informed Lavin that Mr Shawn gave 'The Lucky Pair' the green light: '"Extremely interesting" he says, and we all say the same, and feel that we're lucky, too, having it and having you.'[29]

'The Lucky Pair' was the fourth story purchased within the bonus period, making it Lavin's second four-story quantity bonus and so earned her an additional 15 per cent bonus on each of the texts sold. She was paid $1,533 for 'The Lucky Pair', which included the bonus. The additional retrospective bonus for the other three stories amounted to $589.50.[30] Lavin was naturally delighted with the windfall but the fact that Shawn found the story of interest 'was a source of great pleasure' to her. She revealed that although she 'found it so interesting to write', she was also guilt-ridden for spending so much time on a story that she ultimately thought the magazine would reject.[31]

After the Easter break Lavin resolved to work solidly until June, when the family would be returning to Italy. As always, her work revolved around her children: 'I am going to try hard for the bonus but summer days or Spring I should say – make shorter hours for mothers.'[32] MacKenzie was also travelling to Italy for her vacation and she remarked, 'wouldn't it be fun if we were near enough to meet? I feel that sometime we must know each other.'[33] Lavin was equally enthusiastic at the prospect of their meeting: 'How I'd love to meet you – anyway, anywhere, but specially in Florence.'

Lavin asked for MacKenzie's holiday schedule but was doubtful that their dates would overlap.[34] MacKenzie would be in Florence from 28 May until 7 June, where she would be staying at the Helvetia Hotel, and from there she was going to travel to Siena until 17 June: 'Wouldn't it be fun if we were able to meet in either of these lovely places! Is there any chance?'[35] Unfortunately, it was not to be as Lavin was now not leaving for Italy until 15 August. However, she was planning to go to New York in the autumn and was contemplating taking one of her daughters with her. It was not to be as restful a summer for MacKenzie, who again had to cover Howard Moss's duties, in addition to her own, while he was on a seven-week vacation from 10 July.

Lavin queried whether the magazine considered suggestions for cartoons: 'They keep coming into my head which is a shame since I can't sketch.'[36] MacKenzie encouraged her to send any ideas because the magazine purchased them without images. Lavin again enquired whether MacKenzie liked her poem 'Neurosis' that she had sent the previous year. MacKenzie replied 'it made me laugh', although she seemed to take it slightly personally as she reflected, 'Sometimes I jump into another person's sentence and run away with it, and I always hate myself long before I get to the period.'[37] MacKenzie had forwarded it to Howard Moss but it was rejected.

This prompted MacKenzie to report back on Ned O'Gorman, whose poetry Lavin had sent to MacKenzie for consideration, with the brief note, 'No comment from me. I'm not competent – but Ned is a nice person & I hope you'll meet him some time as you are both in New York.'[38] O'Gorman was also a friend of Muriel Spark, who had introduced him to Shirley Hazzard. MacKenzie duly forwarded O'Gorman's poems to Moss and she informed Lavin that they were due to meet O'Gorman at a lunch event: 'You will be our great bond. I'm looking forward to meeting him.'[39] However, the meeting turned out to be a disappointing one for MacKenzie, who reflected afterwards, 'I think what I met was his public self, and the passion and concern of the poems makes me feel there's a quite different private self to be met. Isn't this so?'[40]

Lavin had applied again for the Guggenheim Fellowship but was doubtful that she would be successful in her reapplication, which took her a painstaking ten days to complete: 'No story on earth – not even the Y. [Yellow] Beret took as much out of me, & only the Preface of the Sel. [Selected] Stories come next.'[41] Lavin did not have to fill out the application form for a renewal of the fellowship, but she had to furnish the foundation with an account of her accomplishments since her last application and a statement of purpose for seeking further support. She also had to provide a list of referees who would be au fait with her latest work.

Lavin's hard work paid off and she was granted a second fellowship for twelve months between the period 15 September 1961 until 15 December 1962, due to the fact that she wanted to take three months outside of the fellowship for her daughters' holidays. Lavin was initially offered a grant of $4,500, which the foundation later increased to $5,000 (she had requested $6,000). Lavin was going to return to Florence with her family and the stipend would be paid in quarterly payments in the form of American Express Traveller's Cheques, the first instalment of which would be available at the American Express in Florence.

In May, Lavin was 'almost incoherent' with excitement over her productivity but had to supress her glee as she was in the National Library. She explained that she had finished 'The Bog Light' and also had two half-finished stories, one of which was 'a kind of a readers story rather than a writers story'. It was another piece that she had to '<u>work</u> at – like the Yellow Beret' and she later wrote in the margin of the letter, 'I feel about it like as if I was doing it with a crotchet hook!' The other story was the 'The Cuckoo Spit', which she described as 'a "flowy" story'[42] Lavin feared that if she concentrated her efforts on the difficult story, 'The Cuckoo Spit' would suffer as a result. She was also working on 'A Dream', that she clarified was 'the title – not a description of it!'

By now, Lavin was tired and longing for her holidays, when she resolved to write nothing until September. Satisfied with her earnings thus far, she decided not to push herself for the bonus but instead would take a laid-back approach and 'plod on' until the end of June.[43] But she had a change of heart after MacKenzie coaxed her to attempt to make the six-story bonus. Lavin reasoned that she had to be in Dublin with her daughters, who were busy studying until the end of June, so she saw it as 'a signpost from fate' to make the effort. Lavin was unsuccessful in getting 'The Bog Light' to MacKenzie before she left for Italy and so, in her absence, Lavin reluctantly wrote to William Maxwell for an update on the story. She had been anxious about making contact with him but she eventually plucked up the courage to write, explaining: 'You are not all that of a stranger, since I know your work and hear Elizabeth Cullinan speak of you so often and warmly. Still I am nervous.'[44] Maxwell informed Lavin that he was keeping 'The Bog Light' for MacKenzie's return, but Lavin suspected that he did not like the story. Upon her arrival back to the office, MacKenzie let Lavin know that the story was unsuccessful: 'The trouble is the situation; there's just something too stock about it, and I'm afraid that not even your enormous skill at reworking will change that fact.'[45]

While it must have been frustrating for Lavin to have the story turned down, given that she was encouraged to try for the extra bonus, she was not surprised at the decision. Lavin hated the story and 'dressed [it] up hastily' in the hopes of selling it. She was gracious in the face of rejection and expressed her gratitude to the magazine: 'I will never get over the feeling that it is me should be paying *The New Yorker* – but alas – with what?' Lavin informed MacKenzie that 1961 was a good year for her financially, even without the Guggenheim Fellowship. In fact, it was a great surprise for her to get the bonus at all, since she thought only two of her stories would be published that year, but when MacKenzie encouraged her to attempt the six-story bonus she put herself under such duress 'that it was really madness to try for it'.[46] Lavin was working on another story that she did like but would not dash off just for the bonus since, as she explained, 'it's a lovely fluid story that must flow its own way & make its own course'. Although Lavin was always anxious to make a sale to the magazine, she was not necessarily prepared to force a story's progression.

Lavin compared working on difficult stories to when she lived in America as a child: on occasion, her mother would sort baskets of peaches, giving herself and her father the ones that were 'going off', with the result that the following day there would be more that were spoiling, which they then had to eat. As a result, Lavin wrote, 'we never got a good peach. I am getting like that about not working on my good stories'.[47] Similarly, Lavin deprived herself of the pleasure of working on stories she liked, because she felt a duty to finish stories she disliked. However, her commitment to such stories and her compulsion to complete them often resulted in improved texts that were subsequently accepted by *The New Yorker.* Lavin recognised that her efforts fine-tuned her craft and ultimately improved her as a writer, 'for my part the work I do on these step-stories (I love that name you gave them) is of immense value to me (and later I hope to you) because I am working so consciously on them … and getting into training'.

Lavin noted in her letters that she felt contractually obliged to let *The New Yorker* see all of her new material and, as a result, she submitted stories to the magazine that she would never normally have let them see, which she planned to send to other magazines with a 'small circulation'. The fact is that Lavin *was* contractually obliged to do so since she was bound by the first-reading agreement to let *The New Yorker* have first refusal of her work. She hoped *The New Yorker* would 'not think less highly of me for these failures, or "essais"'. Despite being 'truly appalled & ashamed' of the 'The Bog Light', to the extent that she vowed to 'tear it up at once', Lavin did not give up on it completely and thought she would rewrite it.

The quantity bonus certainly incentivised Lavin to be productive, and she made every effort to earn it. However, while earning money was a necessity and a driving force for Lavin, writing was not a purely financial exercise for her. She explained to MacKenzie that she did not care about the money but had a 'moral obligation' to try for the bonus in order to do her duty towards her family: 'If I honestly try, under dreadful circumstances, I feel that I am doing my duty in full towards the girls and my mother. It does not in the least matter to me that I do not get it.'[48] Lavin appreciated the forthright and honest dialogue with MacKenzie about her work and acknowledged not only the financial gain in writing for *The New Yorker* but also the fact that through her direct dealings with the magazine and its editing of her stories, she acquired more expertise and experience in the business of magazine publications.

On 27 June Lavin gave Edward Rice, the founder of *Jubilee* magazine, the third draft of 'The Bride and the Statue', to deliver by hand to MacKenzie the following day before her bonus deadline of 30 June.[49] She asked MacKenzie, 'as my friend', not to submit the story if she thought it was not ready.[50] 'The Bride and the Statue' was rejected and MacKenzie, expanding upon the 'step-story' metaphor, bluntly told Lavin that it was 'no step story but a pure orphan'. She was concerned that Lavin was pushing herself too hard to achieve the bonus: 'Of course I understand how you must try for the bonus, but I grieve just the same for your driving yourself when you are too tired.'[51] Lavin was unsurprised that the story was rejected but she feared that that the editors would 'think less' of her for sending in 'such efforts'. She explained that she 'had to make a bid for the money', even though she was too worn out and it was a bad time of year for her to write.[52] Lavin must have been greatly relieved to receive another COLA payment for the last quarter that totalled $1,101.[53]

Lavin 'swore' to take a three-month break from writing, even though she revealed that 'the pet stories on which I want to work, dangle like carrots before my nose!' Macmillan were coming over to Dublin to discuss her next book and she caught up with her backlog of work and was spending her time organising her mother's apartment, 'shutting my eyes to the folly of her living in it – alone – at 80'. Lavin lamented the fact that she could not make her mother happy despite all her efforts and wondered how she, who was one of twelve children, could be 'a completely spoiled woman', while Lavin, an only child, was not. She bought a new Triumph convertible for the journey to Italy and hoped that her mother would not give cause for them to be summoned back from the trip.[54]

Lavin wrote to MacKenzie from Rosslare harbour on the day of their departure to let her know that they were on their way and due to arrive in Florence in approximately ten days, but if something was urgent regarding 'The Lucky Pair', she could contact her via the American Express in Nice.[55] They ended up making 'a dash into Spain' before heading to Florence. Lavin expressed a desire to meet Nabokov while in Nice and asked whether MacKenzie knew him and if there was anyone else she should meet with while she was in Europe.[56]

The Great Wave and Other Stories was published by Macmillan London and New York in May and August respectively. The volume comprises all of Lavin's stories to have appeared in *The New Yorker* thus far. An abundance of generally positive reviews featured in the Irish, British and American press including *The Observer*, *The Times Literary Supplement*, *The Guardian Journal*, *The Spectator*, *The Saturday Review*, *The Irish Times*, the *Sunday Independent*, *The Washington Star*, *The New Yorker*, *The Boston Evening Herald*, *The New York Times*, *The Miami Herald*, *The Daily Telegraph*, *The Wall Street Journal*, *The Boston Globe* and *The Chicago Tribune*.

Orville Prescott, in his *New York Times* review of the collection, asserted: 'Mary Lavin is one of the most distinguished of living Irish writers, as complete a master of the short story as Frank O'Connor. Mary Lavin writes in stories that belong to the great tradition of Chekhov.'[57] Mary McGrory, in *The Evening Star*, wrote in praise of the volume: 'Some modern short stories are like strawmats, slippery to walk on, not much to look at. Mary Lavin's are by comparison, like oriental rugs, with a deep pile and a design that glows the more you study it.'[58] Francis Stuart in his *Irish Times* review found the stories to be 'glimpses ... of familiar things seen from an angle that is both unfamiliar and stimulating'.[59] And in *The Saturday Review* Padraic Colum observed of Lavin: 'To my mind, Mary Lavin's great distinction is in the fact that she reverses the turn that the usual short-storyteller gives the narrative – the turn to disenchantment.'[60] Colum had written to Lavin from New York to congratulate her on the new book and informed her that he wrote his review 'with enthusiasm'. He considered the stories 'beautiful and lasting' and 'the best that have come out of Ireland'.[61] Muriel Spark in her 17 December *Observer* review considered the collection 'lovely' and 'undervalued'.

The next contact Lavin made with MacKenzie was towards the end of September. The holiday was proving a success: 'I have had <u>such</u> a holiday – never in my life did I have such rest & such freedom from worry.' Lavin had also stopped worrying about the author's proof for the 'The Lucky Pair' as she believed MacKenzie would have got in touch had there been any urgency.[62] MacKenzie never did because it was not due to be published until the spring and she explained that the author's proofs were normally only set when a story was scheduled.[63]

Lavin immediately resumed writing upon her return from holiday in October. She 'took a plunge' and sent Caroline and Elizabeth to school in Kylemore Abbey in Connemara, although she had intended to send Elizabeth to the Sacred Heart School in Florence.[64] Lavin was sorting out her Irish taxes and enquired whether the Form 1099 that *The New Yorker* sent to her was only issued to writers on contracts or to all contributors. MacKenzie informed her that the form was sent to every writer whose earnings exceeded a minimum amount in a given year.[65]

Elizabeth Cullinan went back to New York in October and MacKenzie informed Lavin that 'our Elizabeth' had returned home laden with Irish wares, 'She and I have a regular review of each other's foreign shopping – I laid in knits in Italy, and I don't need to tell you what she laid in.' Cullinan clearly felt at home in Ireland as MacKenzie imparted, 'What a lovely year she had. I feel that she found the place she belongs – and don't you think she'll be back? She loves you, but I hardly need to tell you that.'[66] Cullinan, in fact, was 'stunned' when she went to Ireland to find that she was not considered Irish. As an Irish American in the US, Cullinan always had a sense of being an outsider but she was not expecting this sense of otherness in Ireland.[67] This feeling of displacement is captured in her stories, for instance, 'A Sunday like the Others', when Cullinan writes of the character Frances Hayes: 'Here in Ireland she was American, though back in Boston she was known as Irish. Irish American.'[68]

Frank O'Connor wrote to Maxwell of how Cullinan 'slipped back to N.Y. without even seeing me, which may be as well, as it would have made me homesick, and I am sick enough as things are'. O'Connor had returned to Ireland after suffering a stroke while teaching at Stanford that year and was living in Dublin in an apartment in Wilton Place, just a stone's throw from Lavin's mews.[69] He had intended to introduce Cullinan to his long-standing friend Dan Binchy, the historian and diplomat, who was an avid *New Yorker* reader (O'Connor told Maxwell that Binchy was his 'alter ego in

Dublin').[70] Earlier in the year, MacKenzie had given Maxwell a photograph of O'Connor 'listening in the most sympathetic way in the world to an upset raccoon'. Maxwell wrote that he placed it 'under the glass top of my desk, along with AE's portrait, which it beautifully complements'.[71] The photograph, taken by Sprague Holden, features in the Middlebury College Bread Loaf Writers' Conference catalogue of 1954 with the caption, 'Frank O'Connor conducts an extracurricular interview.'[72]

In December, MacKenzie sent Lavin her first-reading agreement for 1962 and a cheque for $850 'to bind the bargain'. The sum reflected the fact that, as MacKenzie put it, 'We've had a good year, and you have, too – a good last several years.' Lavin's productivity paid off and enhanced her earnings considerably, making it understandable why she pushed herself so hard to earn the bonuses. MacKenzie enquired after Lavin's health after she heard through Cullinan that she had been unwell: 'Of course I hope it's something short and unserious, but do let me know when you send back the copy of the agreement so my anxiety for you will be in decent proportion. It makes me sad to think of your being ill.'[73]

On 10 December Mary McGrory, in her reflection on the literature of 1961 for her *Sunday Star* article wrote, 'Was it a memorable year in the world of books? To a reviewer, who admittedly read only a fraction of the more than 10,000 books which poured from the presses – possibly the wrong fraction – it did not seem be so.' However, McGrory found Lavin's *The Great Wave* to be 'the finest fiction' that she had read and that it 'simply glowed with artistry and feeling'. It was one of four books that she would remember best from 1961. Frank O'Connor's *An Only Child* also made the cut, alongside Theodore H. White's *The Making of a President* and Russell Baker's *An American in Washington*. McGrory's column carried photographs of both Lavin and O'Connor. She also gave mention to Salinger's *Franny and Zooey*, which was based on two stories originally published in *The New Yorker* that featured the Irish-Jewish Glass family. McGrory noted the passing of literary giant Ernest Hemingway, who committed suicide in July, and the long-serving *New Yorker* staffer James Thurber, who died in November.[74]

The year 1962 got off to a good financial start for Mary Lavin, thanks to *The New Yorker*. Towards the end of January Rachel MacKenzie sent her an unexpected cheque amounting to $821.50 for the cost-of-living adjustment (COLA) for the previous year. MacKenzie asked after Elizabeth Cullinan, who, as she predicted, had returned to Ireland: 'will you tell her that this floor is empty for her absence? Every now and again, when I go down the hall in my reading glasses, I forget myself and wave at her typewriter, and it's disconcerting both to me and the new girl who's sitting at it.'[75] Cullinan had recently spent a long weekend with Lavin at Bective and was also due to spend that coming Easter with the family.[76]

The Scottish writer Muriel Spark forged another link between MacKenzie and Lavin. Spark was in New York in January for the American launch of *The Prime of Miss Jean Brodie* and MacKenzie informed Lavin, 'Muriel Spark is here, and do you know what a great admirer she is of your writing? We speak of you; it is one of our bonds.'[77] Macmillan London had published the first UK edition of *The Prime of Miss Jean Brodie* the previous year. Martin Stannard reveals that MacKenzie entertained Spark and brought her to the Broadway musicals *How to Succeed in Business Without Really Trying* and *A Funny Thing Happened on the Way to the Forum*.[78] It was MacKenzie who first solicited fiction from Spark for *The New Yorker* and she became her editor when the magazine began publishing her stories. After some initial rejections, the magazine accepted Spark's 'The Ormolu Clock' in 1959. It was published in *The New Yorker* on 17 September 1960. In 1961 Spark sent MacKenzie *The Prime of Miss Jean Brodie*. The editors, particularly MacKenzie, were so impressed with the story that the 14 October 1961 issue was dedicated to a condensed version of the work, the publication of which played a major role in establishing Spark's international reputation.[79]

MacKenzie also met with Lovat 'Rache' Dickson of Macmillan London, who handled Spark, and who was also in New York in January scouting for new talent, although according to Stannard, he was there 'ostensibly on general business but really to junket with her [Spark] and to guard his prize author'.[80] On Dickson's return to London, at Spark's request, he sent MacKenzie a copy of *The Great Wave and Other Stories*, and he conveyed how much he enjoyed their meeting. MacKenzie acknowledged the receipt of Lavin's book and informed Dickson, 'I've read all the stories, of course, and worked with seven of them, and it's like having a collection of old friends come to hand.'[81] She told Lovat that she was going to read his biographical work *The Ante-Room*.[82]

Dickson had informed MacKenzie that they had taken on another *New Yorker* contributor, Shirley Hazzard, during his trip to New York.[83]

MacKenzie was Hazzard's editor when she joined *The New Yorker* and she introduced Hazzard to Spark, which initiated a friendship between the two writers.[84] Both women would later share their unease at MacKenzie's overfamiliar approach. According to Stannard, both Spark and Hazzard dreaded MacKenzie's 'claustrophobic Sunday suppers'. MacKenzie, or 'Auntie Rachel', as Spark referred to her, even informed Hazzard that she was moving into a new apartment 'to be nearer to you'.[85] MacKenzie and Hazzard were of the opinion that MacKenzie 'was (unconsciously) a lesbian'.[86]

MacKenzie had also met a young artist friend of Lavin's named Pamela, whom she planned to see again. MacKenzie could not recall her surname but she was more than likely Dublin-born Pamela Matthews, who had travelled to New York in 1962 and exhibited her paintings in galleries including the Ruth White Gallery on 42 East 57th Street. Matthews was a member of a group of modern female artists who exhibited at the Royal Hibernian Academy (RHA) in Dublin. Lavin's opening of Matthews' first solo exhibition at the Dawson Gallery in Dublin was covered in *The Irish Press* on 3 March 1964.[87] MacKenzie continually found herself meeting a diverse group of people with connections to Lavin and yet she had never met the woman herself, prompting her to end one of her letters, 'Of course even more satisfactory than meeting these friends and admirers would be to meet you. Some day, Until then, here's my love.'[88]

In February Lavin was finally back at work after an unproductive winter and a series of unfortunate events that left her drained. She had been ill with bronchitis and Caroline was suffering from earaches and tonsillitis. To add to her woes, there had been a break-in at the farm. It was particularly devastating for Lavin because November was normally one of her more productive months: 'this, I suppose, is easily explained by these two months occurring bang in the middle of term, with the children's holiday out of sight from both decks!' Lavin reckoned that she had not done any work since her 'ridiculous effort' at the 'orphan' story, 'The Bog Light', back in July. She also revealed, contrary to her previous reports, that the family's trip abroad was not such a success as the business of camping and managing the girls proved quite challenging.[89]

On the upside, Lavin's mother was finally happy in her new 'luxury' accommodation in the Mespil Flats in Ballsbridge, which was very close to Lavin's mews. Aside from her mother living alone, it gave Lavin great peace of mind, but she hoped to get someone to share the apartment with her. MacKenzie had told Lavin of her friend Doris's 87-year-old mother, who was suffering from dementia, and reflected, 'What saddens me about the old isn't this kind of confusion but the heaviness of their hearts, and the terrible sense of loss they seem to live with. Perhaps we'll have the luck to die in time.'[90]

Despite the various challenges Lavin remained in good spirits, largely due to the recent generous COLA cheque, the proceeds of which she promptly used to check in to a hotel. Lavin's doctor had recommended that she take some time alone in Italy, even though she had been given a clean bill of health, but she opted to stay in nearby Buswell's Hotel for five days with her daughters.[91] Lavin revealed, however, that it was really the presence of mice in the mews that instigated the brief getaway, which resulted in the adoption of a rescue cat to tackle the problem. Cullinan recounted that Alice, the cat, sorted out the mice infestation.[92] Buswell's Hotel, located on Molesworth Street in Dublin, was just 'two streets away' from Lavin's Lad Lane mews. To illustrate the 'absurdity' of the journey Lavin drew MacKenzie a map of 'our bit of Dublin', on which she indicated the proximity of Lad Lane to Buswell's and she also marked the locations of St Stephen's Green and the National Library. The brief sojourn re-energised Lavin and although she had not fully recovered, she battled on, 'coughing my way (and sniffling & almost crying)' through several drafts of the 'The Cuckoo Spit', which was at last near completion.

'The Cuckoo Spit' was another story Lavin hated and she referred to it as a 'DOG of a story'. She presumed that she found it so difficult to write due to its close resemblance to her own life: 'It's one of those semi-autobiographical stories – like "In a Café" & "The Middle of the Fields" – that I loathe anyway & find very hard. It will be so wonderful to be dealing with purely imagined material again – it never blurs or goes out of focus as the other does.' 'The Cuckoo Spit' features a childless Vera Traske, who has been widowed for four years. She happens upon a much younger man, the nephew of a neighbour, while she is making her way back to her country home after a walk in the field.

Vera later meets him in St Stephen's Green in Dublin but realises that it was a mistake and that there is no future in a May–December relationship.

Lavin was trying to save her Guggenheim money for the following year and possibly use it to travel for a few months and to write 'a really funny short novel' featuring two sisters that she had wanted to compose for some years. Meanwhile, she was surviving on her *New Yorker* bonus until she had a clear run to work and remarked, 'It's such a pity one cannot write with one's fingers crossed!'[93]

MacKenzie was happy to hear that Lavin was writing again and while she was looking forward to receiving the new story, she informed Lavin that she was 'awfully fond of your dogs, too – what an unmerciful name for "In a Café" and "In the Middle of the Fields", those dear good stories –'[94] Lavin's opinion of 'In the Middle of the Fields' seemed to soften somewhat when she later wrote to MacKenzie, 'I hear In the Middle of the Fields is in the O. Henry Collection. I'm glad – I do like that old story.'[95] Again, Lavin seemed to be confusing the *O. Henry Stories* with Foley and Burnett's *Best American Short Stories*, the 1962 edition of which also included fiction by John Updike, Flannery O'Connor and Irwin Shaw.

In early March MacKenzie reminded Lavin to return the signed first-reading agreement as the business office required it for their records: 'Can you put your hands on it without a general house cleaning?'[96] The office had also requested written confirmation from Lavin verifying that she was 'still an American citizen'. In a later letter, MacKenzie thought this needed to be confirmed every second year. Lavin, perhaps slightly taken aback at MacKenzie's supposition of a disorderly household, remarked, 'How very careless you must think me.' However, Lavin admitted that she thought she would 'have to tilt the mews on end and shake it all out' but she was more organised than they both gave her credit for and found it where she had filed away her copy of the contract.[97]

Lavin duly returned the first-reading contract and her declaration of American citizenship. She was now eligible to join *The New Yorker*'s retirement plan, having completed three first-reading agreements.[98] MacKenzie explained that it paid 1¼ per cent of her earnings from the commencement date until she turned sixty and she considered it to be 'a very generous arrangement'.[99] Lavin had already signed and returned the annuity form, 'certain it was something very good & generous'.[100] However, the form had to be reissued to Lavin because there was ambiguity over her relationship to her beneficiaries (her daughters), due to the fact that they did not share the same surname. She was advised to sign it 'Mary Lavin Walsh' in order to avoid any confusion.

MacKenzie sent Lavin the author's proof of 'The Lucky Pair' with her queries placed in the margins, which mainly sought clarity with regard to a character and the time frame. MacKenzie needed the story back almost immediately as it was scheduled for the 7 April issue, which meant that it needed to go to press on 28 or 29 March. Lavin sent the proofs the following day and addressed MacKenzie's queries as best she could and made some minor corrections that could be ignored. She apologised for making corrections in pencil but she was under time pressure due to the fact that she had to travel to Galway and back in one day (approximately an eight-hour round trip then) for the funeral of her uncle's wife, and wished that in such a situation she could be more like Salinger – presumably a reference to his reclusiveness. *Time* magazine had run a profile of Salinger in September 1961, which revealed his hermit-like lifestyle: 'Outsiders trying to reach him are, in fact, reduced to passing notes or letters, to which there is usually no reply.'[101]

'The Lucky Pair' was rescheduled for the later date of 5 May but it was ultimately published in *The New Yorker* on 28 April 1962. Arthur Getz's cover is a view of the string section of an orchestra.[102] Lavin's story spans across eight pages shared with two poems, 'Folk Songs from the Oblivian' by William Walden and 'Hiroshige' by Mark M. Perlberg, and several cartoons. One depicts two men chatting at a drinks party with the caption 'When Allen Ginsberg has three kids and a mortgage, maybe I'll listen to what he has to say.'[103] Ginsberg's poetry would later be published in *The New Yorker*, the first of which, 'Wales Visitation', appeared in the 11 May 1968 issue. A cartoon by Dana Fradon depicts a man sitting with his stern-looking loans manager and carries the caption 'To be perfectly honest with you, sir, when I got the loan last year, I didn't expect any of us to be here this year.'[104] This quip possibly alludes to well-known American psychic and astrologer Jeane Dixon's prediction that the world would end on 4 February 1962.[105] The issue also features the stories 'If It Please Your Honour' by S. J. Perelman and 'Visit the Sick' by Fred Licht.

In March Lavin began to have itchy feet on hearing that the O'Connors had travelled to Italy.[106] Maxwell wrote to O'Connor in response to a postcard he received from him from Pompeii, that he would have 'slapped a habeas corpus' on O'Connor to prevent him from leaving the United States.[107] Perhaps Maxwell had a sense of foreboding, as O'Connor would never return to America. Louise Bogan, the poet and *New Yorker* poetry critic, wrote to let O'Connor know that he was being offered the American Academy of Arts and Letters Award for Literature for 1962. His only issue in accepting the honour was getting back to New York by boat in time for the ceremony on 24 May. O'Connor, like Lavin, had a fear of flying and on 5 April he wrote to Maxwell of his dilemma: 'how the hell do you explain personally that you're terrified out of your wits of aeroplanes?'[108] It probably did not help matters that on 1 March American Airlines Flight 1 crashed soon after take-off at New York International Airport (now John F. Kennedy International Airport), killing all the eighty-seven passengers and eight crew members on board.[109] In the end O'Connor did not make it back to New York, but provided a 'Progress Report' and received the grant of $2,000. Nobel Prize laureate William Faulkner received the Academy's Gold Medal for fiction that year and his acceptance speech at the ceremony was his last before he died from a heart attack six weeks later.[110]

Lavin was planning to travel to the United States in the autumn for a couple of weeks and aimed to be back by mid-November 'for a good winter of work'.[111] She had sent MacKenzie two new stories, 'Let me Come Inland' and 'Assassins, All'.[112] Both stories were rejected but MacKenzie was comforted by the fact that Lavin did not labour over them. MacKenzie believed 'Let Me Come Inland' to be a stronger story than 'Assassins, All', but she thought that it presented 'more like a theatre piece than a story, and, I'm afraid, one belonging to a period far enough back to feel rather remote – at least to us here in this city of New York in this year of 1962'.[113] MacKenzie advised Lavin where she could make cuts and strengthen the story but she explained that as it currently stood it was unsuitable for the magazine.

On 2 April MacKenzie told Lavin that Katherine Anne Porter's hotly anticipated novel *Ship of Fools* was launched that day at the 21

Club: 'I haven't read it yet, but I feel we all should and so I've ordered copy for myself, and one for you, too. For Spring.'[114] In late March William Maxwell wrote to Frank O'Connor to let him know that he was reading the novel in advance of its launch the following week and offered to send him a copy.[115] Mark Schorer was not exaggerating in his *New York Times* review of the book ('the *Middlemarch* of a later day') when he observed that it had been 'awaited through an entire literary generation'. The novel, which Porter began writing in 1940, was based on a journal she kept of her travels from Mexico to Germany while on one of her Guggenheim Fellowships.[116] It was the bestselling novel in America in 1962.[117] *The New Yorker* published a satire of the novel *Nobody's Fool* by *New Yorker* staffer and writer Peter de Vries in the 16 June 1962 issue. MacKenzie promised to keep Lavin informed about Eudora Welty's new novel – likely her only children's book, *The Shoe Bird* – which was published in 1964. She was unsure as to whether the magazine would be publishing any extracts (it did not).

Lavin tended to burn out by April, but she was particularly weary that year because she was disheartened over the lack of work to show for her productivity in comparison to previous years. She estimated that she had spent eight months working on 'The Cuckoo Spit, 'not counting the end of last year when it began in my mind'.[118] Lavin was also working on another story, *First Love*, which she was considering renaming 'The Life of the Red Haired Man', as she wanted to keep the title for another story.[119] Lavin's dearth of stories that year made her fearful of a year when she might have none at all. She was not concerned about a lack of ideas for stories, which she had in abundance, but in getting them all written. Lavin's approach to her writing was in stark contrast to her admirer Muriel Spark, who stated in a *New Yorker* 'Profile' piece, 'I don't correct or rewrite … because I do all the correcting before I begin, getting it in my mind. And then when I pounce, I pounce.'[120]

MacKenzie was troubled that Lavin was so worn down and suggested she take another hotel break or go 'some other place where nothing is being asked of you for a while. Is it out of the question? I feel concerned about you.'[121] Lavin was aiming to finish up for the summer, after her daughters' examinations in June, when she would go to Bective, 'to fix it up & put in an appearance in the village etc.'[122]

MacKenzie urged her to spend the Guggenheim money to give her some respite: 'I can't think of anything that would better nourish your writing, now, can you?[123] Lavin reassured MacKenzie that she was fine and back writing. She explained that the whole point in saving the money was so that it would fund her period of desired inactivity.[124]

On 16 June Lavin was a guest at the opening of the James Joyce tower in Sandycove in County Dublin. Sylvia Beach was the guest of honour and a photograph of Mary Lavin with Sylvia Beach and Niall Sheridan featured in the *Irish Independent*'s 'Picture Special'. The newspaper's coverage of the tower's opening was overshadowed by a photograph capturing the moment President John F. Kennedy's mortar board slipped off his head while he posed for photographs after receiving his honorary doctorate from Yale University. Other attendees at the launch of the tower included Joyce's sisters, Eileen Schaurek and May Monaghan; Brendan Behan, Brian O'Nolan, Seán Ó Faoláin, Austin Clarke, Louis MacNeice, Anthony Cronin, Niall Sheridan, Charlie Haughey, minister for justice; Donagh MacDonagh, chairman of the Dublin Joyce Society; and Frances Steloff, founder of the Gotham Book Mart and James Joyce Society in New York.[125] MacDonagh introduced Beach and wrote a poem for the occasion. Padraic Colum, who was the president of the James Joyce Tower Committee, was unable to attend the event as he was the guest of another Joycean commemoration in New York. (Brendan Gill interviewed Colum for a 'Talk of the Town' piece for *The New Yorker* the previous week, on 9 June, in which he said that the opening of the Sandycove Martello Tower was 'A great day for Joyceans and a great day for Joyce!')[126]

Beach was delighted to have befriended Lavin and she visited Abbey Farm for lunch and toured the countryside with her. She tried to phone Lavin to thank her for 'one of the most wonderful times in my life', but Lavin's telephone was out of order and so she wrote to her from London where she had travelled for an interview (*Appointment with Sylvia Beach* with Malcolm Muggeridge for Granada Television). Beach was clearly impressed with Lavin and contemplated: 'it's hard to say which is the most interesting and fascinating: you or your books' and again she expressed her delight at their meeting: 'I am so thankful to have met you in Dublin, dear Mary Lavin!' Beach asked Lavin to send her photographs that were taken of them together.[127] On the same day

Lavin, having been unable to telephone, wrote Beach 'a note of farewell' in which she was apologetic for missing a trip to Ringsend, where James Joyce's 'The Encounter' was set. Lavin expressed her happiness at seeing the end of a bad year as she explained that she always thought of June as signifying the end of the calendar, rather than January, due to her daughters' summer holidays.[128]

Beach's time in Dublin made a great impression on her. She had stayed with Niall and Monica Sheridan in Dalkey and she wrote to them afterwards: 'The lovely blue scarf and brooch you gave me and my smart Dublin outfits made a sensation when I showed them to my friends in Paris – I am almost a Princess Grace these days.'[129] Beach wrote again to Lavin on 27 July from her chalet in Savoie, where she spent her summers, to convey her thanks for the books she had sent her and she politely reminded Lavin to send the photographs. Beach ended her letter: 'With the sincere admiration and love of Sylvia.'[130] She died in Paris just over two months later on 5 October, aged seventy-five. Lavin kept a clipping of her *Sunday Times* obituary in her files.[131]

In early July Lavin spent a fortnight in Kerry, which revived her spirits enormously and she had been busy writing ever since her return home. 'The New Gardener', which had been rejected by *The New Yorker* in 1960, was published in *Cosmopolitan*'s August Summer Fiction Festival issue, alongside fiction by Rona Jaffe, James Purdy and Gloria Vanderbilt and two novels, *The Creative Urge* by Margery Sharp and *Where the Body Lies* by John D. MacDonald.[132] Fifteen-year-old actress Sue Lyon, who played the title role in Stanley Kubrick's 1962 film adaptation of Nabokov's 1955 novel *Lolita*, graced the cover.[133] Lavin also had an essay, 'The Fields Will Never Leave You', published in *Country Beautiful* the following month.[134]

At the end of August Lavin finally sent MacKenzie 'The Cuckoo Spit', which she estimated took her 'one solid year & several months' to write.[135] She was greatly relieved to put it behind her: 'I feel like the Jesuit father who was asked by a little boy, "Father, do you never wish you were an ordinary human being?"' Lavin acknowledged that the Guggenheim bursary gave her the luxury of spending so much time on the story and yet pondered why it took so many months to write. (This was likely due to the fact that Lavin had originally conceived it as a novella and then tirelessly worked on condensing it to make it suitable for *The New Yorker.*) Although she put all her energy into the story, she had jotted down ideas and drafts for other stories that she planned to work on at wintertime, 'so that I lost nothing as it were'.

Lavin was spending her time tending the garden and doing household chores, which made her reflect that 'sometimes I am filled with wonder & envy at the thought that for some women life is unendingly filled with these simple tasks'. She made the decision to postpone her US trip until March, which would allow her to work in November. Lavin was feeling much more positive and she had a feeling that 'what seemed a bad year is going to be one of my really good years in a queer quiet way'.[136]

Lavin's work on 'The Cuckoo Spit' was not in vain. On 17 September MacKenzie sent her a cable with the good news that the story was accepted: 'We love The Cuckoo Spit. It's a beautiful story, worth every minute.'[137] Lavin was paid $2,375 for the story plus the 25 per cent premium of $593.75 ($44.53 was deducted for the retirement plan) and MacKenzie remarked: 'Isn't it a lovely check – but no more money would ever be adequate for that lovely story!'[138]

On 22 September Lavin set off on a three-week camping holiday with Valentine and Caroline. Elizabeth was already in Italy. Lavin had originally intended to leave Caroline, 'the little one', at home for the first time because she felt that should be attending school, but she declared, 'I never think school important except as a pleasure!' and so Caroline went along too.[139] The *Drogheda Independent* reported on their trip: 'As always on her trips abroad she travelled in her black Triumph Herald coupe, the Tricolour flying from the tip of the radio aerial, with her daughters Valentine (18), now studying law, and Caroline (9). Her third daughter, Elizabeth (13), who had been spending the summer in Florence, was collected en route.'[140]

Lavin suggested that MacKenzie could contact her via American Express at their various European destinations, the first of which was to be Venice. She availed of the opportunity to travel to Turkey and sent MacKenzie a postcard of Soliman's mosque and the Golden Horn in Istanbul, on which she informed her that they had driven 2,576 miles since receiving her cable. They mostly slept in the car 'and although exhausted we are enchanted with every day'.[141] On 5 October they left Athens for Florence and on 14 October they drove to Paris. They also travelled to Menton, because Lavin was due to be awarded the Katherine Mansfield Prize (International PEN). She had not mentioned the prize to MacKenzie because she had been sworn to secrecy until the official announcement. Two prizes amounting to approximately £100 were awarded for the best short story published in English between the years 1959 and 1961. There were entries from Ireland, the United Kingdom, the British Commonwealth and South Africa. The English judges, Muriel Spark, William Sansom and L. P. Hartley, selected Mary Lavin's 'The Great Wave' as the winner.[142] The *Drogheda Independent* reported of the prize, 'As so often happens with our Irish writers, Mary Lavin is better known and more widely acclaimed outside Ireland.'[143]

On 7 December Lavin wrote to MacKenzie after a long silence between them. Caroline had been out of school with tonsillitis for two months and Lavin was making up for lost time by trying to get as much work done before Christmas before she sailed to the US in April: 'I sail about the 19th April and return about ditto of May.' She was slowly working on *First Love* but explained that it was only 'a line a month (and you know how I exaggerate if probably only a line every two monts [*sic*])' Lavin liked the title, which she said, 'cheers me up every time I come on the mss under a heep [*sic*] of sweepings or hockey boots, or turfbricks'. She assured MacKenzie that they were all keeping well 'even if being well and happy takes a lot of time and makes a lot of work, no more, surely I tell myself then [*sic*] misery and worry!'[144]

Lavin read her prize-winning story to Dublin PEN at the Shelbourne Hotel on 8 December.[145] Patrick Lagan covered the recital in *The Irish Press*, erroneously calling the story, 'The Big Wave': 'An odd and unusual story and not really like Mary Lavin. But this adroit and expert writer was, possibly showing us that she could walk outside her own territory and still artistically, be completely at home.'[146] Patrick Lagan was the shared pseudonym under which Lavin's friend and fellow *New Yorker* contributor, Benedict Kiely, and Sean White wrote.[147]

On 2 December Fergus Wright's 'Panorama' section in the *Sunday Independent* carried an article titled 'Frank O'Connor gets a plea for books', which highlighted the author's ongoing concern at the number of out-of-print Irish books: 'Often has Frank O'Connor drawn attention to the great difficulties in finding books by Irish authors, including books by himself.'[148] On 30 December 1962 a *Sunday Independent* article, 'Save those books by Irish authors', highlighted the scarcity of works by Irish writers, including Frank O'Connor and Mary Lavin.[149] The article suggested that it was due to the fact that libraries discarded books that were not getting borrowed: 'They are the treasures of our past and must be preserved.'

MacKenzie posted Lavin her first-reading contract and, as usual, included 'a lovely check to bind the bargain'.[150] The contract ran from 6 March 1964 to 6 March 1965.[151] She mentioned that Muriel Spark was with her: 'Muriel Spark is in tow, and she told me about a prize that has come (is coming?) to you for "The Great Wave". I am so pleased.'[152] Lavin had presumed that she had told MacKenzie about the Katherine Mansfield Prize but it transpired that MacKenzie never received her letters from Menton. She asked MacKenzie to convey her great disappointment to Muriel Spark that she was not present for the ceremony. William Sansom must have attended the prize-giving because Lavin asked MacKenzie whether she was familiar with his work and wondered if she could recommend that he send in one of his stories to her for consideration. MacKenzie was actually an admirer of Sansom's writing as he had previously submitted pieces into *The New Yorker*; yet while she welcomed seeing any new work, none of his stories was ever published in the magazine.

Lavin had asked MacKenzie for suggestions of places to stay for three nights in New York. MacKenzie was pleased that Lavin would be visiting the city, even if only for a brief period: 'You'll save me a piece of it, won't you? I know so many people will want to be with you.'[153] One of those people was Nancy Wilson Ross, who offered to do whatever she could to make Lavin's visit as pleasurable as possible, including introducing Lavin to her private social club if she wished to stay there.[154] MacKenzie correctly thought Nancy Wilson Ross's club was the Cosmopolitan Club, located on the Upper East Side of Manhattan, which she noted was 'a bit less convenient than midtown, if stores and theatres are what you're interested in, but it's not too out of the way and transportation is easy enough'.[155] Wilson Ross's letter to Lavin was written on the Cosmopolitan Club's headed paper with the address 122 East 66th Street, New York.

The Poetry Center in New York had often invited Lavin to give a reading but the director, Elizabeth Kray, had left and Lavin baulked at the idea of having to contact strangers and so she enquired if MacKenzie knew the staff there.[156] MacKenzie promptly phoned Galen Eberl, the new secretary: 'I don't know her, but her telephone voice is lively and attractive.' Eberl was pleased to know that Lavin would be coming to the US and although the centre's spring series had already been scheduled, she was hopeful that they could facilitate a reading with her. MacKenzie trusted that Lavin did not mind her contacting Eberl: 'I know they would love to have you, and after all I haven't committed you to a thing!'[157] Eberl was obviously keen as she wrote to MacKenzie expressing her hope that they could work something out. Nothing came of it on this particular trip.

Lavin was somewhat addled over the question of her nationality and finding herself listed in reference books and anthologies 'as an Irish writer, an English writer & an American writer'. She had consulted with the American consulate, who were investigating the situation. She asked MacKenzie whether *The New Yorker* considered her Irish or American because she had signed a form that identified her as a '"non resident alien" paying tax in Ireland'.[158] MacKenzie let her know that *The New Yorker* regarded her as American. She was unsure what document Lavin was referring to and asked her to return it to them for further clarity, guessing that it was likely a paper sent to non-residents in order 'to determine their citizenship; in the case of aliens, unless the country of citizenship has a tax agreement with the United States, we are required to withhold 30% from all payments'.[159]

MacKenzie was again feeling the festive spirit in the run-up to Christmas: 'It's a season I love, though at the moment I feel a little frazzled by it.'[160] This was because she was under pressure to finish up work before she left for Ohio to visit her sister Ruth and her family for Christmas. MacKenzie flew back to New York on Christmas Day and ended her last letter of the year to Lavin on a high note: 'Yesterday, the plane took off to a rousing rendition of "In Deo Jubilo" and I felt that if anything untoward were to happen, we'd go straight on up and not down. Happy New Year!'[161]

5
'Paperback Writer'
1963–1964

> Do write me when you have a moment, though not at the expense of story-writing time.[1]

> If I could write while walking or talking – I'd be away.[2]

The year's first contact between Mary Lavin and Rachel MacKenzie was towards the end of January when MacKenzie issued Lavin two cheques that covered her regular quarterly COLA payment, in addition to the adjustment of the previous year's COLA.[3] Both came with the magazine's 'affection and our longing for another story'.[4] A month later Roger Angell wrote to inform Lavin that MacKenzie was in hospital and that they were holding her correspondence for her return, 'She has been quite ill, but is convalescing normally. It may be some time, however, before she can take up her editorial duties, I'm sure you will be hearing from her in a few weeks.'[5] He invited Lavin to continue sending in her stories to the magazine. Angell did not indicate the nature of MacKenzie's illness, but a letter from William Maxwell to Harriet O'Connor reveals that she had suffered a heart attack: 'There has been an enormous amount of work at the office, and Rachel MacKenzie had a massive coronary, and is still in the hospital, though perhaps going home this week, for a probably fairly long convalescence.'[6]

Lavin travelled to Paris in March, according to a letter from John McGahern to Michael McLaverty. In the same letter he also mentioned that he was in regular contact with Elizabeth Cullinan, who he most likely met through Lavin: 'she is a very beautiful person. I will miss her very much when she goes home'.[7] The pair had formed a close bond when Cullinan was in Dublin and McGahern had 'reluctantly' accompanied her to a party, hosted by Frank O'Connor, because she 'needed an escort'. It was the only time that he met O'Connor who, according to McGahern, spent most of the night in bed.[8] O'Connor, in a letter to Maxwell, referred to McGahern as 'her [Cullinan's] boy', implying that the two were romantically involved.[9]

Lavin wrote to J. D. Salinger before she travelled to America in the hope of meeting with him during her time there. Although he was not in a position to do so, he expressed his hope to see her one day in Ireland.[10] On 23 April she wrote to MacKenzie from the Canadian Pacific steamship the *Empress of England*: 'I feel so bad not knowing how you are really, but hearing at least good reports.'[11] Prior to journeying to New York Lavin had evidently returned to the town where she grew up because she sent an aerogram to Angell, postmarked from East Walpole, to let him know that she would get in touch when she arrived in New York on 14 May, as she was mindful that he might need to contact her in relation to 'The Cuckoo Spit', if it got scheduled for publication.[12]

Although Lavin described her trip to the United States as a holiday, she was taking part in the Third Annal Boston College Writers' Conference, 'Careers in Writing', on 4 May.[13] Among the authors and journalists participating were Francis Brown, editor of *The New York Times Book Review*; Paul Horgan, a Pulitzer Prize-winner and *New Yorker* contributor; E. K. Thompson, editor of *Life* magazine; and the Irish novelist Brian Moore.[14] Lavin was on the first panel, chaired by Riley Hughes, and was going to 'speak on the short story'.[15] She was also going to read at Notre Dame because she had a friend there, presumably Father Frank Phelan, a Holy Cross priest.[16] Lavin also met with Cecil Scott while she was in New York.

MacKenzie's convalescence did not take as long as Maxwell had anticipated, as she met with Lavin and they worked on 'The Cuckoo Spit' together. Lavin clearly made a good impression on MacKenzie, who was gushing in admiration when she wrote to her while she was in the harbour in New York about to embark on her homeward journey to Ireland: 'There is no way I can tell you how charmed we were by your visit, and I was particularly. You were just as I wanted you to be, and I am so grateful for the time we had together. It made me feel, as few things have, that I am coming back to life.' MacKenzie highlighted William Shawn's queries on the proofs of 'The Cuckoo Spit' and signed off her letter, 'I send you my love.'[17] Three days later she sent Lavin tear sheets of a Sylvia Townsend Warner story that they had discussed in New York. The work in question was most likely 'Their Quiet Lives', which was published in *The New Yorker* on 11 May 1963. The story, about a guilt-ridden daughter who leaves her elderly mother in order to pursue her dream, may well have struck a chord with both women.

Lavin returned to Ireland on the SS *America* ocean liner. The *Irish Examiner* covered its arrival on the morning of 23 May in Cobh, County Cork: 'The United States Lines vessel America, from New York, arrived in Cork Harbour yesterday morning, and landed 280 passengers, 2,339 sacks of mail and three tons of cargo.' The article also named some passengers who disembarked: 'Among those to land at Cobh was Mrs Mary Walsh, the well-known authoress and lecturer, professionally known as "Mary Lavin", who was returning from a nine-day visit to the U.S.A.'[18]

Lavin returned from New York with a chill but was busy working on the proofs of 'The Cuckoo Spit' while bedridden. Despite her illness, she attended the AGM of the Dublin Centre of Irish PEN in the Dublin Arts Club on 27 May, where she was elected vice-chairman. The poet John Hewitt was appointed president and Captain Seamus MacCall was elected chairman.[19] Lavin was equally delighted to have met MacKenzie and to be able to put a face to the name: 'It's so lovely to be able to see you as I write.'[20] She wanted to write a letter of thanks to 'Mr. Shawn' but wondered 'what letter could do justice to that lunch party?'[21] Lavin's respectful referral to William Shawn as 'Mr. Shawn' demonstrates that their meeting did not break down the formality that existed between them. Those on more familiar terms with Shawn addressed him as Bill, but MacKenzie always referred to him as Mr Shawn in her correspondence with Lavin.

MacKenzie was saddened to hear that Lavin was unwell and urged her to take care of herself, noting, 'Oh dear, mustn't we all. I'm learning, and am much stronger, so this recommendation has just a touch of self-righteousness. A good deal more affection, though.' MacKenzie concurred about the gathering, 'That lunch we had together was a very special occasion all round.'[22] The lunch took place in Le Pavillon, a fine-dining French restaurant, that was located in the Ritz Tower on Park Avenue and 57th Street. When Muriel Spark was in New York in January 1962, for the launch of the US edition of *The Prime of Miss Jean Brodie*, she was also taken to lunch at Le Pavillon by MacKenzie and Maxwell.[23]

The Rose Room in the Algonquin Hotel, where William Shawn had lunch most days, was another favourite haunt: 'Almost every day at one-thirty, William Shawn had lunch in the Rose Room of the Algonquin: orange juice, coffee with hot milk, Special K, or, once in a blue moon, toasted pound cake. Occasionally, he ate alone; more often, he was with a friend or a writer; and once in a while he asked one of his editors to join him.'[24] Over two weeks after her return, Lavin wrote Shawn the letter of thanks: 'I might as well never have written two lines in my life I felt so helpless in the face of thanking you for that wonderful lunch. It was so very wonderful. The only thing that I am sure of is that you all knew I loved it at the time, & might possibly have guessed my foolish nervous reasons for not writing sooner to say so.'[25] Lavin regretted sending him the 'inadequate & stupid' letter and wished she had left her appreciation unsaid but understood.[26] MacKenzie assured Lavin that Shawn was very happy with her letter and she expected him to respond.

MacKenzie airmailed Lavin a paperback of *More Stories* by Frank O'Connor that she had urgently requested in order to help inform her own selection of stories for her forthcoming collection *The Stories of Mary Lavin, Vol. I*, due to be published by the UK publisher Constable.[27] Lavin had moved to Constable after being approached by Ben Glazebrook who had heard from Cecil Scott that she was not very happy with her British publisher. Lavin asked MacKenzie to open an account with a New York bookstore on her behalf and suggested Brentano's or Scribner's.[29] After consulting with several people on the matter MacKenzie settled on Gotham Book Mart, which she described as 'rather small but seems to have the best selection of literary things and to be generally most knowledgeable about them'. It was also the bookshop that *The New Yorker* turned to when it encountered difficulty finding books or specialist magazines. In addition to its niche in sourcing rare or out-of-print books, the bookstore was a place where customers could acquire censored material. Gotham Book Mart served as one of the main literary salons in New York City and its patrons and guests included Dylan Thomas, W. H. Auden, John Updike, J. D. Salinger, Eugene O'Neill, Arthur Miller, Edward Albee, Katherine Anne Porter and H. L. Mencken. MacKenzie informed Lavin that the store 'would indeed welcome your account, and being perfectly and admiringly aware of you as a writer they don't want any references'.[29] Gotham

Book Mart's founder, Frances Steloff, had possibly even met Lavin when she attended the opening of the Martello Tower in Sandycove the previous summer.[30]

The end of June was a particularly taxing time of year for Lavin as her daughters were 'frayed with exam tensions'. She was also encountering some problems with Macmillan and she found herself 'deadly tired'. Lavin was working on a new story but she felt 'more & more that my writing is a losing battle – like trying to talk in a high high wind where the words get blown back in one's face. But this dejection may be the weather as much as anything.'[31] The weather was unusually bad for June in Ireland: a thunderstorm had hit the country on 11 June and made headline news. The *Irish Independent* reported that it was 'one of the worst electrical storms in living memory', which saw cars stranded and homes evacuated.[32]

In July things began to settle for Lavin and she was happily writing again, 'I seem to have to go down to the bottom before I come up – to feel the floor of the ocean and be able to give myself a good kick off from it.'[33] She was working on 'An Illness', which she retitled 'One Summer'. It was unusual for Lavin to be working during the summer when her daughters were on their school holidays. She was very proud of her girls who, despite all their pre-exam jitters, excelled in their examinations: Valdi got honours in her first bar exams, 'a real feat', and Elizabeth got a place on the first year arts degree at University College Dublin. Lavin believed that Elizabeth's accomplishment 'justified my rashness' in allowing her to travel to France. She informed MacKenzie that her daughters would be writing to her to thank her for her gifts that she had posted them.[34]

Lavin made another 'rash' decision to travel to Brittany with Caroline for two weeks in August as she reasoned that she would not be able to get much writing done before school reopened on 3 September: 'So I'm knocking off completely.'[35] She was hoping to finish 'One Summer' before her departure and was going to take another story with her on the off chance that she found herself with spare time. Lavin's trip to the US, coupled with the breakdown of her car, had put a considerable strain on her finances but she was hopeful that 'a few weeks work will effect wonders'.

Lavin was delighted to see another of Eudora Welty's stories appear in *The New Yorker*: 'it cheered me up & made me feel – for some reason – like as if it was old times & she & I are young again'.[36]

Welty's story 'Where Is the Voice Coming from?' featured in the 6 July 1963 issue.[37] John McGahern had his first *New Yorker* story, 'Summer at Strandhill', originally titled 'Strandhill, the Sea', published in the magazine on 21 September 1963. Elizabeth Cullinan brought the story to the attention of Maxwell, who wrote to her after the magazine had decided to accept it: 'you must now revise your belief that you don't know how to tell a good manuscript from a bad one. You have changed. You have learned. And if you see any more of this calibre floating around Dublin, start them on their way to me.'[38] Maxwell 'reluctantly' had to pass the story on to Robert Henderson as he had too many writers. He gave Cullinan the opportunity to deliver the good news to McGahern before he received the letter of acceptance in the post.[39]

In November Lavin grew increasingly anxious over the lack of communication from MacKenzie, having heard nothing from her in over four months: 'My vague uneasiness at not hearing from you has given way to a downright worry. Are you well?'[40] When she received no response, she followed up with another letter expressing her great concern over MacKenzie's 'total silence'. Lavin was initially worried in case she had somehow caused offence and wrote that she had 'examined my conscience & indeed there are always plenty of black spots on it', one of which was her daughters not writing to thank MacKenzie for gifts she sent them but, she reasoned, 'I think you'd make allowances for me – in your kindness of heart.'[41]

Lavin noted that 'The Cuckoo Spit' had not yet been published and wondered if it was because the magazine regretted its decision to take it. Despite the various worries and demands made of her, she was very productive after her return from America.[42] By Lavin's own admission, 1963 was not a good year for her, 'I'll be glad to see the end of it – so will the whole world I suppose since it ends with this terrible tragedy in Dallas. We are heartbroken here in Ireland.' Lavin was referring to the assassination of John F. Kennedy in Dallas on 22 November. Kennedy had visited Ireland on a four-day tour a few months earlier on 26 June 1963. It was the first visit by a serving American president (Princess Grace had made the first official visit of a head of state two years earlier, in June 1961). Lavin admitted, however, that, 'With regard to work oddly enough I never worked harder, more speedily or better. It ought to be a bumper year.'[43] She was going to send MacKenzie 'One Summer' and 'Heart of Gold' and she had nearly finished another two new stories.

MacKenzie finally got in touch via a cablegram, in which she acknowledged the receipt of 'Heart of Gold', and she included a brief message to alleviate Lavin's concerns: 'Do not worry, I am getting stronger and all my thought of you is affection. It has just been difficult to get things done. I send love.'[44] In December MacKenzie gave Lavin the good news that 'Heart of Gold' was accepted, 'We love it and are so pleased to have it.' She asked permission to edit the beginning of the story in order to speed it up, 'Oh, it's a lovely full story, done with tenderness and warmth and humor enough for an edge.' MacKenzie also sent Lavin the customary first-reading renewal forms and a cheque for $738.75, which she encouragingly noted 'looks both to the present and the future (the retirement plan)'. MacKenzie sent Lavin her love for Christmas and the New Year and while she agreed with Lavin's overall impression of 1963, she still found reasons to be positive: 'It has been a somber year, and a somber fall, and yet one comes back to find happiness in one's heart – in part, to be alive, perhaps, but more, for friends.'[45]

Lavin responded to MacKenzie on New Year's Eve. Naturally, she was delighted that 'Heart of Gold' was accepted but upon re-reading the story Lavin found it 'longwinded' and so she was going to attempt to condense it further. Lavin had been focusing her efforts on 'One Summer' and noted that 'some devil makes me choose the least likely stories to sell when I most need the money – I suppose it's some fear of writing for money & the work suffering'.[46] Colm Tóibín recalled Lavin explaining aspects of her *New Yorker* contract to him: 'they [*The New Yorker*] only paid for the stories they used, and thus each time she began a new story, she chose to write the one they were least likely to take. And sometimes, she said, she was right and sometimes she was wrong.'[47] Worried that MacKenzie would not like 'One Summer', Lavin began another story called 'The Wake'. She wished MacKenzie the best for 1964 and ended her letter with the words, 'I'm not sorry to see the last of this one.'[48]

Lavin returned the signed contract in January 1964. Things were looking up and she let MacKenzie know that the 'panic has lifted'.[49] Lavin had finished the corrections for two new books but she was determined to finish 'One Summer' even though she found the story 'dull & dreary'.[50] MacKenzie sent Lavin 'a splendid check' for $810.25, as a result of a change to the COLA payment system, which meant that 35 per cent was added to the first cheque instead of being paid quarterly: 'I hope it's enough to take the largest weight of the worry from your heart – I was going to say back, and then I thought Really, it's the heart that grows anxious.' MacKenzie also sent $2,893.75 for 'Heart of Gold', which included the 25 per cent premium: 'It's a dear story – but what have you written that isn't?'[51]

Elizabeth Cullinan returned to New York and rented a room with two beds on East 68th Street. John McGahern reckoned the move was permanent.[52] She was writing a book and told Lavin that the trip to Ireland made her writing 'sharper and clearer and bigger than before'. Cullinan was also buoyed up by Maxwell's encouragement and belief in the work. She passed on the news that Frank O'Connor considered Lavin to be 'the best writer in Ireland today'. Cullinan returned to work in *The New Yorker* fiction department and she informed Lavin that, 'Everyone asks me about you, even Mr. Shawn who never asks about anyone. I tell them about you, about the Mews and about Bective, about Valentine and about Elizabeth and Caroline.' She let Lavin know that Peter Nichols was in *The New Yorker* offices and that she came up in their conversation. Cullinan was financially strapped at the time and was grateful for Lavin's offer of a loan, which she refused, but she did ask her to propose her for the Guggenheim Fellowship.[53]

MacKenzie, who had similarly been living in rented accommodation in New York, had always longed for her own plot of land. She was therefore 'excited almost out of my skin' to find herself on the verge of purchasing 'a small house in Connecticut. With an acre, and a stone wall, and a patch of promising straggly woods.' The experience reminded her of when Lavin purchased her mews. MacKenzie's sister Gennie was living with her at the time. Gennie, Geneva Jacobs, was a 'sister-by-choice'. She had met MacKenzie after losing her family in a disaster as a young adult, whereupon she was taken in by the MacKenzie family. Gennie, who had a master's degree in social work from Smith College, worked for the International Red Cross and was stationed in Japan after the Second World War. She lived intermittently with MacKenzie when she returned to the US.[54]

Lavin was delighted to hear of MacKenzie's news and asked her to send photographs of the farmhouse and she promised to send her some of Abbey Farm. Lavin was having trouble writing due to an infection in her fingers, but she soldiered on with 'Heart of Gold' and had 'ripped the manuscript [galleys] into ribbons'. She put question marks against proposed changes to indicate that she did not feel deeply about them and confessed to MacKenzie, 'There is nothing about this story that I feel very strongly about,' largely because she was engrossed in a new story that was near completion.[55] MacKenzie was sorry to hear about Lavin's 'miserable winter' and her difficulty with her fingers. She found Lavin's changes to 'Heart of Gold' 'all so sure and right', and so the story was reset in revised galleys. The only issue MacKenzie had was trying to decipher Lavin's handwriting: 'You have a challenging hand; it brings out the best in me – the most ingenious, that is.'[56]

Lavin deeply regretted participating in *Dublin Through Different Eyes*, a television programme for the American network CBS, which was due to be televised in the US on 23 February as part of a four-part series, *One of a Kind*. She had reluctantly taken part and was very apprehensive about it.[57] Other interviewees included Valerie Goulding, founder of the Central Remedial Clinic, and Lord Powerscourt.[58] Lavin asked MacKenzie to give her feedback on the programme, figuring that she had 'better know the worst'.[59] Unfortunately, MacKenzie did not receive Lavin's letter in time and was only made aware of its airing when her friend telephoned her while it was being televised. To make matters worse, MacKenzie and Gennie were in the New York apartment and had left their television in Connecticut.[60]

MacKenzie was devastated not to have seen the documentary but she reassured Lavin that 'Everyone who did see the program was genuinely enthusiastic, and most of all about your part in it. I pass that news on happily, but it makes me feel even worse to have missed it.'[61] Jack Gould's review in *The New York Times* the following day described the documentary as, 'Life in Dublin as lived and discussed by four persons of different economic, social and cultural status.'[62] Lavin was relieved that MacKenzie did not see the programme but she was pleased to hear that it was good. She had not seen it herself, which was part of the reason that she was reluctant to tell people about it. She told MacKenzie that she would get the producers to screen it for them both when she was next in New York. Cullinan, who did see the broadcast, thought it was 'heavenly' and that Lavin 'stole' the show. She informed Lavin that *The New Yorker* intended to organise a screening.[63]

The programme was broadcast in the UK on Christmas Eve. The *Irish Examiner's* 'London Letter' reported, 'Over nine million people here in Britain saw the Columbia Broadcasting System's television programme.' In the documentary, Jeremy Simpson, a budding playwright, whose play *The Big Finish* was performed during the Dublin Theatre Festival, commented that 'the older writers function very much as patrons of the younger writer and that Frank O'Connor and Mary Lavin were among those who helped younger writers'. An unnamed commentator is quoted as saying that 'Dublin is a remarkable city of the eighteenth century and is unique. The scale of the buildings are the number one characteristic giving one the sense of unity, peace and charm but the city is now about to explode and how to rebuild it without disturbing its magical eighteenth-century quality is a problem. Some of the new buildings are most unfortunate.' *The Sunday Tim*es television critic, Maurice Wiggin, observed that Dublin city was 'threatened at last by the apparently inevitable population explosion, new hideous building, traffic trouble, supermarkets, the businessmen's blindfold ideology of expansion'.[64] This is particularly ironic given that in 1966 Lavin initiated court proceedings against Goulding Fertilisers, Valerie Goulding's husband's family business, over her objection to the company's erection of Fitzwilton House, a modern thirteen-storey office block that towered over Lavin's mews and blocked her light, demolishing six Victorian villas in the process.[65]

MacKenzie purchased the Connecticut home, which she and Gennie had only viewed in 'heavy snow and towering rain'. Her free time was spent getting it into shape: 'At the moment, outside office hours I'm swallowed up in arrangements: yard cleaning, wall papering, fumigating, tile for kitchen floor. And I don't even get the house until April 1st!' She promised to send Lavin a photograph when she had 'one that looks worthy. By "worthy" I suppose I mean a little better than fact. Why not.' MacKenzie received a 'sweet letter' from Lavin's daughter Elizabeth, thanking her for gifts that she had sent them, but MacKenzie hoped the letter was not written under duress: 'For she mustn't have, at all. Those little things were just a greeting, like a postcard, because I wanted the girls to be included in my affection for you. That was all.'[66]

Lavin once again raised her suspicion that the delay in publishing the 'The Cuckoo Spit' was because *The New Yorker* had reservations about the story. MacKenzie assured Lavin that 'everyone loved' the work and explained that the delay was due to the fact that the magazine was in the process of changing its printers from Condé Nast in New York to the Donnelley plant in Chicago in May.[67] As a result, they had an issue prepared in case of a scheduling emergency and 'The Cuckoo Spit' was earmarked for that particular publication. However, there was no longer a need for a backup and so the story would run when there was enough room for it. MacKenzie asked Lavin when the new book was due for publication in order to ensure that 'The Cuckoo Spit' would get published well in advance, as the magazine had an abundance of long stories that were due for inclusion in forthcoming collections. Cecil Scott, whom MacKenzie had met briefly at her apartment stoop, requested her name from Lavin so that he could contact her directly in order to get publication dates for Lavin's pending stories, which Macmillan were hoping to include in a new collection, *In the Middle of the Fields and Other Stories*.

Lavin and Arthur Rae were appointed official delegates to the PEN International Executive Committee meeting in London on 15 and 16 April. Lavin availed of the opportunity to attend to some business while there and met with Lovat Dickson from Macmillan and with her new literary agent, Michael Sissons, from the A. D. Peters agency, who represented her in London.[68] Lavin had engaged the services of literary agent Harold Matson but decided to terminate the relationship 'after 15 months of no result', ruminating that perhaps she did not need the services of an agent after all.[69] She made the decision to leave Macmillan and gave Sissons her Macmillan sales dockets to review before she progressed with the upcoming Macmillan publication. Sissons found it 'outrageous' that Lavin was not in paperback in America and Lavin told MacKenzie that 'everyone says that unless I am done in a paper back soon in U.S.A it will be decidedly odd & at least 6 universities have said they would have put me on prescribed reading courses had I been in paper back'.

Macmillan seemed to pay no heed to Lavin's paperback dilemma and she found them 'to be very dopey & indeed disorganised'.[70] She noted that, 'Reports in England about Macmillan N.Y. are at the moment very very bad.'[71] Lavin was very grateful to Scott for signing her up when she was at a low point after her husband's death but she was growing increasingly frustrated with his lackadaisical approach and she found her meetings with him in New York 'ludicrous'. She was especially saddened at her decision to leave Macmillan after they filled her London hotel room with flowers. Nevertheless, Lavin was revelling in the London break, extending her stay by a few days and working on the proofs of her new book. The trip also allowed her some rare pampering time: 'These little forays are so good – I do my nails & braid my hair & sew dangling buttons & things I never get time to do at home.'[72]

Lavin had discussed the business of agents and publishers with MacKenzie while she was in New York and she was again looking for some advice on the matter. MacKenzie found it difficult to provide guidance on agents but she noted that they were useful in drawing up book contracts. Lavin did not require an agent to manage her *New Yorker* affairs and so MacKenzie advised her to 'make it clear that you want them excepted from any arrangement you make; a number of agents will do this – I don't know whether they all will'. She recommended the Russell & Volkening agency, having obviously forgotten that Diarmuid Russell had initially been acting as Lavin's agent in her early dealings with the magazine. MacKenzie also mentioned Ivan von Auw of Curtis Brown; McIntosh & Otis, and Marie Rodell, all of whom she thought would be happy to represent Lavin, and she generously offered to contact them on her behalf.[73]

On a personal note, MacKenzie informed Lavin that she 'became a homeowner officially: everything finally recorded: "Map Prepared for Rachel MacKenzie". How's that for a touch of immortality?' She explained that her plot at 'one-and-a-tenth' of an acre was much more modest than a farm: 'It's such a simple house, Mary, and no farm at all – just a place of my own in a moderately rural atmosphere, with some thin woods and lots of birds and lovely, fresh New England air. At the moment, it's buzzing with workmen painting and papering, and tinkering with screens and stubborn doors, and tidying up outside.' She reckoned it would take about five years to get it into shape but it was habitable and she was in no rush.

On 2 June MacKenzie sent Lavin the author's proof of 'Heart of Gold' with minor queries and let her know that it was due to for inclusion in the 27 June issue, therefore she needed it returned as a matter of urgency. She explained that they were publishing the story in advance of 'The Cuckoo Spit' because of its length: 'It's 7 ½ inches shorter, and will just fit in. Did you know this business had such a mathematical side?' MacKenzie was taking three weeks' vacation and she let Lavin know that Mr Henderson would be handling the proof: 'I've told him how amenable you are to editorial interference.'[74] She hoped that Lavin's new work would be awaiting her when she returned from her holidays.

Lavin was anxious about dealing with a different editor, especially when there was such urgency on the corrections, but on the whole she was, as MacKenzie pointed out, amenable to the suggested changes, and told Henderson, 'I agree to all the punctuation. And in fact I will not be stubborn about the other points – especially in view of the need for haste.'[75] An example of where words mattered to Lavin is evidenced when she wrote to Henderson to ask if it was too late to fix a misprint in the story, 'The word arched should have been circled.'[76] It was not too late and the change was made.

'Heart of Gold' was published in the 27 June 1964 issue. The cover by Anatol Kovarsky is of a tour group in a grand hall of a historic building staring up at the trompe-l'oeil painted ceiling.[77] The issue includes a 'Comment' piece by John Updike and fiction by James Stevenson. Lavin's story shares its pages with a poem, 'Song for my First Child, Noah', by Robert David Cohen, and several cartoons. A Robert Weber cartoon features a housewife greeting her husband with pride as he returns home from work with the tagline: 'Guess what! I dialled Westbury, Long Island, today, and I didn't make a single mistake!'[78] In another sketch, two workmen carry an enormous computer into an office after which six dejected-looking employees exit the room, their roles having been replaced by burgeoning technology. There is also a full page with information on The World's Trade Fair, which was held at Flushing Meadows–Corona Park in Queens, New York City. The theme of the fair was 'Peace through Understanding' and it ran for two six-month seasons, from 22 April until 18 October 1964 and then from 21 April until 17 October 1965.[79]

'Heart of Gold' was one of twenty-two stories – the only *New Yorker* one chosen by Martha Foley for *The Best American Short Stories*

1965.[80] Elizabeth Heide, a copy editor at Houghton Mifflin, wrote to Lavin to seek her permission to reprint the story in the collection and to get a short biography. In a handwritten postscript she wrote, 'I read "Heart of Gold" when it first appeared in The New Yorker and I thought it was marvellous.'[81]

Lavin travelled on a partly funded trip to Oslo in June for the 32nd PEN International Congress, which took place from 21 until 27 June. The theme was 'The Writer and Semantics: Literature as Concept, Meaning and Expression'. She wrote to MacKenzie from 'Oslo to Copenhagen', to explain why 'One Summer' was not awaiting MacKenzie's return. Although Lavin had taken the manuscript away with her, she did not find the time to work on it. The break did not 'work its usual spell', but the highlights of the trip began 'to take on a glitter in retrospect'. Lavin intended to finish the story when she returned home and thought it would only require a few hours' work: 'If only I worked differently & not like the swallows who dive in & out under the eaves!' She estimated that, while she wrote every day, it did not add up to more than six months' work.[82] On 15 August Lavin presided over the Dublin Centre of Irish PEN committee meeting at which Frank O'Connor was made an honorary member.[83]

In July Cullinan wrote to Lavin to thank her for sending her newspaper clippings concerning John McGahern. The cuttings would have referenced the banning in Ireland of John McGahern's second novel, *The Dark*, by the Censorship of Publications Board in June, because of its 'indecent or obscene' content. Cullinan thought that 'it all seemed like a real sensation and so much of it nonsense'. McGahern was abroad in at the time, having taken a year's sabbatical from his teaching duties after receiving a £1,000 prize as the recipient of the Macauley Fellowship award the previous year.[84]

Towards the end of May or early June, Lavin's typist posted MacKenzie 'One Summer' and a reworked version of 'The Grammar of Women', which Lavin thought MacKenzie might like to read before she tried to sell it elsewhere. Lavin estimated that she had spent sixteen months writing 'One Summer' in what amounted to approximately 30,000 words, although she was drafting other stories at the same time including 'The Mock Auction' and 'Revisiting Chapelizod', at least of one of which she was hoping to finish before the bonus deadline, despite the fact that she was completely worn out. Towards the end of August, Lavin was in suspense about 'One Summer', having heard nothing further from MacKenzie, and raised her concerns with Cullinan, who in turn got in touch with MacKenzie. MacKenzie then phoned Lavin and followed up their conversation with a letter: 'You must never wait in such suspense again. I never mind being asked if we've made up our minds about a story, when the answer seems too long to be reasonable or customary. And you should remember that once in a while there is a mix-up with overseas mail.'[85] It transpired that the story got lost in the post, which Lavin believed was 'Providence' because 'in spite of the agony of suspense' and the need for money, she felt that she had sent the story prematurely.[86] Nevertheless, getting it off her desk freed her to work on other stories.

Cullinan informed Lavin that 'the nice soft job I had at the New Yorker came to an end when the summer did and the girl I'd replaced reappeared.' She then worked in the typing pool, which she soon regretted: 'I'd sit typing those awful fact articles all day long, and then I'd come home here and sit down and make myself a gin-and-tonic and start crying from sheer exhaustion.'[87] Cullinan was still writing the novel and had also written a new story, likely her next published *New Yorker* story, 'A Swim', which appeared in the 5 June 1965 issue. The story features an American woman, Bernadette Shea, who goes for a swim at Portmarnock beach with her Irish writer friend Jim Delaney, who was possibly based on McGahern. There is an awkward sexual tension between the two in the story. Cullinan, by her own admission, was an 'entirely autobiographical' writer, who 'just changed the time frames'.[88] Despite Lavin's misgivings about 'One Summer', the editors were enthusiastic about the work: 'We like it enormously and are delighted to have it.' Although MacKenzie observed that, 'There are such lovely things in this story; the ending is perfection,' the story needed to be condensed. She was doubtful that it would make a summer issue and so there was no urgency on the revisions: 'Our long stories require the fat issues – Spring or Fall, when the advertising burgeons and pages and pages are available.'

MacKenzie was 'tinkering' with a revised version of 'The Grammar of Women' that Lavin had sent her and although she felt it was improved, it still needed work: 'the first section goes on too long, and the second is not clear enough'. She found it 'interesting', but some of the other editors did not: 'The point of it eluded the men.' MacKenzie informed Lavin that William Shawn declared, 'I had no idea what this story was all about. In fact, it all seemed impossible.' However, he felt that if MacKenzie's understanding of the story was correct, 'that the core is sexual', then Lavin should rewrite it and make it more explicit. Lavin fully agreed with the magazine's appraisal of the work but she thought that making the end more graphic might coarsen the story.

MacKenzie wished Lavin 'a happy sunny Fall – if you get to France, that is. Otherwise, just happy. Or is there sun in Ireland in the Fall?' She reminded Lavin that she could draw down money from her account if she needed it. It was not unusual for the magazine to offer advances and some of its writers had a drawing account or a special arrangement that allowed them to borrow against future work. MacKenzie ended her letter, 'And, whether you go to France or not, don't let Providence give you any more battering.'[89]

Lavin consulted with her bank and tax office to check her finances and to ascertain whether she needed to take up MacKenzie's offer. In the end, she decided to accept the offer via a cable: 'DEAR RACHEL I THINK I HAD BETTER HAVE SOME MONEY AFTER ALL RIGHT AWAY STOP ALL GOING WELL WRITING.'[90] Lavin left the amount of the advance up to MacKenzie. She reasoned that she had worked on 'One Summer' for such a long time and still had further work to do on it and so she did not want to feel anxious about money. She also needed income to stock the farm as a new bill was due to be introduced, 'to take over land that is not "worked" by the owner & so, my hand being forced here'.[91] MacKenzie responded in a cablegram: 'DO SEND CUT PAGES ALONG. WE'LL TRY FOR NOVEMBER 10. CHECK FOR 1500 IS ON WAY.'[92]

Lavin was hesitant to sign the contract for the new American Macmillan book because of the paperback issue: 'I feel I <u>must</u> be put in a paperback at this stage & Macmillan cannot sell one.'[93] She could not fathom why they would not publish her in that format when they owned a paperback house and so was contemplating heading to New York after Christmas to try and sort out the matter. 'The Cuckoo Spit' was eventually published on 3 October 1964. Lavin first mentioned working on this story on 9 May 1961. The magazine cover by Arthur Getz depicts a heavy police escort from the airport.[94] The story spans thirty-six pages that are shared with numerous cartoons including a topical one by Joseph Mirachi, which depicts two construction workers standing by an open trench with the tagline 'Wow! I hear we've backed up traffic clear to Fourteenth Street.' The drawing alludes to traffic jams in New York City caused by the recent building boom. There is an abundance of adverts for products from the UK and Ireland including Scottish tweeds, Hampton Court cutlery and Waterford Crystal, perhaps because of the World's Fair, which was due to end 18 October 1964. The magazine features one of John O'Hara's Gibbsville stories, 'All Tied Up', Brendan Gill's cinematic review of *Mary Poppins* and Saul Bellow's latest work, *Herzog*.[95] It also carries a cinema listing for *Girl with Green Eyes*, the screen adaption of Edna O'Brien's novel *The Lonely Girl* for which O'Brien had written the screenplay.

The Stories of Mary Lavin, Vol. 1, was published by Constable in October. The collection contained two *New Yorker* stories, 'The Great Wave' and 'In a Café'. The Belfast *News Letter* review observed of the volume: 'Here is the quiet voice of sensibility, of compassion streaked with a humour that sometimes verges on the cynical of a half-ironic melancholy' and compared Lavin's 'tone' to that of Chekhov and Turgenev.'[96] Criostóir Mac Aonghusa in his *Irish Press* review did not see the universal appeal of Lavin's stories: 'Her stories are highly thought of abroad, but they are not written for a foreign market, but for us Irish people, and it is obvious that no one but ourselves can fully appreciate any of her stories. She writes in the Irish-English of Ireland, and there is preciseness in her dialogue not found in any of the many other English dialects. It is the blending of two languages.'[97] The *Sunday Independent*'s P.T. Hughes observed, 'Her gentle style contrasted with the earthier quality of Frank O'Connor's stories and she tended to remain overshadowed by his richly masculine probing of the Irish character and scene.'[98]

On 7 October Lavin travelled to Paris for six days for a holiday, where she stayed with a friend. She was enjoying the trip immensely but decided to return home because she wanted to host a small party for Valdi's twenty-first birthday on 4 November at their farm and she also wanted to finish 'One Summer' before they left for the Continent on 14 November. The Paris trip greatly revived Lavin: 'I don't think I was so happy for many and many a year!' and although she returned home in great spirits, the energy of her daughters was tiring her out again: 'the noise – the fuss – the very happiness itself of those girls – is wearing me out. The party will about kill me!'

Lavin continued to tweak 'One Summer' while she awaited MacKenzie's edits, in the hope that they could finish work on the story before she went away. She would then get it retyped and send MacKenzie the new version, as well as the one with the corrections to make it easier for her to identify the amendments: 'We will have our old arrangement that if the old version seems better than the new one we will leave it at your discretion.' Lavin had also been working on 'The Mock Auction', 'like a wheel keeps turning for a while after the motor is shut off', but decided to put the story on ice until after Christmas. She was going to take the manuscript away with her, 'in case I get a few minutes in bed to work on it – which would be a great recreation in actual fact'. She enquired about her bonus dates as she was aiming to get as many stories completed before the deadline.[99]

MacKenzie received three letters from Lavin one morning and declared, 'what a feast!' She confirmed that Lavin's quantity bonus commenced on 20 January. MacKenzie was doubtful that they would manage to put 'One Summer' to bed by 14 November but she was happy to try. She felt that it needed some minor cuts throughout and a quicker pace. MacKenzie proposed that she would cut the story and then she would amalgamate their joint changes and get the story set in a working proof, which she would send to Lavin in France. Importantly, once the story was set in working proof, Lavin would get paid, which MacKenzie estimated would be in early December. She advised Lavin not to overdo things before her holidays, 'you deserve a rested spirit to enjoy your happiness. With that bit of sententiousness I send you my love.'[100] Lavin only managed to reduce the story by twelve pages but she was confident that she could cut it further. While she was grateful for MacKenzie's endeavours to get her paid for the story, she did not want to rush it, but then she reasoned that 'this may be as good a way as any to tackle it!'[101]

Valdi's twenty-first birthday party on 4 November was a great success but Lavin came down with bronchitis after the event and was bedridden again. Despite her condition, on 7 November she had to meet four young men who had flown in from Scotland to explore the possibility of filming 'The Green Grave and the Black Grave', a story that was first published in *The Atlantic Monthly* in the May 1940 issue. Lavin also attended the Irish PEN annual dinner, which was held on Thursday 12 November at the Shelbourne Hotel. Frank O'Connor, president of the organisation, officiated the event. Ogden Nash, who was due to be the guest of honour, had suddenly taken ill in London and was admitted to the London Clinic. It befell Lavin, in her role as chairman, to explain his absence to the attendees and also to let them know that their next choice, Edna O'Brien, was unavailable at such short notice.[102] However, they managed to get His Excellency Dr Francis-Léo Goffart, who was the newly appointed Belgian Ambassador to Ireland.[103] Arthur Rae wrote instructions for Lavin's speech, in which she was to note the deaths of Richard Hayward and former Irish PEN chairman Seamus MacCall. Hayward, an actor and writer, was killed in a car crash in Ballymena in October and Seamus MacCall died at his home, Tower Hill, in Dalkey on 29 October 1964. Rae suggested that Lavin could mention that they were both with Hayward for the annual International PEN congress in Oslo 'and that he was always a gracious and kindly figure who dearly loved to visit Dublin at any time'.[104] He also observed that Hayward had intended to travel to Budapest for the International PEN Executive Meeting, but when Lavin and Rae could not attend he cancelled the trip: 'The tragic fact is that if he had gone to Hungary, he would have left Ireland on the day before he was killed near Ballymena.'[105]

In O'Connor's toast, 'Our Guests', he decried that Ireland was 'without a proper system of education, without a publishing house, without a first-rate library, and without a Chair of Irish Literature'.[106] He also spoke of important books that were missing and being exported: 'In this country we could not collect a complete edition of O'Flaherty's works and there are no books by Mary Lavin in the libraries. Edna O'Brien is entirely suppressed here.' The Library of Congress solicited O'Connor's manuscripts but he questioned why an Irish library did not approach him, 'People far more important than myself were not asked for their manuscripts – Synge, Yeats, Lady Gregory, Joyce, O'Casey. I doubt very much whether O'Flaherty or Mary Lavin were approached, and I am quite sure Edna O'Brien was left alone, otherwise half Dublin would be queuing up to have a peep.' Reportedly, the speech was 'listened to in a glassy-eyed silence induced by liberal helpings of roast stuffed white turkey, Limerick ham and Brussels sprouts'.[107]

The following day, Lavin set off for the Continent with Caroline in tow. Valdi and Elizabeth were going to join them at a later stage. On the day of her departure, Colm P. O Briain, a university student friend of Valdi's, who was handling Lavin's correspondence in her absence, informed MacKenzie that Lavin would still correspond directly with her and intended to write to her from the boat.[108] He let her know that Lavin did not manage to finish 'One Summer' earlier due to illness. O Briain sent her a list of forwarding addresses for poste restante, namely, Madrid (until 23 November); Lyon (until 6 December); Geneva (until 15 December); Munich (until 22 December) and Paris (until 5 January). He reported that Lavin thought it would be wiser to send any cheques to her bank in Dublin while she was travelling abroad.

Lavin did not manage to write to MacKenzie from the boat but from Orléans. She had posted the edited manuscript of 'One Summer' before her departure but neglected to cut the letters as MacKenzie had requested. Lavin had another copy of the story with her and was working on the amendments. She noted that she could reinstate any cuts that she regretted losing in book versions: 'In other words don't worry – we will I am sure work this out together.'[109] The only problem Lavin envisaged was them both having to work around her travel. A few days later she wrote to MacKenzie from Madrid and explained that she was finding it difficult to write as she had to mind Caroline. Lavin expected that once her other daughters arrived, she would have more flexibility. She was enjoying the holiday immensely: 'But I am having a great time & terribly happy & getting very rested.'[110]

'One Summer' was only set into galleys in December, due to the amount of time it took to revise it. While MacKenzie found Lavin's cuts useful, the story was still too long at over 20,000 words and William Shawn ideally wanted it condensed to 12,000 words. MacKenzie worked tirelessly on the text and managed to reduce it to just over 15,000 words and she felt that there was not much more that could be shaved off: 'The story is more compact at this length, but I don't feel that its quality suffers or that it has lost its sense of time passing or of growth, or its largeness, or its sadness. And I didn't take out any writing that I loved.' MacKenzie, despite being under orders to prune significantly, remained faithful to Lavin's story. She thought it would be published in early autumn and recommended that Lavin review the galleys where she had made notes in the margins. Lavin would then have a final opportunity to revise it when she received the author's proof. MacKenzie was of the mind that the story only required some tweaking, 'just small surface changes where a word has been used too often, or perhaps a softening here and there where you may feel that cutting has made something too abrupt'.[111] Lavin intended to work on the manuscript 'with great energy and enthusiasm' when she returned home.[112]

As instructed, MacKenzie sent a cheque for $4,101.54, which covered the balance of the payment for 'One Summer', and the cost-of-living adjustment, to Lavin's bank manager. She also posted Lavin the voucher and a copy of the cover letter for her files. On 10 December MacKenzie posted the first-reading agreement renewal forms and was holding on to the payment of $788 until it was signed. MacKenzie ended her letter, 'Be happy. I send you special love for Christmas.'[113] Lavin promptly returned the first-reading agreement as she was relying on the contract fee to 'satisfy the bank'.[114] Incidentally, that same year, John Cheever had the same word rate as Lavin. However, his first-reading agreement payment was considerably higher: 'The highest (rate) the magazine would go for in 1964 was an annual bonus of $2,500 for signing the first-reading agreement, and a minimum word rate of eighteen cents a word for the first two thousand words and nine cents a word after that.'[115] Cheever felt cheated and undervalued by the magazine and in 1964 he sought a raise from William Maxwell. He acquired an agent and was offered a deal with the *Saturday Evening Post* for $24,000 a year for a first-look agreement and four stories. Yet he chose to remain with *The New Yorker.* His daughter, Susan, estimated that the total sum he was paid by *The New Yorker* for the 121 stories he sold to it between 1935 and 1982 to be less than $173,000.[116]

On 21 December Lavin sent the revised story from Bologna. It was quite a challenge for her to do the revisions, 'in bits in one town after another – but I think I finally saw it as pieces'. Valdi and Elizabeth had joined the family and they were enjoying the holiday together, 'it's a great break – you've no idea – & I hope to get back to work in great form'.[117] However, Lavin was growing very concerned about her mother at home. On 29 December she wrote to MacKenzie from Basel in Switzerland, where they were staying at the Hotel Krafft. Valdi and Elizabeth had returned home the previous day. Lavin received the copy of the cheque for her records while in Geneva, which 'made such a difference'. Although the weather had been bad at Christmas, they were still having a wonderful time and were going to Austria before returning home on 6 January. She ended her letter to MacKenzie, 'Many thanks & gratitude – & lots of love.'[118]

6
'Right Side Up'
1965–1966

> Your stories matter to us, you know. It's lonesome when there isn't a new one around.[1]

> I do feel that you are most whole when you are writing, most vulnerable when you are not.[2]

In early January Mary Lavin returned from her travels and resumed writing with gusto, incentivised by the looming quantity bonus deadline of 20 January.[3] Time was tight and 'One Summer' was the only story accepted to date in her current bonus cycle. Lavin sent Rachel MacKenzie a revised and cut version of 'The Grammar of Women'. She was also working on 'The Mock Auction', 'Happiness', 'Tomb of an Ancestor' and the novel *First Love*, which she hoped to finish within the year. Lavin feared that she would appear grasping in striving to make the bonus and instead should be content with the generous payment for the renewal of the first-reading contract, which she received before Christmas, but she explained that it was more a case of unburdening herself of the work so that she could move on to new stories.[4] This was mainly because Lavin's writing time was limited as she was due to travel to the United States in February. The English department at the University of Pennsylvania had invited her as a spring guest, as part of the Visiting Authors Program, and she was also going to judge a story competition and give readings at various venues including Swarthmore College.[5] In a letter to John McGahern, Michael McLaverty mentioned Lavin's impending trip: 'she's still on the go as usual and I hear she's going to the States again on a lecture tour. She's wonderful and God has endowed her with tremendous energy.'[6]

Lavin was a warm and engaging raconteur and reading tours boosted her income considerably – they paid handsomely. Nevertheless, it meant sacrificing precious writing time. She intended to return to Ireland before 1 April as Valdi was due to sit her final bar examinations in May. Lavin hoped to meet with MacKenzie during the course of the trip and wrote to her, 'if you are able to spare me time, we really will have some good long chats'. She was also planning to meet with some publishers MacKenzie had recommended. Although Lavin had not severed ties with Macmillan, she had become exasperated with Cecil Scott and wanted to explore her options. Houghton Mifflin were the only house to reply and Lavin wondered if perhaps other responses got lost in the post. She shared a rumour with MacKenzie that she was in line to receive an honorary degree from Trinity College Dublin.[7]

At the end of January MacKenzie informed Lavin that the 'The Grammar of Women' was again unsuccessful. The reasons for the story's rejection included the readers' lack of engagement with the characters and MacKenzie reasoned, 'Perhaps we're just the wrong magazine for this one; that often turns out to be the case.'[8] She hoped that Lavin would be successful in trying it elsewhere and that the generous cheque for the adjustment of the previous year's COLA, sent the previous day, would soften the blow.[9] It did. Lavin wrote to MacKenzie, 'How magically you time things' upon receiving the substantial payment of $1,905.86.[10] She had put a 'dear friend' in touch with MacKenzie in order to get Elizabeth Cullinan's address while he was in New York. The 'dear friend' in question was Father Michael Scott, who duly got in touch with MacKenzie.[11] MacKenzie was pleased to have met him and was looking forward to Lavin's own imminent trip to New York, when the two would 'meet for pleasure!'[12]

Lavin sent MacKenzie a brief note from the boat train on the day of her departure to let her know that she was embarking on her journey and would arrive in New York on 1 March and would be staying with Elizabeth Cullinan.[13] She had a fairly packed schedule but unfortunately fell ill on the voyage over. William Maxwell wrote to their mutual friend Frank O'Connor, telling of Lavin's visit to his home on 4 March. He found her 'enchanting' despite her ailment:

> On the boat coming over she got an abscess in her throat, and didn't know what it was, and was, I suspect, afraid to find out. But anyway, the morning of the day she came to dinner Rachel

> MacKenzie carried her off to her doctor, who diagnosed it as that – she had had ferocious headaches as well as the swelling – and said she was getting over it all right. She was in no way dimmed, and carried the whole evening on her capable shoulders … She was going off somewhere for a week and then coming back through town for five days, and I think then going home.[14]

The symptoms must have been worrying and bothersome for Lavin, given that she had been due to perform readings. Nevertheless, she soldiered on and travelled to Boston to meet with Dorothy de Santillana, a senior editor at Houghton Mifflin.[15] The meeting was initiated by MacKenzie, who had contacted de Santillana in January to inform her of Lavin's impending visit. Lavin wrote to MacKenzie from the Ritz Carlton in Boston to thank her for her kindness during her illness and informed her that she would hold off contacting her doctor until she was sure how she felt, 'no headache again today – but I did have it yesterday morning – you will see what I mean about wanting to be clearer before I write to her'.[16]

Lavin lunched at the Ritz Carlton with de Santillana, who told MacKenzie afterwards that she found Lavin to be 'a wonderful joy': 'I found all the truest charm and freshness of the Irish in her, and not one tiny trace of that brogue-ish layer of seduction which so many of them can assume like a cloak. She is as good a person as a writer – and that's saying superlatives.'[17] De Santillana was eager to sign Lavin and told her that Houghton Mifflin 'would be extremely proud' to have her as a client but, much to de Santillana's disappointment, Lavin said she could not leave Macmillan due to her allegiance to Scott. De Santillana understood and admired Lavin's loyalty to Scott, whom she knew and thought was 'a real pro'. She thought Lavin was wise to stay with him but asked her to keep them in mind, 'tuck our interest away in the back of your head', should Scott retire.[18] Lavin had clearly had a change of heart about leaving Macmillan and Scott.

After meeting with de Santillana, Lavin journeyed to Philadelphia to embark on her reading tour. She was due to return to New York on 18 March, when she would be meeting with Scott, and she told MacKenzie that she hoped 'to see as much of you as I can do without feeling I am tiring you'.[19] Lavin visited the University of Pennsylvania from 9 until 12 March, where she 'addressed classes and met with students interested in creative writing and literature'.[20] Ralph Ellison, probably best known as the author of *The Invisible Man*, which won the National Book Award in 1953, visited the university from 22 until 26 February, and May Sarton, a returning guest and fellow Bread Loaf colleague of MacKenzie's, was on campus from 22 March until 2 April.[21] Hortense Calisher was the writer-in-residence at the university's College of Women for the month of April.[22]

Lavin and MacKenzie met several times and worked on 'One Summer' together. On her journey back to Ireland on the Cunard Line RMS *Franconia*, she scribbled MacKenzie a quick note of thanks while the boat was offshore from Bermuda: 'I am dashing off a line of very inadequate thanks for so many things that I can hardly specify them. Perhaps our last dinner was best of all.'[23] Lavin only began to feel better on the boat journey home.

It was not until early May, on the anniversary of her husband's death, that Lavin contacted MacKenzie again: 'It's hard to believe so long has passed since I saw you & that I wrote only scattered lines of thanks for <u>all</u> the wonderful things – the beautiful meals – the talks, the help & the lovely gifts.' Lavin had been preoccupied with various familial worries, particularly concerning Valdi, who was thinking about getting engaged. Although Lavin was fond of her intended, she was concerned that it might scupper her daughter's plans to take up a possible scholarship in the US. Lavin's daughter Elizabeth 'got a sudden lucky break to interpret for the Paris press all over the luxury hotels & tourist spots of Ireland for the advance publicity of Le Bal des Petits Lits Blancs which is being held in Dublin this year.'[24] Le Bal des Petits Lits Blancs was a charity ball hosted in Princess Grace's honour, which took place, not in Dublin, but at Wicklow's Powerscourt Estate in July 1965. It was the second time the event took place outside of France. Valerie Goulding was seemingly instrumental in getting Princess Grace to come to Ireland for the event and her clinic was one of several charities that benefited from the funds raised. Gloria Emerson covered the ball for *The New York Times* and her article recounted how 'One impatient Frenchman, Raoul Lévy, a film producer, pushed over a table set with champagne, white wine, chinaware, silver and flowers because he was told it was reserved.'[25] Perhaps he was irked upon discovering that French guests were charged $300 a ticket while Irish guests only paid $45.

MacKenzie likewise addressed the gap in their correspondence: 'It's hard for me to think I haven't written you a dozen letters, for at least that many have gone out from my mind to you. The time we had together still gives me such pleasure; your visit was very dear to me – all of it.' She let Lavin know that at the beginning of April she and Gennie sublet their New York apartment and moved to their country house in Connecticut. MacKenzie brought with her a splash of glamour, having purchased 'a fine fat pale-pink 1957 Oldsmobile – a big heavy car – and I trundle along to and from the station four days a week'.[26] She was not finding the commute to New York too arduous and enjoyed living in the countryside where she busied herself weeding and planting trees. MacKenzie was looking forward to spending her three weeks' annual leave in Connecticut, where she was going to bring *The Stories of Mary Lavin, Vol. 1* as 'company for my holiday' and she informed Lavin, 'It will be as if you were making me a little visit.'[27]

Lavin was apologetic for not writing MacKenzie a 'holiday-reading letter' but she explained that Valdi was going to announce her engagement on Lavin's birthday, which fell on 10 June. She was delighted with this news and let MacKenzie know that she was completing 'The Mock Auction' and 'used the time in between to write a sad little story – typically called Happiness!!'[28] Despite its title, Lavin said that the story was about death. Upon completion of 'The Mock Auction' she hoped to 'take the plunge & work on my pet story – the one I am 20 years tinkering at! After all what am I waiting for?'[29]

MacKenzie was on vacation when the letter containing news of Valdi's engagement arrived: 'I only wish I had got it in time to send you a cable for that double celebration.' She was riveted over which of Valdi's suitors was to become her fiancé: 'Not knowing is like having to wait for the next instalment when you want to know now.' MacKenzie's sister Ruth, her husband and twelve-year-old son visited from Ohio during her vacation, which prompted her to reflect: 'We are together so seldom, and I miss them.'[30]

Unfortunately, towards the end of June things were not so great with Lavin, who found herself 'pretty low & tired' due to personal and financial reasons. She had locked horns with Valdi's fiancé, which greatly upset her and, to add to the mix, the family had a French exchange student staying with them. Lavin was wondering if 'The Mock Auction' had any chance, explaining to MacKenzie that 'things are pretty bad again in the money line' but, true to form, she had another story in the works if it proved unsuitable. Amid the mounting pressures, Lavin took comfort in her 'beautiful' farm and told MacKenzie that it made 'the sadness lighter'.[31]

In early July 'The Mock Auction' was rejected. Aside from being too long, the editors did not find the ending 'credible' and MacKenzie felt it needed to be 'rewritten into a tighter, more astringent story'.[32] Lavin had two other endings for the story and reflected, 'You know I do not believe in the completely inevitable end – or shall we say that I do not believe that a story need inevitably end at a particular place.'[33] Lavin thought she could make 'a few thousand dollars (or one anyway)' if she signed a new contract with Macmillan, as she had planned to do in New York. Yet she was hesitant to commit as she was encountering the same frustrations again, 'no reply to letters etc'.[34] MacKenzie advised Lavin to send them a 'firm letter', reasoning that, 'The best test of their interest and intention will surely be their response to your need for money' and that if she did not hear back from them promptly, she could reassess her situation.

MacKenzie suggested that Lavin should move on to her new story and hoped that she could manage to steal some time and space for her writing as she felt that 'The Mock Auction' and 'Grammar of Women' 'suffered from a lack of it, and I suspect that your happiness has, too, now hasn't it?' She trusted that she was not overstepping the mark in giving her opinion but she reckoned that, 'My own nature has enough of yours in it that I know firsthand how easily it disperses itself.' MacKenzie and her sister were still commuting to work in New York from Connecticut: 'The city steams, but we just shuttle through it, from our air conditioned office to air conditioned train to the country.'[35]

In early August, having heard nothing from Lavin in over a month, MacKenzie worried that her blunt words of advice had caused upset. She told her that they had been hoarding water for their plants as water restrictions had been imposed due to a drought in the northeastern US, yet the weeds were thriving: 'we're fighting a losing battle with crabgrass. Monday I bought a book on weeds, feeling that I should have closer acquaintance with any living thing I was giving so much energy to, and I think we have most of them – Nimble Will and Creeping Jenny and

Carpet Grass and on and on. Nice names.' MacKenzie ended the letter entreating Lavin to let her know that she was alright: 'Please tell me you're fine, or at least that you aren't worse because I wrote you as I did.'[36]

MacKenzie subsequently sent Lavin the author's proof of 'One Summer', which was due to be published in the 11 September issue, with some queries that she did not think would take much time or effort and she mused: 'But then this story has had time. Didn't we have fun going over it together!'[37] 'One Summer' was published as planned on 11 September.[38] The cover by Charles E. Martin is of Wall Street with a view towards Trinity Church imprinted with stock exchange newspaper articles.[39] There is an advert for a Fifth Avenue women's clothing store on the third page with the caption: 'There is a certain kind of woman who would gladly do a rain dance if it would end the drought. For this woman, there is a certain kind of store: Peck & Peck.' Lavin's story shares its forty-eight pages with Hilary Cloke's poem 'Freya Observed' and numerous cartoons, including one by Charles Addams and another by Alan Dunn, in which one woman remarks to another, as she looks out at the rain, 'It's simply teeming. Now we won't have to drink Lake Erie!' (Both the advert and cartoon allude to the current water shortage mentioned by MacKenzie.)

Cullinan passed on the news to Lavin that Maxwell 'told me it was the best thing of yours he'd ever read. My sister Claire also loved it. As did Claire's sister, me.'[40] 'One Summer' and Maxwell's 'Further Tales about Men and Women' were the only *New Yorker* stories selected for Foley & Burnett's *Best American Short Stories 1966*. The collection also featured fiction by William Faulkner, Shirley Jackson and Flannery O'Connor.[41]

Towards the end of September Lavin acknowledged the long gap in communication with MacKenzie and explained that she had been preoccupied with Valdi's on-off engagement and with her mother, who had fallen ill. However, she was at last back working on *First Love* and had finally signed a contract with Macmillan for her next collection of stories, *In the Middle of the Fields and Other Stories*, which was to feature the title story and four other *New Yorker* pieces, namely 'The Lucky Pair', 'Heart of Gold', 'The Cuckoo Spit' and 'One Summer'. Scott wanted to include another story to fatten up the volume and Lavin had suggested 'The Mock Auction'. Lavin received a $2,000 advance for the book, which she used to pay off mounting bills and for a three-day break at Buswell's Hotel with Caroline: 'I bet you anything you like I'll have a story in the post on the night of the 3rd day!!'

Lavin did not wish to appear 'obstinate & a nuisance', but she wondered if MacKenzie would have another look at 'A Grammar of Women'.[42] MacKenzie did reconsider the story but returned the manuscript to Betty (Elizabeth Cullinan), as Lavin had requested, with the note, 'She said she knew there wasn't much chance, but where would we be without hope?' Maxwell had informed MacKenzie that there was a new Cullinan story ('The Old Priest') in the works and she told her, 'I can't think of anything nicer, except reading it. No galleys yet.'[43] MacKenzie also wrote to Lavin directly to let her know that the revisions did not work out. Almost two years later, *The Kenyon Review* purchased 'The Grammar of Women' and Lavin pondered, 'I don't know if they pay any money, but it has prestige value, I think.'[44]

By the autumn the fifty-mile commute to Manhattan from Connecticut was beginning to take its toll on MacKenzie and Gennie and so they made the decision to move into a small hotel apartment in the city from Monday to Friday for the winter months: 'The apartment is crummy, but I don't care; it's near the office and convenient to the things we'll want to be doing, and I expect we shall enjoy ourselves enormously. I'm looking forward to a place I don't have to be responsible for, though I shouldn't like it if I didn't have another.'[45]

Lavin wrote to MacKenzie about her dire financial situation, which was 'a direct result of being too shattered over the summer'. Instead she put her efforts into selling old stories, including both rejected *New Yorker* stories and previously published work. Lavin had some income from the farm and she sublet a room in her mother's flat. She hired a young secretary, Gerry Breen, a fellow law student friend of Valdi's, who was putting her affairs in order by settling her income tax and meeting with her accountant in order to address paying off her overdraft. He was also following up on Lavin's unanswered letters from anthologists and magazines. Breen 'worked a miracle' and did a big cull of Lavin's papers and organised her office and desk 'to make them exclusively literary & not a hotch-potch of everyone's activity as it was'. Lavin was delighted that Valdi, having broken off her engagement, had returned to the nest.

Although Lavin told MacKenzie that 'the worst is over', she was nevertheless reliant on receiving her *New Yorker* first-reading contract.[46] MacKenzie assured Lavin that the agreement would be renewed and she sympathised with her over her financial concerns and mused: 'there's enough weight to this life without having that added, and if I had been at your cradle with a wand I'd have seen to it'.[47] Lavin took on board MacKenzie's advice and resolved not to work until she was out of her current financial bind, noting, 'The stories in my mind are too good to be damaged. Don't worry about me. People always seem to survive.'[48]

Lavin eventually made the difficult decision to part ways with Macmillan due to their 'inefficiency and their impersonal methods'.[49] Her main gripes with Macmillan were that her books were out of print and circulation in the US and that they did not publish them in paperback. Another issue she had with Macmillan was that Scott believed that *In the Middle of the Fields* was 'an alternative' to publishing the *Collected Stories*, which was to be the American publication of *The Stories of Mary Lavin, Vol. 1*.[50] Lavin wrote to Scott of her decision and told him that it would be to their mutual benefit if she returned the advance and he in turn cancelled the contract for *In the Middle of the Fields*.[51]

Lavin wanted to sign a contract with Houghton Mifflin for *Collected Stories* because she found them to be 'so enthusiastic', especially after de Santillana sent cables to Buswell's Hotel, Abbey Farm and the mews, declaring, 'passionately interested in anything you have to offer'. She also telephoned Lavin and even proposed travelling to Ireland to review the situation. The wooing gave Lavin a much-needed 'boost to morale'.[52] The fact that de Santillana agreed with Ben Glazebrook's opinion that Lavin needed 'a "body" of work on the market' was 'a decisive factor' in Lavin's reckoning.[53] Lavin was keen to seal the deal as she wanted to concentrate on her current *New Yorker* story.

Houghton Mifflin offered to pay Lavin a $2,000 advance for *In the Middle of the Fields*, which was still under contract to Macmillan. De Santillana cabled Lavin to inform her that she was preparing the contract but needed to know whether it was Lavin or Constable who held the US rights to the stories. Her understanding was that the advance included the rights to *The Stories of Mary Lavin, Vol. 1* and *In the Middle of the Fields*.[54] Lavin thought she held the US rights and de

Santillana advised her to get Michael Sissons to handle the business side of things.

In December Lavin decided to let Macmillan publish *In the Middle of the Fields* after all because Scott was upset over her decision to leave and Ben Glazebrook advised her that it was the right thing to do. Therefore, she offered de Santillana the *Collected Stories* followed by a new book. This was not an attractive deal for Houghton Mifflin as the advance they offered was for the new volume. If they were successful in acquiring this they would then consider publishing the collected stories at a later stage.[55] Houghton Mifflin also clarified that they wanted to be the only American publisher of Lavin's stories.

On 9 December Lavin received her *New Yorker* contract, which was due for renewal on 6 March 1966: 'It's first-reading agreement renewal time at last, and here are the forms and the check that binds us to one another.' MacKenzie was disappointed that the sum of $500 (minus the retirement plan contribution of $7.50) was less than the previous year's payment of $800: 'The amount is arrived at by some arithmetical computation from what we've bought over the last several years, and when there's been a small year the check comes out smaller. Is there anything less heartening than logic? It doesn't mean that we cherish you any the less. But you know that.' MacKenzie then gave a flavour of the bustle in New York in the run-up to Christmas:

> Here, the whole city seems to be embarked on Christmas; the streets are all legs and bundles. I spent an hour and a half of concentrated shopping – that is, I had a list of exactly what I wanted to find – at Lord and Taylor's this noon and came away with two dishtowels. I don't know where I'll find the courage to go back into a store unless it's in the country this weekend. About this time every year I think I'll retire from Christmas and I never do, so I suppose I'll manage. Anyway, I love it, clutter and all. I just don't like getting tired.

She ended the letter, 'I love you, too.'[56]

Lavin was grateful for the payment, regardless of the amount, noting that 'it's better than a kick in the teeth of which I've had plenty'. She concluded her letter on a positive note: 'But things are looking up definitely. Merry Xmas to you & to all.'[57] MacKenzie's last correspondence with Lavin that year was an undated telegram wishing her 'Special love for Christmas and the New Year.'

MacKenzie, in her first letter to Lavin of 1966, expressed concern over her well-being and productivity. There must have been a phone conversation, or perhaps a missing letter, in which Lavin discussed her publishing predicament, as MacKenzie wrote, 'I've grieved for you all weekend and longed for a way to send you comfort. Are you too upset to start buying them off this minute by finishing a story?'[58] Lavin was upset because Cecil Scott had written to her on 21 January to confirm that Macmillan owned the American rights to *Selected Stories* and *The Great Wave and Other Stories* and he explained that if another American publisher wanted to reprint them they would need to liaise with them.[59] His statement, 'I am sure that something can be arranged,' greatly upset Lavin due to its ambiguity. Scott did, however, offer to release her from her contract for *In the Middle of the Fields* if she returned the advance.

It was March before Lavin was 'beginning to come to life again'. Unfortunately, things were not looking too rosy on the publishing front and she informed MacKenzie that her dealings with Houghton Mifflin were on the verge of collapse, for which Lavin laid the blame squarely on Scott, although she believed that Houghton Mifflin thought she was at fault. Lavin was consoled by the fact that Constable said that she behaved honourably.[60] In February Gerry Breen had written a polite but direct letter to de Santillana of Lavin's anguish over the whole matter in an effort to progress matters. The situation, combined with various 'domestic difficulties', he told her, were distracting Lavin from her writing (her mother had recently been staying with the family but Lavin had organised for her to stay at a convent in Meath because of rising tensions in the household due to her presence). Breen explained that Lavin would only sign with Houghton Mifflin if they agreed to publish *Collected Stories* and *In the Middle of the Fields*.[61]

On 10 March Lavin was dealt another blow. Frank O'Connor, who had been suffering from ill health since his stroke in 1961, died suddenly of a heart attack at his Dublin home at the age of sixty-three. Among the mourners at his funeral were Lavin, Michael Yeats, the son of O'Connor's friend William Butler, Patrick Kavanagh and Brendan Kennelly, who later gave the oration at O'Connor's graveside at Deansgrange cemetery.[62] After the funeral some of the mourners, including Kavanagh, Robert MacBryde, Seán O'Kissane, an Irish translator, Vivien Igoe, the curator of the James Joyce museum in Sandycove and Joseph Dever, an American writer, gathered at the Grosvenor Hotel at Westland Row in Dublin for a drink. During the course of conversation Dever asked Kavanagh who he considered to be 'Ireland's greatest contemporary writer'. Kavanagh 'without hesitation' replied, 'Liam O'Flaherty. And Mary Lavin is Ireland's greatest lady writer.' On the subject of Irish writers making a living from their writing, the group agreed that O'Connor and Lavin 'were well taken care of' because they wrote for *The New Yorker*.[63]

O'Connor's death made the front page of *The Irish Times*.[64] *The Irish Press* covered the author's passing with the news that 'Ireland lost its most distinguished short-story writer' and described O'Connor as 'The Irish Chekhov'. W. B. Yeats once said that O'Connor was 'doing for Ireland what Chekhov did for Russia'. The article quoted Lavin as saying, 'He was a close and dear friend. It is hard to make any statement going beyond that of personal sadness, but I think Ireland can better afford his loss as a great writer than as a truly good man.'[65] *The New York Times* covered O'Connor's death with the subheading 'Irish Short-Story Writer Contributed to New Yorker' and quotes William Maxwell, who said, 'After he [O'Connor] was published, he rewrote and was republished. Everything he wrote was an unfinished work, not so much because of any dissatisfaction, but because of the pleasure he got out of a story.'[66] In this aspect, O'Connor's approach to writing was very similar to Lavin's. The article observed that O'Connor 'was probably best known to Americans through the 47 stories published in *The New Yorker* between 1945 and 1961. The magazine had bought a story from him last year and had recently sent him proofs of the type for correction.'[67]

Lavin was grateful for MacKenzie's offer to work on a story with her 'to try to pull me out of the gripe'.[68] She had started writing two stories that she liked but she felt compelled to finish 'The Mock Auction' and get it 'coffined in a magazine or a book', even though she thought it was 'the worst & most hated story I have ever wrestled with since the Yellow Beret, only it's worse'.[69] But she began to feel more hopeful about it after she had brought it to a standard that had 'come alive' for her, explaining that beforehand, 'it was just like a sticky mess [of] plasticine, that I would keep imagining was stuck to my fingers no matter what else I tried to do'.[70] Once again she sent the story to MacKenzie.

Towards the end of March relations with Houghton Mifflin appeared to have improved and Lavin was expecting a contract and an advance. She was determined never to get into such a bind again. With her daughters getting older and freeing her of certain responsibilities, she resolved 'go away somewhere for about a week each month – or a month every three months – or some such plan to work undistracted (& get physical rest at the same time) on a few stories which I must write before I stop'. Lavin was on tenterhooks because Caroline was due to undergo an eye operation. She was also mourning the loss of O'Connor and told MacKenzie, 'After all I got a great fright on the death of Frank O'Connor apart from personal loss.'[71]

Less than a month after O'Connor's passing, Lavin attended the funeral of Brian O'Nolan (Brian Ó Nualláin), who died of a heart attack on 1 April at the age of fifty-four. Other attendees included O'Nolan's UCD college friends Niall Sheridan and Niall Montgomery. *The Irish Times* poignantly noted the absence of the recently deceased Frank O'Connor and Brendan Behan, who died on 20 March 1964, aged forty-one. An interesting sidebar concerns Cullinan, who met Behan at the Old Ground Hotel in Ennis, County Clare, most likely in 1961, and found him 'splendidly awful and awfully funny'. This was despite the fact that he had pursued her Benny Hill-style through the hotel until she managed to take refuge in the ladies' room where she remained, 'trembling', for ten minutes.[72] In a letter to MacKenzie on 12 April, Lavin mused, 'It would be better for you, but not for me if I could go out in the true fashion of Irish literature & get drunk for a week (they're only coming home now from the funeral of Myles na Copaleen.' It prompted her to think of O'Connor and how much she would 'love if we could be going – say tonight – to dinner with Bill Maxwell (& Mick there too to make better still) to talk about Michael & the strange strange days after his death'.[73]

Lavin explained to de Santillana that although her *New Yorker* payments were 'fantastically high', she only managed to complete two stories in the last two years because 'they were very long & one of them ['One Summer'] very difficult'. The other story was 'The Mock Auction' that she said 'hung like an albatross' over her. She told de Santillana that if *The New Yorker* rejected the story, she would be in dire need of money, therefore she sought an advance for the *Collected Stories*, and she was going to use the money to pay back Scott. Lavin was adamant that the new collection needed to be in paperback for universities and she reckoned that had she been in paperback, 'my reputation today would be at least as high as O'Connor & O Faolain'. Lavin informed de Santillana that she was confident of having a new collection, *First Love and Other Stories*, the following year: 'If I live a few years more & don't die of strain & worry my best stories will yet to be written. Seems to me lately I am only beginning to understand what a story is – much less a good story.'[74]

Much to Lavin's great disappointment, 'The Mock Auction' was again rejected. MacKenzie explained that they felt it was 'more a novella than short story' and she still had an issue with its 'credibility'. MacKenzie gave some suggestions for an alternative ending and marked passages that she felt could be excised from the first twenty-five pages. However, she advised Lavin that unless she took a different approach with the story, it would not be suitable material for the magazine, 'which, of course, is no reason not to go on with it and write it as a full novella, but is perhaps a reason not to do it now, when you need money'. She wondered if it was time for Lavin to move on to one of 'those gift stories waiting for you in the wings!'[75] Lavin rewrote the ending but finally accepted that it was not right for *The New Yorker*. It would, however, be anthologised in the new collection. She thought the story had a 'clodhopping quality' and wished it was more 'frank, and beautiful' like 'The Eve of the Holiday. I did love it – did you?'[76] This was Shirley Hazzard's story, published in *The New Yorker* on 17 April 1965.[77]

Lavin had some paintings that she could sell if she found herself 'in a really dire position'.[78] Mick had been urging her to sell one of her works by Jack B. Yeats.[79] Padraic Colum was looking into selling some of Lavin's correspondence with Lord Dunsany to Binghamton University, having sold them his own papers the previous year. Lavin told MacKenzie that rereading her correspondence with Dunsany 'was like making a voyage with my own past'. She had a 'brain wave' and was looking into the possibility of publishing the letters, prior to selling them in order to make some extra money.[80] MacKenzie thought it a good idea if she could get a publisher; she did not think it would devalue the letters. Lavin was going to discuss it with Dunsany's wife, Beatrice, and she sought Milton Greenstein's advice on the copyright side of things (she had lunched with Greenstein and met him again at Maxwell's home while she was in New York).

Many other universities and colleges expressed interest in Lavin's papers around this time, including Colby College, the University of Toronto, Binghamton University and New York University. Lavin was seeking a valuation of her letters and Terence de Vere White, literary editor of *The Irish Times*, put her in touch with Anthony Robert Alwyn Hobson, a director of Sotheby's in London. The American book dealer Dr Jacob (Jake) Schwartz contacted Lavin in his role as an 'American University Library Agent' to offer to sell her papers. John D. Gordan from the New York Public Library expressed an interest in Lavin's manuscripts and typescripts, but he forewarned Schwartz that the library would not be in a position to make a generous offer.[81] Schwartz pointed out to Lavin that 'original works entirely written by hand … are the most precious'.[82] The tentative proposition came to nothing: Lavin had written on a couple of the letters 'No use' and 'No good.' MacKenzie later suggested that Lavin might write something concerning the correspondence but Lavin responded, 'I can't be bothered really – its stories for me – all the time & all the way.'[83] Yet she was contemplating doing a profile of Dunsany, as suggested by Maxwell, and wondered if *The New Yorker* would be interested in such an article. Ultimately, Lavin abandoned the idea and decided that 'the money is quicker and surer by selling'. She also found correspondence from Seamus O'Sullivan, and James Johnson Sweeney, whom Lavin encountered during her Guggenheim Fellowship, was trying to sell her manuscripts to Texas University.

Lavin had been elected President of PEN on 16 October 1965 and so she was invited to the International PEN congress that was taking place in New York in June.[84] Arthur Miller was hosting the event, having been elected the first American president of International PEN in 1966, a role he held until 1969. Lavin did not attend as she was expected to pay for her own fare and she also did not want to lose any writing time: 'I'd love it of course. But better write a few more stories & some day be a guest of honour – for free!'[85]

The conference, 'The Writer As Independent Spirit', ran from 12 to 18 June. A photograph of Lavin at the airport seeing off the Irish delegation, consisting of Austin Clarke, Arthur Rae and Charles E. Kelly, was published in *The Irish Press*.[86] Ralph Ellison and Saul Bellow were among the 650 attendees.[87] Arthur Miller delivered the closing address, in which he asked writers to 'emphasise that which is similar among us, isolate that which separates us, resolve our differences and put aside those things that we cannot resolve'.[88]

In early September Lavin explained that the long gap in correspondence over the summer was because she had no 'time or energy'. She took on board MacKenzie's advice and took a complete break from writing, 'I did not lift a pen – not once.' Lavin was only beginning to recover properly from the throat complaint that she had in New York, for which she was taking vitamin pills. Upon receiving an advance from Constable for *In the Middle of the Fields*, Lavin and Caroline checked into a hotel. Lavin was looking for the notebook in which she jotted down the outline for a story named 'Happiness'. She reckoned that it would only take her a few hours or days to write it, after which she intended to go away with Valdi for a week.[89] Lavin's self-declared 'First Idea for Happiness' was handwritten on a page of a *Vogue* magazine advertisement for Bounce hair gel, dated November 1965.[90]

Lavin was relieved that the summer was over and the girls were back in school and college and 'not around my ears all day'. Valdi impressively came fourth in her bar finals and was sitting her Bachelor of Law exams the following week, after which she would be leaving home '(where we know not – but somewhere)'. Elizabeth was looking to join the Peace Corps and she was due to leave home also.[91] Meanwhile, Lavin's mother had absconded from the convent and gone to her sister's house in Galway.

In a last-ditch attempt to sell 'The Mock Auction' to *The New Yorker*, before it was published in January in the new Constable collection, Lavin airmailed the book proof to MacKenzie for her to reconsider the revised story. Although MacKenzie thought that Lavin's amendments improved the text, it was nevertheless rejected again on the basis that it was too long at over 20,000 words and there was no space in the magazine in the autumn schedule: 'Please don't grieve; it's fine in the book, and the book is lovely. All stories I have great affection for. Opening it was like opening the door to a roomful of very dear friends.'[92] Lavin asked MacKenzie if she noticed its dedication: 'Did you see that at last I was able to dedicate it to him name & not just by initials?'[93] Lavin dedicated the book to 'Michael Scott, S. J.' and told MacKenzie that he was the 'M.S.' of some other dedications, which MacKenzie had already ascertained.[94] MacKenzie was pleased to hear that things were looking more positive for Lavin: 'It's time for an upswing, don't you feel? I do.'

MacKenzie sent 'The Mock Auction' to Jeff Brown at *The Saturday Evening Post* for consideration but it was not suitable for that publication either, as MacKenzie explained: 'He took time to read it at once and has just sent it back with word that it would not do for them – length partly, but subject even more; it seems that they have had a run of stories about older women in financial trouble (isn't that a funny description of Miss Lomas?).'[95] It was also an unintentional description of Lavin, who had declared in an earlier letter to MacKenzie that Miss Lomas in the story was her. MacKenzie did not know of any other magazine that would take such a long story.

Lavin sought feedback on a query raised by Constable's proofreader regarding the use of the word 'aphis' in 'The Cuckoo Spit' (in the story, during Vera Traske's encounter with the young man, she picked him a rose on which there was a cuckoo spit and they both watched as an aphis emerged from it). The proofreader thought it should be 'nymph'. Lavin, knowing first-hand how rigorously the *New Yorker's* checking department scrutinised texts, observed, 'I feel it would never have escaped the eagle eye of your proof reader if it was very inaccurate & for me all the meaning is altered by this poetical suggestions of the word "nymph".'[96] MacKenzie queried it with the checking department, which in turn got in touch with the Museum of Natural History. MacKenzie provided the following feedback: 'Technically, it seems, "nymph" is correct. But the nymph of the cuckoo spit looks like an aphis, and is the same family and the same order, so it isn't so very inaccurate.' She suggested that Lavin substitute 'insect' for aphid: 'The nymph is an insect in immature form. I feel with you about "nymph". The connotations of the word are too strong, and in this story they matter.'[97] 'Aphis' remained in the collected version of the story.

In October Lavin travelled to Brussels as the guest 'for a Belgian writer's centenary' organised by the Belgian Friends of the French Language Society.[98] She was the only English-speaking guest amongst members from Luxembourg, Belgium and the French Academy. Lavin spent an additional four days in Belgium and frequented cafés at Ostend, from where she wrote to MacKenzie before getting the boat back home. She was badly in need of the break, which had thoroughly revived her: 'I can put right side up at last & may even with a bit of luck have turned inside out as well – something one has to do every other decade or so in life – or I have had to do it – in order not only to progress lest even to survive.' She intended to return home 'to crack the whip over them all' and make a 'vital change in my life'.[99]

Meanwhile, MacKenzie was braving a cold winter in Connecticut: 'we have hoar frost these mornings almost as thick as a fine fall of snow. And a new roof going on, and the snow-plowing contract signed to take care of the driveway, and snow tires put on the cars. I cherish the turning of the seasons, even to shingles and tires.' She was hoping that she and Gennie could remain in the countryside for December: 'The hotel last winter was marvellously convenient and moderately comfortable, but so ugly I can hardly face it again – not for so long a stretch anyway.' MacKenzie was looking forward to brighter days and planted bulbs for the spring: 'These were crocus and grape hyacinth and miniature tulips and anemone. No daffodils, though there are a few from last year. But nothing like the lovely masses of "One Summer," which are what I want to have one day, stragglers and all.'[100] In the story, Lavin writes, 'It was only March and early in the month, but the daffodils were out on either side of the drive. As they walked by them, the massed flower heads shone like a lake of light ... They'd spread into the pastures, indeed, where many of them were trampled and broken by the cattle, and far off, in the very middle of the field, there were a few stragglers.'[101] Cullinan told MacKenzie that Lavin had 'the most beautiful garden in the world' at Bective.

Although Lavin loved hearing all about MacKenzie's farm, she was sorry to have received such a long letter from her, knowing how busy she was: 'You know I can always – so easily too – take your sympathy & affection for granted without a letter.' Colum was successful in his dealings with Binghamton and Lavin sold some letters to the university for $2,000.

She put MacKenzie as a contact on the insured package of letters that she posted to the university, 'just in case – & to save them having to cross back all the way across "the wild & stormy sea" (that last to be sung)'. The University of Illinois offered Lavin $4,000 for the manuscripts, which she did not think was an adequate sum, but she thought she might have to accept it if her money situation did not improve.

Constable had put Lavin forward for a British Arts Council bursary, which she was awarded, but the day after she received the news the offer had to be withdrawn because as an American citizen Lavin was ineligible for the grant. External Affairs in Ireland appealed the decision on the basis that Lavin held dual citizenship, but she did not think that she would, or should, satisfy the conditions: 'It feels a bit like having your loaf and eating it.' They were unsuccessful in their appeal. John McGahern was among the recipients of the award that year and received a grant of £800.[102]

The protracted dealings between Macmillan and Houghton Mifflin took such a toll on Lavin that she declared, 'my belief in my being a writer at all seemed to wither away'.[103] Ben Glazebrook from Constable even travelled to the US in October to try sort out the muddle. De Santillana wrote to Lavin on 21 December, expressing her confidence that Lavin would be on their list in 1967. On 29 December Paul Brooks, the editor-in-chief at Houghton Mifflin, wrote to Gerry Breen to inform him that Macmillan held the copyright for nine of the stories that were due to be anthologised in *Collected Stories*, only two of which were in print. Macmillan were seeking a fee of $200 per story for hardback rights only. This meant that Macmillan could potentially publish paperback editions of their two collections. Brooks sought permission to issue a cheque to Macmillan for $2,000 to buy the contract for *In the Middle of the Fields*, which they would then publish in the autumn. Houghton Mifflin would continue their negotiations with Macmillan for the rights to Lavin's stories. Brooks noted that *Selected Stories* (1959) and seemingly *The Great Wave* (1961) were out of print in the USA and he wondered if that meant that the rights should revert back to Lavin, which was usually standard in a contract.[104] Lavin did not agree to his proposal because she felt it 'would only be reversing the situation now existing with Macmillan'.[105]

On 9 December MacKenzie sent Lavin the first-reading agreement cheque for $300 with the note: 'I wish it were larger, but perhaps its arrival is well enough timed for it to be particularly welcome, large or small. It comes with our gratitude and our love.'[106] Lavin was 'thunderstruck' to receive a larger amount than the previous year as she feared she was 'not being worth my keep this year', but she figured it was something to do with the word count. She saw the increase as an 'omen' but she was obviously confused as the amount she was paid the previous year was $500. After wishing MacKenzie 'a beautiful beautiful Christmas', Lavin ended her letter with a reflection on her new work: 'It has just occurred to me that, although without arrogance I hope, the new story is good – strong & true and moving like an arrow, it could well be unsuitable for you because it's a bitter story but I don't think I am bitter & that may save it – I mean there will I hope be chinks in its darkness.'[107]

7
'Happiness for Sure'
1967

> I hope to Heaven that my own letters are never sold by anyone, when I think of what a long, boring wail about money they must all surely boil down to.[1]

On 13 January 1967 Gerry Breen wrote to Cecil Scott seeking a reversal of the rights for *Selected Stories* back to Mary Lavin as it was out of print. He also wanted to get Lavin out of the contract for *The Great Wave*, if it was also out of print, and he enquired after the number of copies in stock.[2] Macmillan were not prepared to revert the rights to *The Great Wave*, which Scott confirmed was still in print, or *Selected Stories*, when Macmillan could profit from the works in the future. Scott said that any permission fees for the stories would be shared equally with Lavin. This was not a viable arrangement for Houghton Mifflin, who made it clear that they wanted to hold the American rights to all of Lavin's work.

On 23 January 1967 Constable brought out the collection *In the Middle of the Fields and Other Stories*.[3] A flurry of mixed reviews appeared in the Irish and UK press including *The Irish Times*, *The Tribune*, *The Sunday Telegraph* and *The Times Literary Supplement*. Augustine Martin wrote in *The Irish Press* that the volume 'forces us to look forward even more eagerly to her next collection while consolidating her position in the first rank of modern Irish writers'.[4] Terence de Vere White did not share Martin's enthusiasm. He thought Lavin was 'making heavy weather with incidents that are insufficiently dramatic' and observed that Lavin was 'one of the select few who are under contract to the *New Yorker*, a fate which those who don't enjoy it are apt to say is detrimental to the storyteller's art'. He singled out 'Heart of Gold' as 'the nearest to Miss Lavin's high best' and concluded his article, 'If Miss Lavin were not a national asset I would not have spoken from my heart and damned the consequence.'[5] Ronan Farren of the *Irish Independent* found the book to be 'an uneven collection', but maintained that 'it would be ridiculous to use any but the highest standards in the writing of Mary Lavin'.[6]

Lavin had asked Rachel MacKenzie for her thoughts on a poem 'about the air hostess', which she said 'nearly tore me to bits – in a queer way'.[7] She was referring to James Dickey's haunting poem 'Falling', which commanded three pages in *The New Yorker* on 11 February 1967.[8] It was inspired by the true story of a 29-year-old Allegheny Airlines stewardess who was sucked out of an airplane's emergency exit and tragically fell to her death in October 1962.[9] MacKenzie, unsurprisingly, had a similar reaction to the poem: 'The tension of it is almost unbearable.'[10] It was unfortunate timing, not to mention a *New Yorker* oversight, that the same issue carried adverts for seven airlines.[11] The poem probably spooked Lavin in particular, given her well-known fear of flying.

Lavin had planned to travel to the US – by boat – for six months the following January and expressed a desire to see MacKenzie's farm in Connecticut during her stay. She invited MacKenzie to visit her own farm at Bective that coming summer. In her last letter to MacKenzie before Christmas of 1966, Lavin had mentioned that 'a spark flew out & ignited another little blaze' while she was composing the story 'Happiness'.[12] The 'little blaze' resulted in 'A Pure Accident', which was written in two days. It was February before Lavin sent a rough draft to MacKenzie, fearing that it might be 'too savage' for the magazine. Although the story was written with 'speed & ease', Lavin did not care for the work.[13] Nevertheless, she was grateful to it and acknowledged its value in getting her writing again under difficult circumstances. It would appear that William Shawn did not care for 'A Pure Accident' either, as it was promptly rejected. MacKenzie was particularly saddened by Shawn's decision because she expected that the story would be taken, despite the need for significant cutting and revision. She greatly sympathised with Lavin, telling her, 'And I grieve for your disappointment. The only comfort I have is knowing that there's another story on the way.' MacKenzie was heartened to hear about Lavin's impending trip and noted the stark difference in the weather between New York and Connecticut, with the city 'clear and bright and dry' while the country was 'white with snow and every branch and twig on the place is coated with ice'.[14]

Lavin was not surprised at the outcome and she described the timing of a $250 cheque that she received from the magazine as a 'New York miracle'. She divulged that she would 'have been terribly depressed – or perhaps more correct to say panick-stricken [*sic*] otherwise.'[15] This was due to the fact that Lavin was yet again experiencing financial difficulties, but she remained positive and aspired to have another bonus year. She also expected that her money situation would 'be easier by nine tenths!' with both Valdi and Elizabeth finished with their studies. Lavin recounted that when 'dear Bill Maxwell' asked Harriet O'Connor if she and the girls were 'ever hungry', Harriet responded that they were not as they would often dine with them, but Lavin explained that 'it was because I could never let them be hungry that things were a strain'. Then on the day of O'Connor's death, Harriet told Lavin about his concern for her financial situation and that when he had broached the subject with Lavin she had responded, 'don't worry, Michael [O'Connor's birth name], I might buy a villa in Florence'. They were both amused by her response but Lavin said that they were 'missing the whole point that I would be selling the farm'.[16]

When Lavin sent MacKenzie the second draft of 'Happiness', she was cognisant of the fact that it needed further work but, as was her habit, she was eager to move on to another story. Lavin revealed that 'Happiness' was somewhat semi-autobiographical: 'I'm a bit ashamed at your seeing it because it's a queer mixture of truth & fantasy.'[17] MacKenzie was 'moved' by 'Happiness' and was tentatively of the opinion that it would make 'a lovely story'.[18] In April Shawn accepted 'the story with the understanding that it required further revision and cutting. MacKenzie proposed that they take the same approach to the alterations as they had done with 'One Summer', with MacKenzie cutting and tightening the story and Lavin polishing the edited version.[19] MacKenzie was comforted to be working on another of Lavin's stories. Recognising that the substantial revisions would take some time, she offered to send her an advance payment of $1,000, which Lavin promptly accepted via a Western Union telegram: 'AGREE STORY ADVANCE APPRECIATED.'[20] Lavin was especially grateful for the money because she was awaiting the payment of $4,000 for the manuscripts of *The Great Wave* and approximately another ten stories, which she decided to sell to the State University of Southern Illinois.

MacKenzie sent Lavin the cheque and hoped that Lavin did not have every penny earmarked because $15 had been deducted for the retirement plan. The money was timely as Lavin revealed to MacKenzie that she had travelled to London 'on borrowed money' for a couple of days, staying with friends. To celebrate her advance, Lavin extended her visit by a night and booked into a hotel as a treat. She had combined attending a PEN event with visiting Valdi, who was then based in London, in addition to taking the opportunity to try and straighten out the business between Macmillan and Houghton Mifflin that was 'now going into its 3rd depressing year'.[21] Lavin also thought that she may need to travel to New York to sort out the Macmillan situation after negotiations appeared to take a nasty turn, 'the glow was taken out of it. I think, for both of us, by the dance [Cecil] Scott has led us'.[22] At some point Lavin mentioned to Houghton Mifflin that she was working on the novel because Scott informed Breen that it was his understanding that Houghton Mifflin would only publish *Collected Stories* when they received this new novel.[23] Lavin was sorry that she ever mentioned that she had a novel, 'or long story as I prefer to call it', in the works as she feared it would 'interfere in the reputation I have built up [as a short-story writer], with so many sacrifices over the years'.[24]

Lavin was keen to send one of her *New Yorker* stories, possibly 'Happiness', to *Vogue*, if it was permitted after publication in *The New Yorker*, noting, 'I always saw F. O'Connor in other magazines but they [A. D. Peters] never sold mine.'[25] Frustrated by A. D. Peters's inefficiencies and Michael Sissons's refusal to handle the issue of American rights with Macmillan, Lavin decided to part ways with the agency.[26] She dealt with the matter herself and spoke with Scott, who agreed to amend her current contract for *In the Middle of the Fields* with any changes she wanted, including the reversal of rights. Lavin followed up their conversation with a letter in which she told him that she thought she might stay with Macmillan after all because the 'rigidity of her contract' made it difficult for her to leave, but also because she valued her friendship with him.

Lavin enquired as to the likelihood of Macmillan publishing her *Collected Stories*, which was her original bone of contention with them, and she also asked about the reversion of rights for her books that were out of print. She told Scott that she had finished 'Happiness', which was going to be the title of her next collection, and when that book was finished, she was going to go away and work on the novel, possibly in January and February when she was due to travel to Spain. On a personal note, she wrote, 'Meanwhile, dear Cecil, do please write me a note, because we have a lot of lost time to make up.' She let him know that she would likely be in New York in October or November when she hoped that 'everything between us will have been settled, and plans for the future on the way'.[27] In the end, Macmillan agreed to revert the rights of the books that were out of print to Lavin.

Lavin was badly in need of the remaining money for 'Happiness' and wondered how the payment could be expedited. MacKenzie proposed that once they agreed on the revisions, she would get it set in a working proof, which would mean that Lavin could be paid for the story. MacKenzie suggested that they could then work on the story together when Lavin came to the US in the autumn, as they had done with 'One Summer': 'Would you like that? I know I would.'[28] Despite her difficulties in deciphering Lavin's writing, MacKenzie thought she captured most of the changes and she felt that it only needed some slight changes: 'It will be lovely to go over it together.'[29] Lavin was greatly relieved when MacKenzie sent the remaining money for 'Happiness', which amounted to $2,062.50.[30] Coincidentally, the cheque arrived on the same day as the payment for the manuscripts she sold to the State University of Southern Illinois, which had been delayed by State Treasury. Although the majority of the money was owed to 'snarling creditors', it gave Lavin great satisfaction to be able to settle her bills.[31]

By Lavin's own admission, 'Happiness' was semi-autobiographical: 'It's not <u>me</u>, of course, but near enough to make me want it <u>harder</u> for personal as well as technical reasons.'[32] There are obvious parallels to be drawn between the text and Lavin's own life. The story portrays a widow, Vera, who features in many of her stories and is the character who most strongly resembles Lavin. In 'Happiness', she lives with her three daughters on a farm in County Meath and has befriended a priest, Father Hugh, loosely based on Father Michael Scott.[33] The story is told through the eyes of Vera's eldest, unnamed daughter. Mindful that the story draws from Lavin's life, we see Lavin writing the story from the perspective of Valdi. However, Colm Tóibín has noted that Lavin 'found a voice which was close too to Caroline's'.[34]

The story also makes reference to Vera's beloved dead father and her difficult and demanding mother, whose selfishness drove an exasperated Father Hugh to exclaim at one point, 'God Almighty couldn't make that woman happy.'[35] Lavin's own mother's happiness was playing on her mind during the composition of the story, as evidenced when she informed MacKenzie that she did not think her mother was 'capable of happiness – or certainly not of letting you see that you can give it to her – poor little dear'.[36]

In the story, Vera reminisces back to when she 'dragged you children after me all over Europe' in her 'battered and dilapidated red sports car', mirroring Lavin's journey across Europe with her daughters.[37] She had taken the children to Fécamp in France in the summer following her husband's death, but her emotions were still raw and her concerned daughters realised that she was in a state of semi-breakdown. Lavin brought her own daughters to Saint Briac in Brittany after their father died, where they had all been together as a family the previous year. Her daughter Elizabeth recollected that they went on 'the same holiday, in the same house, except without him. Mother nearly lost her mind over there. The grief must have been appalling.' It was the last time that Lavin travelled by plane.[38] While travel provided a form of escape, it was also an incentive and reward, which carried Lavin through more difficult times. It comes as no surprise then that Lavin told MacKenzie of her plans to go for a week's holiday with Valdi as soon as she finished the story.

Gardening is another form of escape for Vera, who immerses herself in her garden mentally, physically and spiritually. Her garden offers a diversion and place of refuge and her daughter reflects that, 'There was only one place Mother found rest. When she was at breaking point and fit to fall, she'd go out into the garden – not to sit or stroll around but to dig, to drag up weeds, to move great clumps of corms or rhizomes, or indeed quite frequently to haul huge rocks from one place to another.'[39] Lavin, likewise, retreated to her garden when she was worried or stressed and unable to write, such as when she received the offer of the first-reading agreement from *The New Yorker* and a paralysis overcame her and 'spread to cover all my intellectual efforts, and I did nothing but dig in the garden'.[40] Gardening and flowers feature in many of Lavin's stories and daffodils play a significant role in 'Happiness'.

After Lavin's death, her daughters sent acknowledgement cards with the following quotation from 'Happiness': 'If anything ever happens to me, children, suddenly, I mean, or when you are not near me, or I cannot speak to you, I want you to promise you won't feel bad. There's no need! Just remember that I had a happy life – and that if I had to choose my kind of heaven I'd take it on this earth with you again, no matter how much you might annoy me!'[41] Lavin's words obviously resonated strongly with her daughters and Lavin, in composing them, effectively wrote her own epitaph.

Lavin had been reappointed as president of Irish PEN, which took up a considerable amount of her time. In March she attended the Belfast PEN annual dinner, where Loyd Moyne was the guest of honour.[42] On 20 April Lavin was a speaker at the Irish PEN symposium 'The Writer in Ireland To-day' alongside the publisher Liam Miller, the poet Brendan Kennelly and the writer Francis Stuart. In May, Lord Moyne succeeded her as the new president of Irish PEN. Lavin had been elected to a sub-committee of Irish PEN and the Irish Academy of Letters, whose aim was to 'revive and enhance the importance of the Irish Academy of letters and to consider ways in which both organisations could co-operate for the benefit of Irish writers in general'.[43]

By the end of May, Lavin's fortunes took an upturn. She had been appointed writer-in-residence for three weeks at Denison University in Ohio that coming November, 'during which they say they expect me to do very little more than allow my name to be printed on the syllabus'.[44] The university was paying for first-class round trips and providing board and accommodation for both herself and Caroline, in addition to paying Lavin a stipend of $1,500 'all profit'.[45] Lavin saw it as an opportunity to work on her novella. She proudly informed MacKenzie that Elizabeth was writing 'very beautiful & "spare"' poetry and that her work had been accepted by prestigious publications such as *Poetry Ireland*.[46] Valentine had applied rather late in the day to American universities, including Yale, Harvard, Columbia and Cornell, for postgraduate scholarships. Having received no response from Columbia, and the wrong information from Cornell, she wrote to MacKenzie to see if she would contact them to get the applications on her behalf.[47] MacKenzie promptly wrote to the universities seeking applications. In the end, Valdi got a scholarship to the Southern Methodist Graduate Law School in Dallas, which Lavin felt was 'a bit creepy for us Europeans', but she did not elaborate on this sentiment.[48] MacKenzie was delighted to hear all of Lavin's good news: 'Things really have turned, haven't they. I see this as meaning a whole string of new stories. Happiness for sure.'[49]

The trip to Denison ended up getting postponed until 1968, but it was an ill wind, as Lavin subsequently received a cable from the University of Connecticut (Storrs) offering her the position of writer-in-residence for twelve weeks commencing that coming September, for which she would be paid $6,500.[50] She was going to take Caroline with her while Elizabeth stayed at Buswell's Hotel to continue her university degree. Lavin was hoping to get a short break in a hotel 'doing nothing' before her voyage to New York: 'For me heaven will be a hotel. I know for some it's hell. Not me.'[51] However, she faced many difficulties before her journey, including rehoming her mother, who turned up unexpectedly in a taxi one evening after having left the convent where she had been residing. Lavin managed to get her 'poor little mother' settled in a hospital as a stopgap until she returned from America but she was broken-hearted at seeing her looking 'so sad & lonely'.[52]

On 14 August David Carver, the general secretary and treasurer of International PEN, wrote to Lavin of his disappointment that she would not be present for the International PEN executive committee meeting and the round-table conference in Dublin that was being held from 1 to 4 November 1967. Carver was hopeful that Arthur Miller would be able to attend the meeting. He offered to put Lavin in touch with Miller, who was spending a lot of time in New York for rehearsals of his new play, *The Price*, which was due to open in Philadelphia on 8 January and in New York on 30 January.[53] Disappointingly, Miller could not make the Dublin event due to illness.

On 31 August Lavin and Caroline set sail for the United States. They were going to stay with Elizabeth Cullinan upon their arrival in New York on 5 September. When Valdi travelled to the US in August she also stayed with Cullinan before going on to Dallas. Lavin had hoped that she would get the opportunity to meet with MacKenzie but this never panned out as she was on vacation. Douglass Paige, who handled Lavin's work while Cecil Scott was away, assured Lavin that one or both of them would meet with Valdi. In the event, Paige suffered a coronary and ended up in hospital.

Lavin's six-month residency at the University of Connecticut began on 16 September. On 29 September *The Hartford Courant*, the largest daily newspaper in the state of Connecticut, carried the headline 'Irish Author Tutors U of C Students' and publicised: 'One of the world's foremost short-story writers, Mary Lavin Walsh, has been engaged as 1967–68 writer-in-residence at the University of Connecticut, it was announced Thursday by President Homer D. Babbidge Jr.'[54] Lavin and Caroline were living 'in a lovely wood, but dark & far from the campus'. She went to her office in the university every day to work while Caroline attended the university-owned E.O. Smith High School. Lavin was clearly relishing the experience and told MacKenzie, 'I am looking forward so much to seeing you! I love being here & Im so glad I came.' She frequently met with MacKenzie in New York. On one visit she only managed to talk to MacKenzie on the phone because she had to escape the city due to the intense heat: 'It was tantalising to talk to you on the phone & not see you, but I was so hot & bothered in the literally sense of the expression that my only hope was to get out of N. York fast.'[55]

On 11 October 1967 George Starbuck, the director of the Iowa Writers' Workshop, wrote to Lavin to let her know that they 'would be pleased and honored' if she would 'give a lecture or reading or perhaps both'.[56] He offered Lavin a fee of $300, which could possibly be stretched to a little more, plus her travel expenses to 'spend several days here and meet informally with some of the young novelists and storywriters in the Workshop'.[57] Lavin let Starbuck know that January was the only month really feasible for her to take up the offer. In a later letter, she sought clarification on the fee offered, her understanding being that they would 'pay $300 for a reading (& discussion of course, but I do not lecture)', but that they 'could pay a larger fee if she stayed for a few days and met with the students'.[58] The honorarium was lower than Lavin was normally offered, but she was nonetheless very appreciative of the proposition. William Cotter Murray then got in touch to let Lavin know that the most they could offer was $400 – Starbuck had asked him to 'plead with her to come anyway'.[59] Murray suggested that

Lavin could visit for two or three days if she planned to go to Southern Illinois; he also let her know that because she did not fly, the journey from Illinois to Iowa was a rather cumbersome one.

MacKenzie later asked if it was George Starbuck who invited Lavin to Iowa, as she recalled recommending Lavin to him when he was seeking a lecturer for the school of creative writing.[60] While MacKenzie may well have recommended Lavin, it was the Irish writer Bryan MacMahon who instigated the invitation.[61] On 14 September 1967 MacMahon wrote to Paul Engle, the former director of the Iowa Writers' Workshop, to let him know that Lavin was at Storrs.[62] He informed him that there was the possibility of her reading at Kansas and thought Engel might wish for her to speak at Iowa also, although MacMahon alerted him to the fact that Lavin could not remain too long in America as she had to return home to her ageing mother. Engle subsequently got in touch with Starbuck suggesting Lavin as a speaker, noting 'she might help represent the cause of fiction among all of the poets'.[63]

Lavin had been partnered with John Updike to do a joint reading at the Poetry Center in New York on Sunday 19 November at 8.30 p.m. She was a great admirer of Updike's work and so was excited about the pairing and meeting him, 'teamed with – of all writers John Updike – whom I most wanted to meet – but would not have tried achieving other than thus by accident'.[64] Although they had never met, their work appeared in the same issue of *The New Yorker* on five occasions and they were both awarded the Guggenheim Fellowship in 1959. Lavin and MacKenzie ruminated over which story Lavin should read at the event. MacKenzie was curious as to what Updike would be reading. She suggested that 'The Living' would be a good choice if 'In the Middle of the Fields' was too long: 'And after all it's not so old; 1958, isn't it? I have a special affection for both stories.'[65]

'The Living' and 'In the Middle of the Fields' were both collected in *The Great Wave and Other Stories* but Lavin was struggling to find copies of the book in New York bookstores for the upcoming reading. She had heard rumours that it was out of print but knew from the book sales that this could not be the case.[66] Macmillan were insistent that the book was in stock although Lavin explained that 'when forced by the Houghton Mifflin situation to give figures, it appeared that "in stock" meant a handful of copies, and sales dockets showed this had been the situation for a long time'. Macmillan were unable to locate the three copies of the book that were stored in their New Jersey warehouse. Lavin discovered that *The Great Wave* had been out of circulation 'for over a year & now turning out to be lost', causing her to lament, 'Oh Rachel I cannot help being filled with despair.'[67] She confided in MacKenzie that the whole debacle 'depressed me more than anyone could ever know'. It was a very frustrating situation for Lavin as she explained, 'It is NOT the money – as you know – but the loss of readers – that is so disheartening.' To add to her woes, the move to Houghton Mifflin broke down and de Santillana told Lavin that they had to back off 'as the situation was so impossible'.[68]

On the night, Lavin read 'In the Middle of the Fields' and Updike read three of his *New Yorker* poems, 'Youth's Progress' (26 February 1955), 'The High-Hearts' (24 February 1962) and 'Telephone Poles' (21 January 1961) and two *New Yorker* stories, 'Toward Evening' (11 February 1956) and 'The Astronomer' (1 April 1961).[69] The event was a great success and Lavin 'got three curtain calls', but it must have been hugely frustrating for her to have no books for signing afterwards, especially when Updike, who received no curtain call, spent 'half the night' signing his books. The incident made Lavin reflect on her 'obscurity' as a result of her work being out of print, especially as she did not envision 'a sudden spectacular sale that would bring me into the literary limelight'. Lavin believed that she and other writers such as O'Connor, Welty and Bowen 'had really a sort of cumulative reputation'.[70] Despite Lavin's three curtain calls, it would appear from correspondence from Maxwell, who attended the reading, that the audience were so in awe of Updike they failed to appreciate the quality of Lavin's 'classical short story, the art at its highest, a sample of perfection'.[71] This conflicts with MacKenzie's appraisal of Lavin's recital when she informed her: 'Since then, so many people have spoken to me about your reading; it made a lasting impression. Well, you were very endearing up on that platform, and the quality of the story as well as your own, carried.'[72] May Sarton also attended the event with her friend, the author Rozanne Knudson and some of Knudson's students, who were 'interested and thrilled by the readings'.[73] Sarton wrote a letter to Galen Eberl the following day to apologise for not going to the afterparty. While Sarton thought 'both readings were excellent', she was greatly impressed by Lavin: 'And what a lovely person Mary Lavin is. I drank her in. They both presented their work superbly. It was one of the most enjoyable events I've ever been to at the "y".'[74]

Lavin returned to Storrs after the reading as she was unable to book accommodation at the Algonquin or Westbury hotels that night but she had to travel back to New York the following day to work on 'Happiness' with MacKenzie.[75] Lavin subsequently thanked MacKenzie for the 'lovely lunch & all the incidental fun'.[76] She was also due to give a reading at Fairfield University in Connecticut on Saturday 9 December. MacKenzie had hoped the event would fall at the weekend because she wanted Lavin to visit her home in Weston, a town in Fairfield. Lavin offered to visit her that Sunday or else wait until nearer Christmas. She also let MacKenzie know that she might be in New York from 18 until 22 December, 'if I agree to let Helen Roelofs do a bronze head of me – which seems a hateful idea, but I've been putting her off for years'. Roelof's first husband, Ernie O'Malley, and her son, Cormac, were Lavin's neighbours in Dublin in the 1950s. Roelofs befriended Lavin in 1957 and the two remained good friends.[77]

Life at Storrs was not going too well due to an uncomfortable living arrangement, which saw Lavin and Caroline sharing a home with a rather disagreeable family: 'I gave you no idea of how bad it is in Storrs & after the brief visit here I realise how absurd as well as outrageous of them to bring me across the world & have no place for me to live – except to share a house with someone – anyone – much less really awful people.'[78] Although the situation was unpleasant, Lavin resolved to 'stay in America long enough to get the [Macmillan] contracts over from Dublin & get that straightened out – or else what use in trying to write stories anymore?'[79] Scott was supposed to have furnished Lavin with copies of her contracts and sales figures to review, so when Ben Glazebrook informed her in November that Macmillan were planning to publish *In the Middle of the Fields* in March, she was naturally taken aback and requested that they cease the publication until they had an opportunity to address her concerns.

Fortunately, Lavin and Caroline were subsequently rehomed with Professor George Saul and his wife, Eileen, who proved a far more suitable match, and she remained friends with the couple after she returned to Ireland. Saul was a scholar of Anglo-Irish literature and had been teaching at the University of Connecticut since 1924. He had spent the previous year in Ireland researching modern Irish literature.[80] Towards the end of their stay, Lavin and Caroline lived with the Medlicott family, who had three children, and so Caroline had company. Lavin also kept in touch with the Medlicotts and the family visited Bective in 1977.

On 27 November James Wade wrote to let Lavin know that Paige, who had been dealing with her predicament, was still very ill and would be out of the office for the foreseeable future. Paige had another coronary, the second in three months, and was back in hospital. He had written to Lavin during his first hospitalisation to try and rectify the situation with Macmillan. Wade had been asked by the editor-in-chief of his department to handle the affair in Paige's absence and informed Lavin that Macmillan were now intending to publish *In the Middle of the Fields* in October of 1968.

Lavin sought Milton Greenstein's counsel on the matter and had given MacKenzie a copy of her Macmillan contract for him to review.[81] On Greenstein's advice, Lavin phoned Macmillan and talked to Wade, who was 'was <u>very</u> concerned on the phone & spoke of a new leaf etc & doing everything they could to keep me on their list & make amends etc'. She had a change of heart and thought that perhaps she should remain with Macmillan after all: 'I can trust them & if they give me new retrospective contracts this should be allright [*sic*].'[82] She had discussed with Wade the possibility of publishing some of her other work and of having the same clause regarding rights that was in her Constable contract put into her Macmillan one but Wade said that this would require the president of the company's authorisation. However, he noted that they were both essentially the same as the 'out of print' clause in their current contract, which meant that the stories in *In the Middle of the Fields* would either remain in print or would revert to Lavin within a specific time period.[83] Wade proposed that they should meet the following week in order to get a better grasp of her situation and to address any uncertainties.

MacKenzie passed on Greenstein's advice, which was for Lavin to meet with Wade and focus on 'one single request: that the reversion clause of your 1965 contract be incorporated into all prior contracts, and that a letter from an officer of the company (not an editor) be sent to you, stating this'. This was 'standard in contracts' and Greenstein believed that it was just an oversight.[84] A lunch meeting with Wade was scheduled for 11 December and Lavin was going to stay in a hotel in the city that night. MacKenzie asked Lavin to phone her with an update after the meeting and wondered if she would be free to meet for dinner that evening or for lunch the following day.

On 12 December MacKenzie posted Lavin her first-reading agreement contract along with a cheque for $295.50, after $4.50 had been deducted for the retirement plan. Lavin was due to visit New York the following week and MacKenzie had Thursday 21 December 'circled in red crayon'. Paige sent Lavin a Christmas card from Lenox Hill Hospital on 17 December in which he was apologetic that his illness had delayed matters. He hoped to return to the office on 15 January but told Lavin that if she was planning to return to Ireland before then that she could visit him in hospital. Paige had spoken with the vice president of Macmillan, Gerald Gross, who more or less told him that they could publish Lavin's *Collected Stories*. He was also going to telephone Lavin's newly appointed US agent, Phyllis Jackson.[85] It was February before Lavin responded to him with the reassuring words, 'Through all the worry & unhappiness the past few months I have thought of you always with affection & sympathy.'[86]

8
'Haggling and Bargaining'
1968–1969

> Is not it nice to be able to tell you, and everyone interested in 25 West 43rd that things are at last not too bad.[1]

On 12 January Mary Lavin wrote to Rachel MacKenzie from the Morris Inn, a hotel located on the University of Notre Dame's campus. She had given a reading at Ashland College in Ohio on 10 January and 'been shuttling from one state to another – in most cases just to see a friend & have dinner!', a result of being unable to shake the 'village idea' of calling in on friends when she found herself in their neck of the woods.[2] Unfortunately, one friend Lavin did not manage to visit during this trip was Eudora Welty, who had hoped that she would get the opportunity to come to her home in Jackson, Mississippi. Lavin was planning to travel up to New York on 17 January, where she would be staying at the Westbury Hotel on Madison Avenue. She hoped to have 'at least one good long visit' with MacKenzie, before she sailed home on 19 January, and so gave her first dibs on her brief time in the city. John Beary, another connection between the two women, had mentioned to Lavin that MacKenzie hoped to work on the proofs of 'Happiness' with her before she returned to Ireland. William Maxwell read the proofs of the story and thought that Lavin had 'outdone' herself – 'I feel personally indebted to you for writing it.' He reminisced about being on Eighth Avenue one day with Frank O'Connor, who told him that Lavin was 'one of the really great short-story writers.[3]

Lavin and MacKenzie evidently had a successful meeting and the letters between them became much more intimate after this trip. MacKenzie was particularly smitten with Lavin and a letter she wrote to her before her departure back to Ireland bordered on the romantic: 'I looked out my apartment window at the United States the night before you sailed, and felt forlorn because there was no longer a possibility of your turning up for lunch or dinner or a between-times visit. Oh, well, you will surely soon be coming back. And those visits we did have were altogether satisfying.' She signed off the letter, 'Love. I miss you.'[4] Lavin shared and reciprocated MacKenzie's tender sentiments and responded, 'I miss you too – very much.'[5]

Lavin had 'at last' met Edna O'Brien on the boat journey home but she did not elaborate any further on their encounter.[6] At this juncture *The New Yorker* had published six of O'Brien's stories, and her first collection, printed in June of that year, took its title from her *New Yorker* story 'The Love Object', which appeared in the magazine on 13 May 1967.[7] Lavin was delighted to return to 'a small welcome-home greeting' from MacKenzie in the form of a cheque for $528.33 for the adjustment of the 1967 COLA retirement plan.[8] However, she was somewhat downcast because she was unable to travel to the farm due to foot-and-mouth disease. The 'deafening' din from construction work taking place across from the mews, presumably on Goulding Fertilisers' new office block, compounded the confinement.[9] In addition, Lavin's brother-in-law had passed away the day after she arrived home from New York. She did not elaborate further on his death in her letter to MacKenzie but she informed George and Eileen Saul that he had passed away in his sleep.[10] The final blow was losing $1,000 in traveller's cheques. Despite the distractions and worry, Lavin was working on the typescript of 'Happiness' and her review of Elizabeth Bowen's novel *Eva Trout*, which was published in *The Irish Press* on 1 February.[11] She was trying to conserve her energy to finish other stories 'before the worries gather force & come down again in an avalanche'.[12]

New Yorkers had also been experiencing a lockdown of sorts due to the 'great garbage strike' that hit the city on 2 February as well as the garage strike which shut down public parking spaces in Manhattan and the Bronx: 'we have been locked in by the garage strike – the car, that is—and it's kept us in the city'. On 5 February *The New York Times* reported that the city resembled 'a vast slum as mounds of refuse grow higher and strong winds whirl the filth through the streets'. MacKenzie described a similar scene to Lavin the following day, 'the air uptown is full of blowing, highly questionable debris'. However, it did not prevent MacKenzie and Gennie, who were stuck in New York for four weeks, from venturing outdoors and making the most of their time in the city, where they took in a ballet and two plays. The garage strike ended on 4 February and the garbage strike ended on 10 February.[13]

Lavin felt her union with her new literary agent, Phyllis Jackson from the Ashley Famous Agency in New York, was fate. She had yet another change of heart and Jackson was in negotiations with Macmillan to get Lavin out of her contract with them and to get them to revert the rights to her stories back to her, but the response from the president, Jerry Kaplan, 'after a long, hard fight', was a resounding no.[14] MacKenzie had a knack of inserting herself into Lavin's affairs. Having inadvertently opened a letter that Lavin had sent to her intended for Jackson, MacKenzie telephoned Jackson to apologise for her blunder and the two women ended up chatting about Lavin's publishing predicament. MacKenzie thought that Jackson had a very sensible view on the matter and Jackson promised to keep her abreast of any developments. They tentatively made plans to meet for lunch.[15] While all agreed that Lavin could take Macmillan to court, and probably win, everyone, including Greenstein, Breen and Jackson, felt that it would not be worth the stress, time and money.

Lavin asked Jackson to go gently in her negotiations with Macmillan as she needed time to understand her position more fully. Although she did not want to stay with the publisher, she realised that she might have no choice in the matter and so needed to know what Macmillan were offering in terms of reverting the rights to her, 'making the old contracts good retroactively as it were – and as they promised'.[16] Lavin wondered if she could get another American publisher to publish books that Macmillan would not, such as *Collected Stories* and *The Becker Wives*, but excluding any stories for which Macmillan held the rights.

Jackson was endeavouring to get Lavin set up with a new publishing house and suggested Alfred A. Knopf, mainly due to the fact that Bob Gottlieb, Edna O'Brien's longtime editor, who had been the editor-in-chief at Simon & Schuster, had recently joined the firm.[17] Gottlieb was an admirer of Lavin and keen to publish her work. However, the fact that he was also a good friend of Jerry Kaplan understandably made Lavin uncomfortable.[18] Jackson suspected that the poet Marianne Moore had a similar problem to Lavin because Viking and Macmillan jointly published her latest book of poetry and Lavin wondered if something similar was an option for her.[19] Jackson sounded out Viking Press, which MacKenzie considered an established and respectable publisher, but Viking was not interested.[20]

Macmillan finally relented and agreed to revert the rights to Lavin. In March they sent Jackson all the relevant documents, which were signed off by Tim Seldes.[21] Jackson contacted MacKenzie to update her with the good news and she in turn wrote to Lavin, who she expected was 'half delirious with relief and joy' and only wished that they could mark the occasion together.[22] Wade was genuinely sorry to lose Lavin as a client as he was a great fan of her work and he told her that he considered her to be 'a very fine writer, a master of the most demanding prose form to my mind'.[23]

Jackson thought Macmillan were going ahead with the publication of *In the Middle of the Fields* because Lavin never returned her advance and they heard nothing further from her on the matter.[24] She therefore urgently needed to know how Lavin wished to proceed. Lavin had assumed that Macmillan had decided not to go ahead with the book but she thought it best to let them publish it, a decision greatly influenced by her fondness for Douglass Paige. Both Glazebrook and Jackson thought it was the right call. In May Paige made the decision to leave Macmillan and New York 'for something more rural and tranquil' and moved to Connecticut, where he took up a teaching post as a professor of English at Middlesex Community College.[25]

On 29 March the President of Ireland and Chancellor of the National University of Ireland, Éamon de Valera, conferred an honorary doctorate on Lavin.[26] Ironically, Lavin had written a PhD thesis on Virginia Woolf when she was a student at University College Dublin but she began writing her first story on the reverse side of the script and never submitted it. Six men and one other woman, Lady Goulding, were also conferred. There must have been some degree of tension between the two women given that Lavin was still embroiled in the case against Goulding's husband's company, which ended up in the High Court four months later. In introducing Mary Lavin, Mr Justice John Kenny said, 'This degree is not only our tribute to her as an artist: it is also an expression of our gratitude because she has continued to live and work in Ireland. Many of our great artists have left because they did not get the appreciation which they felt they had merited. She has stayed with us and her international reputation gives happiness to her fellow graduates.'[27]

Lavin was due to travel to Spain with Mick but the nuns finally ousted her mother from the convent. Clearly, she was not exaggerating her mother's difficult nature if even the 'dear holy creatures of God', as Lavin referred to them, could not tolerate her. The unfortunate timing caused Lavin to declare, 'She really seems to be my nemesis.' Lavin cabled Mick, who was in Mexico, but he had already made his way back to Dublin. On his advice, Lavin took her mother to Bective for a fortnight, where her daughters could enjoy a holiday. He then arranged for the girls to look after their grandmother in the mews while he and Lavin travelled to Spain: 'It was really heavenly.'[28] Lavin had been reinvited back to Storrs for 1970 but she had to sort out the matter of rehoming her mother, who was now living 'on top' of them, before she could commit to anything. However, Lavin was convinced that 'survival for all means my going out – regardless – & trying to do the novel (I hope you know that old Dublinism?)'[29]

Lavin was still tidying up some loose ends from her stay at Storrs. She asked MacKenzie to send a cheque for $68 on her behalf to George Saul to cover a telephone bill that she would repay at a later stage. MacKenzie issued a personal cheque as it was not professional business. Saul returned a cheque for $5.08 as Lavin had overestimated the bill and MacKenzie remarked of his 'refined penmanship': 'Doesn't it put us to shame!'[30]

Lavin asked MacKenzie if she knew the name of the owner or director of Horizon Press, where Coburn Britton was the editor. The man in question had taken Lavin out to dinner and attended one of her readings and she wished to write and thank him.[31] MacKenzie confirmed that Ben Raeburn was both the president and owner and she thought she recalled Lavin mentioning him.[32] MacKenzie remembered correctly: back in March 1966, Lavin had asked her for information on the publishing house as they had been in contact and she was considering them as a publisher.[33] Lavin later asked MacKenzie to airmail her the Horizon Press catalogue and, feeling guilty with all the demands she was making of her, reflected, 'I always imagine that you have a few embryonic Truman Capotes to run messages for you in 25 (I think of those huge letters over the door).'[34]

Jackson told Lavin that she needed a new novel in order to get her signed with a new publishing company, and on that basis, she reckoned that she could manage to negotiate a contract for two books: a new novel and a collection of stories.[35] Lavin revealed that she was 'always very hesitant to commit myself to a novel since I consider myself to be essentially a short-story writer'.[36] Ben Glazebrook had recommended Farrar, Straus and Giroux and was having a business lunch with them on on 26 March.[37] On 2 April Henry Robbins, a senior editor at the house who was present at the meeting, wrote to Jackson to express how keen they were to publish Lavin's work: 'I wish Mary Lavin could have seen the enthusiastic response by Roger Straus, Bob Giroux and myself when Ben Glazebrook mentioned at lunch the possibility that she might change American publishers with her next book.'[38] All three men were 'great admirers' of Lavin's writing and 'followed her stories as they've appeared in The New Yorker with admiration and delight'.[39] They promptly offered Lavin a two-book deal for the new novel (*First Love*), which they would publish first, followed by a new collection of stories, which Lavin was going to title *Happiness*.

Jackson and Lavin both thought Farrar, Straus and Giroux would be a suitable home and so Jackson was going to approach Giroux, the editor-in-chief, on the matter. Although Lavin was delighted at the prospect of going to Farrar, Straus and Giroux, she was disappointed that they wanted a novel and were not willing to accept her as a short-story writer; a point she wanted Jackson to emphasise in her dealings with them. Lavin made it clear that she would not normally have committed to a novel but for the fact that she was already writing one. However, she understood that the novel was the carrot and so was agreeable to Jackson going for a two-book deal. As it was more of a novella, Lavin was hopeful that it could also 'be squeezed into the New Yorker too'.[40]

Lavin let Jackson know that she had promised Constable *First Love*, which she was hoping to finish in June (Glazebrook had sent Lavin an advance for the novel but was agreeable to publishing her new collection, *Happiness*, first and then waiting to see the developments with *First Love*). She told Jackson of her urgent need to be in paperback because universities such as Notre Dame, Vermont and Connecticut would have placed her on their curriculum had her work been available in that format. Lavin therefore asked Jackson to push for the prioritisation of a paperback version of the Constable collection (*The Stories of Mary Lavin, Vol. 1*).

Farrar, Straus and Giroux issued two contracts and paid Lavin an advance of $2,250 for *First Love*, after Jackson's commission, which presumably was 10 per cent. The other contract was for *Happiness*. They also agreed, outside of the contract, to import copies of Constable's collection, *The Stories of Mary Lavin, Vol. 1*, 'either bound books with our imprint or sheets'. They took on board Lavin's request to be in paperback and intended publishing her in paperback via an offshoot of Noonday Press.[41] However, it soon transpired that there was a major issue with Lavin's contract, due to a 'stupid mistake' on Jackson's part, which Lavin feared could not be remedied, and she was beginning to get cold feet about the move.[42] Trusting Jackson, Lavin inadvertently signed a contract for the delivery of a new volume of stories in October, which was not feasible for her and therefore she wanted them to publish the Constable collection in October instead.

Lavin wrote to Roger Straus in the hope that he would be of the same mind, but if not, she offered to return the advance. The frustrating part for Lavin was that the protracted negotiations and stress over the matter were deterring her from concentrating on completing *First Love*, the novella that all of the publishers seemed insistent upon acquiring. One can see why at times Lavin opted to handle her own affairs rather than engage the services of an agent. Straus was sympathetic to Lavin's situation, but there were several difficulties. Macmillan were going to publish *In the Middle of the Fields* in February and he felt that it would be too soon to publish *Happiness.* The contract issued for *First Love* was on the basis that it would be a novella and so Lavin was paid more money than she would have received for a collection of short stories. His suggestion was to hold off until *In the Middle of the Fields* was published and Constable published *Happiness*. They would then be in a better position to ascertain whether *First Love* would be novel material. This left Lavin unsure as to where they stood with the *Collected Stories* if she could not produce a novella.

Ultimately, Farrar, Straus and Giroux offered to publish *Collected Stories* at the same time as *First Love*, whether the latter was in form of a novella or new collection of stories, but not until at least six months had elapsed after the publication of Macmillan's *In the Middle of the Fields.* If

First Love turned out to be a novel, they would pay Lavin an additional $1,000, but if it was a short story, then the advance she already received would be her total payment. Farrar, Straus and Giroux would then wait at least three months after its publication before making a decision on bringing out another collection. While they were hopeful that Lavin would remain with them, they also offered to release her from her contract if she returned the advance.

On 25 April Lavin sent MacKenzie an uncorrected draft of 'The Lost Child' 'to glance at', but she did not think it was suitable for *The New Yorker*.[43] Lavin mentioned that she almost completed the story while sitting in a 'Whamburger' on Madison Avenue. This was most likely Phebe's Whamburger, which was located on 813 Madison Avenue.[44] MacKenzie was keen for the magazine to take the piece, but there were two major concerns. First, the story was too long and even if cut significantly it would have to be held for one of *The New Yorker*'s monthly 'all-fiction front' issues, which had more space for lengthier works. However, as the magazine had over a year and a half's stock of such stories, Lavin's story would have to wait in line until after they were published. This also meant that she could not publish it elsewhere in the interim. The second unease the magazine had was the story's 'bloodiness', which 'made Mr. Shawn sick', but MacKenzie reassured him that, with Lavin's permission, they could 'drain a good bit of it off in the editing'.[45]

'The Lost Child' features a miscarriage and is an attack on the notion of limbo. One of the offending passages is most likely the following line, or a version of it, describing the moment of the miscarriage, 'For of course those blobs and clots that had flowed out of her – those ice floes! – remember – remember – those were her liver, her kidneys, her lungs, her heart.'[46] While the graphic and gory details in the story were a departure from Lavin's more circumspect work that the magazine had published to date, it also shows how Shawn's prudishness majorly influenced the type of fiction published in *The New Yorker*. There was obviously a lighter side to Shawn, as revealed in a postcard he sent to Maeve Brennan from Deauville in August 1967, on which he thanked her for seeing him and his party off on their travels with a bottle of champagne and told her of losing $100 at the casino while his companion won $2,000.[47]

Understandably, especially given Shawn's reaction, Lavin was hesitant about letting Mick read 'The Lost Child' and 'The Pure Accident', so she was taken aback when he considered them 'better than anything I'd written'.[48] MacKenzie agreed with Mick about the 'quality' of 'The Lost Child' and she personally found that it was 'honest and has great strength, and I love all the levels it moves along'.[49] Lavin was pleased that MacKenzie liked the story and she 'loved' her observation about its differing levels. She had intended to cut and improve it further but the delay in publishing the work was problematic for her because she felt the piece was 'topical now – with the birth control issues'.[50] Back in 1964 Lavin wanted to write a story about Dr Rock's pill: '(what a vulgarity – the expression is – "the pill" don't you think?)', but she put it on hold until she achieved another quantity bonus. Lavin checked whether it would be alright for her to consult with Jackson on the matter, explaining that while she would prefer for the story to appear in *The New Yorker*, she feared the subject matter would be 'stale' come 1970. Lavin responded with a mixture of sympathy and sassiness in addressing Shawn's queasy reaction to the story: 'I feel so bad about Mr Shawn feeling sick. All I can say is he'd feel worse if I'd enlarged on the baptism bit & I may yet! But not necessary in your version.'[51]

The magazine had no problem with Lavin consulting with Jackson about 'The Lost Child'. MacKenzie even offered to send Jackson the manuscript to facilitate her in deciding where it could be placed, if she thought it needed to be published sooner than the magazine could accommodate it. MacKenzie agreed that it was a substantial amount of time to wait for publication but she did not think that 'a change in the church's attitude toward birth control would mean a change toward the unbaptized'.[52] She conceded that Lavin would have a more informed opinion on the matter. Lavin was still sitting on the fence with regard to the placing of 'The Lost Child' but she was happy for MacKenzie to send Jackson the manuscript in case she had a plan for it. Otherwise, she reasoned, it could be included in the forthcoming collection or 'wait for the lovely N.York Money'.[53]

MacKenzie had warned Lavin that unless her other stories were shorter, they would encounter the same problem: 'Scheduling is difficult all round these days, we have so many stories and so many book publication dates to meet.'[54] Lavin sent MacKenzie a greatly improved version of 'A Pure

Accident' but she wanted MacKenzie's feedback before she edited it further. It was another story that she felt was topical due to its subject of celibacy. Although MacKenzie agreed that Lavin enhanced the text, the story was rejected, primarily because of its length of approximately fifty pages. MacKenzie let Lavin know that Shawn was very apologetic for its rejection.

MacKenzie was sorry for being 'troublesome' about 'The Lost Child' and informed Jackson that she had returned 'A Pure Accident' to Lavin. Naturally, Lavin was disappointed that the story would not be published in *The New Yorker* and reaping the benefit of MacKenzie's 'wise cutting on it' but it became essential for her to supply stories to her publishers.[55] Time was not just an issue in terms of the topicality of the stories; Lavin was also under pressure to have stories available for a new collection due to be brought out by Constable in the spring of 1969.[56] In the end *The Southern Review*, much to MacKenzie's relief, purchased 'The Lost Child' and 'A Pure Accident'.[57] She let Lavin know that 'Happiness' was provisionally scheduled for 14 December and assured her that it would be published in time for it to be included in the forthcoming Constable collection.

MacKenzie passed on the news to Lavin that 'Bill and Emmy Maxwell' were flying to Dublin on 5 June and that Maxwell planned to get in touch with her.[58] The Maxwells often visited Frank O'Connor and his family in Ireland and continued to visit Harriet O'Connor and Hallie Óg after O'Connor's death.[59] They were staying at the Russell Hotel on St Stephen's Green and met Lavin at Dan Binchy's nearby club.[60] Eudora Welty wrote to them while they were in Ireland and asked them to pass on her regards to Lavin: 'Do give my love to her. (I really feel sure she never got my letters till she got home, and it was so like her to make no provision for getting the answers to the ones she wrote. But anyway, it is all right, but give her my love especially.)'[61] Maxwell responded to Eudora Welty on 10 July 1968 and told her that they had planned to visit Bective but it never transpired as Lavin was feeling out of sorts:

> She was keeping away from her mother. From her description it didn't sound very real, the difficulty, but it was obviously real to her. And the last day she and I met on Molesworth Street, while Emmy was down below, buying more Avoca rugs and blankets in Cleo's, and we stood and talked for half an hour, and every person that walked by said hello Mary. Just like Lincoln. Or Jackson, I would guess.[62]

Bill Maxwell was delighted when MacKenzie passed on Lavin's fond recounting ('loved seeing Bill') of their meeting and let her know that he would be dropping Lavin a line immediately.[63] Lavin must have been apologetic for not seeing more of them while they were in Ireland because Maxwell responded reassuringly: 'I had what I wanted, which was your undivided attention, in conversation, for half an hour on Molesworth Street, so you have nothing to feel guilty about.'[64] Maxwell had obviously passed on Welty's good wishes to Lavin because in October, Welty informed him that Lavin had written to her:

> Had a note from Mary Lavin speaking of seeing you, and I could see you (from your letter) talking on the street, with Dublin walking by. So glad of a word from her – the rest of the letter said she couldn't write now – how well I understand, here I think if it would just rain I could write a letter, while thinking of my friends all day long all the time. But she is having me sent galleys of her new book, which I'll be pleased to see. So thanks for passing us news of each other, on your wonderful trip.[65]

On 28 June Henry Robbins sent Lavin Marjorie Kellogg's first novel, which was due for publication in the autumn, hoping for Lavin's appraisal and permission to use some of the quotes on the book sleeve. Lavin obliged and the following quote appeared on the dust jacket, 'I loved *Tell Me That You Love Me, Junie Moon*. It is one of the strongest, deepest, and most touching books I have read in many a day, and as well as that it has the liveliness of a thoroughbred.'[66] However, unable to decipher Lavin's handwriting, 'liveliness' was printed instead of 'lively step'.

Towards the end of July Gerry Breen travelled to New York to try and sort out the mess with Farrar, Straus and Giroux. After meeting with MacKenzie and Jackson and discussing Lavin's predicament with them, his opinion was that time was of the essence and that Lavin should stick with them, noting that it was reasonable for them to want to publish new material first. He explained that Farrar, Straus and Giroux would then consider publishing the collected stories based on the sales and reception of the first publication. Jackson would push for a contract for this but it was highly unlikely she would get one. He also thought Lavin should trust that they would bring out future work.

Lavin had divulged to Jackson that she was anxious about the looming court case against Goulding Fertilisers, which was due to take place on 17 July, and enquired how Jackson got on with her recent lawsuit (Jackson had been involved in a rights case brought by her client Theodor Seuss Geisel, better known as Dr Seuss, against Poynter Products). Lavin expected to lose her 'classic case of an action for loss of light, under the Ancient Lights Act' but she explained that it was 'a matter of principle, which one could only understand on the spot. When your friends see the terrible rape of this beautiful city they will be able to tell you that I could not hold my head if I did not take this action.'[67]

On 26 July MacKenzie had an early start to her day as she was busy finishing up work before going on her 'mish-mash' holidays for a month, during which she planned to meet with good friends and travel to Bruges, while in between times she would be at her Connecticut home. Writing to Lavin was first on her list that morning. Lavin had informed her that the mews case was finished but she never told her of the outcome, which prompted MacKenzie to write, 'Your letters are like installments of the old Pearl White serials, each one ending with some unresolved happening that leaves the reader breathless.' MacKenzie hoped Lavin 'got a decent settlement'.[68]

On 31 July the High Court awarded Lavin damages of £1,700 and costs. *The Irish Times* reported that Lavin had been 'seeking damages and an injunction to restrain the company from continuing with the construction of a building which, she claimed, would materially obstruct and diminish the light going into her residence at 11 Lad Lane, Dublin'. The presiding judge, Justice Teevan, found that Lavin's 'residence and its pleasant setting had lost much of its charm because of a large office building erected by the company' and he observed that Lavin's mews 'conversion was carried out with taste and discrimination of a high artistic order and has evoked the praise of the expert witnesses on both sides'.[69]

In August Valdi's former fiancé, Dermot, suffered serious injuries during a climbing accident in the Zillertal in Austria, which left him in a coma. The prognosis was not good and the family were naturally devasted: 'I think it is true to say that our hearts are broken, and for me at times the shafts of anguish for him are almost unbearable.'[70] It was a dark and upsetting time for the family, especially for Valentine, and Lavin told MacKenzie 'our hearts that were broken are now just frozen'.[71]

In September James Wade asked Lavin for names of people who might endorse *In the Middle of the Fields* and Lavin suggested Lionel Trilling, Eudora Welty, Padraic Colum and Elizabeth Bowen, 'a friend of mine who has never lost an opportunity to speak well of me'.[72] He was also going to send copies to Mark Schorer and possibly Muriel Spark, John Updike, Eliot Fremont-Smith, Peter Taylor and William Alfred.[73] Welty responded promptly and observed of the collection, 'Her powers are revealed at their finest in these stories; they have her strong insights, her generosity of feeling, her surety of command over her subject and its world. Their vividness and beauty bring the same pleasure as always in her work.'[74]

Lavin had chosen *Happiness* as the name for her next collection, but was unhappy with the extended title the publishers subsequently decided upon, namely *Happiness and Other Stories of Ireland*, as she did not think it reflected the stories contained within the volume. There was time enough for the title to be changed to *Happiness and Other Stories*. Lavin struggled writing the blurb for the book as she 'felt too much of a fool' and so asked an assistant professor at UCD who was very familiar with her work, most likely her good friend Maurice Harmon, to write it on her behalf. Understandably, she wanted to move on from references to Dunsany and the Tait prize and comparisons of her work to Ó Faoláin and O'Connor because she rightly felt they undermined her writing, 'since what was always said was that I was "nearly as good as them" or, much worse that "her stories could almost have been written" by them'.[75]

It was October before the author's proof of 'Happiness' was prepared. Shawn had some queries and the proofreader had suggested minor changes while MacKenzie made some notes on the story. Although it was not yet scheduled for publication, MacKenzie explained that the production of the author's proof usually indicated that it would be. MacKenzie again likened the 'great gaps in [their] writing and seeing each other' to 'the waits between the old Pearl White serials – pure suspense. You and Mick in the air. The suit for the mews only awaiting the announcement of a verdict. The new book in the balance between Ashley Famous and Farrar, Straus, to say nothing of the author.'

MacKenzie condoled with Lavin and the family on the tragic situation with Dermot: 'It strikes me that there's an extraordinary amount of grief to share these days.'[76]

First Love was shaping into more of a short story and Lavin explained her writing process in a letter to Straus: 'If my work has any value at all it probably lies in an instinctive sense of the proper proportion between matter and form, and this is not always apparent to me until the last stages of composition. My method of work has been to compose very freely and fully, and then offer to cut down drastically in the last stages.'[77]

In 1967 Lavin and Mick had agreed to get married and so in early 1968 Mick requested to be released from his vows. There was a deafening silence from Rome on the laicisation, which left the pair in limbo, but Mick remained philosophical about the situation. He had to reside in a monastery in Bruges for a set time in order 'to establish domicile for the civil wedding which much [*sic*] accompany the church ceremony'. The situation dragged on for so long that Lavin revealed to MacKenzie that 'at times I forget we are <u>not</u> married' and remarked, 'How most people – Catholics most of all – are begining [*sic*] to despise the Vatican.'[78] The fact that they were not married posed an obstacle when a former unnamed US commissioner with the British embassy had tentatively organised for them to travel to Iran for Lavin to give readings and Mick to lecture, but they were unable to take up the offer due to their marital status. Although the marriage was supposed to be a secret, Lavin was unable to keep it under wraps and shared the news with MacKenzie, Wade, Jackson, Glazebrook and Maxwell.

Lavin also shared the secret with Evelyn Hofer, the German-born photographer known for her portraits of daily life in New York City during the 1960s and 70s. Hofer likely befriended Lavin when she was in Dublin to take photographs of the city and its people for the 1967 book *Dublin: A Portrait*, which she produced in collaboration with their mutual friend V. S. Pritchett, who Hofer revealed 'had enormous admiration' for Lavin.[79] Lavin, Frank O'Connor and Patrick Kavanagh were among the people Hofer photographed over the course of six months between 1965 and 1966 and she became another regular visitor to Lad Lane. It would appear that Lavin was not too happy with her portrait as she found it somewhat sombre, but V. S. Pritchett thought it 'conveyed strong emotional power'.[80] Hofer was delighted to hear the news of Lavin's impending nuptials – at least she surmised that the letter she received with news of a wedding was from Lavin as she could not make out the handwriting – and wanted to hear all the details.[81]

Hofer, who was at the time living in New York, told Lavin that the city was 'ghastly' and in a later letter, she informed her that she and her husband, Humphrey, who was a book designer, were looking to move apartments because their rent was so high.[82] At Hofer's suggestion, the trio were looking to collaborate on a book about Ireland and Hofer asked Lavin to type her ideas for the project because she found it difficult to interpret her handwriting: 'it sweeps and flies so generously over the pages and I follow you almost, limping behind … then I try again … !'[83] Lavin had suggested that they do a book on 'the literary panorama of Ireland', which Hofer thought was an excellent idea because of the current 'trend' for educational literature.[84] Hofer had a sure publisher (Bodley Head) for the UK volume but she wanted to get it published in the US first, so their only obstacle was in securing an American publisher in order to make the project financially viable. On 10 January 1969 Hofer sent Lavin photos that she had taken of her and gave her permission for Lavin to use them professionally.

Mick had been busy working on his own book of photographs of modern churches with accompanying architectural descriptions and Lavin wondered if *The New Yorker* would be interested in some articles from him that might be placed in the 'Reporter at Large' section of the magazine, which she later corrected to a 'Profile' piece. She suggested that the title of his book, *A Church for the People of God*, could work for the article title also. Lavin had been reluctant to approach MacKenzie about his article 'because one always hates to appear to be asking a favour which was not what I meant at all'.[85] Lavin was also trying to get Mick to write about his childhood in Australia: 'The really beautiful autobiographies are so often written by people who have NOT led public lives.'[86] Prompted by Lavin, Mick, writing as Reverend Michael Scott, S.V., wrote to MacKenzie directly to enquire about the prospect of writing a piece for the magazine. He provided her with some background and informed her of his various trips abroad and grants and scholarship received to conduct his recreational research whereupon he amassed 10,000 colour slides and revealed his knowledge in the area of 'great modern churches of the world'.[87]

Lavin's union with Mick signified a new beginning and chapter in her life and writing. He was getting Lavin's affairs in order, 'licking me into shape', as she referred to it, which freed her up mentally and physically and enabled her to focus on the business of writing. Lavin was keen to return to the US for both 'the extra money and the stimulation', and so she got in touch with George Starbuck again, almost a year after he had invited her to Iowa.[88] She explained that she had been unable to follow up on the offer because the journey to Iowa – with Caroline in tow and in the middle of winter – proved too complicated in the end but that she was considering returning to the US after Christmas because Macmillan wanted her there for the US launch of *In the Middle of the Fields and Other Stories*, which was due to be published in the spring and she reflected, 'It often amazes me that American Universities are so anxious to have me visit them considering that for some years there has not been a single book of mine in print in America, due to a protracted argument with Macmillan about reversal of rights.'[89]

Lavin suggested that she could visit the university in the spring, a short stint being preferable to a full semester, if the offer was still on the table and if Starbuck could make it worth her while.[90] She also expressed interest in Paul Engle's new European Writers' Workshop, as, she reasoned, 'it is very easy to hop over to the Continent whereas that Atlantic is pretty broad!'[91] Starbuck explained that Engle was establishing an International Writing Program at Iowa rather than in Europe. He was gladdened to hear Lavin was still interested in visiting the university and as luck would have it, he was looking for someone for the spring term, which ran from February until May. Starbuck invited her to come for a semester, or as much as a semester as Lavin could manage, and offered to be flexible about how she made up her time there. For such an arrangement, he could offer her $7,000.

Lavin was keen to go to Iowa and thought that, although some aspects of the visit needed to be 'thrashed out', they could reach a happy agreement.[92] She was particularly appreciative that she would be paid the highest fee for a visiting author thus far and was also relieved to hear that her fare would be covered, in addition to the stipend. Lavin reflected that she actually could have gone immediately to Iowa when they first approached her, but as she had failed to mention this at the time she accepted that it was 'no use crying over spilled milk'.[93] Lavin assured Starbuck that she would 'endeavour to give you good value' and related how at Storrs they grew concerned that she was devoting too much time to the students and was setting 'a dangerous precedent by being in my office so much!'[94] Lavin also mentioned that she kept 'an unofficial correspondence course' with students afterwards. The only possible fly in the ointment was the lack of boats crossing to America but she was looking at all options including cargo ships. She proposed leaving on Stephen's Day, provided there was a boat, and then staying from January until March or possibly April.[95]

The previous winter MacKenzie had mentioned to Lavin the possibility of a fellowship at Wesleyan University at Middletown, Connecticut. MacKenzie had spoken to Anne Fremantle about her experience as a fellow there and reported back to Lavin: 'She's been there and found it excellent for work (money, an apartment, secretarial help, no teaching).'[96] MacKenzie offered to get in touch with the director, if Lavin was interested, as a writer could not apply directly. When MacKenzie heard nothing back from Lavin on the matter, she presumed that she was not interested until Lavin got in touch to let her know of the Iowa offer, which she had accepted 'on the principle of the bird in the hand'. However, she expressed her preference to go to Wesleyan if it could still be organised and so she asked MacKenzie to sound it out before she finalised her plans with Starbuck.[97] Although Lavin was open to all dates, January to April was the best time for her, followed by mid-October to mid-December. Lavin planned to meet with MacKenzie when she went to Iowa and suggested that they work on the proofs of 'Happiness' together, as she 'did so love' the two occasions they worked together in her office on 25 West 45 Street.[98] MacKenzie agreed that the timing would be good: 'I shall concentrate on everything's working out for that to come to pass.'[99]

On 25 November MacKenzie wrote to Mr Hallie of Wesleyan recommending Lavin for a fellowship to the Institute for Advanced Study: 'I know she would value the opportunity to work at Weslyan [sic]. I know she would be a responsible member of the Institute. Besides, she is a delight to have around.'[100] She provided him with Lavin's Bective address. MacKenzie presumed that Hallie would be familiar with Lavin's work but explained that, while much of it was hard to obtain in book form, Macmillan were publishing *In the Middle of the Fields* and Farrar, Straus and Giroux were due to publish a volume of stories in the autumn. She confirmed that the new books would contain stories that had been published by *The New Yorker* and she offered to send tear sheets of them if required.

Lavin informed MacKenzie that John Beary was due to get married. According to *The New York Times*, his marriage to Susan Cora Steven, an actress and singer and a graduate of the American Musical and Dramatic Academy in New York, took place on 10 November. The article reads more like a society piece than a wedding announcement: the bride's father, we are told, is a neurosurgeon, while her stepfather, 'an optical physicist, is president of the White Development Corporation of Stamford'.[101] The article also reveals that Beary, whose late father was 'a noted horse trainer', was the godson of the late Prince Aly Khan.[102]

MacKenzie had moved into Robert Henderson's former office and after settling into the desk the decision was made to buy a new one, which ended up being 'catastrophic' for the normally well-ordered MacKenzie: 'I just shoved things under cover, and it will take a couple of days to get reorganised.'[103] Lavin was reading Benedict Kiely's novel, most likely *Dogs Enjoy the Morning*, and wanted to discuss it with MacKenzie. She added that they were all very troubled by the problems he had with his visa, presumably to remain teaching in the US. In 1968 Kiely had returned to Ireland after four years of appointments in various American colleges including Hollins College in Virginia, the University of Oregon in Portland and Emory University in Atlanta, Georgia.[104]

Lavin asked MacKenzie 'very privately & personally' if she thought it would be 'a mistake' to remain with Macmillan. She felt that Wade 'seems so good & kind & generous & I am getting a bit old for all the haggling & bargaining that seems to go with changing publishers'. Lavin did not want to put MacKenzie under pressure to give advice but it gave her comfort to confide in her as she would understand the complexities of the situation. She later wrote to MacKenzie: 'That one mistake of Phyllis Jackson's was really like leaving out a leg of a table & then trying to make it work by balancing the delph different ways.' There was still no word from Rome about Mick's laicisation and they were all on edge as a result, which she figured was the intent: 'Let us hope our courage & our trust in God will withstand this.'[105] The trip to

Ohio was also in doubt but despite her various woes, Lavin was looking forward to seeing MacKenzie again: 'I am just simply longing to see you & hope we can have a few hours together no matter how short a time I stay in New York.'[106]

'Happiness' appeared in *The New Yorker* in the 14 December issue. The cover, illustrated by William Steig, depicts a seasonal snowy scene of a boy and his grandmother watching snowflakes fall. The story commanded eight pages shared with cartoons and a poem, 'Thyme Flowering Among Rocks' by Richard Wilbur.[107] One cartoon depicts a female secretary asking the male author of children's books what he would like for his 'din dins'. The issue also features fiction by Roger Angell and Mollie Panter-Downes's 'Letter from London'. With its proximity to Christmas the issue is brimming with adverts for luxury brands and indulgences. An advert for a Sony 5-inch screen, carrying the caption 'Wouldn't it make more sense to eat a big dinner and squeeze the TV into the tiny package?' depicts a glamorous couple eating a lavish meal at the dinner table while looking at their individual television sets.

'Happiness' was selected for Martha Foley's *Best American Short Stories 1969* collection, which also featured fiction by Maeve Brennan, Bernard Malamud, Joyce Carol Oates, Isaac Bashevis Singer and Sylvia Plath, whose story 'Johnny Panic and the Bible of Dreams' was published posthumously in *The Atlantic Monthly* in September. Lavin 'nearly died of surprise & joy' when she saw the book's dedication and she asked whether MacKenzie had seen it.[108] MacKenzie had not and so ordered a copy declaring, 'Whatever it is that made you happy will make me happy, too.' The dedication reads, 'To Mary Lavin'.

On the 28 December Lavin wrote to MacKenzie to wish her a happy New Year and explained that she had not written before Christmas because 'things were pretty grim'. Her mother's health had declined and she was back staying with the family and causing a bit of a stir, which prompted someone to declare that Lavin 'ought to be proud to come of such durable stock!' Lavin was concerned that she had not received her *New Yorker* contract and she wondered if they were 'tired of me – or have I the dates wrong'. MacKenzie had sent Lavin a private letter, which she typed herself, on the matter of publishers. She obviously considered giving advice to Lavin on the matter, in her professional capacity, to be a conflict of interest. Lavin felt like 'an idiot' for asking MacKenzie about the Macmillan situation but she was simply broaching with her that she might remain on their books, on the principle of 'the devil you know'. She did not like the contracts offered by Farrar, Straus and Giroux and she had become completely disillusioned with Jackson. On a happier note, Lavin had received a 'lovely letter' from Bill Maxwell and informed MacKenzie that she would be writing him a letter that evening. She ended her letter, 'all my love – dear dear Rachel'.[109]

On 3 January 1969 MacKenzie sent Lavin her first-reading agreement cheque, 'late but loving', and explained that the reason for the delay was because she had come down with the flu: '(I had the new kind hard and really am just over it, after four weeks.'). MacKenzie had clearly contracted the Hong Kong flu, also known as the 1968 flu pandemic, that became widespread in the United States in December of 1968. She divulged that the payment was calculated 'by some complex manner that has never been explained to me on what we've bought over the three preceding years, and this one is much less than I wish it were'. MacKenzie reassured Lavin by letting her know that it would be 'unthinkable for us not to have a first-reading agreement with you' and that they hoped 1969 would be a productive and lucrative year for Lavin. She told Lavin that everyone including Hawley Truax admired 'Happiness' (Truax was a poet and former chairman of the board of *The New Yorker* and one of its directors for forty-six years). MacKenzie was looking forward to seeing Lavin and getting an update on her publishing situation in person. On the subject of Lavin's mother, she comforted her with the fact that Lavin had three daughters 'to share you out when it comes your turn to exert yourself at the end' and she ended her letter with words of encouragement: 'My love to you both, and wishes for your happiness in this new year, along with strength to manage whatever betides.'[110]

On 7 January Macmillan New York sent Lavin a 'first off-press copy' of *In the Middle of the Fields*', which was due to be launched in February. They were going to use Eudora Welty's quote in the first advertisement for the book and a photograph by Evelyn Hofer in a later advert, towards the end of March. Wade was hoping to get more endorsers and sent a copy to Padraic Colum via *The New Yorker.* Eudora Welty shared with Maxwell that she regretfully had to turn down reviewing the book for *The Southern Review* and she was also sorry that she could not write the review for Frank O'Connor's 'A Set of Variations'.[111] In April Wade let Lavin know that the book was doing well: they had shipped nearly 3,500 copies to date. As books in the US were fully returnable he was unable to give her an idea of sales. He sent her some reviews from newspapers including *The Washington Post* and *The Boston Herald* but he was unsuccessful in getting *The New York Times* to review it.[112]

Much to the great disappointment of both Lavin and Starbuck, the trip to Iowa did not work out due to scheduling. Lavin asked if he had seen 'Happiness' in *The New Yorker* and let him know that it was going into her new book of stories due out that month. Starbuck had indeed seen the story and liked it, as did his students, who approached him with the published story and asked if Lavin was going to come to Iowa. He was saddened to deliver the news that she was not. Starbuck did not close the book on the offer and asked Lavin to let him know if a visit ever became a possibility for her in the future.[113]

Lavin received a lot of letters about 'Happiness'. Her advance copy of *The New Yorker* featuring the story never arrived at the mews and she asked if another could be sent to her at Bective. Lavin complained that she only received one-tenth of letters at the mews due to it being located on a lane. Macmillan had written to her on 21 November but she never received the letter. As a result, Lavin advised MacKenzie to get in touch if she received no response to urgent letters. She had great hopes for her new story that she thought would 'sing too (like a telegraph wire – with a bird!)' and so she abandoned 'Trastevere' and 'The Wake' in order to work on it, even though she was in dire need of money, 'but as you know I sink or rise on putting the work before the money always'.[114]

At home, Maurice Harmon delivered Lavin news of 'a very exciting offer': Irish University Press were interested in publishing a collection of her work titled *Stories from the Novels* and she was busy 'chopping them [her novels] up in odd moments'. University College Dublin, her alma mater, offered her a lectureship on the short story '(an unheard-of departure for Ireland)' the following spring. In addition, the lecturers there were trying to sort out her affairs. Lavin was looking after Caroline, who was trying to study at home due to a teachers' strike, but the older girls were becoming independent young women. The family were 'stunned' when Elizabeth was impressively appointed the women's editor of the paper where she worked after only one year and Valdi was due to travel to Strasbourg the following week.[115]

MacKenzie was 'horrified' to hear, through Maxwell, that Lavin had burned herself. MacKenzie had her own health woes. She had been in the hospital for three weeks in January to get her spine 'straightened out' and she declared that she emerged 'three inches taller than I went in'. She had to wear a 'a five-pound molded, absolutely rigid jacked (so-called) that makes me feel like a turtle. If you could see me struggling out of my boots.'[116] It would appear that MacKenzie had scoliosis and was fitted with a corrective spinal orthosis known as the Milwaukee brace. Lavin was delighted to hear about MacKenzie's 'restored stature': 'I was so pleased oh so pleased you'd defied the biblical saint & added to your stature – physically – & why not since you do so every day mentally & spiritually.'[117]

Lavin took a break from her new story in order to gain some perspective on it and returned to 'Trastevere' and 'The Wake'. She sent 'The Wake' to MacKenzie but stated that it was, 'rotten – no good –no point – no nothing'.[118] The story was promptly rejected. Ultimately, the quality of the work came first and MacKenzie professed, 'But what good are we to each other if we aren't first responsible to the work?'[119] Lavin expressed her relief that 'The Wake' was rejected, even though she badly needed the money.

Mick wrote to MacKenzie to let her know that Lavin was back writing after her mishap and had reworked 'The Wake' into a cheerier and shorter story, which she would try to sell elsewhere. Lavin was still working on *First Love* for Farrar, Straus and Giroux and he advised Lavin to write it as a short story, rather than a novel, and if they were willing to take it in that form, then she should remain with them. Despite all of Lavin's hard work on *First Love*, it was not published in either form. *The Stories of Mary Lavin, Vol. 1* was being translated into German. Elizabeth Schnack, considered the most important translator of Irish writing into the German language in the 1950s and 60s, translated Lavin's writing as well as works by Elizabeth Bowen, Brian Friel, Benedict Kiely, John McGahern, Michael McLaverty, Edna O'Brien, Frank O'Connor, Seán Ó Faoláin, Liam O'Flaherty and Oscar Wilde. She also translated works by *New Yorker* writers Truman Capote, J. D. Salinger, Muriel Spark and Eudora Welty.[120]

On 16 September 1966 McLaverty had invited Lavin to his home alongside a small group of young writers, to meet with Schnack who was actively seeking new Irish authors.[121] On 5 June 1969 McLaverty encouraged Schnack to visit Lavin at Bective: 'She'd be delighted to see you for I heard her speak of you with great admiration and referred to you as "the great German translator".'[122] It is quite possible that she visited Lavin on this occasion: in an undated letter from Schnack to Lavin, written from the Old Ground Hotel in Ennis, she wrote that she had 'a lovely stay in your house: I dream of it and will write a very fine article on it!'[123]

On 20 March Lavin wrote to MacKenzie from Bruges to let her know that she and Mick had finally tied the knot following his papal dispensation and she asked her to pass on the news to Maxwell.[124] They travelled to Bruges with Caroline. Valdi, who was bridesmaid, had joined them from Strasbourg. Elizabeth did not attend because at the time she opposed the marriage.[125] *The Irish Press* reported on their quiet wedding, which took place in the Benedictine Abbey of Zevenkerken Loppem. The civil ceremony took place in Bruges City Hall, both of which:

> were conducted in great secrecy. No one was at either but those whose presence was necessary. The best man was Rt. Rev. Mgr. Armando Vandenbunder, a domestic prelate of the diocese of Bruges. The secrecy of the wedding was assured by the royal attorney in Bruges, who agreed to waive the law requiring public notice of weddings to be made 10 days beforehand.[126]

They returned soon afterwards on doctor's advice as Valdi had fallen ill. MacKenzie was delighted to hear that Lavin and Mick had wed at last: 'That things worked out for you to marry at peace is the very dearest of news of this year.'[127]

In April, in their newly married state, Lavin and Mick put their focus into getting a neglected and rundown Abbey Farm in order. Now that things were in better shape, Lavin invited MacKenzie to visit. Valentine's former fiancé, Dermot, died in June and Lavin divulged that her 'grief was almost unbearable', but she concealed it from Valentine, who was due to marry Desmond 'very quietly' in July, 'someone who has supported her throughout this terrible year by his kindness, gentleness

& generosity'.[128] Lavin was certain that Valentine had made a good match in Desmond and would be very happy. MacKenzie was happy to hear about Valdi's upcoming nuptials and sympathised with Lavin's grief over Dermot: 'isn't it curious how often the extremes of joy and sorrow present themselves to be absorbed at one and the same time'.[129]

In June Lavin decided that Farrar, Straus and Giroux was not a right fit for her. Jackson had offered to 'bow out' if dealings with the publisher did not work out and Lavin held her to her word. She again asked MacKenzie to check the situation with Wesleyan University and she asked if it was the Center for Advanced Study where Frank Kermode, the British literary critic, had a fellowship. Lavin was correct; Kermode held a fellowship at the centre in 1963 and 1969. The idea of going was 'like a dream of paradise' to Lavin but she thought she was 'too little known really to make it very acceptable an idea'.[130] MacKenzie received no response to her letter of proposal from Wesleyan and she was unsure if one could even suggest a writer for the fellowship. She advised Lavin to forget about it and thought it might be an opportunity to write some of her stories, especially now that there was more order in her life. 'I think there's nothing more releasing than the strict charting of order.' MacKenzie made no mention of a visit to Ireland but she hoped that Lavin would make it to the US: 'Oh Mary, I do long to be working on a story with you. Pawn a little silver if time has to be bought!'[131]

In August MacKenzie sent Lavin a telegram with the news that they wanted 'Trastevere' – 'WE'RE DELIGHTED WITH THE STORY.'[132] She cut the story and set it in working proof before taking her summer holidays. Towards the end of August Elizabeth Tingom, in MacKenzie's absence, sent the new Mrs Scott a cheque for the story.[133] Lavin used the payment for 'Trastevere' to repay the advance given to her by Farrar, Straus and Giroux and so they released her from her contract and she moved to Houghton Mifflin, which was a great comfort to MacKenzie: 'Much as I admire Farrar, Straus, I think Houghton Mifflin wanted you in such a particular way that you can't help but be happier there.'[134]

'Trastevere' was another semi-autobiographical work inspired by Lavin's trip to Italy while on her Guggenheim Fellowship. It features the widow Vera Traske, who is a novelist in this story, and fits into the pattern of Lavin's own life. Lavin did not think it would be suitable material for *The New Yorker* due to its 'strong editorial taboo about writers and artists' but the magazine evidently relaxed its rule on stories featuring writers. 'Trastevere' reflects Lavin's artistic struggle, her role as the primary wage earner, her nurturing of young artists and her subsequent remarriage. With its setting in both New York and Rome, it is the only one of Lavin's *New Yorker* stories to be located outside Ireland. Vera and her daughter, Gloria, visit Rome where they are introduced to a mismatched couple, Simon and Della, by their mutual acquaintance, Paul. Both Paul and Simon are poets and Paul remarks light-heartedly that 'Della doesn't think writing poetry is work at all.' In defence of the artist and her mother, Gloria remarks that, 'Writers are sometimes working when we think they're only looking out the window.' For Vera, the act of composition is all-consuming.

Back in New York, Gloria learns from Paul of Della's suicide, which makes her reassess her relationship with her partner Mack: 'Widowed young herself, and having enough good sense not to make public by marriage a second, late but deeply satisfying relationship, she had her own concept of love (Mack).' However, Vera considers that marriage is a possibility, 'In spite of how often they thrashed things out and discarded the idea of marrying – laughed at the mere notion – perhaps after all ...'[135] Lavin began writing the story in February 1968, around the same time that Mick asked to be laicised after they made the decision to marry. Usually in Lavin's stories about widowhood, the widow clings to memories of her deceased husband and is prevented by grief from moving on. However, in this story, while the deceased husband is referred to, Vera has found a new love and it would appear that she is ready to embrace it and move forward in their relationship.

Mick was very encouraging to Zack Bowen, a professor of English at the State University of New York at Binghamton, when he got in touch about writing a 'biographical-critical study' of Lavin as part of a series for Bucknell University Press:

> I think I can say what Mary herself could hardly say without appearing vain, that it is time someone of the stature of yourself did this, not so much for Mary as for her readers, present and future. As she is about to sign a contract this week with a new American publisher for a new book of stories, and

> more important, a large volume of her collected stories, your suggestion comes at a very opportune time. Up to now her past work has not been in print for a long time in America, which is tragic. Needless to say, Mary and I will both give you all the assistance we can when you come to the writing of the study.[136]

In November Lavin informed MacKenzie that she was sending *McCall's*, an American women's magazine, 'a little children's poem' that was about a thousand words long: 'they are words that depend utterly on being illustrated I am hoping that they will come out here in book form, and if it does it will be illustrated by Edward Ardizzone who is a friend of mine (now) and whom I admire madly'.[137] Even though Lavin was sure that it would not be suitable for *The New Yorker*, she thought she ought to inform MacKenzie about it. She did not send MacKenzie a copy in case she thought it was submitted for consideration and think that Lavin had 'gone nutty'.[138] The magazine had no issue with Lavin submitting the children's poem *Round the World & Back Again* to *McCall's* and in any case, MacKenzie did not think that Lavin's first-reading contract included poetry: 'Of course this doesn't mean that we wouldn't want to see any adult poetry you wrote – we would, but I'm pretty sure the agreement leaves you free to send it where you will.'[139] MacKenzie was correct: Lavin's contract only covered 'fiction, humor, reminiscence and casual essays'.

Lavin wrote that she was looking forward to reading Elizabeth Cullinan's new story, likely 'Nora's Friends', which was published in *The New Yorker* on 29 August 1970, and her new novel *House of Gold*, which was also published the following year. 'Nora's Friends' was inspired by Cullinan's visits to Bective and as previously mentioned the title character, Nora Lynch, was based on Lavin, while Cecilia Bell was based on Cullinan. Cullinan had many concerns about the piece when it was in galleys and was clearly anxious about Lavin's opinion of it, informing her that the story was 'pure praise' for Lavin: 'My own reservation is that trying to speak in your voice I didn't get it quite right—anywhere <u>near</u> right.' Cullinan did not think the story 'good enough' and asked Lavin to 'Bear in mind, when you read it, that I wrote it last summer with no air-conditioning in this room and the temperature almost 100.'[140] Her fears were justified because Lavin was not too happy about her portrayal in the work, which Cullinan felt was due to one's perception of oneself being 'so firm and fixed … to see yourself in someone else's story image doesn't come close to our own sense of self'.[141]

In late November Lavin received her author's copy of *Happiness and Other Stories*, which the publisher had forgotten to send her. Constable published the collection at some stage in late October or early November.[142] The book was due to be published by Houghton Mifflin in the following year. The title story was the only *New Yorker* story to feature in the collection, which also contained 'The New Gardener', 'One Evening', 'A Pure Accident' and 'The Lost Child'.[143] William Trevor, in his *Irish Press* review of the volume, observed that the five stories are 'moving, gentle, intensely involving'. He concluded his article by comparing Lavin to Chekhov, Gogol, Carson McCullers and William Faulkner: 'She sets a story in a faraway corner, which she then succeeds in making familiar to all who visit it. Her men and women are people first, and Irish people second. And who can argue with that?'[144] Lavin sent a copy of the book to MacKenzie, who received it 'just in time for Christmas' and she wrote, 'How dear of you to send it. It will go to my shelf of very special books, next to "In the Middle of the Fields".'[145]

Lavin was delayed in sending MacKenzie two new stories because her typist, Claire L'Estrange, whom she deemed to be the only person who could read her manuscripts, had been unwell. Lavin had hoped to send them before the end of the contract in the hope of increasing her next first-reading agreement fee. She liked the stories and although they were long, she was confident that MacKenzie would too. Lavin was looking forward to working on the novella, possibly abroad, that 'was so fatal' in the summer.

Mick was concentrating on getting Lavin's affairs in order and found that her financial situation was not as bad as they had initially thought. They had managed to settle smaller debts and had consolidated bigger ones using a line of overdraft. Lavin was actively seeking out fellowships, not out of necessity as in the early days when she 'would not survive without it', 'but because Mick has got me into such order that I would be in a position, for the first time in my life, to be really professional about doing a piece of work'. Nevertheless, she still relied on selling her stories for her livelihood, 'and <u>that</u> worry no one can take from me'. While Lavin believed that her output was not as great as other writers, she felt that she worked hard given her circumstances and she was greatly heartened to discover that Flannery O'Connor only wrote about two stories a year.

In December Lavin's mother was hospitalised and there was a possibility that she would not be discharged in time for Christmas. Lavin was broken-hearted over the situation: 'It seems that every time I hear a snatch of a song on the radio or even a boy whistling in a Dublin street there is a heartbreaking reminder of her.' Yet she recognised her own limitations and was not prepared to upset the family dynamic by providing a hospital set-up at home for her mother. Lavin clearly felt guilty about this, having always accommodated her mother, 'a tiny little creature', as much as possible. She was greatly comforted by the letter MacKenzie wrote to her about her own 'little mother'.[146]

On a more positive note, the newly married Valdi was 'radiant' and expecting her first child in April. The couple were living in a thatched cottage by the sea in Waterford. They had intended to travel to Jamaica but their plans were thrown up in the air when Desmond, a civil engineer, was offered the position of heading up a new branch of his firm's marine engineering company in Ireland. In the end, they opted to travel. Lavin only hoped that they would remain long enough for Valdi to have the baby in Ireland as she was particularly keen for her mother to see her first great grandchild.

MacKenzie informed Lavin that *In the Middle of the Fields* was included in *The New Yorker*'s Christmas list, which consisted of a selection of books by *New Yorker* writers published that year. Maeve Brennan's *The Long-Winded Lady* and *In and Out of Never-Never Land*, Frank O'Connor's *A Set of Variations*, Edna O'Brien's *The Love Object* and *The Collected Stories of Jean Stafford* were among the books that also got a mention. MacKenzie was pleased to hear of Valdi's news and asked Lavin to keep her informed of the birth. She sent Lavin the first-reading agreement and cheque, which again came to $197 after the retirement plan contribution of $3 was deducted: 'We must see that it's bigger next year – more stories! But this one does say that you're loved and cherished hereabouts, and that we rest on hope.' She ended her letter: 'From such an ordered and happy life as yours sounds, only good can come (along, of course, with some suffering – how else could we be sure we were alive?) Nineteen seventy has to be an extraordinary year.'[147]

On 30 December Lavin wrote to MacKenzie to let her know that her mother, 'the poor little creature', died on 23 December and was buried on Christmas Eve: 'I'm telling you because I know you'd want to know but there's no need in the world to write or anything because I know how you'll sympathise.' Her mother was eighty-eight years old and Lavin remarked of her passing, 'As for my own feelings – it seems to me that she was cheated out of them even by dying at Xmas but of course Xmas doesn't last forever.'[148]

Mary Lavin with her mother, December 1912. Mary Lavin Personal Papers, UCD Special Collections. (© The Beneficiaries of the Estate of Mary Lavin)

Mary Lavin with her father at Bective. Mary Lavin Personal Papers, UCD Special Collections. (© The Beneficiaries of the Estate of Mary Lavin)

Mary Lavin outside Abbey Farm with her three daughters (l to r) Caroline, Elizabeth and Valentine 'Valdi' (1959). Mary Lavin Personal Papers, UCD Special Collections. (© The Beneficiaries of the Estate of Mary Lavin. Photograph by John Sarsfield)

Mary Lavin in front of her portrait by Ernest Hayes. (© Albert Fenton, 1985)

Mary Lavin Place, Wilton Park, Dublin, 2024. Courtesy of IPUT Real Estate Dublin.

Dipping the Other Wing, sculpture by Eilis O'Connell at Wilton Park. The name is taken from Lavin's short story 'One Evening'. Courtesy of IPUT Real Estate Dublin.

December 20, 1974

Dear Mary,

A quick letter to send you the renewal forms of your first-reading agreement. It says, as it does each year, that we value you especially and know how you have enriched this magazine; we know that you will again.

And then, Mary, it sends you my love. For Christmas (which will probably not reach you in time), and for the new year. The new year is not a matter of goodbye; it's a year's leave I'm taking because I want to get a novel written. It's started, but I haven't been able to do any work on it since summer. I'm going to my sister's big, comfortable house -- big enough for three people to live in in whatever degree of privacy they need -- and needing both us, for laughter and affection, and our furniture. Her father-in-law died (96) and left Ruth the house, but the furnishings were divided equally among the seven children. Besides, she hasn't money enough to keep it up. So we shall make a home together, and when I come back to New York I'll probably stay in a hotel. Wish me good luck -- I feel bereaved to be leaving -- but don't think goodbye.

Please blossom in the sun of Lake Como and know I shall be hoping that you're working on your memoirs. Are you?

Mary Lavin
The Abbey Farm
Bective
County Meath, IRELAND

The last (known) letter from Rachel MacKenzie to Mary Lavin, 20 December 1974. *New Yorker* records. Manuscripts and Archives Division. The New York Public Library. Astor, Lenox, and Tilden Foundations. (© The Estate of Rachel MacKenzie)

Mary Lavin with her three daughters. Mary Lavin Personal Papers, UCD Special Collections. (© The Beneficiaries of the Estate of Mary Lavin)

Mary Lavin in the garden of her Dublin mews (1977). Helen Hooker O'Malley Roelofs Collection (© Helen O'Malley Trust). This image is reproduced courtesy of the National Library of Ireland [NPA ROE705]

The Poetry Center

OF THE 92ND STREET YM-YWHA / 1395 LEXINGTON AVENUE, NEW YORK CITY 10028 / TELEPHONE Fi 8-1500

MARY LAVIN and JOHN UPDIKE

Sunday evening, November 19
1967 8:30 o'clock

*Poetry Center Members: Free
Others: $1.50

MARY LAVIN was born in Massachusetts and taken to Ireland as a child, where she has lived ever since; she is known as an Irish writer and most of her writing is about Ireland and its people. She has a farm in County Meath where she now lives permanently, although this year she is a guest writer-in-residence at the University of Connecticut at Storrs. Her first book, Tales from the Bective Bridge, a collection of short stories, was published in 1943 and was awarded the James Tait Black Memorial Prize for the most outstanding work of fiction of that year. She has also written two novels - The House in Clewe Street and Mary O'Grady - and three other books of stories - The Becker Wives, The Long Ago and The Great Wave and other stories, published in 1961 by Macmillan.

JOHN UPDIKE was born in 1932 in Shillington, Pennsylvania, and holds a B.A. degree summa cum laude from Harvard College. From 1955 to 1957, he was a reporter on the staff of The New Yorker magazine. His literary awards and honors include an O. Henry Memorial Awards first prize and two awards for his novel, The Centaur (1963); the National Book Award and a National Association of Independent Schools Award. Mr. Updike's other novels are The Poorhouse Fair (1959), Rabbit, Run (1960) and Of the Farm (1965). Collections of his short stories include Pigeon Feathers and other stories (1962) and The Music School: Short Stories (1966). He is also the author of books of poetry, the most recent of which is Telephone Poles and Other Poems (1963); and of children's books, among them, A Child's Calendar (1965). Assorted Prose (1965) is a collection of his essays. A new novel, Couples, will be published in April by Knopf.

There will be an intermission of ten minutes between the readings.

The audience is invited to ask the authors questions at the end of the program.

*MEMBERSHIP INFORMATION

$10.00

will entitle you to free admission to all unreserved-seat events (approximately 35) and to a 50¢ reduction on reserved-seat events (approximately 5).

Flyer for Mary Lavin and John Updike's reading at the Poetry Center, New York, on 19 November 1967. *New Yorker* records. Manuscripts and Archives Division. The New York Public Library. Astor, Lenox, and Tilden Foundations. (© Poetry Center)

ML/1/39(3)

1959 slow

Lavin

HAPPINESS

- by -

Mary Lavin

Mother had a lot to say, which does not mean she was always talking, but that we ~~could~~ ~~feel~~ felt she drew ~~her wisdom from well~~ upon wells deep and wonderful.

Her theme was happiness; what it was: what it was not: where to find it: where not: and how ~~we~~ it must, if found, ~~guard it against its many enemies~~ be closely guarded.
Never must ~~we~~ it be confounded ~~it~~ with pleasure. Nor ~~think~~ must it ever be thought that sorrow was ~~its~~ its opposite.

"~~Like~~ Take Father Hugh," she said ~~once~~, flashing her eyes at him, "he ~~claims~~ 'd have you believe that sorrow is an ingredient of happiness — a necessary ingredient if you please !" ~~and here~~, As he tried to protest, ~~she~~ Mother put up her hand.
"There may —" she allowed, "there may be a freakish truth in ~~this~~ your theory for some people. But not for me."

~~And she~~ Turning and looked severely at us, "~~Her~~ And not, I hope, for ~~you~~ my children," she said. ~~"It is a dangerous theory: it could lead one to make one a~~ "I've seen people make a substitute of ~~the~~ sorrow ~~for the other. I've seen it happen.~~" ~~She shivered.~~ She shuddered.

Mother had a habit of asking ~~us~~ at ~~the seemingly people~~ if ~~they were~~ one was happy?

1.

Corrected manuscript of 'Happiness' (undated). Mary Lavin Literary Papers, UCD Special Collections.

Christmas card featuring an illustration of Abbey Farm in County Meath and the Mews in Lad Lane in Dublin. Mary Lavin Personal Papers, UCD Special Collections. (© The Beneficiaries of the Estate of Mary Lavin)

Merry Christmas

from

Mary and the Children

The Abbey Farm
Bective, Co. Meath.

Mews eleven
Lad Lane, Dublin.

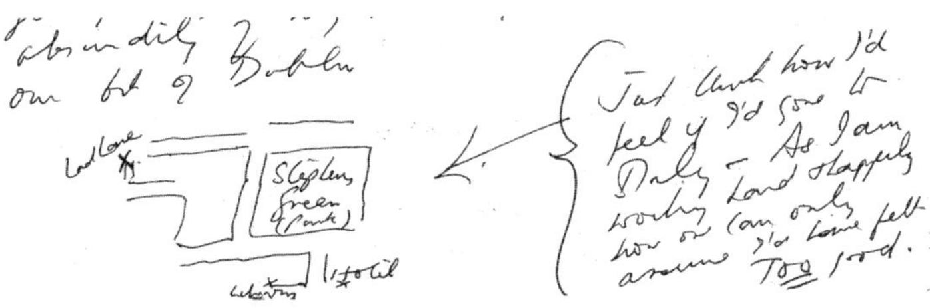

Lavin's map of the 'absurdity of our bit of Dublin', 14 February 1962. *New Yorker* records. Manuscripts and Archives Division. The New York Public Library. Astor, Lenox, and Tilden Foundations. (© The Beneficiaries of the Estate of Mary Lavin)

Lavin's notes for the 'First idea for Happiness' written on a page of the November 1965 issue of *Vogue*. Mary Lavin Literary Papers, UCD Special Collections. (© The Beneficiaries of the Estate of Mary Lavin.)

Rachel MacKenzie (undated). Photograph by Rollie McKenna.

Elizabeth Cullinan (1982). (© Estate of Elizabeth Cullinan)

Mary Lavin in the 1960s with her three daughters. Mary Lavin Personal Papers, UCD Special Collections. (© The Beneficiaries of the Estate of Mary Lavin)

I think I told you how much it meant to me when you first wrote to me, and then when you took a story ! So now, you can perhaps imagine something of what I feel, and why I am a bit stunned still by the good fortune. I needed the money so desperately at the time it came last year, and now this money can put up so many bulwarks between us and the hardship and tension I've endured for so long. The strange thing, that frightens me, is that it was only when appalling burthen was lifted that I really was aware of its weight. I felt more like collapse when you took it fr om my shoulderw than ever I felt dragging alomg with it. Isn't that odd?
I was filled with all kinds of fears too; that I wouldn't be able to do any more good stories, or enough to make it worth your while and so on. I don't think I ever felt this before altough it is supposed to be a common complaint.

But don't worry about it. I am really only telling you because I want to explain as well as apologise for the delay; the paralysis that came over me. Usually I reply to your letters at once.

And one last thing of all. I was so touched by the way your letter ended - affectionately. Indeed it is the way I felt like ending all my letters to the New Yorker, and specially to you since the first one I got from you.

And so,
gratefully and affectionately,

Mary Lavin

No time to re-read,

Letter from Mary Lavin to Rachel MacKenzie, 6 April 1959. *New Yorker* records. Manuscripts and Archives Division. The New York Public Library. Astor, Lenox, and Tilden Foundations. (© The Beneficiaries of the Estate of Mary Lavin)

'Frank O'Connor conducts an extracurricular interview', Bread Loaf Writers' Conference (1953). Courtesy of Middlebury College Special Collections.

'Setting off for the trip to Florence, Guggenheim', 15 September 1959. Mary Lavin Personal Papers, UCD Special Collections. (© The Beneficiaries of the Estate of Mary Lavin)

Rachel MacKenzie teaching a class at Bread Loaf Writers' Conference (1952). Courtesy of Middlebury College Special Collections.

Bread Loaf Writers' Conference, staff photo (1952). MacKenzie is seated in the third row, second from right, next to Robert Frost. Courtesy of Middlebury College Special Collections.

9
'Small Comfort'
1970–1974

> I am writing more than ever in my life but I seem to be writing further & further from the New Yorker but I don't think anyone really cares.[1]

It was February before Mary Lavin got in touch with Rachel MacKenzie as she had been preoccupied with proceedings in the Supreme Court in Dublin after Goulding Fertilisers appealed the High Court ruling, but the judgment was deferred. Ultimately, Goulding Fertilisers won their appeal. Lavin queried whether Mick was correct in thinking that the quantity bonus arrangement had ceased, thus alleviating the pressure to submit work within a set time frame. She had almost completed four stories and reasoned, 'If I was still in time I'd race on & finish one – if there was no need I'd have a few days holiday.'[2]

MacKenzie confirmed that there was no change to the bonus system. 'Trastevere' was the only acceptance in her current cycle, therefore in order to make the bonus, Lavin needed three more stories accepted by 31 July, which MacKenzie deemed 'Child's play, if you're in as good writing fettle as you sound.' She gently reminded Lavin that lengthy stories due for imminent book publications were problematic for the magazine. Lavin was looking to sell her work in the UK and she enquired how soon after a story appeared in *The New Yorker* she could get it published in England. MacKenzie explained that a period of six weeks had to elapse, 'time to allow for slow-boat mail to get copies of the magazine to England and Scotland, and breathing time for reading'. She sent Lavin the end-of-year COLA adjustment for 1969, which amounted to $638.2 after the retirement plan of $9.72 was deducted: 'I hope it's just in the nick of time for something or other. Of [*sic*] if you've weathered the most recent nick that you can look at it and see indulgence.'

MacKenzie had been intending to write to Lavin about the recent loss of her mother: 'I have thought of her more than you might guess over the years, and of your guilt and frustration and responsibility and love all in that terrifying mix that separates out at intervals and confounds you.' She revealed that it took her two years to gain perspective when her own mother died, which she believed was due to the fact that her 'little mother had changed so sorrowfully and I grieved for what had happened to her life, which had been so full of love and giving'. Meanwhile, MacKenzie was coming to terms with her own 'private Christmas grief': her beloved brother-in-law suddenly took ill on Christmas day and died shortly afterwards, leaving behind her sister Ruth and their seventeen-year-old son in Ohio.

On a happier note, MacKenzie informed Lavin of a lunch she attended in the company of Richard McAdoo, Dorothy de Santillana, Bill Maxwell and Elizabeth Cullinan to celebrate Houghton Mifflin's publication of Cullinan's first novel, *House of Gold*: 'You were a member of that party to an extent that would surprise you. (Or would it?) Dear to us all, that's why.' MacKenzie remarked that, 'Elizabeth looked so pretty. Well, she had reason to. Reviews have been so good, and they'd come fast, which, as you know, doesn't always happen.'[3] Cullinan had evidently informed Lavin of the gathering because Lavin acknowledged the lunch in an earlier letter to MacKenzie, 'it was great to think that you, Dick McAdoo & E C were all together talking about me but I'd rather have been there myself too'.[4]

House of Gold centres on the Irish American Devlin family as they gather for the impending death of their powerful matriarch, Julia. Richard M. Elman, in his *New York Times* review of the book, wrote: 'The truth is Elizabeth Cullinan has had the courage to compose a moving and original work of fiction, out of unlikely materials that have hitherto been largely overlooked.' *Kirkus Reviews* described Cullinan as a 'rough-cut Maeve Brennan … and highly promising'. Maeve Brennan, in her *New Yorker* review of the novel, recognised Cullinan as 'a contemplative writer of great natural power'.[5]

Lavin's first grandchild, Kathleen, was born in early April. That same month MacKenzie underwent open-heart surgery, a relatively new and radical procedure at that time. She was recuperating in the Iroquois Hotel home in Midtown Manhattan. William Maxwell handled Lavin's work during MacKenzie's absence. He assumed Lavin knew about the operation and so kept her updated on MacKenzie's progress: 'I talked to her a few minutes ago. She has been home from the hospital about ten days, has no fever, but also, not too much strength. It will take a while. But the operation was successful, she gambled and won, which means she can lead a different life once she has totally recovered from the surgery.[6]

Lavin was shocked at the news as she had no idea that MacKenzie was due to undergo the procedure. Maxwell was apologetic that she had not been notified. After some postoperative complications, including phlebitis and running a fever, MacKenzie was recovering well and back reading manuscripts, one of which was Lavin's 'Tomb of an Ancestor'. Maxwell did not sugarcoat the reasons for the magazine's rejection of the story. Although the editors enjoyed the opening, the children were not compelling enough to sustain interest. However, he reasoned that an Irish audience might feel otherwise: 'Some stories simply do not cross the Atlantic Ocean and this could be one of them.' He had waited until MacKenzie had the opportunity to read the story, in case she could redeem it, but she concurred with their decision: 'But she too agrees that the story isn't right for The New Yorker. Alas, alas. How I hate to do this to you!'

Maxwell empathised with Lavin's grieving process following her mother's death, having experienced something similar when his father died. He explained that writing about their relationship provided a form of catharsis: 'My stomach produced all the symptoms of an ulcer without my actually having one, and it bothered me very much that I hadn't gone to see him before he died. So finally I decided that if I could get him down on paper, in a story, the exact way he was, and particularly the relations between us, which were very funny in a sort of awful way, my stomach would get better. And I did and it did.'[7]

On 5 May Lavin wrote to MacKenzie of her upset over her illness: 'I just can't bear to think of you laid-up, and worse still that I DID NOT KNOW IT.' She had suspected something was amiss when she had not heard from her but put it down to a delay in the postal service. Lavin shared her news of her granddaughter's birth and ended her letter: 'Oh do get better quickly Rachel for the sake of your millions of friends, but for our sakes specially, we love you so much.'[8] MacKenzie was unsure herself as to whether she would need surgery until she was admitted to the hospital: 'I had marvellous medical care. And here I am!'[9]

Houghton Mifflin released *Happiness and Other Stories* in mid-April and it was met with positive reviews. Anne O'Neil Barnes's *New York Times* review observed of the collection: 'Thanks to The New Yorker, I think, more than to anything else, one can speak of a sort of prototype Irish short story which strikes first as being Irish and only secondly as the work of an individual. Mary Lavin is a frequent contributor to The New Yorker; at least one of the five stories in this slim collection was previously printed there, and her work is richly representative of Ireland. But it is also richly, uniquely, individual.'[10] The publisher sent MacKenzie, Maxwell and Cullinan copies of the book. Cullinan thought it 'the most beautiful looking book I've seen in ages' and Maxwell was full of praise for the collection: 'I am enchanted to have it. Such a beautiful looking book. And the stories so remarkable.'[11] Fittingly, given the flower's strong presence and significance in its title story, the cover of the book features a daffodil. MacKenzie also admired the cover and informed Lavin that she had the book in her 'New York hotel apartment – one of the prettier things there, I must say – where I'm living these days, and I give it a little pat of affection whenever I go by it. Isn't that about the best daffodil you ever laid a hand on?'[12]

Daffodils play a significant and symbolic role in 'Happiness'. When Vera's husband is ill in hospital in Dublin, she stays in a hotel nearby so that she can be with him 'all day from early to late'. They do not realise that he is dying. Similarly, when Lavin's first husband, William, was in hospital, she stayed in a hotel in the vicinity. In the story, Vera's daughters made little bunches of daffodils for their father, but for their mother it was not the same as him seeing them grow. On her way to the hospital, after a brief return home to check on the girls, Vera gathers a huge bunch of daffodils to place on his bed. However, she is accosted by a nun at the hospital, who 'Reached out and grabbed the flowers, letting lots of them fall.' The nun proceeds to admonish Vera for being so foolish when her husband was clearly dying, telling her, 'Your prayers are all you can give him now!' Vera admits that she was foolish, but that she 'wasn't cured'. Despite her traumatic associations with the flower, she still has vases of them in her home because she believes their beauty is 'absolute and inviolable'.[13]

Lavin was delighted when Maxwell let her know that she could send MacKenzie her next story, 'Villa Violetta' and so, on 25 May, Lavin posted two separate copies 'to make sure they ship it with a slow boat'. She acknowledged that the story was very long but she reassured MacKenzie that she had a shorter one in the works. Lavin asked when MacKenzie would be coming to visit her in Ireland now that she was likely feeling more up to the journey: 'I was thinking that in the garden the other day & realising that now you will probably feel more like it. I'd hope so dear Rachel.' Lavin informed MacKenzie that her granddaughter, Kathleen, was 'a darling & I don't think it's just because she's mine I feel that'.[14]

Lavin had some good news on the paperback front: Mentor Library (New American Library), New York, was going to publish her first paperback after many years.[15] The book, *The Becker Wives*, was also going to be translated into German and Dutch.[16] In a reversal of roles, Lavin told MacKenzie to take care of herself and not to write until she had regained her strength: 'I hope you are getting better & better every minute.'[17] Rather than disturb MacKenzie, Lavin asked Maxwell to see if he could reactivate her account with Gotham Mart and get them to send her Eudora Welty's latest work, *Losing Battles*: 'She nearly always sends me a copy & vice versa but this time I just <u>can't wait</u>.'[18] MacKenzie subsequently sent Lavin Welty's novel as a gift.

In early June Lavin travelled to Cologne 'as a guest of the Dept of Education' in order to partake in 'Irish Week', which took place from 1 to 7 June.[19] The event, described as 'one of the most intensive programmes of Irish culture ever produced in Germany', was a government initiative with the Abbey Theatre and the Irish embassy in Bonn.[20] The Abbey Theatre staged Brendan Behan's *The Hostage* and Micheál Mac Liammóir performed *The Importance of Being Oscar*. Lavin took part in the Symposium on the Irish Short Story alongside Bryan MacMahon and Augustine Martin.[21] Elizabeth Schnack, who had recently been awarded an honorary doctorate by the National University of Ireland in recognition of her work, gave readings from her translations of Irish literature. Lavin told Maxwell that the University of Frankfurt were 'doing a seminar on my work and Michael's'.[22] Although Lavin had a wonderful time in Germany, she was relieved to be back home as she usually preferred to be in Ireland for the month of June.

MacKenzie gave Lavin the disappointing news that 'Villa Violetta' was rejected because it was too sentimental and long for the magazine '(maybe you're too happy; do you think that could be it? A joke.)'.[23] She suggested that Lavin might have better luck with a women's magazine.[24] MacKenzie managed to visit her Connecticut home on the weekend of 19 June for the first time since the autumn. She spent the Saturday inspecting her acre of land, which left her so exhausted that she had to retire to bed, but she was looking forward to recuperating from her 'real miracle' of an operation: 'I can hardly wait for the months of convalescence to gallop by to see where I come out.' MacKenzie had returned to the office for a few hours each day, but she was hoping to go in for longer stretches.[25] Her operation made her address inefficiencies in her dealings and she asked if Lavin had secured a New York agent as it would speed up their communications considerably in addition to saving on postage fees. MacKenzie had consulted with Joyce Hartman at Houghton Mifflin to see if she had any insight on the matter but she did not.[26]

In November Lavin addressed the significant gap in their correspondence but let her know that she would be seeing her soon as she had been invited back to Storrs.[27] Mick was going to accompany her this time. They were going to travel first class and stay in a stateroom on the *Bremen*, which was due to sail on 15 January from Southampton.[28] Meanwhile, Lavin was busy revising old stories for the next Houghton Mifflin book and for another Constable collection: 'It doesn't boil the pot but it stirs the heart!' Lavin hoped that MacKenzie would not consider her a 'stubborn pig' for resubmitting 'Tomb of an Ancestor', which she had heavily revised and renamed 'The Cousins'.[29] She asked MacKenzie to glance at it before sending it on to Bill Carrington Guy, her new American literary agent, at James O. Brown Associates.[30]

MacKenzie shouldered the blame for the long silence between them. She was delighted to hear that Lavin was returning to the States and had already heard from Joyce Hartman about the new Houghton Mifflin book. MacKenzie told Lavin to peruse the following week's issue of *The New Yorker*: 'It will face you, and I hope you will read it. And it's going to be a book – imagine. Sixty-four pages on last estimation. So we shall have a lot to talk about over at the Algonquin.'[31] MacKenzie was referring to her aptly titled story, 'Risk', inspired and informed by her recent heart surgery and its post-operative complications, which was published in the 21 November issue. The story commands forty-five pages shared with W. H. Auden's poem 'The Aliens', advertisements and cartoons. One of the cartoons by Barney Tobey, sexist but typical of its day, depicts a stylish woman entering a business in response to a 'Girl Wanted' sign posted on its window, only to find herself pounced on and groped by the predatory male boss once inside.[32] Other poetry featured in the issue includes 'Gigolo' by Sylvia Plath, 'The Woman on the Mall' by Robert Dana and 'Echo for the Promise of Georg Trakl's Life' by James Wright.[33]

In 'Risk', the unnamed patient is advised by her doctor that she will need to see a 'super-super heart man' and undergo more intensive examinations if a change in medication does not improve her congestive heart failure and murmur. The patient responds, 'I work you know. Is it something I could come in and have done in a day?'[34] One can picture the diligent MacKenzie posing this question to her own doctor. After the operation, the heart specialist informs the convalescent that it will take six months to a year for her to get back to normal. When back for a check-up, she enquires how many of these operations they had performed at the hospital: '"Between fifteen and twenty – seventeen is the exact number, I believe." Dr Rudd had said the risk was 35 per cent or a little more … Had they lost six? Seven? … They sat for a moment, unsmiling, looking at each other. Oh God, she thought, those nightmare days. Dear God, the miracle.'[35] Perhaps it was not the most appropriate story to place alongside advertisements for brandy, liqueurs, party cheeses and a goose that cooks in twenty-five minutes, but the issue was jam-packed with such adverts due to its proximity to Thanksgiving, which fell on 26 November that year.

Lavin asked MacKenzie to send her the tear sheets of the story as she was eager to read it and it would take an age before she received her copy of the magazine in the post. MacKenzie posted them to Lavin with the warning, 'Don't read it if you find it too distressing. It's not meant to be.'[36] MacKenzie was grateful for Lavin's subsequent appraisal of the story: 'Your letter about "Risk" was so generous. I was touched. It mattered to me to have you value it as a piece of writing.'[37] Curiously, the letter from Lavin referred to is not in the archives – it may have been lost, or retained by MacKenzie. William Shawn considered 'Risk' to be 'an extraordinary piece of writing'.[38] On 15 December MacKenzie posted Lavin her new contract and a cheque for $98.50, after $1.50 was deducted for the retirement plan. She consoled her with the news that everyone received disappointing payments that year. MacKenzie, always one to look at the positive side, remarked, 'Still, I thought, sounding like my mother in my ears, isn't it splendid to have something!'[39]

In January 1971 MacKenzie was sorry to deliver the news that 'The Cousins' was still not right for *The New Yorker*. She encountered the same issue with the story, namely, that 'the children aren't interesting enough; there's not enough life loose'. She was holding the story for Lavin's arrival, in case she wished to try other magazines, and reassured her with the words, 'Don't you dare be humiliated by our not taking a story. Ever. You are too professional for that.'[40] A weary Lavin responded, 'I'm not professional enough not to care – but I am human enough!!'[41]

Elizabeth Cullinan was going to meet Lavin and Mick when they arrived in New York on the *Bremen* on Friday 5 February at 8 a.m. and Lavin wondered if there was a possibility of MacKenzie meeting her for lunch that day. She was then going to travel to Storrs on the Saturday or Sunday.[42] Cullinan's book *The Time of Adam* was released a few days earlier, on 1 February. Before it was published, she expressed her fears to Lavin that it would be 'torn apart'.[43] The collection, which she dedicated to her mentor William Maxwell, features ten *New Yorker* stories including 'Nora's Friends', which was published under the title 'Maura's Friends'.[44] Lavin was not happy about the name change, probably because Nora was her mother's name. Cullinan was deeply apologetic that the new title upset Lavin and explained that two earlier stories in the collection, 'Le Petit Déjeuner' and 'The Old Priest', featured a young girl named Nora Barrett and she thought it would cause confusion. The collection also contains 'A Swim' and Cullinan confided in Lavin that the character of Michael Callan in another of the stories, 'A Sunday Like the Others', was based on the Irish writer Desmond Fennell.[45]

Cullinan had read McGahern's latest collection, *Nightlines*, and thought it 'a perfect book'; she considered the story 'Lavin' to be 'the most erotic piece of writing I've ever read, thoroughly and truly erotic'.[46] She informed McGahern that Mary Lavin was adamant that the story was based on her, although she had not yet read it (in fact, the Lavin in

McGahern's story is an elderly blacksmith). Cullinan was delighted to find that two bookshops had sold out of *Nightlines* when she tried to purchase it in New York. She noted the coincidence that reviews for both of their books appeared on the same day: Joyce Carol Oates's review of *The Time of Adam* and David Pryce-Jones's review of John McGahern's *Nightlines* both appeared in *The New York Times* on 7 February 1971. Cullinan sent John McGahern a copy of her book during the postal strike and in a letter to him wrote that it 'got knocked around'.[47] She informed him of her plans to travel to Ireland in the summer or autumn 'if I can pull myself together'. She revealed that she had been romantically involved with someone but the relationship was complicated and she wished that she could confide in McGahern about it. If Cullinan and McGahern had been romantically involved, they obviously emerged as friends and confidants. Cullinan received an award for *The Time of Adam* from 'some midwestern college' in October.[48]

Risk was published by Viking in April 1971 and was fifty-nine pages long. MacKenzie dedicated the book to her sisters, Gennie and Ruth. M. F. K. Fisher wrote of the publication, 'I rarely use words like "unforgettable" "extraordinary," "masterpiece," but all of them fit this story.'[49] Anatole Broyard wrote a generally positive review for *The New York Times* but only wished MacKenzie:

> had laid her heart as wide open as the doctors had, that she had let us read her own secret charting of her situation. She reports, but she doesn't speculate; she tells us more about her body's struggle than her spirit's. We expect her to bring back from her brush with death some drastic kind of poetry. (One thinks, unfairly, of Sylvia Plath.) But her fastidiousness and her dislike of melodrama have impelled Miss MacKenzie to play down that dimension of her 'miracle' that no cardiogram can record.[50]

Another less favourable *New York Times* review stated that the 'minimum of hard information' provided was 'a pure New Yorker approach – shot through with little emotion'.[51]

Risk featured in the summer edition of the *Reader's Digest Condensed Books* (Volume 86) in 1971. The series comprised hardback collections of abridged versions of current best-selling novels and nonfiction books. As MacKenzie made her way to cash in her first royalty cheque from

Viking for the *Reader's Digest* reprint, she met Andy Logan, a *New Yorker* reporter, who informed MacKenzie that she had received a royalty cheque for twelve cents the previous week for an 'old book'. The two women laughed uncontrollably at the amount: 'we stood and laughed ourselves almost into the gutter'.[52]

There was little correspondence between Lavin and MacKenzie while Lavin was at Storrs. On 20 February, on University of Connecticut headed paper, Lavin wrote the following note for her students: 'There's nothing I can do to make writers out of you – you've got to dig the gift – if you have it – right down out of the pit of your belly. BUT even when you've done that – if you'd done that – you've got to shed everything else – that comes from outside – from others. You've got to be yourselves & after that it will not be easy but it will be easier.'[53]

Lavin was again invited to Bill Maxwell's home, where she met *New Yorker* staffer and contributor Philip Hamburger and his wife, Anna. They clearly had met before as Hamburger subsequently wrote to her of how much they enjoyed meeting her again.[54] He had informed Richard Ellmann of their discussion and Lavin later sent Hamburger some material to pass on to him.[55] It is likely that MacKenzie also attended this gathering. The next correspondence between Lavin and MacKenzie was in July, after Lavin had returned to Ireland. She was busy writing and only hoped to 'have time enough left in my life to polish' all the stories she was jotting down. Lavin held off sending a new story, 'A Memory', until MacKenzie returned from her holidays, but she did not think that it would be suitable as it was 'long and without much action'.[56]

In August MacKenzie got in touch with the 'wretched news' that 'A Memory' was rejected, even though she was impressed with the story, because it was a novella and she did not think that it could, or should, be shortened: 'One of its strengths is the slow, careful, building pace and the devastating acceleration of the end. You should be pleased with the writing; it shows your work. I see your next volume gathering.'[57] Lavin was not upset by the rejection as she wanted it to go in the next book, *A Memory and Other Stories*, due to be published before *The New Yorker* would be able to find a slot for the story.

Cullinan empathised with Lavin over her string of *New Yorker* rejections and shared her own feelings on the matter:

> The way I feel about how they do it though – the way I've come to feel – is that they probably do it the only way there is. That's what I've realised about William Maxwell, anyway. I think he almost can't stand having to send a story back and he does it in a way that he means to look as if it doesn't matter in the slightest; as if we'll both just forget about it. The first time it happened to me I lay down on the bed and cried. But now I galvanise myself and get by – which isn't to say that I wouldn't feel the way you do after a cumulative blow like that.

Cullinan mentioned that Sylvia Townsend Warner was the one writer who continued to get published in the magazine 'come hell or high water'. She informed Lavin that MacKenzie 'now lives down the street from me – which is to say I could now produce documents on that subject, but not for a letter'.[58]

Houghton Mifflin published *Collected Stories* in August. The volume features twenty-two stories, five of which had appeared in *The New Yorker*: 'The Great Wave', The Living', In the Middle of the Fields', 'The Cuckoo Spit' and 'Happiness'. Cullinan thought the collection was 'so beautiful, and the reviews I saw were marvellous'.[59] MacKenzie thought Lavin would be pleased with the reviews, which she sent on to her: 'It is a beautiful book, as most of the reviewers seem to have the sense to recognize, and it kept me loving company in Vermont.' It is possible that MacKenzie had been in Vermont to attend the Middlebury College Bread Loaf Writers' Conference, which took place from 30 June until 15 August that year. The first month of her holidays was a bit of a letdown because she was sickly but once she resigned herself to the fact that she was ill she began to 'rest mindlessly' and felt better than she had in a long time and 'even became mildly active (depending on your definition), like walking out to the mailbox at the road, or up to the old apple tree, or across the meadow after it had been mowed'. The lesson MacKenzie took from the whole experience was to try to stop overstretching herself; nevertheless she still pondered, 'wouldn't it be sinful to stop short!' She did not manage to get any writing done, but she had a solid plan for the book; all she needed now was some stamina.[60]

In September Lavin and Mick were taking a 'much much needed' week's holiday. Mick had been appointed Dean of the School of Irish Studies in Dublin.[61] Initially established as an international summer school in 1969, the school expanded in 1970 to become 'a year-round school offering courses in Irish literature, history, politics and Irish culture', principally aimed at North American and Canadian students. As a result, Scott made numerous trips to the USA to promote the school. The lecturers were mainly from University College Dublin and Lavin also participated as a guest lecturer.

On 27 September MacKenzie attended a Houghton Mifflin afternoon cocktail party at Sardi's to celebrate the launch of Anne Sexton's *Transformations*, 'a modern, horrifying rendition in poetry of Grimm's fairy tales, so they say'.[62] She had not read the book but wrote that Howard Moss would 'do the honour on that score'.[63] MacKenzie admitted to Lavin, 'This going forth to a cocktail party is something new for me' but she had wanted to go as she expected to see their mutual friends Dorothy de Santillana, Joyce Hartman and Dick McAdoo at the event, where they would all 'speak lovingly' of Lavin. She recognised that her desire to attend the event was a good sign as it meant that she was getting better, which she put down to being back on a drug that she had been taken off in February and also because she was not overdoing things. She asked Lavin, 'And wouldn't you think there's just a chance that I might be better?' MacKenzie revealed that she had felt wretched when Lavin was over in New York. The book event was near to MacKenzie's hotel and she figured that she could leave early if there was nowhere for her to sit.[64] In the end, only Dick McAdoo attended the launch. MacKenzie passed on the news that he was happy with the reception of the *Collected Stories* and subsequent sales. MacKenzie told McAdoo that she thought 'A Memory' would be suitable for a book and offered to send him a Xerox copy of the story and of 'Trastevere', if Lavin were agreeable.

Lavin was concerned that 'Trastevere', which the magazine had accepted two years earlier, had not yet been published and worried that the editors had had a change of heart. She thought it could be included in the new collection, but *The New Yorker* would have to publish it before the spring to make this feasible. MacKenzie was embarrassed by the delay in publishing stories and assured Lavin that 'Trastevere' was 'cherished'. The reason for the hold-up, she explained, was due to a lack of space in the magazine, although she noted that the magazine was 'beginning to fatten up'. The best MacKenzie could do was to prompt the schedulers, who had given her a tentative date of 27 November for its publication, but she assured Lavin that it would be published in time for the book.

MacKenzie sent Lavin the author's proof of 'Trastevere'. They excised a reference to a wet nappy sagging like an udder which left a trail on the ground but they retained 'the rain from the child held out over the street'. William Shawn objected to the allusion due to his 'great sense of delicacy'. He also felt that 'three reference to babies wetting are excessive'. MacKenzie thought that he would prefer if there were no references: 'He just wants such matters referred to as little as possible in this magazine.' The subject of soiled nappies was clearly not suitable *New Yorker* material. Although MacKenzie was sorry to lose the image of 'the udder and the snail', she took comfort that Lavin could keep it in the book version. Lavin accepted that perhaps there was 'just too much nappy stuff' and so was agreeable to the deletions, telling MacKenzie, 'You know that in the end you can make up your own mind about some of them.'

MacKenzie had mentioned the word 'dangling' in her revisions, which Lavin presumed referred to the rhythm of the piece. 'Dangling,' MacKenzie explained, meant 'that grammatically a part of a sentence is loose, without anything to modify, or modifying the wrong thing.' MacKenzie wrote to Lavin upon receipt of the author's proof and was apologetic for her lack of clarity in her notes. She was going to send Lavin 'a copy of the proof that's set from the author's proof (pink sheets called overmatter)' so Lavin could read the amended text on which she could make minor changes.[65]

'Trastevere' was published on 11 December 1971. André François's abstract cover depicts an artist in his studio who has painted falling snow on a canvas.[66] Lavin's story shares its pages with two poems, 'Consequences of a Dime' by Jonathan Aaron, 'The Fish' by Greg Kuzma, and several cartoons.[67] The issue features *The New Yorker*'s Christmas list of books by its contributors: MacKenzie's *Risk* and Elizabeth Cullinan's *The Time of Adam* appear in the selection. It also carries an advertisement for William Steig's album of drawings, 'Male/Female', and oodles of suggestions for Christmas gifts including a special Christmas rate for a subscription to *The New Yorker* ($12 for the first year and $8 for subsequent years). A Western Electric advertisement, 'Did you say you want to marry me?' declares, 'It can handle 3,000 proposals a second.' Cullinan wrote to Lavin four days after its publication to let her know how much she loved the story: 'I raced through it on the spot. It had absolutely everything I love in your stories and then something new. It seemed like a new character you were writing about. Well, anyway, I thought it was marvellous.'[68] She had been badly in need of money and it did not help matters that a movie deal collapsed in May but she thought *The New Yorker* was taking another story and so she splashed out and bought a coat.[69]

On 5 November 1971 James Wade expressed his wish that Lavin was still with Macmillan even though he had left the company. He mentioned that he had had lunch with Lola Szladits, the curator of the New York Public Library's Berg Collection, whereupon they embarked on a discussion about Lady Gregory, whose papers had been acquired by the library. Wade suggested that Lavin write a biography of Gregory but she had no interest in the proposition. Szladits got in touch with Lavin and expressed the library's interest in purchasing her papers, but as they were not permitted to evaluate material, Lavin needed to name her price.[70]

On 12 November MacKenzie sent Lavin *The Nation*'s review of *Collected Stories*.[71] She presumed Houghton Mifflin had already done so but figured that she might like to have an extra copy. She hoped the positive review would help generate sales: 'Those collected stories have had lovely attention – lots of it and all full of praise.' MacKenzie told Lavin that although *Risk* was not selling well, she was receiving an award for it from the American Heart Association on 15 November in California. It was a big indulgence for MacKenzie, who admitted, 'I'm sure that people around here fly off to far parts for occasions as casual as high tea, but I have never done such a thing in my life and it amuses me. The place I'm flying to adds to the amusement: Anaheim, which is the home of Disneyland.'

The lunch ceremony was taking place at the Disneyland Hotel, 'The Official Hotel of the Magic Kingdom', where MacKenzie would also be staying.: 'I'm one of five "journalists" being gathered to award, I think for doing good. Oh, well. For whatever, I'm touched.' The award was named after Howard W. Blakeslee, who died of heart disease and who was the founder of the National Association of Science Writers.

Each recipient received a $500 prize, which was given 'for outstanding reporting on diseases of the heart and blood vessels'.[72] MacKenzie suspected that she would be the only one of the group 'to be carrying her most recent cardiogram' that her doctor recommended she take with her, in case of any complications.[73] MacKenzie must have been concerned about her health as she was reviewing her will. There was a bomb scare on her flight back to New York and Derek Morgan recalled, 'It dismayed her not a bit.'[74] The next communication between the women was in December when MacKenzie sent Lavin the first-reading agreement contract and 'a wee bit of money'. She also included some additional tear sheets of 'Trastevere' and noted 'The rest of the space is taken up with my love.'[75]

On 31 January 1972 Lavin wrote to MacKenzie, 'We are all so plunged in grief, sadness & despair at the Derry Killings that it's hard to write a letter at all.' Lavin was referring to the previous day when British had soldiers opened fire on unarmed civilians during a civil rights march on the Bogside area of Derry in Northern Ireland, killing thirteen people. The massacre became known as Bloody Sunday. The events of the previous day put a black cloud on the good news Lavin wanted to share with MacKenzie, which was that Harvard had awarded her the Ella Lyman Cabot Award and a 'small university in Massachusetts' was awarding her an honorary degree and 'bringing me over by ship, first class etc with three weeks luxury accommodation, study etc and a car'. The university was also giving Lavin $2,000 to give a reading. However, it was difficult for her to enjoy her good news 'when the black flags are going up for tomorrow's day of mourning'.[76]

In April Lavin sent MacKenzie 'A Mug of Water' but she was feeling 'a great lack of confidence' because the magazine had rejected so many stories. She noted, 'The sad thing about this is that without a story to hold us together we are both so busy we don't get to writing the letters – personal letters of concern & love – but both are there.'[77] 'A Mug of Water' was promptly rejected: it was too long and Shawn felt that the ending was out of place.[78] MacKenzie took consolation in the fact that Lavin's work was being published in America again. She agreed with Lavin about the need for a story to keep them in touch, but only with regard to correspondence, for she often thought of Lavin and spoke of her with mutual friends. One of those acquaintances was

Joyce Hartman, whom MacKenzie had recently lunched with, and she was happy to pass on the news to Lavin that Houghton Mifflin were 'so proud to have you on their list'. MacKenzie also met Cullinan for lunch during which they spoke of Lavin and MacKenzie expressed how 'proud' they were to have her as a friend. MacKenzie was looking forward to Lavin's impending trip when she hoped they could 'have lunch and wail together'.[79]

In May 'The Shrine' was rejected. Again, length was an issue and the editors felt that some of the characters were not engaging enough. MacKenzie hated returning stories to Lavin: 'I'd save them all and have a Mary Lavin Annual Supplement.'[80] She suggested that both stories could go to into a literary quarterly or a new collection. She also advised Lavin to try *Redbook* and *McCall's* as they paid well for stories. 'A Mug of Water' was subsequently published in *The Southern Review* and 'The Shrine' was published in the *Sewanee Review* and both stories were anthologised in *The Shrine and Other Stories* (1977).[81] Lavin sent in another two stories, 'The Lily and the Rose' and 'The Motor Mower'.

While MacKenzie was on her three-week June vacation, Howard Moss let Lavin know that 'The Lily and the Rose' was rejected.[82] They were holding on to 'The Motor Mower' until MacKenzie's return on 22 June, but a day after she arrived back, she wrote to Lavin to let her know that it too was unsuccessful. 'Length and pace' were the main reason.[83] MacKenzie's sisters and some friends joined her during her holiday in Vermont. MacKenzie and Gennie were given the gift of a garter snakeskin when they were leaving, with instructions to rub it with Vaseline for preservation: 'We brought it along to New York – what else could we do? – and it's rubbed with Vaseline and waiting for disposition.'[84] MacKenzie returned from her holidays to the 'torrents' of Hurricane Agnes. *The New York Times* reported that 'It was one of the worst storms in half a century – and the most wide spread flood disaster in the nation's history. The toll: 18 dead in Florida ... more than 95 dead in the North ... scores missing ... thousands of homes and offices evacuated in Virgian [sic], Pennsylvania, New Jersey, Westchester and the southern tier of New York ... damage in the billions.'[85]

On 19 July 1972 Lavin sent MacKenzie the story 'Tom', and let her know that she would be revising it further. The story, titled after Lavin's father, Tom Lavin, contains many semi-autobiographical elements.

Lavin even wondered whether she should refer to him by his full name in the story.[86] In 'Tom', the narrator observes that her self-made father, who left school early, 'could read and write, but with difficulty'. She even wonders if his bad grammar is the reason her mother destroyed her love letters from him. The narrator, on the other hand, has hers treasured away. While Lavin's mother may have been embarrassed by his letters, *The Atlantic* saw fit to publish one that he wrote to his American boss and owner of Bective House, Charles Sumner Bird. 'The Race at Aintree' by Tom Lavin appeared in its December 1944 issue alongside one of his daughter's 'Gabriel Galloway' stories and articles by Jean-Paul Sartre and Raymond Chandler.[87] Tom Lavin wrote the letter on 17 November 1931 from Bective House in which he describes with delight the win of the estate's racing horse, Heartbreak Hill, at the Grand Sefton Steeplechase in Liverpool: 'The only thing I can say about the mare is that she must have wings on her heart, or otherwise she could never have performed as she has done.'[88] While it is possible that his daughter or the magazine corrected his grammar, there is no doubt as to where Lavin got her power of observation and gift of storytelling from, as is evident from the following passage:

> I had a good pair of field glasses and I never lost sight of the mare from start to finish. She was first across the first jump, – 2 lengths ahead, – then she was on even terms with 'Polorus Jack' and 'Cold Punch.' She came to the water jump with desperate determination as she was fighting for her head and she crossed the jump 3rd, taking off about 3 yards in front of it, and landing about 2 yards clear of it. You could hear everybody on the stand say 'Oh! what a jump!'

On 1 August MacKenzie sent Lavin a cable to let her know that they were accepting 'Tom', much to Lavin's relief after the string of rejections.[89] In October MacKenzie sent her the galleys and she was hopeful that it would be published before the end of the year. MacKenzie felt that Lavin ought to focus on the narrator's relationship with her father and not muddy it with 'the remorse she felt for loving her mother less' as she felt that was for a different story.[90] MacKenzie went ahead and made the necessary changes because Mick, who was in New York at the time, was confident that Lavin would approve of them. She would have preferred to have sent Lavin a working proof but, due to cutbacks at the magazine, they were no longer provided.

Lavin had revised all the rejected stories and they were anthologised in the new book, *A Memory and Other Stories*, which was published by Constable in the autumn. The collection contained the title story and only one *New Yorker* story, 'Trastevere'. It also included 'Asigh', 'Tomb of an Ancestor' and 'Villa Violetta'.[91] Benedict Kiely in his *Irish Times* review of the collection observed that the stories 'show her at the height of her powers, so that, as we should all know, is very high indeed'.[92] His article also mentioned Lavin's 'lovely little story for children', *The Second-Best Children in the World*. Lavin first mentioned the book, originally titled *Round the World & Back Again*, to MacKenzie back in November 1969.[93] As Lavin had hoped, Edward Ardizzone illustrated the volume.

MacKenzie sent Lavin the author's proof of 'Tom' on 6 December. The story was scheduled for 9 January, so she needed it returned as a matter of urgency. By 20 December the proof had still not arrived and so they had to push its publication back by a fortnight. MacKenzie gave Lavin her Christmas greetings and dispatched the first-reading agreement 'with gratitude and pride that we have your stories. The fact that we don't always keep [in touch] doesn't diminish one jot (isn't that your word?) our affection and admiration.'[94]

MacKenzie received the proof of 'Tom' on 8 January and endeavoured to make all the necessary changes including restoring sentences that Lavin regretted losing. She did not think that the final-query editor would have many questions. MacKenzie hoped that Lavin was enjoying her trip to London: 'Love for the new year, And I hope you're soon taken over by a new story you are really smitten with.'[95] She thought the publication of 'Tom' would be 'a good way to start the year'.[96]

'Tom' was published on 20 January 1973. Arthur Getz's cover depicts skiers on the slopes of a mountain. The issue contains one of Maeve Brennan's Long-Winded Lady pieces in the 'Talk of the Town' section, in which she describes getting a coffee at Bickford's on an 'icy cold' morning at 5 a.m.: 'I am wearing fur mukluks I bought at Lord and Taylor, and I pad along making no sound.' Bickford's on Eighth Avenue and 34th street was one of a chain of restaurants frequented by Jack Kerouac and Allen Ginsberg and other members of the beat generation. Woody Allen's 'The Early Essays' features on pages 32 and 33 of the magazine, followed by Lavin's 'Tom' on page 34. The story shares its nine pages with a poem, 'Rouault', by Van K. Brock and cartoons by William Steig, William Hamilton, Charles Addams and Mischa Richter.[97] Hamilton's cartoon depicts a couple getting dressed for a party, with the woman telling her husband: 'Now, remember. The Cochrans are not intellectuals, so please don't go on and on about "Jonathan Livingston Seagull."' According to *The New York Times*, 'the book dotting every beach towel' in the summer of 1972 was this bestselling novel by Richard Bach.[98]

MacKenzie sent Lavin a cheque for the end-of-the-year COLA and she passed on the news that Betty (Elizabeth Cullinan) 'spoke of that story ['Tom'] so warmly, of how much she had liked it' during their lunch the previous week.[99] Cullinan subsequently wrote to Lavin to tell her how much she enjoyed the story: 'I loved it so, and it was so exciting besides because reading it I kept thinking "She's into something different."'[100] In a later letter, she told her that it was 'the best of everything of yours'.[101] Lavin sent MacKenzie $5 for the magazine to airmail her some copies of the issue and asked her to send tear sheets if she had them. Five copies of the magazine were 'air-mail printed' to Lavin as MacKenzie explained: '(it's only 12 hours later than straight air-mail and a third as expensive). The mail desk says that $5.00 would pay for only one magazine sent first-class air-mail, or whatever they call it.'[102] 'Tom' was selected for *The Best American Short Stories 1974* collection, which also features stories by John Updike, William Sarayon, Arturo Vivante, Shirley Jackson and Alice Walker.

In February Benedict Kiely informed Lavin that MacKenzie was possibly retiring. Lavin was 'appalled' at the thought and wrote to MacKenzie, 'I feel as if the magazine was retiring'.[103] MacKenzie assured Lavin that she was not retiring and thought Kiely must have got that impression because she gave one of his recent submissions to Derek Morgan to handle because she had too much work on her plate, plus she thought they would both get along.[104] There then followed a long gap in their correspondence, but Lavin had been busy travelling and giving readings, among other engagements.[105] In June, Maxwell wrote to let Lavin know that MacKenzie was on holidays that month and had asked him to contact her about 'The Face of Hate', her story about the troubles in Northern Ireland, which she had sent to the magazine. Maxwell was sorry to deliver the news that it was not suitable because it was too long and was 'so openly tendentious'. He had been in Ireland with his family for a week and they stayed with Frank O'Connor's widow, Harriet, and her second husband, the former priest Maurice Sheehy, in Dalkey. Maxwell reminisced about his encounter with Lavin a few years earlier and told her, 'When I came to Molesworth Street I looked for you, and was disappointed when you didn't materialize.'[106]

In late July or early August, Lavin had written to Kay Boyle to compliment her on her work and to let her know that she had met her blonde daughter when she was in Paris. Boyle was a foreign correspondent for *The New Yorker* until she lost her job during the McCarthy era. In 1951 Boyle, who was then a European correspondent for the magazine, and her third husband, Baron Joseph von Franckenstein, were falsely accused of being members of the Communist Party, after which Boyle found herself blacklisted by publishers for many years. Boyle was equally complimentary about Lavin's writing and was curious as to which of her five daughters Lavin had met, since two of them, who were fair-haired, resided in Paris. Boyle reckoned that Lavin had met with Sharon, whose father was Ernest Walsh, the Irish American poet and editor of the short-lived but influential literary magazine *This Quarter*, which published work by Ezra Pound, James Joyce and Ernest Hemingway. Boyle delighted in informing Lavin that Sharon had remarried, this time to an Irishman, her 'favourite son-in-law'. She told Lavin that she was trying to finish a novel before classes began at San Francisco State University, where she taught creative writing.[107]

In September Houghton Mifflin brought out *A Memory and Other Stories* and sent Cullinan an advance copy. She loved the stories, particularly 'Villa Violetta' and in a Christmas card to Lavin said that the reviews were 'marvellous'.[108] Cullinan was working on another book of stories but she thought it unlikely that Houghton Mifflin would publish it. She was delighted that Lavin enjoyed her recent *New Yorker* story 'The Perfect Crime', which was published on 27 August 1973. Cullinan was looking forward to seeing Mick, who was due to travel to New York on 18 October for a few nights. Lavin hoped that MacKenzie would also be free to meet with him. However, the trip was postponed, much to MacKenzie's disappointment. She noted the long silence between them and let Lavin know that Joyce Hartman was very happy with the reaction to the new collection. The one review that MacKenzie read was 'lovely' and she hoped it would encourage people to purchase the book: 'Certainly your reputation is enriched.' The review she read may well have been the one Joyce Carol Oates wrote for *The New York Times*, in which she observed that Lavin 'has long been recognized as one of the finest of living short-story writers'.[109] MacKenzie enclosed two cuttings of reviews that the press clipping office sent to her because she thought it would be nice for Lavin to give copies to loved ones 'who care that you are being written of as the literary personage you've been for a good many years'. She asked Lavin to let her know how she, her daughters and 'grandbaby' were keeping and was curious to know what Lavin was writing: 'I long for a story from you that we will take. I was thinking the other day that there is a difference – that a difference exists – between a story that settles right into a magazine and a story that settles comfortably only into a book. I have to give some thought as to why.'[110]

On 13 December MacKenzie airmailed Lavin her first-reading agreement contract and cheque in time for Christmas: 'It's no gift, being the expression of our gratitude to you – well, maybe a reverse gift – and it's surely no surprise after all these years. But it is Christmas and a special feeling comes with it. My love, too.'[111] Lavin wrote to MacKenzie on St Stephen's Day to let her know that she never received the first-reading agreement forms. She also had not received a letter from Valdi, who was now in Nicaragua with her family. Lavin blamed the dire postal system but she must have been worried about Valdi because she mentioned to MacKenzie that it was the one-year anniversary of the Managua earthquake.[112] Lavin was quite deflated because although she was working away on stories, she was not producing any that *The New Yorker* wanted: 'I am writing more than ever in my life but I seem to be writing further & further from the New Yorker but I don't think anyone really cares … I've reached the age when nothing matters very much anymore except for learning that fact. And it's a big, big living fact.' Lavin was going to write to Cullinan for the first time that year: 'She may not be a great writer – what woman can be? – but she is made of the same stuff that great writers are made of – & – for a woman that's pretty good!'[113]

On 1 January 1974 Lavin was sent an advance on the next Houghton Mifflin volume, which was near completion.[114] She received

The New Yorker first-reading contract the following day. MacKenzie was sorry that they were not accepting Lavin's work and told her, 'Of course we care about you – as a writer and a person, too – and I've been sadder than you probably realize that so many recent stories have had to go back to you.'[115]

Lavin had written a new story that she thought would appeal to MacKenzie. She had torn to pieces the recently rejected ones, but thought they were still too long for *The New Yorker*. MacKenzie was saddened at having to reject Lavin's next story, 'The Check-out Girl': 'I know that your prestige as a writer does not rest on The New Yorker, but I feel that you have enhanced our prestige as a literary publication and it fills me with sadness that we have not taken a story from you in such a long time.'[116] She was consoled by the fact that Lavin's work was being published elsewhere and had 'an unfailingly intelligent and appreciative critical reception, and readers'.[117] MacKenzie acknowledged that this was 'Small comfort! No, it is; we seem not to be the magazine for a number of stories that I wish to be published.' She explained that the delay in returning the story was because she had been back in hospital and was on reduced hours at the magazine but let Lavin know that she was recovering well.[118]

Lavin was sorry to hear that MacKenzie had taken ill and hoped that she would be 'in flying form' for her impending visit to New York in April.[119] She was travelling to the United States to receive the Éire Society of Boston Gold Medal at the society's annual dinner on 20 April 1974.[120] Cullinan invited her to stay a few nights with her but she could not extend an open invitation due to the fact that her father was ill and she was 'living on borrowed New Yorker money' after having a story rejected.[121] She met Lavin at the boat, the SS *France*, when it arrived in New York on 11 April.[122] In the end, Lavin never made contact with MacKenzie when she was in the city because she had injured her knee and ended up spending most of the time laid up in bed in the Algonquin. Lavin returned home very sick and bedridden and in her downcast state she did not think she would ever return to America.

Lavin had heard that MacKenzie was back in hospital after an accident – this perhaps relates to when she was knocked down by a car.[123] Lavin was also told that MacKenzie was busy writing a book.

The novel, *The Wine of Astonishment*, was published in 1974 by Viking Press and MacKenzie dedicated the book to her friend Doris Fletcher Borner.[124] *The Wine of Astonishment* centres on two unmarried sisters in New York State who find love after the death of their domineering mother. Isaac Bashevis Singer wrote of the novel, 'With this book Rachel MacKenzie has entered American literature … her voice is both tender and vigorous.' Josephine Jacobsen, whose poetry was published by *The New Yorker*, thought the novel captured, 'A marvellous sense of place, and time, and the nuances of a most acute perception, make *The Wine of Astonishment* an exceptional joy.'[125] Anatole Broyard in his *New York Times* review, 'Good Wine, but Not Vintage', considered it 'a good novel' but 'not a novel for everybody'.[126]

In September Lavin wrote a letter to MacKenzie and Maxwell letting them know that she had given their names as referees to the Rockefeller Foundation for the Villa Bellagio residency on Lake Como and asked them to, 'Speak as well as you can of me if they write which they may not.'[127] MacKenzie responded that they would be 'honored' to vouch for her and wondered how she could think otherwise. She could already envisage Lavin 'basking on Lake Como – studying, writing' and lapping up the sunshine.

MacKenzie broke the news to Lavin that she was taking the following year off to write another novel that she had already begun. MacKenzie and Gennie were going to their sister Ruth's 'big, heavy, comfortable house' in Ohio, where they would have their own space and privacy. The arrangement suited Ruth after her father-in-law, who was ninety-six when he died, left his house to her but its contents were distributed equally among his seven children and so Ruth wanted them both 'for laughter and affection, and our furniture'. Ruth also did not have the financial resources for the house's upkeep so the three sisters were setting up home together for the year. MacKenzie would likely stay in a hotel when she returned to New York.[128] She assured Lavin that she would be well looked after because William Maxwell, Robert Henderson and Derek Morgan, 'a long admirer of yours', would still be at the magazine. She hoped Lavin would be successful in getting the residency: 'I will wish for you the Rockefeller gift, and you wish for me the gift of a novel. How's that for an exchange? Oh Mary, I wish Lake Como for you without one thing in exchange. What's more, I think it will be yours.'[129]

Lavin was delighted to hear that MacKenzie was writing another novel and she told her, 'I refuse to say goodbye till Jan – & it's not goodbye anyway.' She let her know that Mick was going to purchase *The Wine of Astonishment* for her while on a flying visit to the United States in November and that he would try to meet up with her and Maxwell. Lavin wondered if MacKenzie would consider the Rockefeller residency for herself as a break from Ohio. She also enquired after Cullinan because all the letters she posted to her were returned marked 'address unknown' and she wondered if she had 'gone to earth so deep she can't be found'.[130]

On 20 December MacKenzie mailed Lavin the renewal contract for her first-reading agreement with the encouraging words, 'It says, as it does each year, that we value you especially and know how you have enriched this magazine; we know that you will again.' She also sent her love for Christmas and the New Year and hoped that Lavin was writing her memoirs. MacKenzie assured Lavin that her sabbatical was 'not a matter of goodbye' and ended her letter, 'Wish me good luck – I feel bereaved to be leaving – but don't think goodbye.'[131]

10
'Hanging Crêpe'
1975–1992

Rachel MacKenzie's hopes for Mary Lavin's Bellagio residency came true and she went to the writers' retreat in the winter of 1975.[1] From 1975 onwards there was no further written communication between Mary Lavin and Rachel MacKenzie, although MacKenzie continued to work part-time until 1979.[2] The two women remained in touch and met when Lavin was in New York in 1979.[3] *The New Yorker*'s correspondence with Lavin in the magazine's records declines dramatically after MacKenzie's departure, totalling ten letters in thirteen years, only one of which is from Lavin, compared to over four hundred exchanged, mostly with MacKenzie, over a seventeen-year period.[4]

It is harder, therefore, to give a comprehensive picture of Lavin's interaction with *The New Yorker* during this later period. The gaps in the archive are significant in themselves. The possible reasons for the decline in correspondence are manifold. It is possible that Lavin was not submitting many stories during this period or that she was not in as frequent contact with her new editors as she had been with MacKenzie. In addition, a lot of business was conducted over the telephone, as indicated on her drafts from this period. Clearly, some of Lavin's letters are missing, as evidenced in the responses from the editors.[5] The archives, to some extent, reflect Lavin's career trajectory. At the pinnacle of her success with *The New Yorker* in the late 1950s and 60s, the letters are fittingly copious, but in the 1970s and 80s, when she was having less work published, there is congruently a sharp decline in the correspondence. Lavin became increasingly despondent about the long string of rejections during her later years with *The New Yorker*, having failed to make a sale to the magazine in the final twelve years of her contract.

It must have been a source of comfort to Lavin that her contribution to literature was getting recognition in Ireland during this period. On

24 January 1975 she was awarded the Irish Academy of Letters' Lady Gregory Medal, having served two terms as its president between 1971 and 1975. The medal was presented by the Irish president Cearbhall Ó Dálaigh at an event at the Shelbourne Hotel.[6] In March she was voted Meath Personality of the Year 'for the consistent beauty of her literary work'.[7] Zack Bowen's book on Lavin was also published that year.[8] In November 1977 Lavin became a member of the Irish Academy of Letters Council alongside Seamus Heaney, Benedict Kiely, Mervyn Wall, Monk Gibbon and John Montague. She was bestowed the American Irish Foundation Literary Award in 1979. William V. Shannon, the United States Ambassador to Ireland, wrote to inform Lavin that she was chosen for the award 'in recognition of your outstanding contributions to Irish and, indeed, world literature'. She was to be paid $10,000 in five instalments over a five-year period, commencing August 1979, with the condition that the recipient reside 'in Ireland for ten of the twelve months and devote his or her time to creative work'.[9]

Significantly, in January 1976, after the mandatory retirement policy came into effect, there was a turnover of staff in *The New Yorker*'s fiction department.[10] William Maxwell and Robert Henderson left and new editors were appointed, including Charles 'Chip' McGrath,[11] Frances Kiernan and Daniel Menaker. The correspondence from this latter period is with Lavin's later *New Yorker* editors, Derek Morgan and Chip McGrath. Cullinan promptly wrote to Lavin about the reorganisation: 'Maxwell has retired and I miss him though the fellow I have is fine and I like him a lot.' She explained that Maxwell gave her the 'choice of the lot and I picked Chip – Charles McGrath. Very intelligent, very sympathetic and very receptive. Think about it.' Cullinan thought he was going to travel to Ireland that autumn and wondered if Lavin would meet him: 'With an eye to when Rachel retires permanently?'

Lavin had asked Cullinan to buy her a nightdress but Cullinan was not in a position to purchase it for her as she was 'at rock bottom as far as money and money prospects go', having had two stories rejected by *The New Yorker* and none in store and so she was 'terrified of spending a dime that I can't instantly recover'. Nonetheless, she was heartened to see that Lavin had a story, 'Perpetua', in the works and reflected: 'New Yorker acceptance and New Yorker money and New Yorker dealings are purely and simply the most satisfactory.'[12] Cullinan's story 'Life After

Death' appeared in the magazine on 26 January and she was greatly relieved when *The New Yorker* accepted 'Estelle' towards the end of February.[13]

The New Yorker had rejected Lavin's story 'Perpetua' in 1961 under the title 'The Bog Light'.[14] She renamed it 'Eterna', a name conjured by Mick, after William Shawn pointed out that the magazine had already published a story by that name.[15] Derek Morgan worked on the revisions with Lavin, mainly via lengthy telephone conversations.[16] 'Eterna' was published in *The New Yorker* on 8 March 1976. The cover by Charles E. Martin is of a young child leaving a swanky Manhattan apartment block about to walk a dog. Lavin's story shared its pages with Richard Hugo's poem 'The Sandbanks' and several cartoons. Stan Hunt's cartoon depicts a group of arguing businessmen with the caption 'Never mind giving us the facts; we know the facts. The question is: What are we going to put out for public consumption?' The issue contains Roger Angell's obituary of the Irish American humourist Frank Sullivan, who contributed his first *New Yorker* piece in 1926 and was known for his Christmas poems. When the staff of *The New Yorker* learned of his death, they read his clip book and found a reference to Lord Dunsany and then the parentheses '(short for "Dunsanything to the wife about where you seen me last night")'. Cullinan wrote to Lavin on the day the story was published: 'I loved Eterna and it was such a treat to open the magazine and find it. It was like such a breeze, such a breath of fresh air.'[17]

A few days after 'Eterna' appeared in *The New Yorker*, an interview with Lavin featured in *The Irish Times* in which the interviewer, Maev Kennedy, observed:

> One of the problems peculiar to the form [the short story] was that Mary Lavin's writing brought her no real financial security until she was offered in 1960, a contract by *The New Yorker* magazine, still her main market. She says that she felt as grateful to *The New Yorker* in those early days as she was for the Guggenheim Fellowships which she was awarded in 1959 and 1960, because they gave her enough financial security to risk everything on the short story, a perilous business.

In the interview Lavin admitted that there were times when she regretted being a writer: 'Life could have been much easier. I love family life, I love my house and my garden, and I've never had enough time to devote to them.' But she felt compelled to write and vowed to continue until she was 'no longer able to do the job well'.[18]

After the publication of 'Eterna', Charles McGrath began handling Lavin's work. McGrath was also a *New Yorker* writer. His first contribution to the magazine was a fiction piece, 'The Worst', which appeared on 14 October 1974. McGrath knew Lavin's daughter Caroline and hoped to meet Lavin as well one day. It is possible that he met Caroline, who had joined *The Irish Times* as a journalist the previous year, when she visited New York in 1976.[19] Cullinan had invited Caroline to stay with her on her first night in the city during that excursion as she presumed that she would prefer to reside with the Bearys or O'Malleys for the remainder of her visit. McGrath met Lavin only once when she was in New York, likely visiting Cullinan, and has fond memories of working with her: 'I remember her with great warmth and vitality, and I got the sense that she had become a mentor – a mother figure – to a whole generation of younger Irish writers.'

McGrath encouraged Lavin to send in her stories, in the hope that one would be accepted. He was courteous and affable in his dealings with her and it is clear from his correspondence that he held her in high regard. McGrath was a 'huge fan' of Lavin's writing since his high school days and always looked forward to reading her stories.[20] In May of 1977 they had been working on her story 'A Walk on the Cliff'. McGrath was impressed with Lavin's revisions to the story and thought the ending was 'just about perfect'. He liked the story and gave her expansive and considerate feedback. Although Lavin had cut the text in half, they were both of the opinion that it needed further editing.[21] Despite his hopes, the story was rejected due to its length. The editors also took issue 'with the emotional shape of the story'. McGrath was apologetic for the decision. [22] Lavin, as usual, was free to rework the text and return it for consideration, but he let her know that the other editors were not as keen on the work, so as not to get her hopes up. McGrath took comfort in the fact that Lavin had a stock of new stories.[23]

In May Constable published *The Shrine and Other Stories*. The collection featured Lavin's final two *New Yorker* stories, 'Tom' and 'Eterna'; two previously published stories, 'The Shrine' and 'The Mug of Water'; and 'Senility'. 'Senility' was not mentioned in Lavin's correspondence with *The New Yorker.* However, according to A. A. Kelly, it was rejected by the magazine because it featured 'the shame of incontinence'.[24] Benedict Kiely, in his *Irish Times* review of *The Shrine and Other Stories*, wrote in praise of Lavin: 'She also seems to me to be a writer who wrote at her best and then, next time round, manages to be a little better: and with her you are always meeting new people.'[25] Anthony Burgess revealed in his *Irish Press* review of the collection that he did 'not go much in awe of novelists, even the great ones', yet he admitted, 'I envy the skill of Mary Lavin, and have done so for years.'[26] It was some months later before Cullinan wrote to Lavin to express her great admiration for the book: 'But I love these stories so, all of them. Reading them one after the other it becomes so immaterial whether or not The New Yorker even published them; the great thing is that they were written and that there are more to come. There's no one else whose work I enjoy and in the particular way as much as I do yours.' She was deeply apologetic for her delay in getting in touch about the book but she had only had recently returned to New York after a teaching stint at the Iowa Writers' Workshop.[27]

Lavin sent Kiely's review to McGrath, which he duly returned, remarking, 'It's a fine piece, by another fine writer, and I'm grateful to you for letting me see it.'[28] He enquired whether *The Shrine and Other Stories* would be published in the US, to which Lavin responded, 'Of course I have a publisher for the new book. At my age it would be a poor job if I hadn't!'[29] It seems a rather flippant remark given all the difficulties she encountered in trying to secure a suitable American publisher, but Lavin was now happily housed with Houghton Mifflin, who brought out the collection in the autumn. *The New York Times* literary critic Anatole Broyard was not as enthusiastic about the collection as Burgess and Kiely.[30] He observed that 'Tom' 'opens with the sort of stylized reminiscence that sometimes appears to be endemic in stories in The New Yorker magazine, where this one was first published. It is the kind of material that is written too well to dismiss, but exists for no other reason.' Broyard found 'Eterna' implausible and considered 'The Mug of Water' to be the best story in the collection.

In July McGrath rejected the 'The Check-Out Girl', which Lavin had resubmitted. MacKenzie was still working behind the scenes as McGrath informed Lavin that she thought she had read an earlier draft of the story. MacKenzie remembered correctly: she had rejected it on 27 February 1974. Although it was a close call, the overall view was that 'the story was just a little too slight for its length'. McGrath found the story 'both very light and funny' and so was sorry about the decision. Again, he was confident that Lavin could sell the story to another publication.

McGrath informed Lavin that he was taking his annual leave in August but that other editors could handle her work if she urgently needed feedback – if not, her stories would be held until his return.[31] Lavin opted to wait until McGrath came back from his holidays, when she sent him a 'fairly final draft' of 'The First Snow', that was 'totally uncorrected for readability'. Lavin told him that she loved Elizabeth Cullinan's story 'A Good Loser', published in the magazine on 15 August 1977. In the story, a woman who works for an ad agency in New York City returns to Dublin for a month's visit, ten years after she had lived there when she was twenty-six. Lavin let McGrath know that Mick was due to go to New York in October, where he would be staying at the Algonquin, and that he might pay a visit to *The New Yorker* offices.[32]

'The First Snow' was rejected and this time McGrath agreed with the decision. The editors felt it was 'too strong' and unbalanced and needed to be more subtle.[33] In December McGrath was incredibly sorry to deliver the unhappy news that 'A Family Likeness' was also rejected due to it being 'too long and drawn out' and that the strained relationships between the mother and daughter was somewhat exaggerated. He wished Lavin a happy Christmas and passed on his regards to Caroline.

Lavin did in fact return to America in the autumn of 1978 and she and Mick visited Eudora Welty in October. Lavin revealed in an interview that it took her 'a lifetime to get to Jackson, Mississippi' and that the three days she stayed with Welty would 'always be a highlight in my life'.[34] Mick wrote to Welty of how important the trip was to Lavin, that it had given her back 'her own sense of place'.[35] They also visited William Faulkner's home in Oxford, Mississippi. Cullinan had asked Lavin if she wished to give a reading at her alma mater, Marymount College in New York, while she was in America but nothing seems to have come of this proposition.[36]

In the next and final letter in the records, dated 2 July 1979, McGrath rejected Lavin's story 'Lethe', because the ending was 'really a kind of false climax, I think, and one that's a little unfair to the reader'. He was sorry to be giving Lavin such a disappointing response, especially when she had only returned to writing after encountering a number of personal difficulties in the previous months: Mick had undergone a back operation and Caroline had been in an accident. She had also revised 'A Walk in the Cliff', but it too was rejected. Although McGrath thought the story was much improved, the other editors, including Shawn, felt it was 'a little too flat'. McGrath was particularly regretful because he had advised her to cut it but he did think her revisions had improved the story considerably and that she would be able to sell it elsewhere.

McGrath was heartened to see that Lavin was back writing again and looked forward to receiving more stories from her. He also hoped that the 'damned strike' would end. McGrath was referring to the Irish postal strike that began on 19 February 1979 and lasted eighteen weeks. McGrath got wind of the strike because he wrote a letter to Neil Jordan to thank him for sending him his book, which he really enjoyed, but his letter was returned to him. McGrath had subsequently made contact with Jordan's agent in London but he asked Lavin to thank him on his behalf if she came into contact with him. The book was Jordan's first novel, *The Past*, which was published the following year by Jonathan Cape. Although the strike was officially over when McGrath mentioned it to Lavin, the backlog of post took over two months to clear and first-class mail or parcels were not being accepted for a number of weeks.[37]

It must have been disheartening for Lavin to have received so many rejections in a row. The same issues kept arising with each of the rejected texts: they were too long, too slow to start, and the magazine felt that she had a tendency to over-embellish them. Lavin, by this stage, was familiar with the magazine's formulae and requirements, but she still continued to submit stories that did not meet them. Lavin did not move with the trends in order to fit in but instead remained true to her stories. Mary Gordon notes Lavin's resistance to writing for popularity: 'Her [Lavin's] lightly worn insistence on writing what it was she wanted to write – even though no one else thought it was important, would constitute a daring, even dangerous position.'[38]

Lavin travelled again to the US with Mick in September of 1979 to embark on a reading tour, which included a reading with the poet Elizabeth Bishop at Harvard and a reading at the Library of Congress in Washington, while Mick was on a recruitment mission for international students. The couple travelled on the Russian ship SS *Mikail Lermontov*, which arrived in New York on 18 September, where they were met by Elizabeth Cullinan, John Beary and the Irish Consular Service.[39] Lavin's reading with Bishop, which was a benefit for *Ploughshares* literary magazine, was due to take place at the Sanders Theatre in Harvard on 7 October. Lavin's friend Anne Francis Cavanaugh recalled Lavin receiving a phone call to inform her that the reading was cancelled after Bishop died during the night. This was followed by another call telling her that the reading would become a tribute to Bishop: 'The reading was on – friends, students, faculty and writers would read favorite passages from the work of Elizabeth Bishop. The first half of the evening would be a tribute. Then Mary would read. We all sat in silence. Then Mary, who always wore black, stood, pulled herself to full courage and stated, "I will wear my new black dress."' Lavin read 'Happiness'.[40]

Lavin and MacKenzie dined together at the Algonquin during this trip but by then MacKenzie's health had deteriorated considerably. She died only a few months later, on 28 March 1980, aged seventy, at Fieldston Lodge nursing home in the Bronx, two months before she was due to be bestowed the Wells College Alumnae Award.[41] Sadly, MacKenzie never got to publish her third work. Reacting to the news of her death, William Shawn commented that MacKenzie was 'one of the strongest and most passionately devoted of our editors and gave an enormous amount of affection, support and a sensitive response to the writers she worked with and what they were doing. And they seemed to flourish when working with her.' Isaac Bashevis Singer, who had a deep admiration for MacKenzie, declared: 'I think that American literature has lost a giant, one of the last people who understood literature thoroughly from the beginning to the end.' He added, 'It is for me personally a sad day to have lost such a great person, and I intend to write about her and to think about her as long as I live.'[42] Singer, true to his word, dedicated his next book, *The Collected Stories*, to the memory of Rachel MacKenzie.[43] *The New York Times* obituary mentioned that MacKenzie was 'an accomplished cook and hostess and an avid gardener' and noted: 'She is survived by her two sisters, Geneva Jacobs of New York City and Ruth M. Rhodes of Wooster, Ohio.'[44]

A memorial service was held at Madison Avenue Presbyterian Church and her ashes were interred in Auburn, New York.

There are no *New Yorker* records concerning Lavin from 1980 onwards except for contracts.[45] In 1985 Constable brought out *The Stories of Mary Lavin, Vol. 3*, which featured six *New Yorker* stories: 'Happiness', 'In the Middle of the Fields', 'The Lucky Pair', 'Heart of Gold', 'The Cuckoo Spit' and 'One Summer'. That same year Constable also published *A Family Likeness and Other Stories*. This was Lavin's only collection since she started writing for the magazine – with the exception of *Selected Stories* brought out by Macmillan in 1959 – not to include a *New Yorker* story. With this collection Lavin made a clean break from *The New Yorker*.[46]

In 1985 S. I. Newhouse's Advance Publications took over *The New Yorker* magazine with the initial promise that nothing would change.[47] In January 1987 William Shawn, the magazine's editor of thirty-five years, was forced to retire, which led to great dissent at the magazine. Shawn had intended for McGrath, his deputy editor, to be his successor but Robert 'Bob' Gottlieb was announced as his replacement.[48] Gottlieb was sent a letter signed by 154 *New Yorker* staff and contributors, including J. D. Salinger, Howard Moss, Saul Steinberg and Janet Malcolm, calling on him to resign.

The New York Times observed that the 'protest letter was drafted by a committee of six whose names were not revealed. It was also scrutinized and corrected by the magazine's fact checkers and proofreaders – as with any piece of copy at The New Yorker.' According to *The Los Angeles Times* Calvin Trillin, Roger Angell, Janet Malcolm, Philip Hamburger, Lawrence Wechsler, Bill McKibbin and Mark Singer drafted the document, which stated, 'it is our strange and powerfully held conviction that only an editor who has been a long-standing member of the staff will have a reasonable chance of assuring our continuity, cohesion, and independence'.[49] Gottlieb delivered his reply to Shawn during Shawn's regular lunch at the Algonquin. While Gottlieb understood the concerns conveyed in the letter, he declined to relinquish the post and was 'looking forward to knowing and working with you all'.[50]

Many viewed Shawn's departure as the beginning of the end for *The New Yorker*. Elizabeth Cullinan said that when Shawn was fired it became a different magazine and lost its originality.[51] With Shawn out of the picture, the company took a more business-like approach in its dealings with writers.

Lavin did not receive her customary first-reading renewal agreement that December. She was one of many. Charles McGrath recollected that there were significant changes in the magazine in the 1980s: 'As I recall there was a general pruning of the contract list which had grown so large that even the modest payments we made to writers for signing on were beginning to add up, and we regretfully stopped offering contracts to writers who hadn't been productive for several years. Lavin was not the only one, in other words. There were several, and it was painful all around.' Lavin, who had been on a contract with *The New Yorker* for eleven years with no acceptances, would have been an obvious target for culling. Although McGrath was very keen to get Lavin's work published in the magazine, he observed of her later writing, 'That we didn't publish more, frankly, is because most of the work we saw then didn't seem as good as the earlier stories.'[52] Lavin understandably felt somewhat abandoned by the magazine that had once championed her writing and paid her so generously. However, the cold truth was that *The New Yorker* was publishing a different kind of story in the late 1970s and 80s.

Although Lavin was no longer writing for *The New Yorker*, her friends and fellow authors kept her informed of happenings at the magazine. In 1988 Cullinan discussed a book she was writing about *The New Yorker*, titled *Harm's Way*.[53] Cullinan, who once told Lavin that she would 'give her right arm to be an editor' at the magazine, had now lost hope in it and commented that she could not 'imagine that any of my *New Yorker* stories could have got published today; fads and gimmicks are the style, shallow and pretentious stuff'.[54] Cullinan completed her third novel shortly before she died in 2020, under a different title, *Starting From Scratch*.[55] The as-yet-to-be published work is a semi-autobiographical account of her early days at *The New Yorker*. Cullinan's second and most recent novel, *A Change of Scene*, was released in 1982. It features a 26-year-old New Yorker who travels to Dublin for a year where she befriends Oona Ross, who is described in the book's blurb as 'the chaotic and generous novelist'. Cullinan revealed that Ross was based on Lavin: 'Yes, Maura is Mary Lavin and so is Oona in *A Change of Scene*.'[56]

In the story, Lad Lane is clearly identifiable: 'It was only a couple of blocks to Merrion Square, and another short block brought us to the lane, a dirt road between two stone walls with a row of wicket doors. Parked next to one was a dusty Morris Minor that I recognized as the car

Oona Ross and her daughters had been leaning against in the newspaper picture I'd seen.' Cullinan's story is particularly poignant because the mews was auctioned on 2 June 1982.[57] Lavin and Mick, who were suffering from ill health, made the decision to sell the mews as they were spending most of their time in Bective. They then bought an apartment in Gilford Place in Sandymount, so as to have a base near the city.

Despite her problems, Lavin continued to manage her career and sought advice from fellow authors. Letters from Eudora Welty and the poet and translator Patience Ross from the late 1980s reveal that Lavin was still encountering difficulties with literary agents and publishers and with the reprinting of her work.[58] On 4 April 1988 Eudora Welty wrote to Lavin of her great concern that she was not receiving her letters as she was unable to decipher the address from her handwriting, so she was unsure as to whether it was Gilford Acres or Gilford Pines ('only a masterpiece of handwriting could bring that off'). She sympathised with Lavin's various predicaments and wrote to her, 'I think about you every day. Your plight about your whole life's work being at the present moment out of print in the U.S., your native land, and the blow this has been to you now in the ordeals you and Mick have been going through with your health – it's absurd and outrageous on the face of it.'[59]

Lavin informed Welty that Patience Ross was going to try to sort out her publishing dilemma and Welty hoped 'that the tide has turned in all of it, and your mind and heart have been relieved and lifted'.[60] She longed to see Lavin again and suggested that she come over to Ireland. With all the confusion over Lavin's address, Welty was going to use their 'dear friend' Ross as an intermediary. Ross told Lavin that she had suffered a minor stroke and thought that Welty had suffered one also. The friendship between Ross and Lavin went back many years. Lavin and her first husband, William, used to visit her in Sussex, where she lived with her long-term partner, Louise Hoyt Porter.

Ross had been a literary advisor at A. M. Heath and was one of the agents who handled Brian O'Nolan.[61] She consulted with one of the house's literary agents, Mark Hamilton, on Lavin's predicament but he gave her the disheartening news that after the significant gap and changes in the arena of publishing and literary agency, they would not be a suitable firm for Lavin.[62] Ross suggested that Lavin try Virago or Women's Press, both feminist publishing houses, to see if they would consider reissuing her work.[63] Ross died the following year, in 1989. Lavin kept in contact with Ben Glazebrook and on 12 January 1989 she observed that she had been with him for twenty-five years since Constable published *The Stories of Mary Lavin, Vol. 1* in 1964: 'They have been good years, Ben, and I am grateful for them, but I think the time has come now to reconsider what to do with the past work.'[64] She also mentioned that she was working on her autobiography.

In 1989 Lavin sold her beloved Abbey Farm, as she explained in a letter to Welty: 'It was due to the fact that Mick and I were becoming increasingly unable to maintain it, so lonely and far from the road, and particularly after the unexpected series of illnesses and operations we both had. It was essential to come to Dublin.'[65] In 1987 Lavin had been successfully treated for bowel cancer and Mick was suffering from heart issues on top of other ailments including a damaged hip. Lavin was broken-hearted at the decision. On 12 December 1989 Lavin wrote to John McGahern and divulged that she sold Bective 'in sheer panic' after a spate of unfortunate events, 'and that loss I will never get over'. Lavin had intended for one of her daughters to inherit the farm, but none of them wanted it.[66]

Mick died on 29 December 1990. Their good friend Maurice Harmon observed in his *Irish Times* tribute to Scott: 'Known to many as Mary Lavin's husband, he was content to live in the shadow of her brilliance' and he concluded the piece: 'It seems certain that his unquenchable loyalty to the slip of a girl he met in UCD 60 years ago and who was at his bedside on the afternoon of his death will be remembered forever.'[67] Lavin had to cope with her great loss and living alone. In 1992 the members of Aosdána elected Lavin as the first woman Saoi (wise one), the highest honour awarded, 'in recognition of creative work which has made an outstanding contribution to the arts in Ireland'.[68] Louis le Brocquy was also awarded the title that year for his achievements in the visual arts. The previous three Saoithe were Samuel Beckett, Seán Ó Faoláin and Patrick Collins. At this juncture Lavin was eighty years old and living in Newtownpark House nursing home in Blackrock, County Dublin. Despite ill health she attended the ceremony on 23 February, accompanied by her daughters, where President Mary Robinson presented her and le Brocquy with a gold torc.

In June 1992 *An Arrow in Flight*, a documentary to mark the occasion of Lavin's eightieth birthday, was televised on RTÉ One and featured her daughter Caroline, Eavan Boland, Thomas Kilroy, Maurice Harmon and

Nuala O'Faolain amongst others, paying tribute. On 11 July the writer and editor Janet E. Dunleavy sent Lavin 'clippings concerning a major event at *The New Yorker*', presumably relating to the controversial appointment of 38-year-old Tina Brown as the magazine's new editor, after Gottlieb resigned.[69] Deirdre Carmody reported, 'The news, which spread like wildfire throughout the publishing industry, was as juicy as it was unexpected.'[70] Dunleavy divulged that 'everyone says that's the end of the magazine as we've known it, and all sorts of *New Yorker* writers and readers are hanging crêpe'. She suggested that Lavin should write her reminiscences of the magazine, which she offered to include in her upcoming G. K. Hall book: 'It would be a great story to tell – and certainly would be publishable.'[71]

The last apparent correspondence from *The New Yorker* to Lavin was on 28 October 1992 when Owen Ketherry wrote that he would happily pass on a letter to Elizabeth Cullinan on her behalf.[72] Sadly, Lavin seemed to have had lost contact with Cullinan.[73] It is also sad to reflect that Lavin, whose work featured in the magazine during its heyday, now received an impersonal one-line response from an anagram of *The New Yorker.*

Although *The New Yorker* began publishing fewer of Lavin's stories in her later years and ultimately ended her contract, it is comforting to know that she only wrote what pleased her during this period, as she revealed to Eavan Boland in 1988: 'I wrote only what I wanted to write. I like to think that, especially in my middle and later years, anything I wrote was something which I wanted very much to say.'[74] *The New Yorker* has to be credited with inspiring Lavin to write after the death of her husband William and for elevating her profile internationally. Also due recognition must be given to J. D. Salinger for introducing Lavin to *The New Yorker*, as she acknowledged in a letter to the magazine: 'And as I have said before, but could not say too often, if you NEVER take a story you have done a great deal by your encouragement, and I will never cease to be grateful to you, nor to be amazed at the fact that my friend Mr. Salinger should go to the trouble of bringing us together.' Had Salinger not suggested Lavin as a potential *New Yorker* contributor to William Maxwell, it is possible that her work would never have appeared in its pages.

Postscript

Mary Lavin never wrote about her years with *The New Yorker* but she continued to revise her stories for a new collection, which her daughter Elizabeth began to assemble before Lavin moved to the nursing home: 'Mary had been reshaping certain stories on and off since before I left Ireland in the late seventies, for inclusion in a collected volume. I returned home in September '92 to find the residue of this work, not yet in book form. I was invited to step into her shoes. This is the result.'[1] The 'result' was *In a Café and Other Stories*, which was edited by Elizabeth and published by Town House and Country House in 1995. Of the sixteen stories selected, four were originally published in *The New Yorker*, including 'In the Middle of the Fields', 'Tom', 'Trastevere' and the title story. Lavin, whose health had deteriorated considerably, was noticeably 'perkier' after the launch of the book.[2]

Mary Lavin died on 25 March 1996 at the age of eighty-three. Her passing was front-page news in the Irish press and was reported in *The New York Times*, *The Los Angeles Times* and *The London Times*, among other international newspapers. Maurice Harmon in *The Irish Times* observed that Lavin 'holds a commanding position as a short story writer, nationally and internationally, a position all the more likely to endure because it has not been dependent on political and social developments in Ireland or on international literary trends'.[3] William Trevor in his *Guardian* obituary of Lavin noted that, 'The short story of today owes her a very great deal.'[4]

Benedict Kiely, Maeve Binchy, Maurice Harmon, Justice Hugh O'Flaherty, Pauline Bewick and Taoiseach John Bruton were among the 300 mourners who attended Lavin's removal at the Star of the Sea Church in Sandymount. Lavin was buried in the family plot in Saint Mary's Cemetery in Navan by the River Boyne, near to her beloved Abbey Farm in Bective. Michael Holohan composed the aptly titled piano piece *By a River* for the funeral. Lavin's daughters had the epitaph 'Let me come inland always' inscribed on the headstone, taken from her poem of the same title. Valdi believed that the line 'must have been written for her [Lavin's] parents from the west of Ireland'.[5] The final stanza of the poem reads:

> I fear those long blonde beaches
> As I fear the shores of the past
> Lest looking down their reaches
> I should see with slanted mast
> The keeled up happiness of days
> That once sailed free.

On hearing of Lavin's death, the Irish president Mary Robinson commented: 'Mary was held in great esteem by people both in Ireland and abroad and her sad departure will be a profound loss to Irish writing.'[6] Maeve Binchy, who taught Elizabeth and Caroline at Pembroke School in Dublin and attended gatherings at the mews, remembered Lavin with great fondness in her regular *Irish Times* column, 'Maeve's Week': 'In years to come when Mary Lavin is remembered in history books and in literary criticism, I don't want people to forget that she was also a benign, enthusiastic parent – loved and remembered by a generation of school teachers whose true worth she was able to recognise and acknowledge.'[7] Lavin held famous authors in such high esteem that she revealed to Eavan Boland: 'In some strange way I had always thought of great writers – of writers of importance – as having passed over the divide between life and death into a world of the preserved dead; as having left the world of pots and pans and dances and parties.'[8] This was certainly not the case for the multitasking Lavin who did not see 'any difference between cooking a dinner or writing a story'.[9] Sadly, she once remarked that she had 'made too much soup for too many people'.[10]

Bruce Arnold's tribute to Lavin in the *Irish Independent* observed that, 'There is an exactitude, an economy, which prevails over everything, and Mary Lavin had it, and used it with great skill and richness through a long and productive life.' He noted that the recent reprinting of Lavin's work 'brought her attention and a following from a new generation of readers'.[11] The issue of Lavin's work being out of print is an ongoing one. Edward P. Jones even raises the difficulty in obtaining Lavin's work in his *New Yorker* story 'Bad Neighbors', which was published in the magazine on 7 August 2006. In the story, the character Sharon Palmer borrows 'A book of Irish stories the library doesn't seem to have.' The book in question is Mary Lavin's *Tales from Bective Bridge*. The owner's brother warns Sharon to return it, telling her, 'I know one thing for sure: he loves this woman's work, so you bet not lose it. I think the almighty reader is part Irish and don't know it yet.'[12] Lavin's centenary in 2012 sparked a revival, republication and reassessment of her work including the reissue of *Tales from Bective Bridge*, Lavin's first collection of stories.[13] Among the various events and readings was a symposium held in Lavin's honour at New York University's Glucksman Ireland House where Colm Tóibín, Mary Gordon and Greg Londe spoke of Lavin's legacy.[14]

Significantly, on 18 October 2024, Mary Lavin Place in Dublin was launched by Colm Tóibín, the Laureate for Irish Fiction, making it the first public space in Ireland to be named after a female writer.[15] The square links Lad Lane, where Lavin lived, to Wilton Park where her good friend Frank O'Connor spent the last years of his life. Ironically the development is on the same site of Goulding's original building that she bravely opposed all those years ago for the loss of ancient light. Tóibín, in paying tribute to Lavin, noted: 'Her work addresses how happiness is won and lost, how grief becomes sorrow, and what solitude means. It's fitting to have a place named after someone whose literary contributions have stood the test of time.'[16] Sadly, Lavin's three daughters, 'the three graces' as she referred to them, were not alive to witness the historic event and great honour bestowed upon their mother – but her grandchildren and great-grandchildren were present, among them Lavin's granddaughters Kathleen MacMahon and Alice Ryan, both successful authors in their own right, who are continuing their grandmother's legacy. Mary Lavin Place gives a permanence to that legacy and has made Mary Lavin an integral part of the city where she chose to live and write.[17]

Notes

GSP	George Starbuck Papers, University of Iowa Libraries, Iowa City, Iowa
MGA	The McGahern Archive at the James Hardiman Library, National University of Galway, Ireland
MLC	Mary Lavin Collection, Howard Gotlieb Archival Research Center, Boston University Libraries, Boston, Massachusetts
MLLP	Mary Lavin Literary Papers, James Joyce Library, Special Collections, University College Dublin
MLPP	Mary Lavin Personal Papers. James Joyce Library, Special Collections, University College Dublin
NLI	National Library of Ireland
NY	*The New Yorker*
NYR	*New Yorker* records, Manuscripts and Archives Division, The New York Public Library

Introduction

1. Rachel MacKenzie to Mary Lavin, *NYR*, 26 July 1968. Pearl White (1889–1938) was an American silent screen actress, known as 'Queen of the Serials'.
2. Lavin to Edith Oliver, *NYR*, 14 January 1958. Mary Lavin was born to Irish parents, Thomas (Tom) Lavin and Nora Mahon, in East Walpole, Massachusetts, on 10 June 1912. In 1921 Lavin, an only child, and her mother returned to Ireland and were followed by her father a few months later.
3. This assumption is based on the last known *New Yorker* contract issued to Mary Lavin in December 1986, for which she was paid $100, which covered the period commencing 6 March 1987 until 6 March 1988 (MLPP).
4. *New Yorker* editor William 'Bill' Maxwell (1908–2000) who handled the work of John O'Hara, John Cheever and John Updike, referred to

the trio as 'the three Johns'. Maxwell edited and cultivated many of the magazine's important writers including Mavis Gallant, Shirley Hazzard, Mary McCarthy, Vladimir Nabokov, Frank O'Connor, J. D. Salinger, Sylvia Townsend-Warner and Eudora Welty. He was also a writer and contributor of fiction to *The New Yorker.*

5. As quoted by Muriel Spark in her autobiography *Curriculum Vitae* (Constable, 1992), 211. By 1965 *The New Yorker* had almost 450,000 subscribers.
6. Eavan Boland began contributing to *The New Yorker* on 19 October 1987 with her poem 'The Black Lace Fan My Mother Gave Me'. Colm Tóibín's first *New Yorker* story, 'Dublin's Epiphany', was published in the 3 April 1995 issue. All the other writers mentioned had work published in the magazine by the mid–1960s.
7. Carey Winfrey, 'Rachel MacKenzie is Dead at 70: A Fiction Editor for New Yorker', *The New York Times*, 30 March 1980, 36. Isaac Bashevis Singer (1903–1991) was a Polish-born American author who won the Nobel Prize for Literature in 1978.
8. Lavin to MacKenzie, *NYR*, 27 February 1958. John P. R. Budlong (1921–1996) spent twenty-five years at Macmillan and became vice president in charge of general books at McGraw-Hill. In 1965 he was appointed president of the New American Library of World Literature, currently an imprint of Penguin Random House.
9. Lavin to MacKenzie, *NYR*, 24 August 1964 (Lavin added a question mark over the date and crossed out the address of 'Abbey Farm' and replaced it with 'Dublin').
10. Lavin to MacKenzie, *NYR*, 16 May 1966, 7.23 a.m.
11. MacKenzie to Lavin, *NYR*, 20 March 1964.
12. Lavin to MacKenzie, *NYR*, 7 April 1959.
13. See 'Mary Lavin Talking with Eavan Boland', *Writing Lives: Conversations Between Women Writers*, ed. by Mary Chamberlain (Virago Press, 1988), 137–45.
14. Lavin to MacKenzie, *NYR*, 2 May 1967.
15. See Charles McGrath's 'Muriel Spark: Playing God', *The New York Times,* 22 April 2010, and Martin Stannard's *Muriel Spark: The Biography* (W. W. Norton & Company, 2010), 277.
16. See Suzanne Marrs, *What There Is to Say We Have Said: The Correspondence of Eudora Welty and William Maxwell* (Houghton Mifflin Harcourt, 2011); *The Happiness of Getting It Down Right: Letters of Frank O'Connor and William Maxwell, 1945–1966* (Knopf, 1996) and *The Element of Lavishness* by William Maxwell and Sylvia Townsend Warner (Counterpoint, 2003).
17. See Standard, 277.
18. MacKenzie to Lavin, *NYR*, 26 February 1962.
19. Lavin to MacKenzie, *NYR*, 28 November 1960.
20. Lavin to MacKenzie, *NYR*, 2 May 1967.

21. Kathleen MacMahon, 'Irish Women Writing Fiction Were Dismissed as "Quiet". Ireland Wasn't Listening', *The Guardian*, 30 July 2020.
22. Recollection by Mary Lavin's daughter Caroline Walsh, 'Mary Lavin – A Personal Perspective'. Trevor/Bowen Summer School 2008. Mitchelstown Literary Society, 25 May 2008.
23. It is curious that Lavin's fellow Irishwoman and *New Yorker* staffer and contributor Maeve Brennan is never mentioned by either Lavin or MacKenzie in their correspondence.
24. MacKenzie to Lavin, *NYR*, 28 June 1965.
25. *NYR*, 11 July 1961.
26. Derek Morgan, 'Rachel MacKenzie', *NY*, 14 April 1980, 176.
27. Ibid.

1 'The Fire Burned Slow' *1957–1958*

1. Edith Oliver to Mary Lavin, *NYR*, 17 March 1958.
2. Upon Lavin's marriage in 1942 to solicitor William Walsh, the couple moved into Bective House, County Meath, where her father was the estate manager and where she spent a lot of her childhood. They purchased land close to the estate with money inherited from her father, who died in September 1945, and from the royalties from her first collection, *Tales from Bective Bridge* (1942). The couple built Abbey Farm on the plot in 1947. Valentine (Valdi), their eldest daughter, was born in 1943, followed by Elizabeth in 1945 and Caroline in 1952. At the time of William's death he was a Meath county councillor.
3. Lavin to Oliver, *NYR*, 12 February 1958.
4. See Leah Levenson's *The Four Seasons of Mary Lavin* (Marino Books, 1998) 93. Edward Weeks had visited Lavin and William numerous times at Bective and on one occasion Eudora Welty travelled with him and his family to Abbey Farm (see Weeks's 'The Peripatetic Reviewer'). William Walsh was forty-two when he died.
5. Lavin leased some land at Abbey Farm and in 1964 she told MacKenzie that she received 'a few hundred pounds' in rent for the farm (*NYR*, undated letter from 1964).
6. Mary Lavin papers, Binghamton University Libraries Special Collections, 13 April 1956. Lord Dunsany (1878–1957) was a contemporary of W. B. Yeats and Lady Gregory and lived in the family's ancestral home, Dunsany Castle in Meath, near to Bective House and Lavin's Abbey Farm. Dunsany wrote this letter from Dunstall Priory, his home in Shoreham, Kent where he had mainly resided since 1947. Anna Julia Child Bird, the wife of Lavin's father's American employer Charles Sumner Bird, introduced Lavin to Dunsany.
7. Eudora Welty (1909–2001) was an American short-story writer and novelist. Her novel *The Optimist's Daughter* won the Pulitzer Prize in 1973.

8. MLPP, undated letter circa August 1956. Elizabeth Bowen (1899–1973) had been struggling to fund the upkeep of Bowen's Court, her family's Irish stately home, and so embarked on a series of lecture tours in the US in order to make money.
9. Welty to Lavin, MLPP, 10 October 1956. Bowen to Lavin, MLPP, 23 August 1956. The headed paper carries Bowen's address, Bowen's Court, Kildorrey, Co. Cork. Bowen was due to stay in Dublin on 12 September after a return from a trip to England. Jammet's was a fashionable French restaurant frequented by celebrities and writers. Shay Harpur, a sommelier at Jammet's, recalled that on 5 August 1955 Frank O'Connor stopped to chat to Richard Harris and Peter O'Toole while on his way out to meet a *New Yorker* editor, most likely William Maxwell. The pair, who were in Dublin for the Horse Show and on their second bottle of Château Palmer '45, invited O'Connor to join them but he declined the offer, telling them: 'you keep a man from *The New Yorker* waiting at your peril, boys'. See *Jammet's of Dublin* (The Lilliput Press, 2011), 88. Coincidentally, Bective House was James Stern's family home before it was sold to Charles Sumner Bird in 1926. In a 1978 review of the reissued *Tales from Bective Bridge*, Stern recalled: 'Just two decades after we left Ireland I was walking down New York's Fifth Avenue one Spring morning when I happened to look in at the window of a famous bookstore. There, staring me in the face, I saw a book entitled Tales from Bective Bridge by Mary Lavin.' He concluded the article recounting his return to Bective with his wife many years later: 'to be welcomed and entertained to tea in "our" schoolroom by the now famous author. I remember thinking how I had never felt so at home.' James Stern, 'Home Thoughts', *The Irish Press*, 5 October 1978, 6.
10. MLPP, 8 August 1956. Nancy Wilson Ross (1901–1986) had contributed three stories, two poems and a 'Footloose Correspondents' piece about a visit to Burma to *The New Yorker* between 1934 and 1956. She was married to the publisher Stanley P. Young, a partner in Farrar, Straus and Young. Ross and Stanley had visited Lavin when they were in Ireland. The Poetry Center, located at 92nd Street Y, New York, often referred to as 'the Y', was founded by Dr William Kolodney. John Malcolm Brinnin (1916–1998) was the director of the Poetry Center from 1949 until he resigned in 1956. He first brought Dylan Thomas to America and T. S. Eliot and Louis MacNeice to 'the Y'. Lavin had also been in contact with Louis MacNeice, who wrote to her from the BBC on 30 August 1956 to express his hope that something fruitful would come out of her contact with the British Council. He offered his assistance and asked that she phone him to arrange a meeting (MLPP).
11. Welty to Lavin, MLPP, 10 October 1956.
12. Little, Brown published J. D. Salinger's *The Catcher in the Rye* in 1951. James Stern wrote a satirical review of *Catcher*, 'Aw, the World's a Crumby Place', in *The New York Times* on 15 July 1951.

13. John Beary informed Salinger that Lavin was also friendly with Eudora Welty (MLLP, 29 May 1957). Information on Beary, who died in 2000, is scant. He directed the premiere of Samuel Beckett's *Happy Days* on 30 September 1963 at the Eblana Theatre in Dublin and the Irish premiere of *The Happy Haven* by John Arden at the Gate Theatre on 2 December. He was the assistant director on the 1973 Broadway production of Seán O'Casey's *The Plough and the Stars*. Jean Stafford (1915–1979) was an American short-story writer and novelist who won the Pulitzer Prize for Fiction for *The Collected Stories of Jean Stafford* in 1970. *The New Yorker* published some of her fiction between 1948 and 1978. She was also a good friend of Eudora Welty.
14. Salinger did not reveal the identity of the mutual friends.
15. Eudora Welty visited Ireland in 1950, 1951 and 1954. Edward Weeks recalled in his book *Writers and Friends* that Lavin's story 'At Sallygap', which was published in *The Atlantic* in October 1941, 'became the title story of Mary's first book and so attracted Eudora that the three of us years later spent a happy day together at Mary's snow-white cottage beside the river Boyne in County Meath' (see *Writers and Friends*, Little, Brown, 1981, 120). *At Sallygap and Other Stories* was published in 1947: it was not Lavin's first book but her fourth. Lavin was initially unwell when Welty was on her first trip to Dublin in 1950, but she recovered and they climbed the Hill of Tara, near Lavin's home in Bective. Welty also paid a visit to Elizabeth Bowen at Bowen's Court, marking the beginning of a friendship that lasted until Bowen's death in 1973 (see Suzanne Marrs's *Eudora Welty: A Biography*, Harcourt, Inc., 2005). Welty's 'The Bride of the Innisfallen' was partly written at Bowen's Court and it was published in *The New Yorker* on 1 December 1951. Bowen had one story, 'Everything's Frightfully Interesting', published in *The New Yorker* on 11 October 1941. Welty visited Lavin again when she returned to Ireland in 1951.
16. MLPP, 1949. Jean Stafford stayed at the Shelbourne Hotel when she was in Dublin. She had intended to send Lavin a John McNulty *New Yorker* article about Ireland, but it irked her and she suspected that Lavin would have the same reaction to the piece. Stafford was likely referring to McNulty's 'Reporter at Large' article, 'Back Where I had Never Been' that was published in the magazine on 2 September 1949. Stafford could not get a copy of the 6 December 1949 issue of *Holiday* which contained Frank O'Connor's controversial article 'Ireland', and she hoped Lavin could throw some light on the rumour that the Catholic Church was picketing the publishers of the magazine. The piece caused a stir because it was considered anti-Irish due to O'Connor's revelations of poverty in Ireland. Stafford sent Lavin a copy of her first *New Yorker* story, 'Children are Bored on Sunday', which was published on 21 February 1948, and hoped Lavin would send her a copy of her book, presumably *At Sallygap and Other Stories*, in return

(MLPP, 21 October). Stafford had written to Lavin of her second marriage in 1950 to Oliver Jensen, a *Life* magazine editor, and of its subsequent collapse (the marriage ended in divorce in 1953). Stafford's first husband was the poet Robert Lowell, whom she divorced in 1948. She married her third husband, *New Yorker* staffer A. J. Liebling, in 1959.

17. MLLP, 29 May 1957. According to Salinger's daughter, Margaret, relations between Salinger and her mother, Claire, were extremely fraught in 1957. Claire had apparently left Salinger in January of that year, taking Margaret with her, but returned shortly after he had written 'Zooey', which was published in *The New Yorker* in May 1957. See Margaret Salinger's *Dream Catcher: A Memoir* (Washington Square Press, 2000).
18. MLLP, 11 September 1957. Salinger contributed thirteen stories in total between 1946 and 1965, a figure that Lavin surpassed.
19. In 1954 *The New Yorker* had a 55 per cent female readership and a random review of the magazine, from January to March of 1958, found that pieces by female authors dominated: '58 percent of the twenty-four stories and reminiscences were by women'. See Ben Yagoda's *About Town: The New Yorker and the World It Made* (Da Capo Press, 2001), 282.
20. See Louis Menand, 'Holden at Fifty: *The Catcher in the Rye* and what it Spawned', *NYR*, 1 October 2001, 82. The novel was turned down by Harcourt, Brace but was subsequently published by Little, Brown. According to Charles McGrath's *New York Times* obituary of J. D. Salinger, published on 28 January 2010, *Catcher* was selling over 250,000 copies a year.
21. Clearly Salinger held no ill feelings towards the magazine. S. N. Behrman's rave *New Yorker* review of *Catcher*, in which he described the work as 'brilliant, funny, meaningful', possibly helped to soften the blow (see S. N. Behrman's 'The Vision of the Innocent, J. D. Salinger's "The Catcher in the Rye"', 11 August 1951). Salinger dedicated his 1953 collection, *Nine Stories*, to *The New Yorker*'s chief fiction editor Gus Lobrano. Eudora Welty reviewed the book for *The New York Times* on 5 April 1953.
22. MLLP, 11 September 1957. 'Zooey' was a 50,000-word sequel to Salinger's *New Yorker* story 'Franny', which was published in the magazine on 29 January 1955. In 1961 the two stories were published together in a book dedicated to William Shawn. 'Zooey' was initially rejected by *The New Yorker* because it operated a rule against publishing follow-up stories (see Yagoda, 286). William Maxwell informed Eudora Welty about the decision to purchase Salinger's 'new long story' 'Zooey' in a letter dated 3 March 1957, and Welty responded: 'Wonderful about the new Jerry Salinger. Soon? Knowing about a good story you haven't read is like watching for a comet'. (See Marrs, *What There Is to Say*, 109–10).
23. Frank O'Connor was the pseudonym of Cork-born Michael O'Donovan (1903–1966). O'Connor regularly contributed stories to *The New Yorker* from 1945 until 1961 and two of his stories were published posthumously.

He formed a very close bond with his chief editor William Maxwell. See *The Happiness of Getting It Down Right.*

24. Dublin-born Maeve Brennan (1917–1993) moved to the US with her family in 1934. She joined the staff of *The New Yorker* in 1949, having previously worked for *Harper's Bazaar.*
25. Author's interview with Elizabeth Cullinan, 20 October 2009, New York.
26. Wolcott Gibbs, letter to Joel Sayre, 31 July 1931 (qtd in Ben Yagoda, *About Town: The New Yorker and the World It Made*, Da Capo Press, 2001, 145). Wolcott Gibbs (1902–1958) joined *The New Yorker* staff in 1928 and was a writer and copy editor. Gibbs's *New Yorker* obituary, 30 August 1958, observed that he was 'professionally ambidextrous: a natural editor, a prolific and good and versatile writer'. The obituary was unsigned but was generally known to have been written by E. B. White. Gibbs's comedy *Seasons in the Sun*, based on a series of *New Yorker* stories, ran on Broadway 1950–1951.
27. Harold Ross (1892–1951) founded *The New Yorker* with his wife, Jane Grant (1892–1972) in 1925. See Harold Ross's *New Yorker Prospectus*, 1925 (cited in Dale Kramer, *Ross and The New Yorker*, Doubleday, 1951).
28. Sally Benson (1897–1972) had been contributing fiction to *The New Yorker* since 1929 but her St Louis stories first appeared in the magazine in 1941 under the title '5135 Kensington', beginning in the 14 June 1941 issue. Benson later added additional stories and compiled them into a book, which became the basis for the 1944 movie *Meet Me in St. Louis*, starring Judy Garland.
29. James Thurber to William Shawn, *NYR*, 21 November 1957. James Thurber (1894–1961) was a *New Yorker* staffer and contributor of stories and cartoons. He is probably best known for 'The Secret Life of Walter Mitty', published in *The New Yorker* on 18 March 1939.
30. Lavin started to write for *The Atlantic Monthly* by way of an introduction by Lord Dunsany who sent her story 'The Nun's Mother' to his friend and editor of the magazine, Ellery Sedgwick. Although that particular story was not published, Lavin became a regular contributor. Lavin's 'The Two Friends' was published in a New York publication, *Modern British Writing*, which includes work by Dylan Thomas, Liam O'Flaherty, George Orwell and V. S. Pritchett. See *Modern British Writing*, ed. Denys Val Baker (Vanguard, 1947) 73–88.
31. Edward J. O'Brien (1890–1941) was the founder and editor of *The Best American Short Stories* from 1915 until his death in 1941, when he was succeeded by Martha Foley. A *New Yorker* story was first included in this compilation in 1930. The O. Henry Award Prize Collection has been awarded annually since 1919. Established in 1919, it is the oldest major award for short stories. *New Yorker* stories were not included in the O. Henry collection until 1935. O. Henry was the nom de plume of the American short story writer William Sydney Porter (1862–1910).
32. *NY*, 30 May 1942, 65. This collection featured some stories originally published in *Dublin Magazine*, *The Atlantic Monthly* and *Harper's Bazaar.*

33. *NY*, 26 May 1945.
34. *NY*, 8 February 1947.
35. *NY*, 28 January 1950, 86. The article has no byline. *The New York Times* Best Sellers list noted that *Mary O'Grady* was of 'particular literary, topical or scholarly interest' (*New York Times*, 19 February 1950).
36. Mollie Panter-Downes (1906–1997) contributed stories, articles and book reviews to *The New Yorker* from 1938 until 1986. Janet Flanner (1892–1978) was an American writer and journalist and *The New Yorker*'s Paris correspondent from 1925 until she retired in 1975. Maeve Brennan's unsigned Long-Winded Lady vignettes, which appeared in *The New Yorker*'s 'Talk of the Town' section between 1954 and 1981, also took the form of letters that are whimsical observations of New York City. It was not until 1969, when the pieces were collected for publication, that the lady's identity was revealed.
37. Gardner Botsford, 'The Victorian Game', 'The Talk of the Town', *The New Yorker*, 10 February 1997, 30.
38. *NYR*, 11 September 1957.
39. *NYR*, 27 November 1957. Edith Oliver (1913–1998) was a *New Yorker* facts editor and reviewer of books, theatre and film between 1947 and 1993. According to *New Yorker* book and jazz reviewer Whitney Balliett, 'When she [Oliver] joined *The New Yorker* in 1947 as a nonfiction reader cum book editor, she made William Shawn, the managing editor, promise that he would never ask her to write anything – and then began contributing sharp, anonymous reviews.' See 'Postscript', 'Edith Oliver: One on the Aisle', *NY*, 9 March 1998, 33.
40. Katharine White to Mary McCarthy, 19 August 1957 (qtd in Yagoda, 279). Katharine Sergeant Angell White (1892–1977) joined *The New Yorker* in 1925, six months after it was founded. When Gus Lobrano died in 1956, she took over briefly as chief fiction editor. The writers White edited at the magazine included Vladimir Nabokov, John O'Hara, Mary McCarthy, John Cheever, John Updike and Ogden Nash. Her second husband was the *New Yorker* writer and editor E. B. White (1899–1985), best known for his popular children's books *Charlotte's Web* and *Stuart Little*. Mary McCarthy (1912–1989) was an American author, critic and political activist best known for her controversial and bestselling 1963 novel, *The Group*, which was banned in Ireland, Italy and Australia. She was married to the literary critic Edmund Wilson (1895–1972). Lavin references Wilson's *The Wound and the Bow* in her *New Yorker* story, 'Trastevere'.
41. John O'Hara contributed more short stories to *The New Yorker* than any other writer. His novel *Pal Joey* was adapted into a Broadway musical and film, and *Butterfield 8* was also adapted for the big screen.
42. Lavin to Oliver, *NYR*, 14 January 1958. 'Asigh', originally titled 'Baboon' (MLLP, 7 August 1951), was due to be published in *Selected Stories* (1959).

In 1940 Diarmuid Russell (1902–1973) co-founded Russell & Volkening, one of New York's oldest literary agencies, which represented important writers including Saul Bellow, Mavis Gallant, A. J. Liebling, Bernard Malamud, May Sarton, Eudora Welty and P. L. Travers. Welty and Russell struck up a very close friendship: Welty was his son's godmother and it was Russell who introduced her to Lavin's work. In 1972 the agency was sold to Timothy Seldes, formerly the managing editor of Doubleday and vice president of Macmillan.

43. Rudd to Lavin, *NYR*, 20 February 1958. Mary D. Rudd Kierstead (1925–2020) joined *The New Yorker*'s typing pool in 1947. She then became William Shawn's secretary and in 1957 a reader in the fiction department. Rudd was also a *New Yorker* contributor and retired from the magazine in 1999.
44. 'My Molly' was subsequently published in *What's New?* No. 209 (Christmas 1958), 14–1, *The Great Wave* (1961), *The Abbott Christmas Book*, ed. Herbert W. Luthin (Doubleday, n.d.), 6–10 and *The Stories of Mary Lavin, Vol, II* (1974).
45. Lavin to MacKenzie, *NYR*, 20 July 1958. 'The Mouse' was subsequently published in *The Great Wave and Other Stories* (1961), *Collected Stories* (1971) and *The Stories of Mary Lavin, Vol. II* (1974).
46. MLC, Correspondence (Guggenheim Memorial Fellowship folder). The list indicates that eighteen of Lavin's stories were sent to various publications including *Harper's Bazaar*, *Mademoiselle*, *The Atlantic*, *Yale Review*, *Harper's*, *Good Housekeeping*, *Saturday Evening Post*, *McCall*'s and *Charm*.
47. See Marrs, *What There Is to Say*, 5.
48. Lavin to Oliver, *NYR*, 14 January 1958. Michael Joseph (1897–1958) was a British publisher and writer. In 1985 Michael Joseph Ltd was acquired by Penguin Books. Lavin was not exaggerating about the condition of the car: 'To signal a turning, Mary had to stick her hand out. There were no windshield wipers and in rainy weather Mary had to get out from time to time and wipe the windshield with her sleeve.' (See Levenson, 110).
49. Ibid.
50. Lavin to Oliver, *NYR*, 26 March, 1958. In Michael McLaverty's article 'A Note on Katherine Mansfield' (*The Belfast Telegraph*, 15 January 1955) he wrote: 'She has a specific grace, too, when writing about children (read "The Doll's House"), for she is able to write of them with complete naturalness and unsophistication – a gift that she shares with Mary Lavin, Katherine Anne Porter and Mary Beckett.'
51. Lavin to Oliver, *NYR*, 12 February 1958. 'They Call Us Children' was the story's alternative title. Although Lavin later mentioned revising the story, it does not appear that she ever submitted it, under either title, to *The New Yorker*. Lavin wrote a handwritten annotation on an unfinished typescript of 'The Glass Hill or They Call Us Children', 'Never finished, never will be.' (MLLP, undated).

52. Oliver to Lavin, *NYR*, 17 March 1958. The 15 March 1958 *New Yorker*'s cover by Abe Birnbaum was fittingly a drawing of Irish dancers, given its proximity to St Patrick's Day.
53. Maxwell to Russell, *NYR*, 17 April 1958. There is no mention of when this story was sent for consideration. A later, revised version of the story was also rejected on 16 December 1958. While the rejection must have been disappointing for Lavin, she was not surprised: 'Of course you didn't take Aubretia. It's not really interesting. It was technically absorbing – to me – that was all.' (Mary Lavin to MacKenzie, *NYR*, 31 December 1958). 'What's Wrong with Aubretia?' was subsequently published under the Title 'The Villas', in *Pick of Today's Short Stories*, no. 10 (London: Putnam, 1959), 131–41 and in *The Great Wave and Other Stories* (Macmillan, 1961).
54. MacKenzie to Lavin, *NYR*, 23 April 1958. 'Lemonade' was published in *The Great Wave and Other Stories* (1961).
55. Harold Ross was opposed to anything he considered 'writer conscious' as defined in Wolcott Gibbs's tenth rule in his tongue-in-cheek essay, 'Theory and Practice of Editing *New Yorker* Articles', in which he states (quoting Harold Ross) that, 'Nobody gives a damn about a writer or his problems except another writer.' He advised that any articles containing 'authors, reporters, poets, etc.' were undesirable and, if these professions featured, they were to be changed to another profession or removed altogether (reprinted in Thomas Kunkel's biography of Harold Ross, *Genius in Disguise: Harold Ross of The New Yorker*, Random House, 1997). See author's essays 'Trying to Get the Words Right: Mary Lavin and *The New Yorker*' in *Mary Lavin*, ed. Elke D'hoker (Irish Academic Press, 2013) and 'To Cut a Long Story Short: The Shaping of Mary Lavin's *New Yorker* Stories' in *Genesis and Revision in Modern British and Irish Writers*, eds Jonathan Bloom and Catherine Rovera (Palgrave Macmillan, 2020).
56. Lavin to Rudd, *NYR*, 25 April 1958.
57. Lavin to MacKenzie, *NYR*, 20 July 1958.
58. *NYR*, 15 April 1958. *Selected Stories* (Macmillan, 1959). The collection, originally due to be published in the autumn of 1958, was published in the summer of 1959. 'In a Café' was not selected for the volume.
59. MacKenzie to Scott, *NYR*, 22 April 1958 (MacKenzie responded to Scott as Rudd was on vacation).
60. *NYR*, 29 October 1958.
61. Lavin to Rudd, *NYR*, 25 April 1958.
62. William Maxwell confirmed the acceptance in a letter to Diarmuid Russell and included a cheque in part payment for 'Second-Hand'. (*NYR*, 2 May 1958). Shortly afterwards, Lavin's story 'Distant Thunder' was rejected. There was no reason given for its refusal: MacKenzie simply informed Russell, 'The decision on "Distant Thunder" by Mary Lavin is no, I'm sorry to say.' (*NYR*, 15 May 1958). The story does not appear to have been published elsewhere.
63. Scott to MacKenzie, *NYR*, 24 April 1958.

64. MacKenzie to Lavin, *NYR*, 23 April 1958.
65. The fee was approximately one-sixth of the average American income of families (see Income of Families and Persons in the United States: 1958 (census.gov). https://www2.census.gov/library/publications/1960/demographics/p60–33.pdf
66. Lavin to MacKenzie, *NYR*, 20 July 1958.
67. Ilonka Karasz (1896–1981) was a Hungarian-American designer and illustrator who produced 186 covers for *The New Yorker* magazine between 1924 and 1973.
68. The issue also contains stories by Arturo Vivante and St. Clair McKelway; a poem by Theodore Roethke and Janet Flanner's 'Letter from Paris'. Arturo Vivante (1923–2008) was an Italian-American writer. Theodore Roethke (1908–1963) won the Pulitzer Prize for poetry in 1954 for his book *The Waking*. St. Clair McKelway (1905–1980) was a *New Yorker* writer and the magazine's managing editor for journalistic pieces from 1936 to 1939. He was briefly married to Maeve Brennan. The pair tied the knot in 1954 and she lived with him in Sneden's Landing, now known as Palisades, which was the inspiration for Brennan's fictional Herbert's Retreat. They agreed to divorce in 1959.
69. Chevrolet at this time was the cheapest choice of car by General Motors, with Cadillac being their most luxurious model.
70. *NY*, 18 April 1959.
71. Delmore Schwartz (1913–1966) was an American poet and short-story writer. Charles Addams (1912–1988).
72. *Sweet Bird of Youth* premiered at the Martin Beck Theatre, now known as the Al Hirschfeld Theatre, on 10 March 1959. Hirschfeld (1903–2003) was an artist best known for his portraits of Broadway stars. His work appeared in *The New Yorker*. Tennessee Williams's 'Three Players of a Summer Game' was published in *The New Yorker* on 1 November 1952. Williams's hugely successful 1955 play *Cat on a Hot Tin Roof*, which won the Pulitzer Prize for Drama, was an adaptation of this story.
73. *Some Like it Hot* was released on 29 March 1959. The movie is also mentioned in the 'Goings on About Town, Motion Pictures' section of the magazine.
74. *NYR*, 23 June 1958.
75. When *The New Yorker*'s founding editor, Harold Ross, died in 1951, William Shawn (1907–1992) succeeded him as chief editor. Shawn joined the magazine in 1933 as a freelance 'Talk of the Town' reporter.
76. William Maxwell (qtd in Yagoda, 282–3).
77. Rachel Maude MacKenzie (1909–1980). From 1936 until 1938 Lavin taught French at her alma mater, Loreto College on the Green in Dublin, after graduating from University College Dublin.
78. The name comes from the Bread Loaf Mountain, near where the college is located. Eudora Welty was also a past fellow, having been nominated by

Katherine Anne Porter, and was listed as an auditor in 1937. Porter was listed as a lecturer at the conference in 1940. Other participants are listed as contributors (attendees who wished to bring manuscripts for criticism by staff), or auditors (attendees who did not wish to do so). The conference discontinued these references in the summer of 2024. All attendees are now referred to as 'participants'. *American Accent: Fourteen Stories by Authors Associated with the Bread Loaf Writers' Conference* was published in 1954 and features work by Wallace Stegner, May Sarton, Richard Wilbur and Carson McCullers among others. Frank O'Connor gave an evening talk at the 1952 conference and was a member of staff in 1953. Kay Boyle was a member of staff in 1957.

79. McCauley 'Mac' Conner (1913–2019) was one of the most influential commercial illustrators. *The Harper*'s issue also featured V. S. Pritchett's story 'The Collection'. According to MacKenzie's staff profile in the Middlebury College Bread Loaf Writers' Conference catalogue of 1954, she also had a story published in *Woman's Day* magazine.
80. Truman Capote (1924–1984) is listed as a contributor on the record of conference registrants that year. Capote had contributed to a 'Talk of the Town' piece published in *The New Yorker* on 20 May 1944.
81. As quoted in Gerald Clarke's *Capote: A Biography* (Carroll and Graf, 1988).
82. 'The Crumb', 1954 (Bread Loaf Writers' Conference). Saul Bellow and Robert Frost also gave evening lectures that year. Bellow was a lecturer at the University of Minnesota at the time. MacKenzie, Bellow, William Sloane and Eric Swenson are listed staff 'In Fiction' in the Middlebury College Bread Loaf Writers' Conference catalogue of 1954. MacKenzie is seated next to Robert Frost in the 1952 staff photograph.
83. Saul Bellow's first *New Yorker* story, 'Interval in a Lifeboat', was published alongside Maeve Brennan's 'The Joker' on 27 December 1952.
84. Charles McGrath, 'Muriel Spark: Playing God', *The New York Times,* 22 April 2010.
85. MacKenzie to Lavin, *NYR*, 2 May 1958.
86. Lavin to MacKenzie, *NYR*, 20 July 1958.
87. MacKenzie to Lavin, *NYR*, 24 July 1958.
88. Lavin to MacKenzie, *NYR*, 20 July 1958.
89. Dublin city centre is approximately 50 km from Bective, County Meath. Lavin attended Loreto College on St Stephen's Green from 1922 until 1930.
90. Lavin to MacKenzie, *NYR*, 29 October 1958.
91. Mary Lavin's father, Tom, was from Frenchpark, County Roscommon. He emigrated to the US, where he found employment with Charles Sumner Bird, who later purchased Bective House in County Meath. Tom returned to Ireland to take up the role of managing the estate.
92. 'The Living'. *NY*, 22 November 1958.

93. Although not a fiction piece, John Hersey's 'Reporter at Large' article 'Hiroshima' was published on 31 August 1946, making it the first time a whole issue was dedicated to one piece of writing. Muriel Spark's 'The Prime of Miss Jean Brodie' was published in the magazine on 14 October 1961, commanding almost the entire issue at 40,000 words.
94. Updike to Maxwell, 17 February 1958 (Yagoda, 204).
95. Philip Roth's first *New Yorker* story 'The Kind of Person I Am' was published in the following issue (29 November 1958.) *The New Yorker* published its first story by Lavin's friend Benedict Kiely, 'The White Wild Bronco', in its 20 December 1958 issue.
96. Arthur Getz (1913–1996) was an American illustrator who for fifty years was a cover artist for *The New Yorker*. He is the most prolific *New Yorker* cover artist, having had 213 covers appear on the magazine between 1938 and 1988.
97. Maeve Brennan had been engaged to the writer and renowned New York theatre critic Walter Kerr (1913–1996), but he broke off the engagement when he met his future Irish American wife, Jean Collins, best known for her book *Please Don't Eat the Daisies* (1957), which was adapted as a 1960 film starring Doris Day and David Niven. Eugene O'Neill (1888–1953) never contributed work to *The New Yorker* but the magazine published his rediscovered 1920 one-act play, 'Exorcism', in its 17 October 2011 issue. O'Neill was thought to have destroyed all copies of the play after only a few performances.
98. Lavin to Oliver, *NYR*, 26 March 1958.
99. MacKenzie to Lavin, *NYR*, 24 July 1958.
100. Michael McLaverty (1904–1992) was a writer and a teacher. He informed Lavin that Jonathan Cape was interested in publishing her work but warned her that both his and Seán Ó Faoláin's Cape publications were out of print (18 August 1956, MLPP). McLaverty initially acted as the intermediary between Lavin and Cecil Scott. Macmillan New York published three of McLaverty's novels, namely *In this Day* (1945), *Truth in the Night* (1951) and *The Brightening Day* (1965). He was an avid reader of *The New Yorker* and on 28 October 1958 he let Lavin know that he had a bundle of them for her but that it 'would break the bank to post them.' (MLPP).
101. Lavin to MacKenzie, *NYR*, 29 October 1958. The Macmillan volume was *The Great Wave and Other Stories*, which was published in 1961.
102. MacKenzie to Lavin, *NYR*, 16 December 1958.
103. Lavin to MacKenzie, *NYR*, 14 February 1962.
104. A. A. Kelly, for example, observes that 'In a Café' is Lavin's 'first autobiographical story about the experience of widowhood' and states, 'Mary Lavin is the Mary of "In a Café".' Kelly, 62.
105. Author interview with Elizabeth Cullinan, 20 October 2009, New York. Cullinan also presumed that the character of Mary was based on Lavin and

was shocked to discover her misinterpretation of the story. See Hurley, 'To Cut a Long Story Short'.

106. *NYR*, 31 December 1958.

107. Benedict Kiely, *A Raid into Dark Corners*, 246. The area became known as 'Baggotonia' in the 1950s due to the presence of artists. See also Brendan Lynch's *Prodigals and Geniuses, The Writers and Artists of Dublin's Baggotonia*, 2011, Liffey Press.

108. *NYR*, 13 January 1959.

109. *NYR*, 31 December 1958.

2 'Direct Dealings' *1959*

1. Mary Lavin to Rachel MacKenzie, *NYR*, 20 July 1958.
2. Lavin to MacKenzie, *NYR*, 29 January 1959.
3. See Michael Kreyling, *Author and Agent: Eudora Welty and Diarmuid Russell* (Farrar, Straus and Giroux, 1991).
4. *NYR*, 13 January 1959.
5. *NYR*, 29 January 1959.
6. *NYR*, 13 March 1959. Lavin later declared in a 1979 interview that the story 'broke off like a splinter' while writing 'The Great Wave' (See C. Murphy, 'Mary Lavin: An Interview', 207–24).
7. William Steig (1907–2003) was a cartoonist, illustrator and author of children's books. Steven Spielberg purchased the book rights to *Shrek!* in 1991 and produced the hit animated film of the same name in 2001.
8. Ogden Nash (1902–1971).
9. Lavin changed the name Eamonn Og to Ruairi Og in a collected version. She did not include any fadas in her text.
10. Gypsy Rose Lee was born Rose Louise Hovick (1911–1970). *The New Yorker* also published her fiction.
11. The play, which was written by William Gibson and directed by Arthur Penn, premiered on 19 October 1959 in the Playhouse Theatre and won five Tony Awards in 1960 including Best Play and Best Actress for Anne Bancroft.
12. *NYR*, 20 February 1959.
13. *NYR*, 13 March 1959. The quantity bonus period commenced with the purchase of the first story in a new cycle, which in this case was 5 December 1958, and ran for twelve months from that date or until four or six stories were purchased. The bonus increased to 35 per cent with the sale of six stories.
14. *NYR*, 6 April 1959.
15. *NYR*, 10 April 1959. As requested, Lavin consulted with MacKenzie about any commissioned work in case it breached her first-reading agreement. In June, for example, she let MacKenzie know that Batsford Ltd, London, were

'bringing out one of their lovely books of coloured plates on Ireland and have asked me if I would do the script and captions. I wonder do I have to ask you about this, and how you feel? It is a "short piece of work" five thousand words, (5,000 words).' (*NYR*, 23 June 1959). *The New Yorker* was not concerned with Lavin undertaking such an assignment.

16. See Adam Begley, *Updike* (Harper, 2014), 109. Katharine White to John Updike, 15 September 1954.
17. MacKenzie to Lavin, *NYR*, 7 December 1961 and 7 December 1962.
18. See Begley 110.
19. In a letter to Lavin, Oliver St. John Gogarty wrote that he called Weeks 'Yearsly' because he had held onto one of his articles for over a year (MLPP, 19 July 1950).
20. *NYR*, 3 June 1959.
21. *NYR*, 24 March 1959.
22. *NYR*, 7 April 1959.
23. *NYR*, 10 April 1959.
24. Mary Lavin, 'The Great Wave', *NY*, 13 June 1959.
25. *NYR*, 7 April 1959.
26. *NYR*, 11 June 1959. This was another cover by Arthur Getz. 'The Great Wave' was subsequently published in *The Great Wave and Other Stories* (1961), *The Stories of Mary Lavin, Vol. I* (1964) and *Collected Stories* (1971).
27. W. D. Snodgrass (1926–2009) was an American poet whose first collection of poetry, *Heart's Needle* (1959), won the 1960 Pulitzer Prize for poetry: the poem 'Heart's Needle', from which the book took its title, is considered one of the earliest examples of confessional poetry.
28. *A Raisin in the Sun*, which took its title from a line in Langston Hughes's poem 'Harlem', was the first play by an African American woman to be produced on Broadway. Lillian Ross interviewed Lorraine Hansberry shortly after the premiere of the play (see 'How Lorraine Hansberry Wrote "A Raisin in the Sun"' by Lillian Ross, *NY*, 9 May 1959).
29. *NYR*, 14 February 1962.
30. Lavin recalled the inspiration for the story many years later in her interview with Catherine Murphy in 1979.
31. *NYR*, 14 February 1962 and 4 November 1958. On 23 April 1958 McLaverty gave a talk on Lavin, Katherine Anne Porter and Katherine Mansfield for the Business and Professional Women's Club in Belfast.
32. *NYR*, 4 November 1958. *The Sign* was a religious publication.
33. Lavin later recalled in an interview that she 'began and finished that story ['The Great Wave'] in twenty four hours' in the National Library of Ireland. In the same interview, she gave an insight into her writing method: 'It usually takes me several months to finish a story, although admittedly I am usually writing three or four stories at the same time … although I often work for a year or more on one story, I am bringing on

several stories at the same time, like a horse trainer with a string of horses, feeding them all, grooming them all, exercising them all. But there is only one I plan or hope to bring up to the post. But *The Great Wave* was an exception. I concentrated my efforts on it alone.' See Catherine Murphy, 'Mary Lavin: An Interview', 207–24. Lavin would often write in the National Library of Ireland on Kildare Street and she was a familiar figure in Bewley's Café on Grafton Street, where she also regularly wrote after dropping her daughters to their school nearby and where she would have lunch with them most days during the school term. The Country Shop on St Stephen's Green and Buswell's hotel on Molesworth Street were also regular haunts. None of McLaverty's stories appeared in *The New Yorker*. His short story collection *The Game Cock and Other Stories* (1947) was reviewed by *The New Yorker* in July 1947.

34. Lavin to MacKenzie, *NYR*, 14 February 1962. The correct quote reads, 'I am certain of nothing but the holiness of the Heart's affections and the truth of the imagination. What imagination seizes as Beauty must be truth.' From a letter written by John Keats to Benjamin Bailey, 22 November 1817.
35. Lavin erroneously, but understandably, translated Inishbofin (Inis Bó Finne) to Boffin Island, when in fact its correct English translation is Island of the White Cow.
36. MLPP, 25 June 1959.
37. Lavin to MacKenzie, *NYR*, 6 April 1959.
38. MacKenzie to Lavin, *NYR*, 10 April 1959.
39. Lavin to MacKenzie, *NYR*, 6 April 1959.
40. *NYR*, 20 May 1959. The letter was written from Buswell's Hotel. Ethan Ayer was a poet and writer. *The New Yorker* published two of his stories, 'The Promise of Heat', on 3 September 1966, which was also selected for *The Best American Stories 1967*; and 'The Treasure Dream', which was published on 11 March 1967. Arnold Sundgaard was Ethan Ayer's drama teacher and wrote the blurb for Ayer's poetry collection *The Beneficiary and Other Poems*: 'His is a lonely voice, as was Frost's, and the underlying cry of protest is directed at the world even though it is based in the New England town and country he knows so well. A touching work.'
41. *NYR*, 26 May 1959. Robert Asprey (1923–2009) was a military historian.
42. Lavin to MacKenzie, *NYR*, 10 October 1959.
43. MacKenzie to Lavin, *NYR*, 20 October 1959. Lavin sent MacKenzie a manuscript by Jean Blanchard, who worked in the diplomatic corps and occasionally sent her his work. As the manuscript was in French, Lavin kindly offered to translate it if the magazine was interested in the piece: 'I would I am sure find time somewhere under a stone or up the chimeny [*sic*] – somewhere anyway – to translate it.' (*NYR*, 30 June 1959). MacKenzie informed Lavin that the magazine did not consider translated work as a rule but that the piece would be read and given due consideration. In October Lavin queried whether MacKenzie would consider 'The Queen

of France' by George Lorimer (*NYR*, 3 October 1959). Neither story was accepted. A few years later, in 1963, she also recommended William Sansom to the magazine. Sansom was most grateful for the referral but had no new work at that time (MLPP).

44. Reverend Michael Scott (Mick) to Mary Lavin, MLC, Correspondence (Guggenheim Fellowship folder), 15 October 1958. The following day Scott sent a telegram to Fox's Hotel on Leeson Street to apologise for the harsh tone of the airgraph and to express his relief that Lavin had done the application. Scott met Lavin when he was sent to UCD to study as a young Australian seminarian from the Jesuit order and the pair formed a very close bond. He developed somewhat romantic feelings for Lavin. They renewed their friendship after William's death.
45. An undated list of referees also features the writer Van Wyck Brooks; academics Professor White of Trinity College Dublin and Professor Jeremiah Hogan, the registrar of University College Dublin; *The Atlantic* editor Edward Weeks; her good friend the Very Rev. Michael Scott SJ; and her father's employer, Charles Sumner Bird. Hogan later served as the fourth president of University College Dublin from 1964 until 1972, during which time he oversaw the development of Belfield campus. See MLC, Correspondence (Guggenheim Fellowship folder).
46. Copy of Michael McLaverty's letter of recommendation to the Guggenheim Foundation (MLPP).
47. *NYR*, 11 June 1959. Roth's story 'Defender of the Faith' appeared in the 14 March 1959 issue of *The New Yorker*. MacKenzie had previously rejected 'Goodbye, Columbus' in part because 'taste would rule out here much of what is essential to the narrative'. See David Remnick's Introduction in *The 50s: The Story of a Decade, The New Yorker* (Modern Library, 2016).
48. Saul Bellow was awarded the Guggenheim Fellowship in 1948 and 1955; John Cheever was awarded it in 1951 and 1960; Vladimir Nabokov received the award in 1943 and 1952 and Eudora Welty was bestowed the fellowship in 1942 and 1949.
49. Lavin to Henry Moe, 25 March 1959, MLC, Correspondence (Guggenheim Fellowship folder). The letter is either a copy of one that was sent to Moe or a draft.
50. It was a very generous award considering that the average American family income in 1959 was $5,400 and women's earnings averaged approximately $1,200.
51. The fellowship grant amount varies but today ranges from $30,000 to $45,000. John Cheever availed of his second Guggenheim, awarded in 1960, to write his second novel, *The Wapshot Scandal* (1964). See *John Cheever: A Biography* by Scott Donaldson.
52. *NYR*, 23 June 1959.
53. *NYR*, 30 June 1959. Wallace Stegner (1909–1993) (misnamed by Lavin as Maurice Stegner) was an American novelist, short-story writer and historian.

This was his third Guggenheim fellowship. He won the Pulitzer Prize in 1972 and the National Book Award in 1977. Stegner founded the Stanford Creative Writing Programme and Writing Fellowships in 1946 and in 1960 he invited Frank O'Connor to teach at Stanford University.

54. *NYR*, 3 March 1959. Goster is slang for a gossip or a chat.
55. *NYR*, 20 May 1959. Arnold Sundgaard (1909–2006) was an American playwright, librettist, lyricist and writer of short stories and children's books..
56. *NYR*, 10 April 1959. Sundgaard's wife, Marge, kept in touch with Lavin and on 4 October 1959 she wrote to inform her that his story, 'Ken', was published *The New Yorker'* on 19 September and that it was very well received. Marge had been looking into lecturing opportunities for Lavin including Adelphi College, Hofstra, C.W. Post College and the State University of New York. Lavin had also asked Marge about the Bread Loaf Writers' Conference and MacDowell.
57. MacKenzie to Lavin, *NYR*, 14 July 1969. Howard Moss (1922–1987) was an American poet, dramatist, critic and, in his role of almost forty years as the poetry editor for *The New Yorker*, discovered and handled the work of some of America's most important poets including Sylvia Plath, Anne Sexton, James Dickey, Theodore Roethke and Richard Wilbur.
58. See 'These Ghostly Archives 4: Looking for New England' in *These Ghostly Archives: The Unearthing of Sylvia Plath*, Gail Crowther & Peter K. Steinberg (Fonthill Media, 2017). The poem was published in *The New Yorker*'s 20 August 1960 issue.
59. *The Bell Jar* was first published in January 1963 under the pseudonym Victoria Lucas. Plath committed suicide on 11 February of that year. She was thirty years old.
60. Lavin to MacKenzie, *NYR*, 20 May 1959.
61. MacKenzie to Lavin, *NYR*, 13 January 1959.
62. Lavin to MacKenzie, *NYR*, 3 June 1959.
63. Lavin to MacKenzie, *NYR*, 30 June 1959.
64. Thurber observed that: 'other magazines, out shopping for writers, began buying New Yorker contributions for from three to five times as much money as *The New Yorker* thought it could pay. It became a great relief to receive a check from another magazine without a complicated voucher attached to it.' See Thurber, 192.
65. MacKenzie to Lavin, *NYR*, undated letter between mid- to end of May 1959.
66. Lavin to MacKenzie, *NYR*, 3 June 1959.
67. MacKenzie to Lavin, *NYR*, 7 July 1959. Brian Friel's first *New Yorker* story 'The Skelper', was published in the 1 August 1959 issue.
68. Lavin to MacKenzie, *NYR*, 12 September 1959.
69. *Sunday Independent*, 13 September 1959.
70. *NYR*, 3 June 1959. Nothing seems to have come of the proposal. A photograph of Lavin with her three daughters beside their Morris Minor

was taken before they embarked on their trip to Florence and is contained in her personal papers at UCD. On the back of the photograph Lavin had written: 'Setting off for the trip to Florence, Guggenheim.' Valdi was sixteen, Elizabeth fourteen and Caroline was aged six.

71. *NYR*, 26 May 1960. *The New Yorker* records contain a clipping of a newspaper reprint of the Preface ('How Is the Story Written') to *Selected Stories*. The title of the paper is not noted on the clipping.
72. Lavin did not send the story 'Brigid' which was included in the collection, to *The New Yorker* as it had been previously published in *Dublin Magazine* in 1944. The story appeared in the short-lived magazine *Arena* in the spring of 1963. The publication was edited by James Liddy, Liam O'Connor and Michael Hartnett. Other contributors included Patrick Kavanagh and Austin Clarke.
73. The volume made the Catholic Book Reading List, which had been 'selected by well-qualified committees for Catholic book week', *The Catholic Times* (Columbus, Ohio), 19 February 1960.
74. 'Books of the Times', *The New York Times*, 15 June 1959.
75 *NYR*, 10 October 1959.
76. MacKenzie to Lavin, *NYR*, 9 December 1959.

3 'Splitting Hairs' *1960*

1. Mary Lavin to Rachel MacKenzie, *NYR*, undated letter in September 1960.
2. Lavin to MacKenzie, *NYR*,19 January 1959.
3. *Cosmopolitan*, 149 (January 1960), 80–7. The actress and comedian Lucille Ball graced the cover. Lavin's story 'Asigh' commanded eight pages with illustrations by Tom Lovell (1909–1997). The issue also included a complete mystery novel, *The Tug of Evil* (later retitled *Slam the Big Door* for book publication), by John D. MacDonald (1916–1986). MacDonald, who was a writer of crime novels and thrillers, is probably best known for his 1957 novel *The Executioners*, which was adapted for film under the title *Cape Fear* in 1962 and remade in 1991. 'Asigh' had previously been included in *Selected Stories* (1959) and was subsequently published in *Dublin Magazine* 6 (Summer, 1967), 45–62 and in *A Memory and Other Stories* (1972).
4. Lavin to MacKenzie, *NYR*, 19 January 1960. Lavin later wrote to MacKenzie that Frank and Harriet O'Connor would be incredulous that she returned from Italy of her own accord (*NYR*, 2 March 1960).
5. Lavin to MacKenzie, *NYR*, 15 February 1960.
6. Lavin revealed that she would love to return to her birthplace, where she spent her early years.
7. Lavin to MacKenzie, *NYR*, 19 January 1959 (the letter was misdated 1959 instead of 1960).

8. Lavin to MacKenzie, *NYR*, 15 February 1960
9. MacKenzie to Lavin, *NYR*, 9 December 1959.
10. Lavin to MacKenzie, *NYR*, 19 January 1960 (Lavin erroneously dated the letter 1959). Lavin restored the birds nesting in later versions of the story (see Hurley, 'To Cut a Long Story Short'). *The New Yorker* published Benedict Kiely's 'The Wild Boy' on 30 January 1960. Michael McLaverty sent John McGahern the issue featuring the story. Clearly McLaverty and McGahern were unimpressed with the story when the latter wrote, 'The story is indeed as bad as you said it was – not really a story at all. Something strung hurriedly together for that fat fee the New Yorker pays and he has probably an easy wicket. His new novel [*The Captain with the Whiskers*] is coming out shortly. It is unlikely to be, on the N.Y. evidence, much of an event.' (MGA, 9 March 1960).
11. Mary Lavin, 'In a Café', *NY*, 13 February 1960, 33.
12. Leonard Dove (1906–1972) was an illustrator and cartoonist. He drew fifty-six covers for *The New Yorker* and also contributed cartoons to Collier's and Look publications.
13. Frank Modell (1917–2016) was an American cartoonist who for over fifty years, since 1946, contributed over 1,400 cartoons to *The New Yorker*, which he described as 'angry men and sexy women and dogs'. Modell also illustrated six covers for the magazine. James Merrill (1926–1995), son of co-founder of the Merrill Lynch investment firm, was an American poet and writer who won the Pulitzer Prize for poetry in 1977 for *Divine Comedies* and the National Book Award in 1967 and 1979. *The New Yorke*r published forty-two of his poems. Robert Wallace (1932–1999) was an American poet. He befriended John Updike when both were studying English at Harvard. Marianne Moore (1887–1972) was an American poet and critic. In 1951 she won the National Book Award, Pulitzer Prize and Bollinger Prize for her *Collected Poems*. Charles Maitland Fair (1916–2014) was an American neuroscientist and writer. Information on Phyllis Graham is scant. This was her only story published in *The New Yorker.* Emily Hahn (1905–1997) was an American journalist and writer. She wrote for *The New Yorker* from 1929 until 1996 and was the magazine's China correspondent. Her literary agent Max Lieber, cofounder of Lieber & Lewis, also represented other *New Yorker* writers including John O'Hara and John Cheever.
14. *Two Weeks in Another Town* was adapted into a 1962 movie of the same, directed by Vincent Minnelli and starring Kirk Douglas, Cyd Charisse and Edward G. Robinson.
15. *Stories from The New Yorker: A Thirty-Fifth Anniversary Volume of Stories that Have Appeared in the Magazine during the Past Decade 1950–1960* (New York: Simon and Schuster, 1960), 247–61. The previous two volumes were for the years 1925–1940 and 1940–1950.

16. The records of royalties show that Lavin received $347.46 for sales through 31 March 1961; $52.58 for sales through 30 September 1962; and $52.75 for sales until 31 March 1966, for the republication of the story.
17. Lavin to MacKenzie, *NYR*, 28 November 1960.
18. MacKenzie to Lavin, *NYR*, 9 December 1960.
19. The volume was retitled *The Great Wave and Other Stories* (Macmillan, 1961).
20. Lavin to MacKenzie, *NYR*, 2 March and 15 February 1960.
21. 'Lemonade' was subsequently published in *The Great Wave and Other Stories* (1961) and *In a Café and Other Stories* (1985).
22. *NYR*, 19 January 1960.
23. Lavin to MacKenzie, *NYR*, 15 February 1960
24. Lavin to MacKenzie, *NYR*, 24 March 1960.
25. Lavin to MacKenzie, *NYR*, 29 March 1960.
26. Lavin to MacKenzie, *NYR*, 19 January 1960.The 'wonderful harvest' comprised 'Second-Hand', 'The Living', 'Bridal Sheets' and 'The Great Wave'.
27. Lavin to MacKenzie, *NYR*, undated but received by *The New Yorker* on 13 April 1960.
28. MacKenzie to Lavin, 13 April 1960. In January, MacKenzie informed Lavin that the magazine would handle the permissions directly with Macmillan (27 January 1961).
29. MacKenzie to Lavin, *NYR*, 19 April 1960.
30. Lavin to MacKenzie, *NYR*, 24 April 1960.
31. Lavin to MacKenzie, *NYR*, 6 July 1960. The amount included a 25 per cent premium of $257.50.
32. *NYR* 20 July 1960. The final version exceeded the wordage of the copy upon which Lavin's original payment was based, and so she received an additional cheque of $56.25 to make up for the shortfall, which included a 25 per cent premium of $11.25.
33. Easter Sunday fell on 17 April in 1960.
34. Lavin to MacKenzie, *NYR*, 2 April 1960.
35. Lavin to MacKenzie, *NYR*, 26 May 1960.
36. MacKenzie to Lavin, *NYR*, 22 June 1960.
37. Lavin to MacKenzie, *NYR*, 6 July 1960.
38. MacKenzie commenced her three-week vacation on 9 July.
39. Lavin to Wade, Correspondence K. Macmillan (1967–1969), MLC, 23 September 1968.
40. Introduction, *The Lonely Voice*, 42–3.
41. *NYR*22 June 1960. Lavin had done further work on 'Loving Memory' while she was on a long train journey in Italy and she decided to change the narration from the first person to the third.
42. Lavin to MacKenzie, *NYR*, 6 July 1960.
43. *NYR*, 29 July 1960.
44. *NYR*, 8 February 1960.

45. *NYR*, 30 August 1960.
46. *NYR*, 3 September 1960 (Lavin later wrote to MacKenzie that the letter should have been dated 6 September 1960).
47. David Langdon (1914–2011) was once described by *The Evening Standard* as 'the greatest comic artist of our time'. He was one of *Punch*'s most prolific cartoonists and a regular contributor to *The New Yorker.*
48. Howard Nemeroy (1920–1991) was an American poet who won the National Book Award for Poetry and the Pulitzer Prize for Poetry in 1978. Burton Bernstein (1932–2017), the younger brother of conductor and composer Leonard Bernstein, was a staff writer for *The New Yorker* from 1957 to 1992. Calvin Tomkins (1925) is a New Yorker staff writer since 1960.
49. Lavin to MacKenzie, *NYR*, undated but sometime in September 1960.
50. MacKenzie to Lavin, *NYR*, 30 August 1960.
51. *The New Yorker* published twenty-three of Cullinan's stories between 1960 and 1981.
52. Author interview with Elizabeth Cullinan, 20 October 2009, New York.
53. See *The Happiness of Getting it Down Right*, 139. *The Château* was originally titled *Displaced Persons*. It was Frank O'Connor who, acting as an editor of sorts on the work, suggested the change in title. The novel was published in the spring of 1961 and Elizabeth Bowen reviewed it for *The Reporter.*
54. Author interview with Elizabeth Cullinan, 20 October 2009, New York.
55. MacKenzie to Lavin, *NYR*, 30 August 1960.
56. Lavin to MacKenzie, *NYR*, 7 September 1960.
57. *A Change of Scene* by Elizabeth Cullinan, reviewed by Maureen Connolly, *Irish Literary Supplement*, Vol. 2, No. 1, 1 March 1983. The article also states that their American publisher introduced them.
58. *NY*, 29 August 1970.
59. MacKenzie to Lavin, *NYR*, 30 August 1960.
60. Lavin to MacKenzie, *NYR*, 9 September 1960.
61. Lavin to MacKenzie, *NYR*, 10 September 1960.
62. Colm Tóibín, 'In Honour of Mary', *Sunday Independent*, 14 June 1992.
63. Lavin to MacKenzie, *NYR*, 10 September 1960.
64. MacKenzie to Lavin, *NYR*, 12 September 1960.
65. MLC (Memorabilia). Lavin recorded the note on the newspaper on 25 January 1971.
66. An excerpt of Liam Nolan's interview with Lavin was replayed on *Bowman: Sunday*, 3 June 2012, RTÉ Radio 1.
67. *NYR*, 12 September 1960.
68. The story was retitled 'A Miscellany of Characters That Will Not Appear' in the collection, which featured six of Cheever's *New Yorker* stories.
69. 'The Catbird Seat' was published in *The New Yorker* on 14 November 1942 and was adapted for film by Monja Danischewsky. It starred Peter Sellers, Robert Morley and Constance Cummings. *A Thurber Carnival* was directed by Burgess Meredith and the cast included Thurber himself.

70. The story features John O'Hara's recurring literary alter ego, the Irish American Jimmy Malloy.
71. MacKenzie to Lavin, *NYR*, 12 September 1960. On the front page of that day's *New York Times* is an article with the headline 'City is Preparing for Gales Today: L.I. Cleared.' The article stated: 'An emergency hurricane advisory issued at the Battery said that winds of 115 miles an hour were confined to a small area around the center of the storm, but that winds of at least seventy-five miles an hour would extend outward 110 miles in all directions.'
72. Hurricane Donna in '60 Was the Last Bad One', *The New York Times*, 10 August 1976.
73. MacKenzie to Lavin, *NYR*, 6 October 1960.
74. Lavin to MacKenzie, *NYR*, 17 October 1960.
75. MacKenzie to Lavin, *NYR*, 29 November 1960.
76. Lavin to MacKenzie, *NYR*, 12 December 1960.
77. *Cosmopolitan*, 153 (Aug. 1962), 60–3. It was also included in *Happiness and Other Stories (*1969) and *Collected Stories* (1971).
78. Lavin to MacKenzie, *NYR*, 28 November 1960.
79. *NYR*, 29 November 1960.
80. MacKenzie to Lavin, *NYR*, 9 December 1960.
81. *NYR*, 12 December 1960. Lavin's 1099 form (US Information Return) for the 1960 calendar year show that her annuities, pensions, and other fixed or determinable income came to $5,850.17.

4 'A Moral Obligation' *1961–1962*

1. Mary Lavin to Rachel MacKenzie, *NYR*, 7 December 1962.
2. MacKenzie to Lavin, *NYR*, 25 January 1961.
3. Lavin's first contract was dated 3 June 1959.
4. Mary Lavin held on to her American citizenship, as per her dying father's request, until she relinquished it in 1981, 'Until recent years I feel obliged to keep this promise until now in my 70th year I feel it is ridiculous, having spent 60 years in Ireland and all my forbears were and my children and grandchildren are Irish, I wish to live an Irishwoman.' (MLLP, 17 August 1981). Anthony Burgess in his *Irish Press* review of Lavin's *The Shrine and Other Stories* remarked of Lavin, 'She is strictly an American, having been born in Massachusetts, but she has been long enough domiciled in Ireland to be regarded as of a distinguished national tradition (I leave her ancestry out of the question)', 'What Literature is About', *The Irish Press,* 2 June 1977. Lavin would have strongly disagreed.
5. *The Best American Short Stories 1961*. Martha Foley (1897–1977), along with her former husband, Whit Burnett, co-founded and co-edited the influential *Story* magazine, which published the first works by J. D. Salinger, whom Burnett taught at Columbia, and Truman Capote,

whom Foley taught at Columbia. She succeeded Edward J. O'Brien as editor of *Best American Short Stories* and her son, David Burnett, later joined her as co-editor. Milton Greenstein (1911–1991), a lawyer, joined *The New Yorker* in 1945, where he checked copy for potential libel. He then headed up the legal department and became vice president in 1962 and assistant secretary in 1976. He continued working as a consultant for the magazine after his retirement in 1976.

6. Peter Taylor (1917–1994) was an American short story writer, novelist and playwright who won the 1987 Pulitzer Prize for *A Summons to Memphis*. He was married to the poet Eleanor Ross Taylor, who was also a *New Yorker* contributor.
7. Lavin to MacKenzie, *NYR*, 20 March 1961. Lavin's story 'The Sand Castle' was included in the O. Henry annual collection of the year's best stories in 1945.
8. Lionel Trilling (1905–1975) was a short-story writer, literary critic and professor of English at Columbia University. André Maurois (1885–1967) was a French novelist, essayist and biographer. The college's first annual Writer's Conference (which featured sixteen writers including Ralph Ellison and W. D. Snodgrass, who gave lectures 'on the tricks and trials of their craft') took place at the end of April, but Trilling and Maurois were not part of this group.
9. Lavin to MacKenzie, *NYR*, 27 February 1961. Lavin wrote the letter in the National Library of Ireland. On 15 October 1967 Lionel Trilling responded to a letter that Lavin had written to him, in which she must have expressed her desire to meet with him. He was teaching at Columbia and suggested that they meet for lunch in New York some Saturday; however, Lavin noted on the letter that it 'came to nothing.' MLC (Correspondence 1935–1975 folder).
10. Lavin to MacKenzie, *NYR*, 20 March 1961.
11. Norah Lavin was born on 7 April 1881.
12. Lavin to MacKenzie, *NYR*, 20 March 1961.
13. 'Loving Memory', *The New Yorker* 20 August 1960 and 'The Yellow Beret', *The New Yorker* 12 November 1960.
14. Lavin to MacKenzie, *NYR*, 24 February 1961.
15. *NYR*, 20 March 1961. MacKenzie was ill with a virus and so her letter was signed by 'LR', as MacKenzie would not have wished to delay the news about the acceptance.
16. MacKenzie to Lavin, *NYR*, 12 April 1961.
17. *In the Middle of the Fields and Other Stories* (Constable, 1967; Macmillan, 1969).
18. 'In the Middle of the Fields', *NY*, 32.
19. MacKenzie to Lavin, *NYR*, 12 April 1961.
20. MacKenzie to Lavin, *NYR*, 26 April 1961.
21. Lavin to Oliver, *NYR*, 14 January 1958.

22. 'It's one of those semi-autobiographical stories – like In a Café & The Middle of the Fields – that I loathe anyway & find very hard' (*NYR*, 14 February 1962).
23. The average (median) income of families in 1961 in the US was approximately $5,700, according to estimates released by the Bureau of the Census, Department of Commerce.
24. MacKenzie to Lavin, *NYR*, 20 March 1961.
25. The cover was by Abe Birnbaum (1899–1996), who illustrated nearly 200 *New Yorker* covers.
26. Donald Davie (1922–1995) was an English poet. He taught at Trinity College Dublin, Cambridge University, the University of Essex, Stanford and Vanderbilt University.
27. Lavin to MacKenzie, *NYR*, 20 March 1961. There is no further mention of 'The Faithful Heart' but it is possible that Lavin renamed the story 'Heart of Gold', which she sent to the magazine in 1963.
28. Lavin to MacKenzie, *NYR*, 16 July 1960.
29. MacKenzie to Lavin, *NYR*, 3 May 1961.
30. Lavin's other three bonus stories in this cycle were 'The Yellow Beret' (1960), 'Loving Memory' (1960) and 'In the Middle of the Fields' (1961).
31. Lavin to MacKenzie, *NYR*, 8 May 1961
32. Lavin to MacKenzie, *NYR*, 20 April 1961.
33. MacKenzie to Lavin, *NYR*, 12 April 1961.
34. Lavin to MacKenzie, *NYR*, 20 April 1961.
35. MacKenzie to Lavin, *NYR*, 26 April 1961. MacKenzie left for Italy on 23 May. In a letter to Lavin before her departure, she wrote: 'The trip to Italy begins to feel as if it might be real. I leave the twenty-third. How I long for sun!' (12 May 1961).
36. Lavin to MacKenzie, *NYR*, 22 March 1961.
37. MacKenzie to Lavin, *NYR*, 26 April 1961.
38. Lavin to MacKenzie, *NYR*, undated but before 26 April 1960. Ned O'Gorman (1929–2014) was an American poet. He received an MA from Columbia University, where he studied with the poet Mark Van Doren. O'Gorman was awarded the Guggenheim Fellowship in 1956 and 1962, during which he travelled, visiting Ireland to trace his family's roots. He also travelled to Africa. *The New Yorker* published three of his poems on 2 June 1997, 25 August 1997 and 30 March 1998. O'Gorman was the literary editor of the Catholic magazine *Jubilee* from 1962 to 1965. A *New Yorker* 'Talk of the Town' piece focused on O'Gorman's running of a library and children's day centre in Harlem (2 December 1967).
39. MacKenzie to Lavin, *NYR*, 26 April 1961.
40. MacKenzie to Lavin, *NYR*,12 May 1961.
41. Lavin to MacKenzie, *NYR*, 20 April 1961.
42. Lavin to MacKenzie, *NYR*, 9 May 1961.

43. Lavin to MacKenzie, *NYR*, 8 May 1961. 'A Dream' was never published in *The New Yorker* and does not appear to have been published elsewhere, unless it underwent a title change.
44. Lavin to Maxwell, *NYR*, 7 June 1961 (had an earlier date of 5 June 1961).
45. MacKenzie to Lavin, *NYR*, 21 June 1961.
46. Lavin to MacKenzie, *NYR*, 27 and 28 June 1961. Lavin's US Information Return for the Calendar Year 1961 was $6,378.92.
47. Lavin to MacKenzie, *NYR*, June 1961 (date is crossed out but appears to be postmarked 19 June).
48. *NYR*, 28 June 1961.
49. Edward J. Rice (1918–2001) was an American author and publisher who founded *Jubilee* magazine in 1953.
50. *NYR*, two dates: 27 June and 29 June 1961.
51. *NYR*, 5 July 1961.
52. *NYR*, 11 July 1961.
53. *NYR*, 13 July 1961.
54. Lavin to MacKenzie, *NYR*, 11 July 1961.
55. *NYR*, 16 August 1961.
56. *NYR*, 11 July 1961. The Russian-born writer Vladimir Nabokov (1899–1977) was a regular visitor to the French Riviera from 1904 until 1961. He wrote *Pale Fire* (1962) in Nice, considered by some critics to be his greatest work.
57. *The New York Times*, 2 August 1961.
58. Mary McGrory, 'Stories of Erin, A Deep Look Into The Irish Heart', *The Evening Star*, 6 August 1961. Mary McGrory (1918–2004) was known as 'The First Queen of Journalism'. Her political journalism career began when she reported on the McCarthy trials in 1954 and later covered the presidency of John F. Kennedy, whom she had briefly dated. She won the Pulitzer Prize in 1975 for her commentary on the Watergate scandal.
59. Francis Stuart, 'Mary Lavin's Short Stories', *The Irish Times*, 3 June 1961.
60. 'A Turn to Enchantment', *The Saturday Review*, 44 (12 August 1961),
61. MLPP, 30 June 1961.
62. *NYR*, 21 September 1961.
63. *NYR*, 23 October 1961.
64. *NYR*, 20 October 1961.
65. The 1099 form is used to report non-employment income to the Internal Revenue Service (IRS).
66. *NYR*, 23 October 1961.
67. Author interview with Elizabeth Cullinan, 20 October 2009, New York. Cullinan noted that John F. Kennedy's presidency changed the perception of the Irish in America. She noticed a stark difference in the power of the Church in Ireland, where it dictated, in comparison to the United States, where there was choice. Cullinan must have shared a certain sense of being an outsider with Maeve Brennan, who she thought

was 'sophisticated and brilliant, a bon vivant' but she always got the sense that Brennan was displaced, which she found heartbreaking. Cullinan thought Brennan's American stories were written in a sophisticated vein but that her Irish stories tell of 'a world she had lost'.

68. *NY*, 18 August 1967.
69. Frank O'Connor's Dublin apartment was 34 Court Flats, Wilton Place, Dublin 2. In November of 1962 O'Connor and his family moved to the larger 22 Court Flats. The new Mary Lavin Place is located in Wilton Park.
70. 10 October 1961 and 5 April 1962, *The Happiness of Getting It Down Right,* 174. Daniel (Dan) Binchy (1899–1989), who was born in Cork, was the first Irish ambassador to Germany from 1929 until 1932. He was the uncle of the Irish novelist Maeve Binchy and a friend of Seán Ó Faoláin.
71. *The Happiness of Getting It Down Right*, 153. George Russell's poem 'Enchantment' was published under his pseudonym, Æ, in *The New Yorker* on 5 April 1930.
72. Frank O'Connor gave 'three lectures epitomizing his own teaching of the short story' at the conference. Holden was a professor of journalism at Wayne State University. MacKenzie was a member of staff that year and Wallace Stegner gave an evening talk. The 1953 catalogue contains a photograph of O'Connor with Robert Frost.
73. *NYR*, 7 December 1961. 'Mrs. Ever's Eiderdown' was published in Aylesford Review, 4 (Winter, 1961/62), 186–91.
74. 'The Literary Scene in 1961', *The Sunday Star*, Washington, D.C., 10 December 1961. According to a *Time* magazine cover story on Salinger, William Shawn was so flattered that Salinger dedicated *Franny and Zooey* to him that *The New Yorker* gave away 6,000 copies of the book. O'Connor, who read the article, asked Maxwell to add him to the list of recipients. However, Maxwell explained that the business department had suggested the book for a promotional Christmas gift, but the idea was abandoned. Shawn did, however, send O'Connor a copy. Hemingway had contributed one story, 'My Own Life', to *The New Yorker*, which was published on 12 February 1927. The magazine published 'Miss Mary's Sorrow' on 24 May 1999.
75. MacKenzie to Lavin, *NYR*, 24 January 1962. Michael McLaverty met Cullinan and found her to be 'a lovely sweet girl'. He 'fished out' some of her stories from past copies of the magazine, which he greatly enjoyed: 'Her stories are good. They are cool and calm and precise.' He advised McGahern to recommend that she borrow *My Darling from the Lion's Mouth* from Lavin, 'if she was still around at Christmas'. (See *In Quiet Places: Uncollected Stories, Letters and Critical Prose of Michael McLaverty*, 1989, 206–7).
76. Easter fell on 22 April in 1962.
77. MacKenzie to Lavin, *NYR*, 24 January 1962. The first American edition was published by J. B. Lippincott Company, Philadelphia and New York, 1962.
78. See Stannard, 257.

79. Spark was paid $6,000 for the story and had a $750 first-reading agreement with the magazine.
80. See Stannard, 257. Lovat Dickson (1902–1987), known as Rache, was a publisher and writer. In his short-lived *Lovat Dickson Magazine* he published works by Frank O'Connor including his 'First Confession' under the title 'Repentance' in 1935. Rache joined the staff of Macmillan & Company in London in 1938 and became a director and general manager of the firm.
81. *NYR*, 9 March 1962.
82. *The Ante-Room* was published by Macmillan London in 1959. It was also the title of Kate O'Brien's second novel, published in 1934.
83. Shirley Hazzard's first published story, 'Woollahra Road', appeared in *The New Yorker* in on 8 April 1961. The following year ten of Hazzard's *New Yorker* stories were published in the book *Cliffs of Fall and Other Stories*. Lovat Dickson was introduced to Shirley Hazzard by Alan Pryce-Jones. See Brigitta Olubas, *Shirley Hazzard: A Writing Life* (Little, Brown Book Group, 2022, Kindle, 189–90).
84. See Olubas, 190.
85. See Stannard, 277–8. MacKenzie, amusingly, played the role of 'an efficient maiden aunt' in a play while at Wells College.
86. See Stannard, 278. The relationship between Hazzard and MacKenzie broke down with Hazzard believing MacKenzie had 'a crush' on her and so William Maxwell, who edited her first *New Yorker* story, was reassigned to her (See Olubas, 192).
87. *NYR*, 26 February 1962. MacKenzie noted that she had met Pamela in the previous month. The Ruth White Gallery was established in 1956 and specialised in contemporary art. The Dawson Gallery was established by Leo Smith in 1944 at 4 Dawson Street, Dublin 2, and was taken over by John Taylor, upon Smith's death in 1978, when he renamed it Taylor Galleries. Pamela Matthews seems to have withdrawn from the art world after she married in 1965.
88. *NYR*, 26 February 1962.
89. *NYR*, 14 February 1962.
90. *NYR*, 26 February 1962.
91. Lavin speculated that had she gone to Italy she would 'have felt too good'.
92. Elizabeth Cullinan, 'Remembering Mary', 'A Bouquet for Mary', *Irish Literary Supplement*, Fall 1996, Volume 15, Number 2.
93. *NYR*, 14 February 1962.
94. *NYR*, 26 February 1962.
95. *NYR*, 25 April 1962.
96. *NYR*, 8 March 1962.
97. *NYR*, 19 March 1962.
98. *NYR*, 2 April 1962.
99. *NYR*, 30 April 1962.

100. *NYR*, 3 May 1962. On 5 May, *The Meath Chronicle* reported that Lavin was the guest speaker at the Mayo Historical Society in Castlebar.
101. 'Sonny: An Introduction', *Time*, 15 September 1961.
102. The cover may have been a nod to the fact that the Metropolitan Opera season had ended in the week prior to Lavin's story appearing in the 28 April 1962 issue.
103. Allen Ginsberg (1926–1997) coined the term 'flower power' and was one of the leading poets of the Beat generation and influencer of the American youth counterculture. He is probably best known for his controversial long poem *Howl* (1956), which was banned in the US and the subject of an obscenity trial due to its sexual explicitness and detail of drug use. Ginsberg's second and third books, *Kaddish and Other Poems*, and *Empty Mirror: Early Poems* were both published in 1961.
104. The cartoonist Dana Fradon (1922–2019), contributed approximately 1,400 cartoons to *The New Yorker.*
105. Jeane Dixon (1896–1981) also allegedly predicted John F. Kennedy's assassination.
106. On 25 March Helen McGrory reviewed Sylvia Townsend Warner's collection *A Spirit Rises*, which took its title from her *New Yorker* story that was published on 8 July 1961, for *The Evening Star*. McGrory deemed the volume 'not brilliant but it is enormously competent' and observed that 'The Irish have now outstripped the English in the short-story field' and noted that Warner 'cannot hold a candle to Lavin; she does not go as deep'.
107. Maxwell to Michael (Frank O'Connor), late March 1962, *The Happiness of Getting It Down Right.*
108. O'Connor to Maxwell, 5 April 1962, *The Happiness of Getting It Down Right.*
109. The crash forms the plot of *Flight 1*, the second episode in Season 2 of *Mad Men* (2008).
110. William Faulkner's (1897–1962) final novel, *The Reivers*, published in 1962, won the Pulitzer Prize for Fiction in 1963 (he had previously won the award in 1955 for *A Fable*). Frank O'Connor was awarded an honorary doctorate by Trinity College Dublin on 5 July 1962.
111. *NYR*, 3 May 1962. Lavin had intended to visit the US from around 28 October until 11 November.
112. This was a very similar title to one of Lavin's poems, 'Let Me Come Inland Always', that was published in *Dublin Magazine*, 15 (Jan.–March 1940), 1–2. Lavin had considered two other titles for 'Let me Come Inland', namely, 'The Inland Woman' and 'Cleggan'. She was excited about the story that had suddenly formed in her mind during the composition of 'The Great Wave', as had happened with 'The Bridal Sheets'. Lavin believed the new work to be an improved version of 'The Great Wave' that was 'so much deeper' and 'truer' than the original. *NYR*, 14 February 1962.

113. *NYR*, 11 April 1962.
114. *NYR*, 2 April 1962. MacKenzie posted Lavin the book on 11 April 1962. Katherine Anne Porter (1890–1980) was a regular contributor to *The New Yorker*. *Ship of Fools* was published by Little, Brown. In 1966 Porter's *The Collected Stories* won both the Pulitzer Prize for Fiction and the National Book Award for Fiction. She was nominated five times for the Nobel Prize in Literature. The 21 Club, frequently referred to as 21, was a traditional American restaurant and former speakeasy located at 21 West 52nd Street in New York City.
115. Late March 1962. See *The Happiness of Getting It Down Right*.
116. Porter was awarded the Guggenheim Fellowship in 1931 and 1938.
117. The novel was adapted for the big screen in 1965 by Abby Mann and was produced and directed by Stanley Kramer. It starred Vivien Leigh in her last film role.
118. *NYR*, 3 March 1962.
119. The story was also titled 'Cressie' at one stage (MLLP).
120. Stephen Schiff, 'Muriel Spark Between the Lines', *The New Yorker* (24 May 1993), 36–43.
121. *NYR*, 30 April 1962.
122. *NYR*, 3 May 1962.
123. *NYR*, 7 May 1962. Lavin had mentioned to MacKenzie that she would hold on to the Guggenheim 'for a really funny short novel about two sisters that I've wanted to do for a few years now', *NYR*,14 February 1962.
124. In her panicked state, Lavin had lost $2,500 in traveller's cheques, but the money would be refunded. 'I'm sure you're thinking it was bad enough for me to be acting like a squirrel without losing the nuts?' *NYR*, undated but a direct response to MacKenzie's 7 May letter.
125. *Sunday Independent*, 17 June 1962. JFK was awarded the honorary doctorate from Yale on 11 July 1961. The James Joyce Society in New York was founded by Frances Steloff, 'the Sylvia Beach of New York', in the Gotham Book Mart in February 1947 ('The New York James Joyce Society' by Zack Bowen, *Joyce Studies Annual*, Vol. 12, Summer 2001). Donagh MacDonagh was the son of the Irish Nationalist and poet Thomas MacDonagh.
126. An interesting sidebar concerning Lavin and a connection to James Joyce was that she knew his friend Oliver St. John Gogarty, who was the inspiration for for Buck Mulligan in *Ulysses*. On 1 July. On 1 July 1950, Gogarty wrote to Lavin from Renvyle in Connemara with news from his New York agent Franz Horch, that a publisher, who Gogarty suspected to be Devin Adair, was interested in bringing out a novel or new collection of stories by either Lavin or Frank O'Connor (MLPP).
127. MLPP, 25 June 1962.
128. Sylvia Beach Papers, 1872–1999, Department of Special Collections, Princeton University Library, 25 June 1962.
129. Letter to Sheridan, National Library of Ireland (7 July 1962). On 19 November 1968 Telefís Éireann broadcast an episode of *Writer in Profile*,

which featured an interview conducted by Niall Sheridan with Mary Lavin on her life and work. Telefís Éireann, Ireland's national broadcaster's first channel, began broadcasting on 31 December 1961. *Writer in Profile* was a weekly television interview with a well-known Irish writer. First broadcast on 29 October 1968, it ran until 1976. Niall Sheridan knew Lavin from their university days.

130. MLPP.
131. The obituary clipping from *The Sunday Times* (14 October 1962), anon. is contained in Mary Lavin's Literary Papers, UCD.
132. The English writer Margery Sharp (1905–1991) is probably best known for *The Rescuers* (1959), which was later adapted into an animated Disney film.
133. The world premiere of *Lolita* was held in New York on 13 June of that year which, ironically, Lyon was too young to attend. Brendan Gill reviewed the movie in *The New Yorker* on 23 June 1962.
134. *Country Beautiful*, 2, No. 1 (September 1962), 18, 20.
135. *NYR*, 29 October 1962.
136. *NYR*, 6 September 1962.
137. *NYR*, 17 September 1962.
138. *NYR*, 10 October 1962.
139. *NYR*, 6 September 1962.
140. *Drogheda Independent*, 10 November 1962. Elizabeth was in fact sixteen at the time.
141. *NYR*, the date is indecipherable but it is late September or early October 1962.
142. 'Focus on Mid-Meath Topics, Won French Story Prize', *Drogheda Independent*, 3 November 1962. William Sansom (1912–1876) was a British author. L. P. Hartley (1895–1972) was a novelist and short-story writer.
143. *Drogheda Independent*, 3 November 1962.
144. *NYR*, 7 December 1962.
145. The acronym PEN stands for poets, playwrights, essayists and novelists.
146. 'New Story', *The Irish Press*, 11 December 1962.
147. Sean J. White (1927–1996) was an Irish writer, journalist and broadcaster.
148. Fergus Wright, 'Frank O'Connor gets a plea for books', 'Panorama' section, *Sunday Independent*, 2 December 1962.
149. *Sunday Independent*, 30 December 1962.
150. *NYR*, 7 December 1962.
151. Lavin's rate was '18–19 cents a word minimum' for 'first-reading of all fiction, humor, reminiscence and casual essays'.
152. *NYR*, 7 December 1962.
153. *NYR*, 20 December 1962.
154. MLPP, 24 January 1962.
155. *NYR*, 20 December 1962. The Cosmopolitan Club, located between Park and Lexington Avenues, was founded as a private women's club in 1909.

Its members have included Jean Stafford, Eleanor Roosevelt, Willa Cather and Pearl S. Buck.

156. In 1954 Elizabeth 'Betty' Kray (1916–1987) became director of the Poetry Center. In 1963 Kray was appointed the first executive director of the Academy of American Poets. In 1985 she co-founded Poets House with US poet laureate Stanley Kunitz. According to her *New York Times* obituary, Kray 'also acted as a personal agent for W. H. Auden, E. E. Cummings, Marianne Moore, Edith Sitwell and Stephen Spender (*The New York Times*, 24 November 1987).
157. *NYR*, 20 December 1962. On 16 April 1956, Leonard Cohen wrote to 'Mr. Galen Eberl' at the Poetry Centre and in a postscript enquired 'Are you a man?' Cohen's first musical performance was at the Poetry Center on 14 February 1966. See Pico Iyer's, "'I Told You When I Came I Was a Stranger", Leonard Cohen's first public musical performance,' *Harper's*, 14 February 2014.
158. *NYR*, Undated letter but written in response to MacKenzie's 7 December letter which enclosed the first-reading contract.
159. *NYR*, 26 December 1962.
160. *NYR*, 20 December 1962.
161. *NYR*, 26 December 1962. MacKenzie mistitled the traditional Christmas carol 'In Dulci Jubilo'.

5 'Paperback Writer' *1963–1964*

1. Rachel MacKenzie to Mary Lavin, *NYR*, 22 January 1963
2. Lavin to MacKenzie, *NYR*, 5 November 1963.
3. The quarterly payment (COLA) totalled $824.13 before the deduction of the retirement plan contribution of $12.35. The adjustment to the previous year's COLA was $684.48 before the deduction of the retirement plan contribution of $10.27.
4. *NYR*, 22 January 1963.
5. *NYR*, 26 February 1963. Roger Angell (1920–2022), the son of Katharine White, was a *New Yorker* fiction editor, staff writer and long-time contributor. The magazine published his first *New Yorker* story, 'Three Ladies in the Morning', in 1944 and his final contribution was a 'Comment' piece, 'The Children's Hour', which he wrote at the age of 100 in 2020. Muriel Spark and Shirley Hazzard felt somewhat contrite when they heard that MacKenzie had had a heart attack. Hazzard telephoned MacKenzie's sister only to be met with a 'cool response' (Stannard, 284).
6. William Maxwell to Harriet O'Connor, undated 1963, *The Happiness of Getting it Down Right,* 201.
7. John McGahern to Michael McLaverty, 21 March 1963. See *The Letters of John McGahern* (Faber & Faber, 2021, Kindle, 117). In a letter of 23

January 1959 McLaverty recommended that McGahern read, for his 'own private enjoyment', Mary Lavin's 'The Small Bequest', Frank O'Connor's 'Uprooted' and Tolstoy's 'The Death of Ivan Ilyich' (see *In Quiet Places*, 195).

8. McGahern to Joe Kennedy, 7 February 1999, *The Letters of John McGahern* (Kindle, 893).
9. 6 January 1963, *The Happiness of Getting it Down Right*, 194. John McGahern became a regular visitor to the mews. On 15 June he sent Lavin a letter of thanks for a lovely evening at her home and revealed that it was the second party he had ever attended, the other being a function at Drogheda's Custom House (MLPP, 15 June 1960). In another letter he wrote 'It was a very lucky day for me to meet somebody like you. I had almost lost faith in men and women.' (MLLP, 9 May, year unknown).
10. In June 1963 Salinger's last published book that contained the novellas 'Raise High the Roof Beam, Carpenters' and 'Seymour: An Introduction' was published. Both pieces originally featured in *The New Yorker* in 1955 and 1959 respectively. It was the third-bestselling book of 1963 in the US.
11. *NYR*, 23 April 1963. The letter was written on the liner's headed paper. *The Empress of England* was launched by Lady Eden, wife of the Prime Minister Anthony Eden, on 9 May 1956. It sailed between Liverpool and Montreal. Its maiden voyage was on 18 April 1957. The liner departed from Liverpool on 9 April.
12. The aerogram was dated 7 May 1963. Lavin had evidently returned to East Walpole, where she spent her early years.
13. *The Heights*, 5 April 1963.
14. Paul George Vincent O'Shaughnessy Horgan (1903–1995) wrote historical fictional and non-fictional works and was a professor of English and American Studies at Wesleyan University. He contributed nine stories to *The New Yorker* between the years 1930 and 1938. In 1957, he received a papal knighthood from Pope Pius XII for his contributions to Catholic literature. David McCullough, writing in *The New York Times Book Review* in 1984, stated, 'With the exception of Wallace Stegner, no living American has so distinguished himself in both fiction and history.'
15. *The Heights*, 5 April 1963. Riley Hughes (1914–1981) was a writer who taught English at Georgetown University and helped found the university's writers' conference.
16. *The New Yorker* published a story by Phelan (Francis Joseph), 'Story of My Life', on 2 August 1958.
17. *NYR*, 17 May 1963.
18. 'S.S. America Lands 208 Passengers at Cobh', *Irish Examiner*, 24 May 1964. There is a discrepancy about the number of passengers in the article.
19. John Harold Hewitt (1907–1987) was a renowned and influential Irish poet and political activist. He was the first writer-in-residence

at Queen's University Belfast. The John Hewitt Society and the John Hewitt International Summer School were both established in 1987 to honour his legacy. Hewitt's and Lavin's work appeared in *Irish Harvest*, published in 1946. Other contributors included Lavin's first husband William Walsh, Michael McLaverty, Elizabeth Bowen, Lennox Robinson, Donagh MacDonagh, Seán Ó Faoláin and Robert Greacen, who was also the editor of the volume. Seamus MacCall (1892–1964) was an Irish writer and soldier. In 1931 he became art editor of *The Irish Press*. In June Lavin, in her role as vice-chairman, was the guest of honour at the annual Irish PEN dinner, which took place in Jury's Hotel, Dublin.

20. *NYR*, undated but postmarked 31 May 1963.
21. *NYR*, 6 June 1963.
22. *NYR*, 20 June 1963.
23. See Stannard, 256. Le Pavillon was a French restaurant founded by Henri Soulé that operated in New York City from 1941 until 1972 (not to be confused with Daniel Boulud's New York restaurant of the same name).
24. 'Remembering Mr. Shawn, Friends and colleagues recall the years with William Shawn', *The New Yorker*, 20 December 1992.
25. Lavin to Shawn, William Shawn papers. Manuscripts and Archives Division. The New York Public Library. Astor, Lenox, and Tilden Foundations. 12 June 1963.
26. Lavin to MacKenzie, *NYR*, 18 June 1963.
27. *The Stories of Mary Lavin, Vol. 1* (Constable, 1964).
28. *NYR*, 6 June 1963. Brentano's was founded in New York City in 1853. Its flagship store was on Fifth Avenue. Scribner's Bookstore, founded in 1913, was housed at 597 Fifth Avenue and closed its doors in 1988.
29. *NYR*, 20 June 1963.
30. The Gotham Book Mart was founded by Frances Steloff (1887–1989) in 1920 and operated in various locations until 2007. At the time MacKenzie set up an account for Lavin, the bookstore was located on 51 West 47th Street.
31. *NYR*, 25 June 1963.
32. 'Fierce Storm Damage', *Irish Independent*, 12 June 1963.
33. *NYR*, 11 July 1963.
34. *NYR*, 25 July 1963.
35. *NYR*, 31 July 1963.
36. *NYR*, 25 July 1963. In an interview conducted a few years before she died, Lavin noted that she and Eudora Welty had 'a long history of parallel careers'. Their early stories were published in *The Atlantic* and their 'first books came out in the same year, and both books won prizes.' 'An Interview with Mary Lavin', L. Robert, Mary Lavin and Sylvia Stevens, *Studies: An Irish Quarterly Review*, Vol. 86, No. 341 (Spring, 1997), 43–50: https://www.jstor.org/stable/30092397.

37. 'Where Is the Voice Coming from?' was inspired by the murder of civil rights activist Medgar Evers on 12 June 1963. Welty wrote the story on the night Evers was shot in Jackson, Mississippi, where they both lived.
38. It was republished in *The Irish Press*, 27 April 1968 and anthologised in *Nightlines*.
39. MGA, undated letter. Lavin's story 'The Small Bequest' was anthologised in the annual collection *Winter's Tales 9*, which also featured Muriel Spark's 'The Gentile Jewesses', originally published in *The New Yorker* on 22 June 1963, and Edna O'Brien's 'Sister Imelda', later published in *The New Yorker* on 9 November 1981 (this was unusual as *The New Yorker* generally only published original works).'The Small Bequest' was first published in *Good Housekeeping* in June 1944 and subsequently in *Irish Writing* No. 7 (February 1949).
40. *NYR*, 5 November 1963.
41. *NYR*, 24 November 1963.
42. On 5 October Lavin was the guest of honour at the Irish PEN annual dinner at Jury's hotel in Dublin. The *Irish Independent* covered the event at which Lavin made 'a plea for more young authors to join the Dublin and Belfast centres of P.E.N.'. At the event, Seamus MacCall, chairman of PEN, 'hoped every member of the organisation would make an attempt to recruit at least one more writer to join the ranks' and RDS librarian Desmond Clarke 'said it was the duty of every Irish writer to be a member'. *Irish Independent*, 7 October 1963.
43. *NYR*, 24 November 1963. Princess Grace visited Ireland with her husband Prince Rainier on 10 June 1961.
44. *NYR*, Western Union Cablegram, 29 November 1963. Claire L'Estrange posted 'Heart of Gold' on 25 November 1963 and MacKenzie sent a Western Union cablegram on November 29 acknowledging its receipt.
45. *NYR*, 10 December 1963. A contribution of $11.25 had been deducted from the retirement plan.
46. *NYR*, 31 December 1963.
47. Colm Tóibín, 'Mary Lavin: Context and Character', *American Journal of Irish Studies*, Vol. 10 (2013), 94–113, Glucksman Ireland House, New York University.
48. *NYR*, 31 December 1963.
49. *NYR*, 24 January 1964.
50. *NYR*, 14 January 1964. *The Stories of Mary Lavin, Vol. I,* Constable, 1964. The next collection, *In the Middle of the Fields and Other Stories*, was not published until 1967.
51. *NYR*, 28 January 1964. Lavin was paid a total of $2,893.75 for 'Heart of Gold', which included a $578.75 premium.
52. John McGahern to Michael McLaverty, *The Letters of John McGahern.*
53. MLPP, undated letters from 1964.

54. *NYR*, 28 January 1964. The background on Geneva Jacobs was imparted to the author by Rachel MacKenzie's niece Joan MacKenzie, who stated that Gennie 'was my aunt as much as Rachel and Ruth [Rachel's sister]'. In MacKenzie's semi-autobiographical story, 'Risk', the narrator lives with her adopted sister Ellie.
55. *NYR*, undated but before 23 February 1964.
56. *NYR*, 20 March 1964.
57. *NYR*, 14 January 1964.
58. 'English Aristocrat Valerie Goulding was Founder and Driving Force Behind Clinic', Michael O'Regan, *The Irish Times*, 20 January 2014.
59. *NYR*, undated letter. *One of a Kind* was a joint venture between Harry Reasoner and Andy Rooney. Reasoner was one of the founders of CBS's *60 Minutes*.
60. MacKenzie received Lavin's letter informing her of the documentary the Monday after it was broadcast but she hoped that there would be a re-run.
61. *NYR*, March 20, 1964.
62. Jack Gould, 'Four Residents Discuss Life in Irish Capital in C.B.S. "One of a Kind"', *The New York Times*, 24 February 1964.
63. MLPP, 27 February 1964.
64. 'London Letter', *Irish Examiner*, 28 December 1964.
65. In 2018 Fitzwilton House was razed and redeveloped into Wilton Park. There had been a public campaign to save the brutalist building. To add to the irony, the new development named its square Mary Lavin Place, the first space to be named after a female Irish writer. See 'Commemorative Essay on Mary Lavin', by Kathleen MacMahon, *The Irish Times*, 27 March 2021.
66. *NYR*, 20 March 1964.
67. R. R. Donnelley was founded in 1864 in Chicago.
68. Michael Sissons (1934–2018) represented John McGahern and it was McGahern who put Lavin in touch with Sissons. August Dudley Peters (1892–1973) founded his literary agency in 1924 and the authors he represented included Frank O'Connor, Hilaire Belloc, J. B. Priestley, Evelyn Waugh and Kingsley Amis.
69. *NYR*, 5 April 1964. Harold Matson (1898–1988) was an American literary agent who founded the Harold Matson Company. The company's clients included Frank O'Connor, Evelyn Waugh, Flannery O'Connor, C. S. Forester, William Styron and John Irving. Don Congdon (1918–2009) joined the company in 1947 and acted as Frank O'Connor's American agent, but they fell out in 1962 and O'Connor moved to Cyrilly Abels (1903–1975) when she set up her own literary agency. Abels also represented Katherine Anne Porter, Zelda Popkin and Christina Stead. She also published posthumously Dylan Thomas's *Under Milk Wood* in the February 1954 issue, the premiere of which was performed on 14 May 1953 at the Poetry Center at 92Y, New York. Thomas, who was seriously

ill at the time, died on 9 November 1953. Congdon started up his own literary agency in 1983.

70. *NYR*, 19 May 1964.
71. *NYR*, 21 May 1964.
72. *NYR*, 14, April 1964.
73. *NYR*, 26 May 1964. Ivan von Auw worked for the Harold Ober agency from 1938 until his retirement in 1973. Some of the writers he handled during that time included Pearl Buck, James M. Cain, Agatha Christie, Langston Hughes, Ross MacDonald, Muriel Spark and Dylan Thomas. The New York literary agency McIntosh & Otis was founded in 1928 by Mavis McIntosh (1906–1986) and Elizabeth Otis. Authors they represented included Richard John Hersey, Sinclair Lewis, Patricia Highsmith, Harper Lee and Thomas Wolfe. Marie Rodell (1912–1975) was a New York literary agent and author. She handled the work of Rachel Carson and Martin Luther King's first book, *Stride Toward Freedom*.
74. *NYR*, 2 June 1964.
75. *NYR*, 8 June 1964.
76. *NYR*, 11 June 1964.
77. Anatol Kovarsky (1919 2016) was an artist and cartoonist who drew for *The New Yorker* between 1947 and 1969. In 1963 he drew the projections for the Broadway productions of *The Owl and the Pussycat*, which ran from 18 November 1964 until September 1965 in the ANTA Playhouse. Edward Lear's work was adapted by Bill Manhoff and starred Alan Alda and Diana Sands. Manhoff was a scriptwriter for many television series including *The Patridge Family*, *The Odd Couple* and *Leave It to Beaver*.
78. Robert Weber drew 1,481 cartoons and 11 covers for the magazine from 1962 to 2007.
79. The Ireland pavilion promoted Irish sports and writers including Jonathan Swift, George Bernard Shaw, James Joyce, Oscar Wilde and W. B. Yeats. Irish arts and crafts such as tweed, pottery and Waterford glass were also displayed.
80. The collection included fiction by Elizabeth Spencer, Jean Stafford, Peter Taylor, Isaac Bashevis Singer and Joyce Carol Oates, among others.
81. MLC, Correspondence (Houghton Mifflin 1965–1967 folder), 5 May 1965.
82. *NYR*, 30 June 1964.
83. 'Honour for Frank O'Connor', *Sunday Independent*, 16 August 1964.
84. MLPP, 30 July 1964. McGahern was both hopeful and worried when he heard that Michael Sissons was sending extracts of *The Dark* to *The New Yorker* (MLPP, undated letter). It was the beginning of what became known as the 'McGahern Affair'. Many people waded into the matter, including Samuel Beckett, who had previously been banned by the Board and offered McGahern his support, and Archbishop John Charles McQuaid, who used his influence

to ensure that McGahern was dismissed from his teaching position and not reinstated when he appealed the decision. Authors banned by the Censorship of Publications Board, which was established in 1929 with the power to ban any work it deemed obscene or morally corrupting, included Brendan Behan, J. P. Dunleavy, Edna O'Brien, Frank O'Connor and J. D. Salinger. Irish writers were particularly hard hit as it meant that they could not make a living from their writing in their own country. The tide changed, largely due to McGahern's case and anti-censorship campaigns led by authors including Frank O'Connor and Edna O'Brien, and a new Censorship of Publications Act was passed in 1967. On 8 August 1964, Terence de Vere White, in his review of *The Stories of Mary Lavin*, made the observation: 'We do nothing for our writers except to ban them occasionally; and really they deserve well of the State. They make us famous the world over. They convey altogether too flattering impression of our charms and our powers. And when they die we do not have to collect money to erect memorials to them. They save us that expense. They build their own in their lifetimes.'

85. *NYR*, 24 September 1964.
86. *NYR*, 22 September 1964.
87. MLPP, undated letter.
88. Author interview with Elizabeth Cullinan.
89. *NYR*, 24 September 1964.
90. *NYR*, 27 October 1964.
91. *NYR*, 25 October 1964. Lavin was likely referring to the Agricultural Land (Relief) Act 1964.
92. *NYR*, Undated but a response to Lavin's letter of 25 October 1964.
93. *NYR*, 22 September 1964.
94. The cover may have been a reference to the arrival of the Beatles at JFK airport in New York on 7 February 1964 on their first US visit.
95. John O'Hara named his fictional town of Gibbsville, Pennsylvania, after Wolcott Gibbs. *Mary Poppins* was adapted for the screen by its author, P. L. Travers.
96. JBR, 'The quiet voice that says so much so well', Belfast *News Letter*, 10 October 1964.
97. Mac Aonghusa erroneously refers to Lavin as an Anglo-Irish writer in his *Irish Press* review, 'Bean a bhuil saothar álainn déanta aici' ('A Woman who has done a beautiful job'), 25 August 1964.
98. 'From the Village Homes of Ireland', *Sunday Independent*, 4 October 1964.
99. *NYR*, 23–25 October 1964.
100. *NYR*, 29 October 1964.
101. *NYR*, 7 November 1964.
102. NLI, Irish PEN papers, 1935–2004.
103. NLI. Goffart was a novelist who wrote under the pseudonym Robert de Ransart.

104. It was the 32nd Congress, the theme of which was *The Writer and Semantics: Literature as Concept, Meaning and Expression.* which took place in Oslo on 21–27 June 1964.
105. NLI, Irish PEN papers, 1935–2004.
106. 'Literature Deplored', *The Irish Press*, 13 November 1964.
107. Tom Hennigan, 'Going Places', *Evening Herald*, 13 November 1964.
108. Colm P. O'Briain was likely Colm O'Briain (1943–2020), a qualified barrister, who founded Project 67 in 1966, precursor of the Project Arts Centre. He was appointed the director of the Arts Council in 1975 and later director of the National College of Art and Design. He was also special adviser to Michael D. Higgins in his post as Minister for Arts and Culture.
109. *NYR*, 16 November 1964.
110. *NYR*, 25 November 1964.
111. *NYR*, 4 December 1964.
112. *NYR*, 5 December 1964. Lavin wrote this letter from Saragossa (Zaragoza) in Spain.
113. *NYR*,10 December 1964. Lavin was paid a total of $4,425 for 'One Summer', which included the 25 per cent premium. She also received a COLA payment of $1,239. On 14 December, Stephen Carroll of the Munster and Leinster Bank in Rathfarnham, Dublin, wrote to MacKenzie acknowledging the receipt of the cheque that he confirmed was deposited into Lavin's account. The contract ran from 6 March 1965 until 6 March 1966.
114. *NYR*, 5 December 1964.
115. Yagoda, 293. Contributors were paid a certain rate for a set number of words and once they exceeded this number the word payment rate was reduced. This was to encourage brevity in stories and lessen the magazine's payments to its writers. Katharine White, in a letter to John Updike on 15 September 1954, stated, 'We price every manuscript separately according to what we think its value is to us,' adding that 'this pricing may, I suppose, often seem whimsical to a contributor. It is.' (qtd in Begley, 110). The inconsistency, or perceived inconsistency, surrounding payments added to the magazine's quirkiness.
116. This information was discovered when Susan Cheever was researching her memoir of her father, *Home Before Dark*.
117. *NYR*, 21 December 1964.
118. *NYR*, 29 December 1964.

6 'Right Side Up' *1965–1966*

1. MacKenzie to Lavin, *NYR*, 17 May 1965.
2. MacKenzie to Lavin, *NYR*, 31 January 1966.
3. The quantity bonus cycle commenced on 20 January 1964 with the acceptance of 'Heart of Gold' (MacKenzie confirmed the date with Lavin in a letter dated 29 October 1964).

4. Lavin's contract began on 6 March 1965 and ended 6 March 1966.
5. See *The Almanac*, University of Pennsylvania, Vol. 11, No 5, 12 January 1965. Lavin also mentioned that she had been invited to Belgium, along with Frank O'Connor, as a guest of Belgian PEN.
6. Letter from Michael McLaverty to John McGahern, 15 January 1965, *In Quiet Places*. McLaverty let McGahern know that he was giving a talk on Lavin and Katherine Anne Porter at the Galway Literary Society in March. However, in the end McLaverty spoke about Katherine Mansfield instead of Lavin. (see 'Notes for a Talk on K. Mansfield and K. A. Porter, March 1965, Galway Literary Society', *In Quiet Places*). In the same letter, he expressed his hope that McGahern was still in contact with Elizabeth Cullinan. Cullinan met with McGahern on a few occasions while he was in New York for the American launch of *The Dark* in February of 1966.
7. *NYR*, 28 January 1965. Lavin thought the other publishers that MacKenzie recommended were Doubleday and Random House. The Trinity College honorary doctorate never materialised but in 1968 Lavin was awarded an honorary doctorate by her alma mater, University College Dublin.
8. *NYR*, 29 January 1965.
9. Lavin continued to work on the 'The Grammar of Women' but it does not appear to have been published unless it underwent a change of title.
10. *NYR*, 31 January 1965. $29.02 had been deducted for the retirement plan contribution. It was a generous sum considering that the median income of American families was approximately $6,900 that year.
11. *NYR*, 2 February 1965.
12. *NYR*, 9 February 1965.
13. *NYR*, 24 February 1965. Lavin travelled on the RMS *Queen Mary* ocean liner.
14. William Maxwell to Frank O'Connor, 9 March 1965, *The Happiness of Getting It Down Right,* 237. O'Connor had health issues of his own. In mid-February he had been hospitalised and had undergone a gall bladder operation.
15. Dorothy de Santillana (1904–1980) was the initial commissioning editor of Child's *Mastering the Art of French Cooking* before it was published by Knopf in 1961. Her first husband was the poet Robert Hillyer.
16. *NYR*, 8 March 1965.
17. *NYR*, 25 March 1965
18. MLC, Correspondence (Houghton Mifflin 1965–1967 folder), 14 June 1965.
19. *NYR*, 8 March 1965.
20. *Almanac*, University of Pennsylvania, January 1965, Vol. 11, No. 5 & March 1965, Vol. 11, No. 7.
21. May Sarton (1912–1995), originally named Eleanore Marie Sarton, was an American poet and writer whose work was published in *The New Yorker*. Sarton was rumoured to have had an affair with Elizabeth Bowen, who

inspired her writing. MacKenzie also knew Sarton, who was a staff member at the Bread Loaf Writers' Conference.

22. Lavin and Hortense Calisher (1911–2009) had much in common. Calisher, a regular contributor to *The New Yorker*, also received two Guggenheim Fellowships, in 1952 and 1955, and she was appointed the president of PEN America in 1986. Calisher was a guest editor of *The Best American Short Story* in 1981. In her introduction she felt compelled to explain the reason for her selection of nine *New Yorker* stories: 'About half are from *The New Yorker*, which publishes fifty-two issues per year and a major portion of the country's short fiction, and will naturally get first look at much of the best of it.' In 1987 she was appointed the second female president of the American Academy of Arts and Letters.
23. *NYR*, 23 March 1965. The letter was written on Cunard Line RMS *Franconia* headed paper. Lavin's parents had met onboard the SS *Franconia* in 1908.
24. *NYR*, 2 May 1965.
25. *The New York Times*, 6 July 1965. Gloria Emerson (1929–2004) was a war correspondent for *The New York Times* and transferred to the paper's London office in 1968, where she covered the start of the Troubles in Northern Ireland. Raoul Lévy (1922–1966) was a film producer, director and writer and probably best known for producing movies starring Brigitte Bardot, including *And God Created Woman* (1956).
26. *NYR*, 17 May 1965.
27. *NYR*, 20 May 1965.
28. *NYR*, 7 June 1965. Salinger's final published work, 'Hapworth 16, 1924' appeared in *The New Yorker* on 19 June 1965 and at approximately 26,000 words it almost commandeered the entire magazine.
29. *NYR*, 2 May 1965.
30. *NYR*, 28 June 1965.
31. *NYR*, 30 June 1965.
32. *NYR*, 9 July 1965.
33. *NYR*, 7 July 1965.
34. *NYR*, 30 June 1965.
35. *NYR*, 9 July 1965.
36. *NYR*, 5 August 1965.
37. *NYR*, 11 August 1965.
38. The 25 September 1965 issue featured the first part of Truman Capote's groundbreaking 'nonfiction novel' *In Cold Blood*. Published in four parts, critics hailed the work as New Journalism, despite Truman Capote's insistence that he was a literary writer and not a journalist. There is speculation that the heroine, Holly Golightly, from his 1958 novella, *Breakfast at Tiffany's*, was based on Maeve Brennan as he had befriended her at *The New Yorker*. Capote dubbed the guessing game the 'Holly Golightly Sweepstakes'. Other contenders include Gloria Vanderbilt and Oona O'Neill.

39. Charles E. Martin (1910–1995) was a self-taught artist whose work featured in *The New Yorker*, *Harper's*, *The Saturday Evening Post*, *Punch* and *Esquire*. Trinity Church is where Alexander Hamilton is buried.
40. MLPP, postmarked 1965.
41. 'Further Tales about Men and Women' was published in *The New Yorker* on 7 August 1965.
42. *NYR*, 29 September 1965.
43. *NYR*, 25 October 1965
44. *NYR*, 2 May 1967. The *Kenyon Review* was founded in 1939 by the poet and critic John Crowe Ransom. Contributors include Samuel Beckett, Elizabeth Bishop, T. S. Eliot, Robert Lowell, Joyce Carol Oates, Sylvia Plath and Jean Stafford. There is no record of 'The Grammar of Women' having been published in the journal or elsewhere. 'One Evening' – which had not been previously published and does not appear to have been sent to *The New Yorker* – was published in the September 1967 issue of *The Kenyon Review*.
45. *NYR*, 2 November 1965.
46. *NYR*, 7 November 1965. The stories published included 'A Glimpse of Katey', *Georgia Review* (Winter 1966), originally published in *The Bell* (November 1947); 'A Gentle Soul', originally published in *Irish Writing* (March 1951) appeared in *Atlantic Monthly* (May 1967) and 'Asigh' was published in *Dublin Magazine* (Summer 1967). *The Bell*, a literary monthly magazine, was founded in 1940 by, among others, Seán Ó Faoláin, Frank O'Connor, Ernie O'Malley, Peadar O'Donnell and Maurice Walsh. Its contributors included Mary Lavin, Michael McLaverty, Brendan Behan, Patrick Kavanagh and Patrick Swift.
47. *NYR*, 16 November 1965.
48. *NYR*, 4 December 1965.
49. Lavin to Dorothy de Santillana, MLC, Correspondence (Houghton Mifflin 1965–1967 folder), 3 November 1965.
50. Lavin to Ben Glazebrook, MLC, Correspondence (Houghton Mifflin 1965–1967 folder), 23 November 1965. *The Stories of Mary Lavin, Vol, 1.* (Constable, 1964).
51. MLC, Correspondence (Houghton Mifflin 1965–1967 folder), 3 November 1965.
52. *NYR*, 7 November 1965. Lavin informed de Santillana that she had revised considerably the stories in the volume so it was preferable for her if Houghton Mifflin set up the book on their own type rather than purchase Constable's.
53. MLC, Correspondence (Houghton Mifflin 1965–1967 folder), 3 November 1965. Constable could only keep the first volume of stories in print in the UK if Lavin managed to acquire an American publisher for them and the publication of the second volume of stories was dependent upon getting an American publisher for the first volume.

54. MLC, Correspondence (Houghton Mifflin 1965–1967 folder), postmarked 1965.
55. MLC, Correspondence (Houghton Mifflin 1965–1967 folder), 31 December 1965.
56. *NYR*, 9 December 1965. The contract ran from 6 March 1966 until 6 March 1967.
57. *NYR*, 13 December 1965. Lavin loved Cullinan's story 'The Old Priest', which was published in *The New Yorker* on 18 December 1965 (*NYR*, 5 February 1966).
58. *NYR*, 31 January 1966.
59. Cecil Scott made no mention of Lavin's children's tale *A Likely Story*, which Macmillan New York published in 1957. It was included in the Macmillan Christmas list that was published in *The New York Times* on 17 November 1957.
60. *NYR*, 2 March 1966.
61. MLC, Correspondence (Houghton Mifflin 1965–1967 folder), 22 February 1966.
62. W. B. Yeats's poem 'Death' was published in *The New Yorker* on 27 April 1927. It was included in his 1933 volume *The Winding Stair and Other Poems*. Frank O'Connor had delivered an oration at Yeats' grave in 1965, on the occasion of the centenary year of his birth.
63. 'Burying Frank O'Connor: Some Dublin Talk over a Jar', Joseph Dever, *The National Catholic Reporter* (30 March 1966). Lavin had told Dever that Kavanagh was 'the writer of some of Ireland's finest contemporary lyrics'. Dever was a fellow at the Bread Loaf Writers' Conference in 1957. James Joyce mentioned the Grosvenor Hotel in the 'Lotus Eaters' episode in *Ulysses*. Robert MacBryde, a Scottish artist and set designer, died on 6 May 1966 after he was knocked down by a car outside O'Neill's pub in Dublin, where he had been drinking with Kavanagh. He was 52 years old. Kavanagh died over six months later, on 30 November 1967, at the age of 63. *The Northern Standard* erroneously reported Lavin as attending Kavanagh's requiem mass in St Mary's Church, Haddington Road in Dublin (8 December 1967, *The Northern Standard*). Kavanagh was buried on 2 December in his native Inniskeen in Monaghan and Seamus Heaney, John Montague and David Wright read poems at the graveside.
64. 'Frank O'Connor Dies in Dublin, An Appreciation' by Terence de Vere White, *The Irish Times*, 11 March 1966.
65. 'Frank O'Connor Dies Suddenly', *The Irish Press*, 11 March 1966.
66. 'Frank O'Connor, Author, 63, Dead', *The New York Times*, 11 March 1966.
67. Four of Frank O'Connor's stories were published posthumously: 'The Corkerys' (30 April 1966), 'The School for Wives' (5 November 1966), 'An Act of Charity' (6 May 1967) and 'Bring in the Whiskey Now, Mary' (12 August 1967).

68. *NYR*, 24 March 1966.
69. *NYR*, 5 February 1966.
70. *NYR*, 29 March 1966.
71. *NYR*, 29 March 1966.
72. MLPP. Cullinan had written the letter when she was in Ireland and Lavin and the girls were in Italy. She also mentioned going to dinner and the circus with John McGahern, who had brought her 'three bunches of chrysanthemums – purple, fuchsia and bronze'.
73. *NYR*, 12 April 1966. Brian O'Nolan wrote under various pseudonyms including Myles na gCopaleen (later, Gopaleen), Flann O'Brien, Brother Barnabas and George Knowall. Mary Lavin, Frank O'Connor, Brian O'Nolan and Micheál Mac Liammóir had contributed work to the 1966 publication of the Irish university students' magazine *Yes*, published on 30 April, the proceeds of which went towards various charities including the Central Remedial Clinic. *The Irish Press,* 30 April 1966. Mick was Father Michael Scott.
74. MLC, Correspondence (Houghton Mifflin 1965–1967 folder), 11 April 1966. Glazebrook warned Lavin that she would only receive a small advance from Houghton Mifflin for *Collected Stories*, if they decided to publish it.
75. *NYR*, 28 April 1966.
76. *NYR*, 12 April 1966.
77. *The Evening of the Holiday* was Shirley Hazzard's first novel. It was published by Macmillan, London and Alfred A. Knopf, New York in 1966.
78. *NYR*, undated letter 1966.
79. *NYR*, 29 March 1966. Lavin sent Jack B. Yeats (1871–1957) copies of her latest books and on19 October 1954 he wrote a letter of sympathy to her on the death of her husband, William, who had spent some time in Portobello Hospital in Dublin where Yeats spent his final years (MLPP). In 1980 Lavin sold two of her four Jack B. Yeats paintings, *The Old Ale House* and *The Man in the Shooting Gallery*.
80. *NYR*, 29 March 1966.
81. Jacob Schwartz was a former dentist who was a dealer in literary letters and manuscripts and founded the Ulysses Bookshop in London. He informed Lavin that it was through him that the New York Public Library published Elizabeth Bowen's manuscripts.
82. MLPP, 23 May 1966.
83. *NYR*, 27 April 1966.
84. At the meeting, held in the Intercontinental Hotel in Dublin, Austin Clarke read his poem 'The Paper Curtain' and Ulick O'Connor expressed his horror that 'the part of Dublin most celebrated in the literature of the Irish Renaissance had been given into the hands of a "developer"'. He was referring to the demolition of 15 Ely Place, once the home of Oliver St John Gogarty. 'Concrete to Cover Literary Part of Dublin', *Sunday Independent*, 17 October 1965.

85. *NYR*, 12 April 1966.
86. *The Irish Press*, 11 June 1966. The accompanying article revealed that Clarke would read one of his latest poems, 'which describes a literary pilgrimage to the birthplace of great American writers' at the event.
87. Bellow told the audience that there were 'clear signs that intellectuals in what American universities call the Humanities are trying to appropriate literature for themselves, taking it away from writers'. ('Bellow Assails Literary "Elite"', *The New York Times*, 14 June 1966.)
88. 'Miller Lauds P.E.N. as Congress Closes', *The New York Times*, 19 June 1966. In July Irish PEN wrote a letter to the Minister of Education, Donogh O'Malley, objecting to the application of a new selective wholesale tax on books. The letter, signed by Lavin, Desmond Clarke and Arthur Rae, noted that 'Ireland will thus become the only country in Western Europe to impose a substantial tax on books.' 'P.E.N. Protests at New Tax on Books', *The Irish Press*, 20 July 1966. PEN was successful in its protest. The government relented and books were exempted from the tax. However, it did not exclude periodicals and in September, Irish PEN wrote a letter to Jack Lynch, the Irish Minister of Finance, opposing the taxation of periodical literature purchased or published in Ireland. Lavin, Desmond Clarke and Arthur Rae signed the letter, which highlighted 'the disastrous effect the tax is likely to have on the few Irish literary and cultural periodicals struggling for survival'. *The Irish Press*, 28 September 1966.
89. *NYR*, 6 September 1966.
90. This page of *Vogue* is housed in MLLP.
91. *NYR*, 6 September 1966.
92. NYR, 20 September 1966.
93. *NYR*, 22 October 1966.
94. *NYR*, 12 November 1966.
95. *NYR*, 20 September 1966. Jeff Brown (1926–2003) is probably best known for his children's book *Flat Stanley*, published in 1964. He worked at *The New Yorker*, *The Saturday Evening Post* and *Esquire* and was a senior editor at Warner Books.
96. *NYR*, 13 September 1966.
97. *NYR*, 20 September 1966.
98. *NYR*, 12 September 1966.
99. *NYR*, 22 October 1966.
100. *NYR*, 7 November 1966.
101. 'One Summer', *NY*, 11 September 1965.
102. *NYR*, 12 November 1966. Ralph E. McCoy, the Dean of Library Affairs at Southern Illinois, visited Lavin to discuss her collection. McCoy informed Lavin that the library had work by Kay Boyle, Hart Crane, Ernest Hemingway, D.H. Lawrence, Ezra Pound and Lawrence Durrell. The amount of the British Arts Council bursary varied but Lavin was to be awarded £800. John McGahern's application was sponsored by the writer and editor Ian Hamilton (1938–2001),

who wrote an unauthorised biography of J. D. Salinger. Kay Dick, Elizabeth Smart, Aiden Higgins and Francis King were among the other recipients of the literature bursary in 1966 and Kate O'Brien received the Council's maintenance grant for £750 that same year.

103. *NYR*, undated 1966 letter.
104. MLC, Correspondence (Houghton Mifflin 1965–1967 folder).
105. Lavin to Glazebrook, MLC, Correspondence (Houghton Mifflin 1965–1967 folder), 10 April 1967. On 27 June 1967 Denison University wrote to Lavin requesting *At Sallygap and Other Stories*, *The Long Ago and Other Stories*, *Mary O'Grady*, *The Patriot Son and Other Stories* and *Bective Bridge and Other Stories* as they were all out of print (MLPP).
106. *NYR*. The contract commenced on 6 March 1967 and ended on 6 March 1968.
107. *NYR*, undated letter, December 1966.

7 'Happiness for Sure' *1967*

1. Mary Lavin, letter to Rachel MacKenzie, 2 May 1967, New York Public Library (*NYR*).
2. *The Atlantic Monthly Press* had confirmed in a letter dated 18 January 1967 that it had reverted the rights to *Mary O'Grady* and *The House on Clewe Street* back to her in 1953, MLC, Correspondence (Houghton Mifflin 1965–1967 folder).
3. The book was published on 30 January 1967, according to Terence de Vere White's *Irish Times* article 'The Art of Mary Lavin', 28 January 1967. On 11 April Ben Glazebrook confirmed with Lavin that sales of the book had reached 2,500, MLC, Correspondence (Houghton Mifflin 1965–1967 folder).
4. *The Irish Press*, 28 January 1967. Augustine Martin, in a later article, 'The Great O'Faolain', mentioned that the American critic Robert Caswell was writing a book on Mary Lavin (Books on Saturday, *The Irish Press*, 2 September 1967). While a book never materialised, Caswell wrote two articles on Lavin: the first, 'Mary Lavin: Breaking a Pathway', appeared in *Dublin Magazine*, 6 (Summer, 1967), and the second, 'Irish Political Reality and Mary Lavin's Tales from Bective Bridge' was published in *Éire Ireland*, 3, i (Spring, 1968). Caswell had also written 'The Human Heart's Vagaries', which was published in *Kilkenny Magazine*, nos 12–13 (Spring, 1965).
5. Terence de Vere White, 'The Art of Mary Lavin', *The Irish Times,* 28 January 1967. Terence De Vere White (1912–1994) was *The Irish Times* literary editor from 1961 until 1977.
6. 'New Stories by Mary Lavin', *Irish Independent*, 11 February 1967. By 6 April 1967, sales of *Middle of the Fields and Other Stories* had reached 2,500 since its release.

7. *NYR*, 28 February 1967.
8. James Dickey (1923–1997) was an American poet and novelist and appointed the eighteenth United States Poet Laureate in 1966. He had fifty-two poems and two fiction pieces published in *The New Yorker* between 1959 and 1998. Dickey was a recipient of the Guggenheim Fellowship in 1961 and won the National Book Award for Poetry in 1966, but he is probably best known for his debut novel *Deliverance* (1970), which was adapted into the acclaimed 1972 John Boorman film of the same name for which Dickey also wrote the screenplay.
9. See 'Stewardess is Swept Through Plane Door', *The New York Times*, 20 October 1962.
10. *NYR*, 8 March 1967.
11. The issue carried adverts for Alitalia, Pan Am, SAS (Scandinavian Airlines), Lufthansa, Japan Air Lines, Ethiopia Airlines and BOAC.
12. *NYR*, undated 1967. This echoed her experience in writing 'The Great Wave'.
13. *NYR*, February, undated.
14. *NYR*, 8 March 1967.
15. *NYR*, 14 March 1967.
16. *NYR*, Spy Wednesday (22 March 1967).
17. *NYR*, 28 February 1967.
18. *NYR*, 10 March 1967.
19. *NYR*, 11 April 1967.
20. *NYR*, 14 1967 April, PM 9 04. In fact Lavin received $985 after $15 was deducted for the retirement plan.
21. *NYR*, 20 April 1967. L. P. Hartley, one of the judges of the Katherine Mansfield Prize the year Lavin won, was the president of PEN from 1967 until 1970.
22. *NYR*, 16 April 1967.
23. MLC, Correspondence (Houghton Mifflin 1965–1967 folder), 8 March 1967.
24. Lavin to Glazebrook, MLC, Correspondence (Houghton Mifflin 1965–1967 folder), 10 April 1967.
25. Lavin to MacKenzie, *NYR*, 2 May 1967.
26. Lavin wrote to Sissons on 21 April to let him know that she would no longer need his services as she would be handling her own dealings.
27. Mary Lavin to Cecil Scott, MLC (Correspondence K. Macmillan 1967–1969), 2 May 1967.
28. *NYR*, 19 May 1967.
29. *NYR*, 13 June 1967.
30. Lavin was paid $3,602.50 in total for 'Happiness', which included a 25 per cent premium of $437.50 plus a COLA amounting to $875. A total of $30.94 was deducted for the retirement plan.

31. *NYR*, 18 July 1967.
32. *NYR*, Spy Wednesday 22 March 1967. For autobiographical readings of the story, see Janet Egleson Dunleavy's 'The Making of Mary Lavin's "Happiness"', Ann Owens Weekes' 'Mary Lavin: Textual Gardens', *Irish Women Writers: Unchartered Tradition*, Leah Levenson's *The Four Seasons of Mary Lavin*, Mary E. Donnelly's essay on Mary Lavin in *Modern Irish Writers: A Bio-Critical Sourcebook* (ed. Alexander G. Gonzalez), A. A. Kelly's *Mary Lavin, Quiet Rebel: A Study of Her Short Stories*, Jennifer Molidor's 'Violence, Silence, and Sacrifice: The Mother–daughter Relationship in the Short Fiction of Irish Women Writers, 1890–1980'; Maurice Harmon's 'Heartfelt Narratives: Mary Lavin's Life and Work' and Sinéad Mooney's '"Stranded Objects": Topographies of Loss in Mary Lavin's Widow Stories' in *Mary Lavin* (ed. Elke D'hoker) and D'hoker's *Irish Women Writers and The Modern Short Story*.
33. 'Happiness', *NY*, 60.
34. See Lara Marlowe, 'Mary Lavin: An Arrow Still in Flight', *The Irish Times*, 30 April 2012 (quoting Colm Tóibín's speech on Lavin at a symposium at New York University's Glucksman Ireland House).
35. 'Happiness', *NY*, 61.
36. *NYR*, 5 February 1966.
37. 'Happiness', *NY*, 64.
38. 'Voyage Round My Mother', interview with Elizabeth Walsh Peavoy, *Sunday Independent*, 28 May 1995.
39. 'Happiness', *NY*, 66.
40. *NYR*, 7 April 1959.
41. Levenson, 338.
42. The event was held at the Conway Hotel, Dunmurry. Lord Moyne, Bryan Guinness (1905–1992) was an heir to the Guinness fortune. He was married to Diana Mitford, and both were part of the 1920s 'Bright Young Things' group. Evelyn Waugh, who was also part of the clique, dedicated his second novel, *Vile Bodies*, to 'B.G. and D.G.' (Bryan and Diana Guinness). Mitford married Oswald Mosley after her divorce from Guinness.
43. *The Irish Press*, 29 May 1967. Lavin became a member of the Irish Academy of Letters, which was founded in 1932 by W. B. Yeats and George Bernard Shaw with the aim of recognising literary excellence and opposing literary censorship. Lennox Robinson wrote to inform Lavin of her election to the Academy when openings became available upon the deaths of James Stephens and George Bernard Shaw in 1950 (MLPP).
44. *NYR*, 2 May 1967.
45. *NYR*, 10 May 1967. *The Kenyon Review* purchased 'The Grammar of Women' and Lavin pondered: 'I don't know if they pay any money, but it has prestige value, I think.' *NYR*, 2 May 1967.
46. *NYR*, 2 May 1967.
47. *NYR*, undated letter but the envelope is postmarked 15 January 1967.

48. 10 May 1967.
49. *NYR*, 19 May 1967.
50. *NYR*, 18 July 1967. Lavin would be based in the university's Department of English, The College of Liberal Arts and Sciences.
51. *NYR*, undated, circa May or June 1967.
52. *NYR*, 4 August 1967.
53. MLPP, 14 August 1967. The theme of the four-day conference was 'History and Literature' and Dudley Edwards and F.X. Martin were among the speakers. Carver served as the Secretary of International PEN from Hermon Ould's death in 1951 until his own in May 1974. Lavin and Carver were acquainted and he and his wife, Blanche, intended to see her before she set sail for America.
54. This newspaper clipping is contained in Mary Lavin's papers, UCD. Homer D. Babbidge Jr was the president of the University of Connecticut from 1962 until 1972. On 2 October Babbidge wrote to Lavin to confirm her salary and appointment (GSP).
55. *NYR*, 20 September 1967. Lavin gave MacKenzie her home phone number and address on Separatist Road.
56. GSP, 11 October 1967. George Starbuck (1931–1996), a writer and poet, was the director of the Iowa Writers' Workshop from 1967 until 1971, when he joined the faculty of Boston University. He had studied at Boston University, under the tutelage of Robert Lowell, with fellow poets Sylvia Plath, Kathleen Spivak and Anne Sexton. *The New Yorker* published eighteen of his poems and one of his stories between 1957 and 1985. He edited Philip Roth's first book, *Goodbye, Columbus*. Roth was a visiting professor at the writers' workshop from 1960 until 1962. Other notable writers who taught there include Robert Lowell, Dylan Thomas, John Cheever, Flannery O'Connor and Wallace Stegner, who was an alumnus of the university.
57. GSP and MLC (Correspondence 1935–1975), 11 October 1967. William Cotter Murray had cabled Lavin twice about the possibility of her coming to Iowa prior to Starbuck's letter.
58. GSP, 24 October 1967.
59. GSP, 28 November 1967. William Cotter Murray (1929–2016) was born in County Clare and emigrated to the US in 1949. He was a writer and poet and joined the staff of Iowa's Writers' Workshop in the 1960s and was a Professor of English at Iowa until his retirement in 1991.
60. *NYR*, 9 October 1968.
61. Bryan MacMahon (1909–1998) had reviewed Mary Lavin's *The Becker Wives* and Frank O'Connor's *Selected Stories* in *The Bell* in April 1947.
62. Paul Engle (1908–1991) was an American writer, poet, editor and director of the Iowa Writers' Workshop from 1941 until 1965 and co-founder of Iowa University's International Writing Program. The New Yorker published four of Engle's poems between 1940 and 1964.

63. GSP, undated letter but after 14 September and before 11 October 1967.
64. *NYR*, undated letter to MacKenzie, 1967.
65. *NYR*, 30 October 1967. 'The Living' was published in *The New Yorker* on 22 November 1958.
66. *NYR*, 5 November 1967.
67. *NYR*, 16 November 1967.
68. *NYR*, 5 November 1967.
69. Assumption based on information of a recording of John Updike's reading of these poems and stories at the Poetry Center New York in November 1967: John Updike, '[Poetry reading at the YM-YWHA, New York City, November 1967] / John Updike', *Digital Collections – University at Buffalo Libraries*, https://digital.lib.buffalo.edu/items/show/54795. Updike was introduced by *New Yorker* staff writer and contributor Gerald Jonas, and there was a question-and-answer session at the end.
70. MLC (Ashley Famous folder), 30 August 1968.
71. MLC (*The New Yorker* folder), undated letter.
72. *NYR*, 29 November 1967.
73. MLC (Correspondence 1935–1975), 20 November 1967.
74. MLC (Correspondence 1935–1975), 20 November 1967.
75. An undated letter/note written on the Algonquin Hotel's headed paper.
76. *NYR*, 28 November 1967.
77. *NYR*, 2 December 1967. Helen Hooker O'Malley Roelofs (1905–1993) was an American sculptor, painter and photographer who was married to the Irish republican and writer Ernie O'Malley (1897–1957). She eventually managed to persuade Lavin allow her to take a plaster cast in 1971. Roelof's bronze bust of Lavin was sculpted in 1973 and is housed in Glucksman Ireland House in New York. The sculptor and former Hollywood actress Marjorie FitzGibbon had been commissioned by the Royal Dublin Society to create a series of busts of living Irish artists and Lavin was one of the writers chosen. The front page of *The Irish Press*, 14 September 1972, carries a photograph of Lavin and FitzGibbon with her bronze bust.
78. *NYR*, undated letter 1967.
79. *NYR*, 19 November 1967.
80. Professor George Saul (1901–1986) only visited Ireland twice due to a fear of flying.
81. *NYR*, 13 November 1967.
82. *NYR*, 28 November 1967.
83. *NYR*, 27 November 1967.
84. *NYR*, 29 November 1967.
85. Phyllis Jackson (1908–1977) was a literary agent at Ashley Famous, whose clients included Ian Fleming, Cornelius Ryan and Robert Lowell. One associate remembered her as 'tough, but a lady' (*The New York Times*, 22 March 1977). Ashley Famous was a talent agency that was originally founded in 1945 by Ted Ashley, who had been a talent agent at the William

Morris Agency. MacKenzie later gave Lavin the address for Ashley Famous Agency, Inc., 1301 Avenue of the Americas.

86. MLC (Correspondence K. Macmillan 1967–1969).

8 'Haggling and Bargaining' *1968–1969*

1. Mary Lavin to Rachel MacKenzie, *NYR*, 5 December 1969.
2. *NYR*,12 January 1969. 'Writer Mary Lavin to speak at AC', *The Ohio Times-Gazette*, 5 January 1968, MLLP.
3. William Maxwell to Lavin, MLC (Correspondence 1935–1975), MLC, undated.
4. *NYR*, 25 January 1968.
5. *NYR*, 1 February 1968.
6. Lavin's review of Elizabeth Bowen's novel *Eva Trout* was published in *The Irish Press* on 1 February 1968.
7. Edna O'Brien, *The Love Object* (Cape, 1968).
8. *NYR*, 25 January 1968.
9. *NYR*, 1 February 1968.
10. NLI, Correspondence between Mary Lavin and George Brandon Saul, 1968–1970, 1 February 1968.
11. *Eva Trout* was published by Jonathan Cape on 1 January 1969 and was shortlisted for the 1970 Booker Prize. Fellow Irish writers Iris Murdoch and William Trevor were also shortlisted for the prize, which was won by Bernice Rubens for *The Elected Member*, making Rubens the first woman and only Welsh writer to win the award. Murdoch was shortlisted six times for the prize and won in 1978 for *The Sea, The Sea*. Trevor made the shortlist four times but never won. Lavin had only one story, 'Happiness', in the fiction bonus cycle that was due to end on 8 June 1968.
12. Lavin to MacKenzie, *NYR*, 1 February 1968.
13. *NYR*, 6 February 1968. The sanitation workers were demanding higher wages and better pensions. The strike lasted nine days. The stage adaptation of Muriel Spark's *The Prime of Miss Jean Brodie* premiered at the Helen Hayes Theatre on 16 January and ran until 14 December 1968.
14. MLC, Correspondence (Ashley Famous Agency folder), 7 February 1968. In 1947, Jeremiah Kaplan (1926–1993) founded Free Press with Charles Liebman. He co-founded Meridian Books in 1958. In 1960 Free Press was sold to Macmillan for $1.3 million whereupon Kaplan headed up a new division for Macmillan, becoming its president from 1965 until 1973 when he moved to London to take up the role of managing director of Cassell and Collier Macmillan Publishers Ltd.. He returned to Macmillan New York in 1977 as president again until 1986. He became president of Simon & Schuster from 1987 until 1989. See *The New York Times* obituary, 11 August 1993.

15. *NYR*, 6 February 1968.
16. MLC, Correspondence (Ashley Famous Agency folder), 14 February 1968.
17. Robert (Bob) Gottlieb (1931–2023). Other writers whose work he handled included John Cheever, Joseph Heller, Doris Lessing and Anthony Burgess. In 1987 he replaced William Shawn and became the third editor of *The New Yorker*. See Robert Gottlieb's *Avid Reader: A Life*. Although Blanche and Alfred founded Alfred A. Knopf, it had been acquired by Random House in 1960.
18. *NYR*, 14 February 1968.
19. *The Complete Poems of Marianne Moore* (Macmillan, 1967).
20. MLC Correspondence (Ashley Famous Agency), 21 February 1968. Viking (now Viking Press) was founded by Harold K. Guinzburg and George S. Oppenheimer in 1925, the same year as *The New Yorker*. Its authors include Saul Bellow, Lillian Hellman, Arthur Miller, Hannah Arendt, Ian Fleming and in 1957 it published Jack Kerouac's seminal Beat and counterculture novel *On The Road*.
21. MLC, Correspondence (Ashley Famous Agency folder), 8 March 1968.
22. MLC, Correspondence (Ashley Famous Agency folder), 21 February 1968
23. MLC, Correspondence (Ashley Famous Agency folder), 7 March 1968.
24. MLC, Correspondence (Ashley Famous Agency folder), 8 March 1968.
25. Douglass Paige taught at Middlesex Community College from 1968 until his retirement in 1981. He died in 1983 aged sixty-five.
26. The conferral took place at Iveagh House on St Stephen's Green, Dublin, now the headquarters of the Department of Foreign Affairs. Incidentally, on 17 February of that year Lavin met with a future president of Ireland, Cearbhall Ó Dálaigh, then Chief Justice, when he was the guest of honour at the annual Irish PEN dinner. Ó Dálaigh (1911–1978) was the ninth and youngest Attorney General in Ireland when he succeeded President Childers in 1974.
27. *Irish Times* clipping in Lavin's papers dated 29 March 1968. Garrett Fox covered the conferral in his 'My Royal Meath Album' section of *The Meath Chronicle* 8 April 1968. In his article he mentioned Valentine's 'brilliant post-graduate academic career in the United States'.
28. *NYR*, 16 April 1968.
29. *NYR*, 22 April 1968.
30. *NYR*, 10 May 1968.
31. *NYR*, postmarked 26 April 1968. Coburn Britton (1935–1997), an American poet, was editor at Doubleday and co-publisher of Horizon Press in the 1960s.
32. *NYR*, 2 May 1968.
33. Horizon Press, owned by Ben Raeburn (1911–1997), was in operation from 1951 until 1984.

34. *NYR*, 5 December 1968. *The New Yorker* offices were located at 25 West Forty-Third Street, near Times Square, from 1935 until 1991.
35. MLC, Correspondence (Ashley Famous Agency folder), 21 March 1968.
36. MLC, Correspondence (Ashley Famous Agency folder), March 1968.
37. Farrar, Straus and Giroux and Company was founded in 1945 by John C. Farrar and Richard W. Straus. John C. Farrar (1896–1974) was an American writer, editor and publisher who played a role in the establishment of the Bread Loaf Writers' Conference. Roger Williams Straus Jr (1895–1980): his mother was the American heiress Gladys Guggenheim and his father's family owned Macy's department store. When Richard 'Bob' Giroux (1914–2008), who joined the company in 1955, became a partner, the company was renamed Farrar, Straus and Giroux. Giroux had grown despondent with his previous company, Harcourt, when it rejected Salinger's *The Catcher in the Rye* in 1951. He took many of his writers with him including T. S. Eliot, Robert Lowell, Flannery O'Connor, Jack Kerouac, Bernard Malamud and Edna O'Brien. Giroux edited and published many regular *New Yorker* contributors including Jean Stafford, Flannery O'Connor, Bernard Malamud, Isaac Bashevis Singer, Katherine Anne Porter, Donald Bartheleme and Elizabeth Bishop. Many years earlier Jean Stafford had written to Lavin to let her know that Charles Reilly and Robert Giroux, her friend and editor, were travelling to Ireland. (MLPP).
38. Robbins to Jackson, MLC, Correspondence (Ashley Famous Agency folder), April 1968. Henry Robbins (1928–1979) was as an editor at Alfred A. Knopf for seven years. He joined Farrar, Straus and Giroux and then moved to Simon & Schuster as editor-in-chief, after which he joined Dutton.
39. MLC, Correspondence (Farrar, Straus and Giroux folder), 16 April 1968.
40. *NYR*, 16 April 1968.
41. MLC, Correspondence (Ashley Famous Agency folder), Wendy Weil at Ashley Famous informed Lavin that the paperbacks would retail at approximately $2.45 versus hardback at $6.95.
42. *NYR*, undated. After 10 May 1968.
43. *NYR*, 25 April 1968.
44. See 'Manhattan revised: Jackie Kennedy's Manhattan in 1967' by Matt Brentin, *Saturday Evening Post*, 23 September 2011.
45. MacKenzie to Lavin, *NYR*, 10 May 1968.
46. *Happiness and Other Stories* (Constable, 1969), 144.
47. *NYR*. The postcard was of Boudin's *Personnages sur la plage de Trouville* from the Musée Eugène Boudin (Honfleur).
48. Lavin to MacKenzie, NYR, 16 April 1968 and 16 May 1968. MacKenzie to Lavin, 10 April 1968.
49. MacKenzie to Lavin, NYR, 10 May 1968.
50. *NYR*, 16 May 1968.

51. *NYR*, 24 August 1964 and 16 May 1968.
52. *NYR*, 21 May 1968.
53. *NYR*,18 June 1968.
54. *NYR*, 21 May 1967
55. *NYR*, 7 November 1968.
56. The collection referred to here is *Happiness and Other Stories*.
57. *NYR*, 28 October 1968. 'The Lost Child' was subsequently published in *The Southern Review* on 5 January 1969 and 'A Pure Accident' appeared in the 5 July issue of that year.
58. *NYR*, 3 June 1968.
59. In an early letter to MacKenzie, Lavin remarked, 'Halliόg [Hallie Óg] (what an inspired name for that baby)', *NYR*, 20 May 1959.
60. In 1963 the Russell Hotel, located at 101–4 St Stephen's Green, was the only hotel in Ireland awarded three stars by the Egon Ronay Guide. The hotel was demolished in April 1974. There were four main gentlemen's clubs on and around St Stephen's Green at this time: the St Stephen's Green Club; the Kildare Street Club, Dublin University Club and the Hibernian and United Services Club.
61. 1 June 1968. See Marrs, *What There Is to Say*, 242.
62. Ibid, 244.
63. *NYR*, 18 June 1968.
64. MLC, Correspondence (*New Yorker* folder), undated letter.
65. See Marrs, *What There Is to Say*.
66. MLC, Correspondence (Farrar, Straus and Giroux folder), 28 June 1968. Marjorie Kellogg (1922–2005) wrote the screenplay of the novel for Otto Preminger's film adaptation in which Liza Minnelli starred as Junie Moon. In the same letter, Robbins recalled that some years back, when he was working at *The Dial*, he had sent Lavin a copy of Richard Power's first novel in English, *The Land of Youth*, for feedback and her 'enthusiastic response' gave them a great boost of confidence. Richard (Dick) Power (Risteard de Paor) (1928–1970). The publication's sleeve featured 'praise' from Padraic Colum and Kathryn Hulme, who is probably better known for her bestselling 1956 novel *The Nun's Story*, which was made into a film starring Audrey Hepburn in 1959.
67. MLC, Correspondence (Ashley Famous Agency folder), 1 July 1968. Friends of Jackson's were travelling to Ireland and Lavin had agreed to meet with them.
68. *NYR*, 26 July 1968.
69. *The Irish Times*, 1 August 1968. Justice Thomas Teevan (1903–1976) was an Irish barrister, attorney general and judge. His first case as a newly appointed judge was presiding over Patrick Kavanagh's libel proceedings against *The Leader* magazine for publishing an unflattering and offensive profile piece on him. He was succeeded by Aindrias Ó Caoimh (1912–1994) whose brother, Brian, a professor of Celtic studies at University

College Dublin, was married to Éamon de Valera's daughter Emer. See also 'Commemorative Essay on Mary Lavin', by Kathleen MacMahon, *The Irish Times*, 27 March 2021.

70. *NYR*, 28 October 1968. *Irish Mountaineering Club Newsletter* Dublin Section, No. 2, May 1969.
71. *NYR*, 7 November 1968.
72. Letter to Wade, 23 September 1968, MLC. On September 1968 Radió Telefís Éireann broadcast Lavin reading her story, 'An Old Boot', a pre-*New Yorker* story that was included in the 1956 collection *The Patriot Son and Other Stories*. In June 1969 Lavin was among twenty people of 'a truly representative cross-section of the Irish literary and artistic world' who wrote to *The Irish Press* to express 'the view that Radió Telefís Éireann should be constantly under scrutiny lest it succumb to pressures which induce mediocrity, trivialisation and subservience to commercial or political-party interest'. The letter was signed by Patrick Boyle, novelist and President of PEN. Other signatories included Benedict Kiely; the publisher Michael Gill; Patrick Masterson, who was then a lecturer in metaphysics at UCD; the actress Siobhán McKenna; the historian and archaeologist Máire de Paor and the artist Patrick Scott. 'Want constant watch on RTE: 20 sign a letter', *The Irish Press*, 6 June 1969.
73. Mark Schorer (1908–1977) was an author, critic and academic who taught at Dartmouth, Harvard and the University of California, Berkeley. He was awarded the Guggenheim Fellowship four times. His work was published by *The New Yorker*. Lavin's 'Gabriel Galloway' and Schorer's review of Robert Frost's comedy play *A Masque of Reason* both featured in the March 1945 issue of *The Atlantic Monthly*. He testified in defence of Allen Ginsberg's *Howl* at the Obscenity Trial in 1957. Eliot Fremont-Smith (1929–2007) was a book critic for *The New York Times* and *The Village Voice*. William Alfred (1922–1999) was born into an Irish family in New York. He was a poet and playwright and taught English literature at Harvard.
74. MLC (Correspondence K. Macmillan 1967–1969), 30 November 1968.
75. MLC, Correspondence (Ashley Famous Agency folder), Sunday 24 1968, likely November.
76. *NYR*, 9 October 1968.
77. Lavin to Straus, MLC, Correspondence (Farrar, Straus and Giroux folder), 8 November 1968.
78. *NYR*, 28 October 1968.
79. MLC (Correspondence 1935–1975 folder), 19 September 1968, MLC, Evelyn Hofer (1922–2009). See also *Evelyn Hofer: New York* (Steidl, 2008). Hofer contributed photographs to V. S. Pritchett's *New York Proclaimed*.
80. MLPP, undated letter.
81. MLC (Correspondence 1935–1975 folder), 19 September 1968.
82. Their address was 147 East 19th Street. Humphrey Sutton was a graphic designer who produced Penguin and Pelican book covers including George

Orwell's *1984* and *Animal Farm*. Humphrey and Evelyn befriended the *New Yorker* artist Saul Steinberg when they lived in Greenwich Village (see Deirdre Bair's *Saul Steinberg: A Biography*).

83. MLC (Correspondence 1935–1975 folder), 28 January 1969.
84. MLC (Correspondence 1935–1975 folder), 18 March 1969.
85. *NYR*, 7 November 1968.
86. *NYR*, 5 December 1968.
87. *NYR*, 29 November 1968
88. *NYR*, 28 October 1968. Another reason for going to Iowa, she later revealed, was the frustration of waiting for Mick's freedom.
89. GSP, 1 November 1968.
90. GSP, 14 October 1968.
91. Ibid.
92. GSP, 20 November 1968.
93. Ibid.
94. Ibid.
95. Ibid. MLC (Correspondence 1935–1975 folder), 17 October 1968. Lavin had also received 'a very exciting offer' to go to Vanderbilt University in Nashville in 1970, which she hoped to accept, and Southern Illinois had also been in touch. The novelist and short story writer, Walter Sullivan, confirmed Lavin's presence at Vanderbilt in his book *Nothing Gold Can Stay: A Memoir* (University of Missouri Press, 2006).
96. *NYR*, 3 June 1968. Anne Fremantle (1909–2002) was a British-born journalist and writer who had reviewed Lavin's collection *Selected Stories* in 'A Certain Craft', *Commonweal*, 70 (18 September 1959).
97. *NYR*, 7 November 1968. Lavin had erroneously referred to it as Wellesley College, a private women's liberal college in Massachusetts, but MacKenzie corrected her that it was Weslyan [*sic*] University at Middletown, Connecticut. Rather confusingly, Lavin said that Mick was going to remain in Ireland to look after her daughters when she went to Iowa, but that he would go to Wesleyan and stay off campus if accompanying her posed a problem. Lavin, ever mindful of her daughters, had enquired whether one of them could au pair while she was there, but MacKenzie was unsure and advised her to hold on to see if she was offered first and then make enquiries.
98. *NYR*, 7 November 1968.
99. *NYR*, 11 November 1968.
100. *NYR*, 25 November 1968.
101. *The New York Times*, 11 November 1968.
102. John Beary's father, Michael, was an Irish flat racing jockey who became the Irish champion jockey in 1920, and was a retained jockey for the Aga Khan.
103. *NYR*, 11 November 1968.

104. Benedict Kiely, *Dogs Enjoy the Morning* (Gollancz, 1968). Kiely contributed 'Letter from America' to *The Irish Times* about his experience travelling across the US in the 1960s. See George O'Brien's *A Harbour Green: Celebrating Benedict Kiely*.
105. *NYR*, 21 November 1968.
106. *NYR*, 5 December 1968.
107. Richard Wilbur (1921–2017) was an American poet and literary translator. He was the second poet laureate of the United States. Among his numerous honours and awards, Wilbur won the Pulitzer Prize for Poetry in 1957 and 1989 and the National Book Award for Poetry in 1957. He was the recipient of a Guggenheim Fellowship for Creative Arts in 1952 and 1963. Wilbur wrote the lyrics for Leonard Bernstein's operetta *Candide*, adapted from a Voltaire novella. He was a staff member in poetry at the Middlebury College Bread Loaf Writers' Conference in 1954 and appears in a group photograph alongside MacKenzie.
108. *NYR*, 11 November 1968.
109. *NYR*, 28 December 1968. As of 31 December, the value of Lavin's interest in *The New Yorker* Magazine Participation Trust amounted to $3,337.50.
110. 3 January 1969. The fee was $200 but the cheque was for $197 after a $3 retirement contribution deduction. Hawley Truax acted as the mediator between Harold Ross and Raoul Fleischmann. He retired in 1971.
111. Eudora Welty to William Maxwell, 12 February 1969. Benedict Kiely reviewed 'A Set of Variations' for *The New York Times* on 4 May 1969.
112. MLC (Macmillan Correspondence 1935–1975 folder), 28 April 1969.
113. GSP, 3 March 1969. 'Happiness' was published in *The New Yorker* on 14 December 1968.
114. *NYR*, 7 January 1969.
115. *NYR*, 5 February 1969. The Association of Secondary Teachers in Ireland (ASTI) members went on an all-out strike on 1 February 1969 because they rejected the Ryan Tribunal's recommendation on pay, that of a common salary scale for all teachers.
116. *NYR*, 13 February 1969.
117. *NYR*, 19 February 1969 and 25 February 1969.
118. *NYR*, 19 February 1969.
119. *NYR*, 28 February 1969.
120. Elizabeth Schnack (1899–1992) was a Swiss author and literary translator. She briefly lived in Dublin as an exchange student from the University of Geneva and had a particular interest in Irish literature. When translating McGahern's *The Barracks* 'she revealed that she laboured over one sentence for three hours' (Barry Houlihan, *The Irish Times*, 2 March 2023).
121. MLPP, 12 September 1966.

122. 5 June 1969. *In Quiet Places: The Uncollected Stories, Letters and Critical Prose of Michael McLaverty*. Lavin befriended the Irish American author J. P. Dunleavy when he moved to Meath in the late 1960s.
123. MLPP. Schnack kept in touch with Lavin over the years and sent her reviews of the German translations of her books. On 19 May 1980 Schnack wrote to Lavin that she turned 80 the previous year and was still translating literary texts, most recently work by Seán Ó Faoláin, John McGahern and J. M. Synge.
124. *NYR*. Scott was the first Australian Jesuit to leave the Society to marry.
125. 'Voyage Round my Mother', *Sunday Independent*, 28 May 1995.
126. *The Irish Press*, 19 March 1969. (On the same page is a photograph of Joan Kennedy, wife of Senator Edward Kennedy, being welcomed by President Nixon and his wife at a reception at the White House: 'Long gowns were informally prescribed, but Mrs. Kennedy's dress was six inches above the knee.' Mrs Nixon, who was wearing a full-length gown, is captured glancing down at Joan's bare knees.) This report conflicts with Lavin's daughter Elizabeth's account that Garret FitzGerald was the best man (See Patricia Deevy, 'Voyage Round My Mother', *Sunday Independent*, 28 May 1995).
127. *NYR*, 2 July 1969.
128. *NYR*, 28 December 1968.12 June 1969. Valdi and Desmond married on 10 July 1969 and the reception was held at Abbey Farm.
129. *NYR*, 2 July 1969.
130. *NYR*, 12 June 1969.
131. *NYR*, 2 July 1969.
132. *NYR*, undated August 1969.
133. *NYR*, 26 August 1969. The cheque totalled $3576.78 after the advance and retirement contribution were deducted.
134. *NYR*, 15 December 1969.
135. 'Trastevere', *NY*, 46.
136. MLPP, Letter from Michael Scott to Zack Bowen, 20 October 1969.
137. *NYR*, 11 November 1969. *McCall's*, initially called *The Queen*, was founded in 1873 by James McCall. It was a high-circulating magazine that published stories by prominent writers including Willa Cather, F. Scott Fitzgerald and John Steinbeck. *The New Yorker* film critic Pauline Kael worked briefly at *McCall's* before allegedly being fired in 1968 for 'her withering review' of the film *The Sound of Music*. See Kate Guadagnino, 'So Long, Farewell', *The Paris Review*, 20 January 2017. Edward Ardizzone (1900–1979) was a well-known British artist and author and illustrator of children's books.
138. *NYR*, 11 November 1969. The story was published by Houghton Mifflin in 1973.
139. *NYR*, 14 November 1969. Lavin later clarified that it was not poetry but prose. MacKenzie hoped it would make her money.
140. MLPP, February 1970.
141. Interview with author.

142. This is conjecture based on the reviews which appeared in November 1969.
143. 'The New Gardener' was rejected by *The New Yorker* on 29 November 1960.
144. *The Irish Press*, 8 November 1969. The newspaper also carried Lavin's short tale 'The Sisters', which was published as part of a new weekly series, 'New Irish Writing'. Edited by David Marcus, it featured new work by writers including Lavin, Patrick Boyle and John Hewitt. The first article to be published in the series was the reprinting of Lavin's preface to the American edition of *Selected Stories* on Saturday 27 April 1968.
145. *NYR*, 15 December 1969.
146. *NYR*, 5 December 1969.
147. *NYR*, 15 December 1969.
148. *NYR*, 30 December 1969. The year ended financially well for Lavin. As of 31 December, the amount of her annuity purchased was $348.52 a year, payable in installments from the normal retirement date and on normal retirement basis. Death benefit before retirement was $4, 967.25. Lavin's contribution to the retirement plan was $418.24 *and The New Yorker*'s contribution was $4,549. The value of the Participation Trust Fund was $3,223.80. MLLP, box 22, folder 24.

9 'Small Comfort' *1970–1974*

1. Mary Lavin to Rachel MacKenzie, *NYR*, 26 December 1973.
2. *NYR*, 7 February 1970.
3. *NYR*, 12 February 1970. *House of Gold* was a Houghton Mifflin Literary Fellowship Award novel. Previous recipients included Philip Roth, for his first book *Goodbye*, *Columbus* and Elizabeth Bishop for *North and South*. Cullinan was the first person to win the New Writers' Award from the Great Lakes Colleges Association for *House of Gold*, when it was launched in 1970.
4. 7 February 1970. Richard Budd McAdoo (1920–2018) was vice president and general manager at Harper & Bros (later Harper & Row) in New York. He resigned in 1968 and began working for Houghton Mifflin. In 1982 he retired as vice president.
5. Maeve Brennan, 'Through a Lace Curtain, Darkly', Books, *The New Yorker*, 14 February 1970.
6. *NYR*, 27 April 1970.
7. Letter from William Maxwell to Mary Lavin, *NYR*, 27 April 1970.
8. MLPP, 5 May 1970.
9. MLPP, 22 June 1970.
10. Anne O'Neill-Barna, 'The Subject is the Struggle of Happiness', *The New York Times*, 24 May 1970. Edna O'Brien's *A Pagan Place* was released on the same day.
11. MLPP, an undated 1970 letter from Elizabeth Cullinan, 27 April 1970 letter from William Maxwell (*NYR*).

12. *NYR*, 22 June 1970.
13. 'Happiness', *NY*, 63. There are many superstitions attached to the daffodil, for example bringing a daffodil indoors or stepping on daffodils is believed by some to bring bad luck. In the hospital scene, after the nun snatches at the flowers, they fall on the ground and are trampled on. Lavin perhaps implies an impending sense of catastrophe here.
14. *NYR*, 25 May 1970. 'Villa Violetta', like 'Trastevere', draws upon Lavin's time in Italy on her first Guggenheim Fellowship.
15. The New American Library was founded in 1948 in New York as an imprint of Penguin USA. It had a particular focus on publishing paperbacks and pulp fiction.
16. *The Becker Wives and Other Stories* (Michael Joseph, 1946; New American Library, 1971) features the stories 'The Becker Wives', 'A Happy Death', 'The Joy Ride' and 'Magenta'. Paperback format published 1 January 1972 by Plume (trade paperback imprint of New American Library).
17. *NYR*, 22 June 1970.
18. *NYR*, end of May 1970. Eudora Welty's final novel, *Losing Battles*, was released on 13 April 1970 by Random House.
19. See *The Evening Herald*, 20 May 1970.
20. *The Irish Press*, 29 May 1970. It was funded by the Cultural Relations Committee.
21. In November 1970 Augustine Martin's *Winter's Tales from Ireland* was published, featuring stories by writers including Mary Lavin, Benedict Kiely, Bryan MacMahon and Michael McLaverty. Benedict Kiely's essay 'Green Island, Red South' on Mary Lavin and Flannery O'Connor was published in *Kilkenny Magazine*, No. 18 (1970), 18–39. Oliver Snoddy wrote that Kiely's study was 'criticism at its best, appreciative, exploratory, explanatory' ('Book Review', 'The Phoenix', *Nationalist and Leinster Times*, 11 September 1970).
22. *NYR*, undated letter. Presumably Lavin is referring to Mick here.
23. *NYR*, 22 June 1970.
24. The story only appeared in *A Memory and Other Stories* (Constable, 1972; Houghton Mifflin, 1973).
25. *NYR*, 22 June 1970.
26. Joyce Hartman (1921–2009) was the New York editor for Houghton Mifflin Co. from 1958 until 1979, where she edited works by Rachel Carson, Carson McCullers and Paul Theroux among others.
27. The letter is undated but it is pre–13 November 1970.
28. The boat Lavin took departed from Southampton on 29 January 1971, according to a Bremen luggage tag that belonged to Mary Lavin (with the name Mrs M. MacDonald Scott), that was gifted to the author by Dr Emer McManus.
29. *NYR*, November (undated) letter in which she informs MacKenzie of her impending trip to the US in January 1970.

30. James Oliver Brown (1910–1992) was a New York literary agent whose clients included Jean Stafford and Katherine Anne Porter, Cecil Beaton and Dominick Dunne. He was the New York editor of Little, Brown & Company from 1944 until 1948 and was working there when it published Mary Lavin's *At Sallygap and Other Stories* in 1947. In 1949 he founded James O. Brown Associates, which in 1978 merged with Curtis Brown, where he was president until his retirement in 1985.
31. *NYR*, 13 November 1970.
32. Barney Tobey (1906–1989) contributed over 1,200 cartoons to *The New Yorker* and illustrated Al Perkins's adaptation of Ian Fleming's 1964 novel *Chitty Chitty Bang Bang: The Magical Car*, in 1968, the same year the musical version appeared. Roald Dahl and Ken Hughes adapted the novel for the musical, which starred Dick Van Dyke and Sally Ann Howes and was produced by Albert R. Broccoli, co-producer of the James Bond movies, based on Ian Fleming's novels.
33. *NY*, 30 November 1970, 56. Robert Dana (1929–2010) was the Poet Laureate for the State of Iowa from 2004 to 2008. Sylvia Plath's 'Gigolo' was written on 29 January 1963, a few days before her death on 11 February 1963. American poet James Wright (1927–1980) was awarded the Pulitzer Prize for Poetry in 1973.
34. 'Risk', Rachel MacKenzie, 21 November 1970, 56.
35. Ibid., 101.
36. *NYR*, 7 December 1970.
37. *NYR*, 14 January 1971.
38. As quoted in 'Rachel MacKenzie is dead at 70; A Fiction Editor for New Yorker', by Carey Winfrey, *The New York Times*, 30 March 1980.
39. Although the contract fee was a disappointing one, Lavin still made good money with the magazine that year. On 31 December the value of Lavin's interest in *The New Yorker* Magazine Participation Trust Fund amounted to $3,178.32 (Annual Report to Participants, Morgan Guaranty Trust Company of New York). Lavin's 1099 form for the calendar year 1970 for 'commissions, fees, prizes and awards, etc., to nonemployees, and foreign items' came to $848.04.
40. *NYR*, 14 January 1971.
41. *NYR*, undated letter 1971.
42. Lavin met with Eudora Welty in May when both women had checked into the Algonquin Hotel.
43. MLPP, 15 October 1970.
44. *The Time of Adam* was published by Houghton Mifflin.
45. 24 July 1967, MLPP, UCD. 'A Sunday Like the Others' was published in *The New Yorker* on 18 August 1967.
46. Elizabeth Cullinan to John McGahern, MGA, 24 March 1971.
47. Ibid. The letter was forwarded from the Faber & Faber London office to The New Forge, Cleggan, County Galway.

48. MLPP, 15 October 1970.
49. M. F. K. Fisher's (1908–1992) praise was published on the dust jacket. She described MacKenzie, her *New Yorker* editor, as 'brilliant, dry, and affectionate, all at the same time', as quoted in Luke Barr's *Provence, 1970: M. F. K. Fisher, Julia Child, James Beard, and the Reinvention of American Taste* (Clarkson Potter, 2013).
50. 'The Odds Are 100% or Zero, Books of the Times'. Anatole Broyard, *The New York Times*, 7 May 1971.
51. *The New York Times*, 16 May 1971.
52. *NYR*, 27 September 1971. Andy Logan (1920–2000) reported on New York's City Hall for *The New Yorker* for 25 years (1969–1994). She was the first woman to write for the 'Talk of the Town' section and also contributed fiction and poetry to the magazine. The 'old book' was *The Man Who Robbed the Robber Barons*, published in 1965. Logan had another book, *Against the Evidence*, published in 1970. See Charles Patrick Crow's *Postscript: Remembering Andy Logan*, 'The Talk of the Town', *The New Yorker*, 4 December 2000.
53. MLC (Memorabilia folder), undated.
54. MLPP, 26 March 1971.
55. The American critic Richard (Dick) Ellmann (1918–1987) had tried unsuccessfully to facilitate a visit from Lavin at Northwestern University, where he taught from 1951 until 1968, when she was in the US in 1967.
56. *NYR*, 30 July 1971.
57. *NYR*, 19 August 1971.
58. MLPP, 28 July 1971.
59. MLLP, 11 October 1971.
60. *NYR*, 19 August 1971.
61. *NYR*, 21 September 1971. The School of Irish Studies was founded by Maurice Harmon.
62. 27 September 1971. Anne Sexton (1928–1974) was an American poet whose work was published in *The New Yorker*. Sexton won the Pulitzer Prize for poetry in 1967 for her collection *Live or Die*. In 1973 Conrad Susa produced the opera *Transformations*, based on Sexton's book. Sexton was a Frost fellow at the Bread Loaf Writers' Conference in 1959.
63. Sexton wrote 'Sylvia's Death' in 1963, after Plath's suicide. Sexton also died by suicide in 1974.
64. *NYR*, 27 September 1971.
65. *NYR*, 5–18 October 1971.
66. André François (1915–2005), considered to be one of the most influential graphic artists of his generation, also contributed cartoons to *The New Yorker*.
67. Given the story's locations of Rome and New York, it is ironic that Greg Kuzma (1944–) was born in Rome, New York.
68. MLPP, 15 December 1971.

69. MLPP, 19 November 1971. The story was 'Yellow Roses', which was published on 25 February 1972.
70. MLPP, undated letter.
71. *NYR*, 12 November 1971. There are two copies of the review in Lavin's archive so it would appear that she received a copy from Houghton Mifflin and Rachel MacKenzie. 'A Queer Place Surely', Vivian Mercier, *The Nation*, 8 November 1971.
72. *The New York Times*, 26 October 1971. In fact the award was given to 'three reporters and two television stations'. The other two reporters who received the award were Harold J. Eager of *The Sunday News*, Lancaster, PA. and Jane E. Brody of *The New York Times.*
73. *NYR*, 12 November 1971.
74. Rachel MacKenzie, Derek Morgan, 14 April, *The New Yorker.*
75. *NYR*, 14 December 1972. Bill Maxwell let Lavin know that the poet, Robert Fitzgerald, was looking for her address (MLPP 17, December 1971).
76. *NYR*, 31 January 1972. See Greg Londe's 'Mary Lavin Memory of 1972', *American Journal of Irish Studies*, Vol. 10 (2013), 130–4, Glucksman Ireland House, New York University. The 'small university' may have been Radcliffe College, MacKenzie's alma mater, where Cabot attended before going to Harvard. Radcliffe was subsumed into Harvard in 1999. On 10 February 1972 David Marcus acknowledged Lavin's letter in which she had to decline attending the Hennessy Awards reception (MLPP). The judges were Brian Friel and James Plunkett and the winners that year were Fred Johnston, Ita Daly, Maeve O'Brien Kelly and Patrick Cunningham. Lavin judged the award alongside John Braine in 1978.On 5 August 1972 Lavin informed MacKenzie that she was working on a story about Belfast, which she was finding 'very painful to write'. 'The Face of Hate', which Lavin sent to the magazine the following year, was inspired by the troubles in Northern Ireland.
77. *NYR*, 15 April 1972.
78. *NYR*, 25 April 1972. MacKenzie received it on 20 April and rejected it on 25 April. This was quite an impressive and rapid turnaround.
79. *NYR*, 20 April 1972.
80. *NYR*, 26 May 1972. On 31 May, Milton Greenstein wrote to inform Lavin that from 1 July she would qualify to receive approximately $30 in monthly payments for life. The total sum amounted to $5,173.72 (MLPP).
81. 'The Mug of Water' was published in *The Southern Review*, 10 (Spring 1974) and 'The Shrine' was published in *The Sewanee Review*, 82 (Spring 1974).
82. 'The Lily and the Rose' does not appear to have been published elsewhere.
83. *NYR*, 23 June. 'The Motor Mower' does not appear to have been published elsewhere.
84. *NYR*, 23 June 2024.
85. 'The Nation', *The New York Times*, 25 June 1972.
86. See Hurley, 'To Cut a Long Story Short'.

87. Tom Lavin died in late September 1945. *The Atlantic* published Lavin's 'The Green and the Black Grave' on May 1940 and 'At Sallygap' on October 1941. The magazine began publishing the series of Gabriel Galloway stories on 1 November 1955 which appeared as the book *The House in Clewe Street* in 1945.
88. The horse was trained by Harry Ussher. Billie O'Grady was the jockey. Heartbreak Hill came sixth in the 1932 Grand National at Aintree.
89. On 7 July, Milton Greenstein wrote to Lavin to inform her that from 1 September 1972 she would receive monthly payments of $50 from *The New Yorker*'s Participation Plan which was worth $3,405.52.
90. *NYR*, 30 October 1972.
91. It was published by Constable in 1972 and Houghton Mifflin in 1973.
92. Benedict Kiely, 'The Greatness of Mary Lavin', *The Irish Times*, 21 October 1972.
93. *The Second-Best Children in the World* (Longman, 1972; Houghton Mifflin, 1972). Kiely also mentioned the reprint of *The Becker Wives and Other Stories*, which was published by New American Library in 1971.
94. *NYR*, 20 December 1972.
95. *NYR*, 8 January 1973. The letter in which Lavin talks of her plans to visit London is not contained in the archives.
96. *NYR*, 15 January 1973.
97. Van K. Brock (1932–2017) graduated from the University of Iowa with an MA in English (1963) and an MFA in poetry (1964) after Paul Engle encouraged him to study there. He returned to undertake a PhD in modern letters, which he was awarded in 1970.
98. 'What Were People Reading in the Summer of 1972', Tina Jordan, *The New York Times*, 14 July 2022.
99. *NYR*, 31 January 1973.
100. MLPP, 22 February 1973.
101. MLPP, 1 October 1973.
102. *NYR*, 12 February 1973.
103. *NYR*, 7 February 1973.
104. MacKenzie informed Lavin that Derek Morgan used to be a senior editor at *The Reporter*. He moved to *The New Yorker* after the magazine ceased publication in 1968.
105. On 16 May Lavin attended the Allied Irish Bank award for literature prizegiving in Sligo. John Banville won the award for his novel *Birchwood*. Bob Ryan, in his book *Memoirs of a Reluctant Banker*, recalls how he befriended Lavin: 'Among the special awards I particularly remember was one presented to Mary Lavin in recognition of her contribution to Irish literature.'
106. *NYR*, 5 June 1973. Maurice Sheehy was a friend of Harriet and Frank O'Connor.

107. Kay Boyle (1902–1992) had apparently written a letter to Houghton Mifflin in admiration of Lavin's work, which prompted Lavin's letter (see Levenson, 241–2). Boyle was awarded the Guggenheim Fellowship in 1934 and 1961 in the field of poetry. Boyle and her third husband, Baron Joseph von Franckenstein, were accused of attending Communist Party meetings while they were in New York. Ernest Walsh (1895–1926) contacted Kay Boyle to invite her to submit work for his magazine. Her poem 'Summer' was published in *This Quarter* in 1925. Walsh then invited Boyle to the French Riviera, where he was suffering from tuberculosis, and the two began an affair. He died in October that year and their daughter, Sharon, who Lavin likely met, was born five months later. Kay Boyle did not reveal the title of her new book but it was likely her novel *The Underground Woman* which was published in 1975. In 1963 she accepted a creative writing position on the faculty of San Francisco State College, where she remained until 1979. In 1976 Boyle, who had an interest in Irish politics, visited Ireland in order to conduct research for a book on Irish women. The book was never published.
108. MLLP, undated 1973.
109. See Joyce Carol Oates, 'Written as if by people from different planets', 25 November 1973, *The New York Times*.
110. *NYR*, 5 December 1973.
111. *NYR*, 13 December 1973.
112. The earthquake on 23 December 1972 destroyed the city of Managua. Thousands of people were killed, injured and left destitute.
113. *NYR*, St Stephen's Day, 26 December 1973. In a later interview with Maev Kennedy, Lavin divulged that she was writing more than ever and put her productivity down to the fact that she was ageing: 'She finds that growing older, and having to go slower on some of her favourite occupations – like swimming – has brought her more time to write than ever before.' 'The Saturday Interview: Maev Kennedy Talked to Mary Lavin', *The Irish Times*, 13 March 1976. Diarmuid Russell died on 16 December 1973 at the age of 71.
114. The next collection brought out by Houghton Mifflin was *The Shrine and Other Stories*, which was published in 1977.
115. *NYR*, 4 January 1974.
116. *NYR*, 27 February 1974.
117. *NYR*, 27 February 1974. Princeton Press had been in touch for Lavin to produce two collections of stories from her novels and Mick was encouraging her to write an autobiography but she would only consider writing about her childhood.
118. *NYR*, 27 February 1974.
119. *NYR*, 25 March 1973.
120. Previous recipients of the Éire Society of Boston Gold Medal include John W. McCormack, Siobhán McKenna, John Huston, Cornelius Ryan, Padraic

Colum, John Fitzgerald Kennedy, Seamus Heaney and more recently, Colm Tóibín, who was presented with the award in 2017.

121. MLPP 22, March 1974. Cullinan had hoped to visit Ireland but her financial situation was pretty dire.
122. David Bowie was on board the same ocean liner and gave an impromptu performance for the crew. Lavin hosted Cullinan's sister, Claire, and her husband when they visited Ireland that summer and their stories of the visit made her homesick. Cullinan returned to Ireland the following year.
123. Derek Morgan reported in his *New Yorker* obituary of MacKenzie that she was knocked down by a Cadillac.
124. Doris Fletcher Borner (1907–1998). Fletcher attended the Bread Loaf Writers' Conference as a contributor in 1944.
125. Josephine Jacobsen (1908–2003) was a poet and fiction writer. In 1997 she was awarded the Robert Frost Medal from the Poetry Society of America.
126. *The New York Times*, 21 May 1974.
127. *NYR*, 26 September 1974.
128. *NYR*, 20 December 1974.
129. *NYR*, 7 October 1974.
130. *NYR*, 23 October 1974.
131. *NYR*, 20 December 1974.

10 'Hanging Crêpe' *1975–1992*

1. Information on Lavin's time in Bellagio is scant. V. S. Pritchett wrote to Lavin on 10 February 1975 and asked how to apply for the residency. He also imparted that he was very impressed by Eavan Boland's speech at the 39th International PEN Congress in Jerusalem in December 1974. Saul Bellow and Heinrich Böll also attended the conference that was held from 15 until 22 December 1974.
2. MacKenzie wrote a review, 'Concerning Pain and Beauty', of *The Verdict* by Hildegard Knef for *The New York Times* on 25 January 1976.
3. See Levenson, 241–2.
4. MacKenzie's last letter to Lavin is dated 20 December 1974. The next letter in the archives, almost two and a half years later, is from Charles McGrath and is dated 20 May 1977. Despite Lavin having a contract with the magazine until 1988, there is no correspondence in the *New Yorker* records for the years 1975, 1976 and 1978 and 1979 is the final Mary Lavin folder in the *New Yorker* records.
5. When *The New Yorker* moved offices in 1991, seventy-two boxes of archival material were discarded: 'The *New Yorker* records were donated to the New York Public Library by *The New Yorker* Magazine Inc. in March 1991. Before it could be transferred to the library, approximately 144 linear feet

of material disappeared during *The New Yorker*'s move to new offices in February 1991.

6. *The Irish Times* carries a photograph of Mary Lavin with President Ó Dálaigh. Ó Dálaigh who was in office from 19 December 1974 until 22 October 1976.
7. *The Meath Chronicle*, 22 March 1975. An exhausted Lavin had just returned a few hours earlier from 'an arduous overland journey from Italy, lasting two days and two nights'. In June 1975 Navan County Library opened an exhibition devoted to Mary Lavin's work.
8. See Zack Bowen, *Mary Lavin* (Bucknell University Press, 1975).
9. MLPP, 31 July 1979. William Vincent Shannon (1927–1988) was the United States Ambassador to Ireland from 1977 until 1981 under President Jimmy Carter's administration. Lavin also received the Allied Irish Banks Literary Award in 1981, which carried a prize of £2,000, and she was a member of the Cultural Relations Committee in 1985 and 1986.
10. This was a new union rule imposed on the age of retirement. Eudora Welty suffered the loss of William Maxwell, especially as her other confidant, her trusted agent Diarmuid Russell died in December 1973. See Marrs, *What There Is to Say*, 279.
11. Charles 'Chip' McGrath is an American editor, journalist and writer from an Irish background. He currently writes for *The New York Times* (he was previously the editor of *The New York Times* Book Review). McGrath still contributes to *The New Yorker*. One of his latest pieces, 'One, Two, Three, Jump!', an adaptation of his memoir *The Summer Friend*, was published in the magazine on 27 May 2022.
12. MLPP, 16 January 1976. Two of Lavin's stories were read at some stage on the BBC's *Woman's Hour* in 1976, for which she was paid a sum of £49.20, from which Constable took 25 per cent commission (letter from Mrs. M. Stevens from Constable to Lavin, 2 March, MLLP).
13. MLPP, 26 February 1976. 'Estelle' was published in *The New Yorker* on 19 April 1976
14. See Chapter 4. The story had also been titled 'Ignus Fatuus' and 'Outside the Gallery'. See Hurley, 'To Cut a Long Story Short' for a detailed account of the revisions made to the story.
15. Donald Barthleme's story 'Perpetua' was published in *The New Yorker* on 12 June 1971.
16. Derek Morgan was also Eudora Welty's new editor. Norman A. Jeffares (Derry) had a chapter, 'Mary Lavin', published in 1976. James Vinson (ed.), *Contemporary Novelists* (St James Press; St Martin's Press, 19762), 788–91.
17. 8 March 1975, MLPP. 'Eterna' was subsequently published in *The Irish Press* on 4 September 1976 as part of David Marcus's New Irish Writing series.

18. 'The Saturday Interview: Maev Kennedy Talked to Mary Lavin', *The Irish Times*, 13 March 1976. Lavin's books being out of print was still an issue. See also Greg Londe's 'Mary Lavin's Memory of 1972'.
19. In 1999, Caroline Walsh was appointed the literary editor of *The Irish Times*.
20. Charles McGrath, email to author.
21. *NYR*, 20 May 1977. This is the first mention of the story in the archives, so it is not clear when it was first sent in for consideration.
22. *NYR*, 8 July 1977.
23. *NYR*, 8 July 1977. 'A Walk on the Cliff' featured in *A Family Likeness and Other Stories* (Constable, 1985). The collection contained the two other stories previously rejected by *The New Yorker*, 'A Family Likeness' and 'The Face of Hate'. The story was also anthologised in *The Writers: A Sense of Ireland*, ed. Andrew Carpenter and Peter Fallon (O'Brien Press, 1980).
24. See A. A. Kelly, *Mary Lavin: A Study*, 171, 1980. MLLP contains drafts of 'Senility' ranging from February 1975 until April 1985.
25. 'Mary Lavin's New Collection', *The Irish Times*, 28 May 1977.
26. See Anthony Burgess, 'What Literature is About', *The Irish Press*, 2 June 1977. Seamus Deane reviewed the collection for the *Sunday Independent*.
27. MLPP, 29 March 1978.
28. *NYR*, 21 July 1977.
29. *NYR*, 9 September 1977.
30. See 'Gallic Chic and Irish Pique', *The New York Times*, 30 October 1977.
31. *NYR*, 21 July 1977.
32. *NYR*, 9 September 1977.
33. *NYR*, 29 September 1977. 'The First Snow' was published in *CARA*, the inflight magazine of Aer Lingus in 1978 and in *The Irish Times* in August 1985.
34. See 'An Interview with Mary Lavin', L. Robert, Mary Lavin and Sylvia Stevens, *Studies: An Irish Quarterly Review*, Spring, 1997, Vol. 86, No. 341 (Spring, 1997), 43–50, https://www.jstor.org/stable/30092397. On 11 December 1978 Mick wrote to Welty that Lavin 'had to a certain extent lost her "sense of place" – the quality in you (both of you) which had drawn you together in the first place. But meeting you again in your place – talking to you again and seeing for the first time your beloved Mississippi – and then later, seeing Faulkner's house in Oxford – and re-reading you both – all this has given her back her own sense of place – and with it a new contentment.' See Marrs, *Eudora Welty*, 437.
35. See Marrs, *Eudora Welty*, 437.
36. MLPP, 21 June 1978. Cullinan informed Lavin that she was going to be teaching at the University of Massachusetts the following year. She got the appointment through Janet Dunleavy who had sent her the advert which was in *The New York Times.*

37. *NYR*, 2 July 1979. 'Lethe' was not published elsewhere. Curiously, 'A Walk on the Cliff' had been previously published in *Good Housekeeping*, London in 1940. The letter was sent to Lavin c/o Allied Irish Bank, 299 Park Avenue, New York, New York. On 14 February *The New York Times* reported, 'The Irish postal service, faced with a strike Monday by 13,000 mail deliverers, telephone operators and counter clerks, asked the public today not to mail letters. Advertisements in newspapers said, "Please do not post any letters from now until further notice." Post offices also stopped accepting parcels.' Maev Kennedy, in her *Irish Times* review of *The Past*, observed, 'It is an extraordinary first novel, and one that certainly leaves me wondering what he'll tackle next.'
38. Eileen Battersby named Lavin 'one of modern Irish fiction's most subversive voices'. Eileen Battersby, 'Short Story Writer Mary Lavin Dies at 83', *The Irish Times*, 26 March 1996.
39. Lavin was invited to the captain's table on the journey over to New York. They also met with Eudora Welty and John Beary at the Algonquin during this trip (see Levenson, 236–40.).
40. See Anne Francis Cavanaugh's account of Lavin's reading for Bishop in 'Remembering Mary', 'A Bouquet for Mary', *Irish Literary Supplement*, Fall 1996, Volume 15, Number 2. Lavin's story 'A House to Let' had been republished in *Ploughshares*, 3 (1976), having previously been printed in *Winter's Tales from Ireland* I, ed. Augustine Martin (Gill and Macmillan, Macmillan, 1970), 158–67.
41. Wells College posthumously awarded MacKenzie the Alumnae Award.
42. 'Rachel MacKenzie is dead at 70; A Fiction Editor for New Yorker', by Carey Winfrey, *The New York Times*, 30 March 1980.
43. *The Collected Stories* was published in 1982.
44. *The New York Times*, 30 March 1980.
45. In 1980 Lavin gave a talk at the Institute of Contemporary Art (ICA) alongside Seán Ó Faoláin, Liam O'Flaherty and Francis Stuart. In September 1984 Liam O'Flaherty died and Lavin was one of the mourners at his funeral; others included Seamus Heaney, Byran MacMahon, John Montague, Garech de Brun and Benedict Kiely, who delivered the eulogy at his grave. On 28 August 1985 Lavin wrote to John McGahern to congratulate him on winning the Irish-American Foundation Award and explained that she could not make the award ceremony due to being hospitalised for an operation (MGA).
46. Lavin dedicated *The Stories of Mary Lavin, Vol. 3* to her grandchildren: 'Kathleen, Kevin, and Margaret MacMahon, Matthew Ryan, Eoghain, Adam and Tadgh and to the memory of Eliza Peavoy.' *A Family Likeness and Other Stories* contained the previously published 'A House to Let' and five new stories, which included three stories rejected by *The New Yorker*, 'A Family Likeness', 'A Walk on the Cliff' and 'The Face of Hate'. The other two new stories were 'A Marriage' and 'A Bevy of Aunts'. There is

no mention of 'A House to Let', 'A Bevy of Aunts' or 'A Marriage' in her correspondence with the magazine.

47. The Newhouses paid $200 million for the magazine.
48. Gottlieb had been editor-in-chief at Knopf, which was a subsidiary of the Newhouse-owned Random House and he was due to commence the role on 1 March 1987.
49. Edwin McDowell, '154 at *The New Yorker* Protest Choice of Editor', *The New York Times*, 15 January 1987; and Barry Siegel, 'Breach of Tradition: *New Yorker* Shake-up Is the Talk of the Town', *The Los Angeles Times*, 12 February 1987.
50. Gottlieb saw it as his job to save the *The New Yorker*, which had been performing poorly, with a decline in its circulation and advertising sales. Eric Pace in his obituary of Shawn, 'William Shawn, 85, Is Dead; *New Yorker*'s Gentle Despot' (*The New York Times*, 9 December 1992) reported that the average circulation per *New Yorker* issue rose, 'from about 485,000 for 1974 to a peak of about 510,000 for 1983 but then dropped back toward 500,000 for 1984 – the year before the magazine was sold'. He also observed that 'the number of pages of advertising in *The New Yorker* rose in the late 1970s and early 1980s to a peak of almost 4,500 pages for 1981 and then sagged in the next three years to about 3,500 pages for 1984'.
51. Interview with author.
52. Charles McGrath, email to author, 19 October 2012.
53. MLLP, postmarked 25 January 1988.
54. MLLP, 22 October (the year is not recorded but conjecture would place it after Shawn's departure). Cullinan's final *New Yorker* story, 'Echoes', was published on 7 June 1981.
55. Elizabeth Cullinan died in Towson, Maryland on 26 January 2020.
56. *A Change of Scene* by Elizabeth Cullinan, reviewed by Maureen Connolly, *Irish Literary Supplement*, Vol. 2, No. 1, 1 March 1983. Cullinan is also quoted in the article as saying of Lavin: 'Her writing always left me breathless and her girls – yes, they're all in A Change of Scene – weren't they like others; they knew so much!!'
57. The advert concerning the auction of the mews was placed in the *Irish Independent* on 12 May 1982, 'On the instructions of Miss Mary Lavin'.
58. Patience Ross (1906–1989) was born Patience Henrietta May Ropes. She was a translator and poet and published two volumes of poetry, *Black Bread* (1929) and *The Glass Rose* (1930) and she translated Maurice Leblanc's *L'Image de la femme nue* (1934) into English as *Wanton Venus* (1935). Leblanc is probably best known for his Arsène Lupin short stories.
59. MLLP, 4 April 1988. Cullinan had recommended Lavin's *Collected Stories* for *Writer's Choice: A Library of Rediscoveries*, a 1983 publication which listed almost 1,000 of the most neglected books ever published. Cullinan wrote of the collection, 'Her characters live in a world that seems, at first glance, small but turns out to be the universe.'

60. MLLP, 4 April 1988.
61. Ross joined A. M. Heath in 1926 and she is credited with saving some of the company's files during the Blitz by taking copies of their records and storing them in her chicken coop.
62. MLLP, 13 April 1988.
63. Ibid. Virago had republished Lavin's *Mary O'Grady* in 1986, and *The House in Clewe Street* in 1987 as part of its Modern Classics series.
64. MLPP, 12 January 1989.
65. MLLP, 'Rough Version' of handwritten letter to Eudora Welty, 28 November 1988.
66. Lavin also informed McGahern that she had sold her silver and her writing library, MGA, 12 December 1989.
67. See Maurice Harmon, 'An Appreciation', 15 January 1991, *The Irish Times*.
68. The ceremony was held at the Arts Council Office in Merrion Square on 22 February 1993. See 'Lavin and Le Brocquy Honoured', Paddy Woodworth, *The Irish Times*, 24 February 1992. The previous year, Lavin had nominated Seamus Deane, Dermot Bolger, Frank McGuinness Michael Longley and Peter Carey for Aosdána membership because 'they were writers'. (MLPP). Subsequent Saoithe include Benedict Kiely, Seamus Heaney, William Trevor and Edna O'Brien who was elected Saoi in 2015.
69. MLLP, 11 July 1992. Janet Egleson Dunleavy was an American literary scholar. Tina Bown, who had been the editor in chief of *Vanity Fair*, was appointed the fourth and first female editor of *The New Yorker*. The magazine needed a major shake-up after seeing a loss in profits, reportedly amounting to $10 million the previous year. 'Tina Brown to Take Over at *The New Yorker*' by Deirdre Carmody, *The New York Times*, 1 July 1992. Graydon Carter was Brown's replacement at *Vanity Fair*.
70. 'Tina Brown to Take Over at *The New Yorker*', 1 July 1992, *The New York Times*.
71. MLLP, 11 July 1992.
72. MLLP, 28 October 1992.
73. Many years later, James Ryan wrote a letter to Elizabeth Cullinan and enclosed an envelope on which Lavin had written Cullinan's address, which Ryan imparted to Cullinan 'would suggest she felt she had something she wished to say to you' (MLPP). The letter was returned to sender. Ryan's letter is undated but is date stamped 27 August, which UCD librarian Eugene Roche believes is the date of return rather than the original posting.
74. See 'Mary Lavin Talking with Eavan Boland', 144.

Postscript

1. Preamble, *In a Café*, (Town House, 1995), xi.

2. See Patricia Deevy, 'Voyage Round My Mother', *Sunday Independent*, 28 May 1995.
3. Maurice Harmon, 'Courageous Chronicler of the Vagaries of the Human Heart', *The Irish Times*, 26 March 1996.
4. *The Guardian*, 26 March 1996.
5. 'Cemetery Sunday in Navan', *The Meath Chronicle*, 20 July 1996.
6. As quoted in Eileen Battersby, 'Story Writer Mary Lavin Dies at 83', *The Irish Times*, 26 March 1996.
7. Maeve Binchy, 'A Special Lesson', *The Irish Times*, 30 March 1996.
8. See 'Mary Lavin Talking with Eavan Boland', 141.
9. Ibid, 142.
10. See Patricia Deevy, 'Voyage Round My Mother', *Sunday Independent*, 28 May 1995. In 2015 *The Irish Times* published a poster of women writers to mark International Women's Day (men only featured on the 'Irish Writers' poster until then). The poster features Mary Lavin, Maeve Brennan, Edna O'Brien, Elizabeth Bowen, Maria Edgeworth, Kate O'Brien, Augusta Gregory, Somerville & Ross, Molly Keane, Jennifer Johnston, Eavan Boland and Anne Enright. The poster image was also available as a tea towel which Kathleen MacMahon said 'caused a great laugh in our family because Grandmother was never much of a girl for doing the dishes.' See Kathleen MacMahon, 'Irish Women Writing Fiction Were Dismissed as "Quiet". Ireland Wasn't Listening', op.cit.
11. Bruce Arnold, 'Queen of Palace of Delight', *Irish Independent*, 26 March 1996.
12. Edward P. Jones, 'Bad Neighbors', *The New Yorker*, 7 August 2006. New Island Books reprinted the collections *Happiness and Other Stories* (2011), *In the Middle of the Fields* (2016) and *The Becker Wives and Other Stories* (2018), as part of their Modern Irish Classics series.
13. Evelyn Conlon in the introduction of the republished *Tales from Bective Bridge* noted that Lord Dunsany in the original 1942 foreword, 'was introducing a new writer, was signalling the depth and unusualness of her work, was painting us a promise to come, whereas now we can see this collection as only part of a consistently interesting lifetime's work.' Introduction, *Tales from Bective Bridge, Mary Lavin* (Town House and Country House, 1996). Elke D'hoker's *Mary Lavin*, a collection of critical essays, was also published to celebrate Lavin's centenary. D'hoker addresses Lavin's work being out of print in her introduction to the volume: 'Despite the honours Mary Lavin received and continues to receive, however, her work itself is now rather hard to come by. Of the nineteen short story collections she published during her lifetime, only two are still in print, having been reissued in the context of the centenary celebrations: *Happiness and Other Stories* (2011) and *Tales from Bective Bridge* (2012). Lavin's two novels, *The House in Clewe Street* (1945) and *Mary O'Grady* (1950) are also still available, but the three-

volume collected edition of her short stories, which Constable published in the 1970s, can no longer be found.'

14. Elizabeth Peavoy was Lavin's only surviving daughter at this point. Valdi died in November 2010 and Caroline, who had organised the symposium, died just over a year later in December 2011. See Colm Tóibín's 'Mary Lavin: Context and Character', *American Journal of Irish Studies*, Vol. 10 (2013), 94–113, Glucksman Ireland House, New York University.
15. Colm Tóibín was appointed the Laureate for Irish Fiction 2022–2024. IPUT Real Estate developed the new public square, Mary Lavin Place, as part of its restoration of the Wilton Park development. In January 2022, in another milestone for Irish female writers, Trinity College Dublin renamed the Berkeley Library after the acclaimed poet Eavan Boland in October 2024, making it the first building on Trinity's City Campus to be named after a woman.
16. 'New Public Space Opened in Dublin Named after Former Aosdána Member and Saoi Mary Lavin', Aosdána website, 24 October 2024.
17. Margaret Kelleher noted that Lavin 'is now recognised as one of the greatest short story writers, but here national recognition has lagged well behind her international standing.' See Mary Lavin papers cast fresh light on the writing life', *The Irish Times*, 11 January 2022.

Bibliography

Archives

George Starbuck Papers, University of Iowa Libraries, Iowa City, Iowa

The McGahern Archive at the James Hardiman Library, National University of Galway, Ireland

Mary Lavin Collection, Howard Gotlieb Archival Research Center, Boston University, Boston, Massachusetts

Mary Lavin Literary Papers, James Joyce Library, Special Collections, University College Dublin

Mary Lavin Papers, Binghampton University Libraries Special Collections

Mary Lavin Personal Papers. James Joyce Library, Special Collections, University College Dublin

Michael McLaverty Archive, Linen Hall Library, Belfast

National Library of Ireland

New Yorker records, Manuscripts and Archives Division, The New York Public Library Astor, Lenox, and Tilden Foundations

Sylvia Beach Papers, 1872–1999, Department of Special Collections, Princeton University Library

William Shawn papers. Manuscripts and Archives Division, The New York Public Library. Astor, Lenox, and Tilden Foundations.

General Bibliography

Abell, E. (ed.) (1954), *American Accent: Fourteen Stories by Authors Associated with the Bread Loaf Writers' Conference*, New York: Ballantine Books

Adler, R. (2000), *Gone: The Last Days of The New Yorker*, New York: Simon & Schuster

Angell, R. (2006), *Let Me Finish*, Boston: Houghton Mifflin

Asprey, R. (1959), *Panther's Feast*. New York: G. P. Putnam's Sons

Averill, D. M. (1982), *The Irish Short Story from George Moore to Frank O'Connor*, Washington DC: University Press of America

Ayer, E. (1967), *The Beneficiary and Other Poems*, Iowa City: The Prairie Press

Bair, D. (2012), *Saul Steinberg: A Biography*, New York: Nan A. Talese

Baker, R. (1961), *An American in Washington*, New York: Alfred A. Knopf

Banville, J. (1973), *Birchwood*, London: Secker & Warburg

Barr, L. (2013), *Provence, 1970: M. F. K. Fisher, Julia Child, James Beard, and the Reinvention of American Taste*, New York: Clarkson Potter

Begley, A. (2014), *Updike*, New York: Harper

Biele, J. (ed.) (2011), *Elizabeth Bishop and The New Yorker: The Complete Correspondence*, New York: Farrar Straus & Giroux

Bishop, E. (1946), *North and South*, Boston: Houghton Mifflin

Bloom, J. (2006), *The Art of Revision in the Short Stories of V. S. Pritchett and William Trevor*, New York: Palgrave Macmillan

—. and Rovera, C. (eds) (2020), *Genesis and Revision in Modern British and Irish Writers*, New York: Palgrave Macmillan

Boddy, K. (2010), *The American Short Story Since 1950*, Edinburgh: Edinburgh University Press

Boland, E. (1988), 'Mary Lavin Talking with Eavan Boland' in M. Chamberlain (ed.), *Writing Lives: Conversations Between Women Writers*, London: Virago Press

Botsford, G. (2003), *A Life of Privilege, Mostly*, New York: St Martin's Press

Bourke, A. (2004), *Maeve Brennan: Homesick at The New Yorker*. New York: Counterpoint

Bowen, E. *(1968), Eva Trout,* London: Jonathan Cape

Bowen, Z. (1975), *Mary Lavin*, Lewisburg: Bucknell University Press

Boyle, K. (1975), *The Underground Woman*, New York: Doubleday

Brennan, M. (1969) *The Long-Winded Lady: Notes from The New Yorker*, New York: William Morrow and Company

—. (1969), *In and Out of Never-Never Land*, New York: Scribners

—. (1974), *Christmas Eve*, New York: Scribners

—. (1997), *The Springs of Affection: Stories of Dublin*, Boston: Houghton Mifflin

—. (1999), *The Rose Garden*, Washington DC: Counterpoint Press

—. (2000), *The Visitor*. Washington DC: Counterpoint Press

Brinnin, J. M. (1955), *Dylan Thomas in America*, Boston: Little, Brown and Co.

Brown, J. (1964), *Flat Stanley*, New York: Harper & Row

Brown, T. and Rafroidi, P. (eds) (1979), *The Irish Short Story*, Gerrards Cross: Colin Smythe

Burkhardt, B. (2005), *William Maxwell: A Literary Life*. Urbana: University of Illinois Press

—. (ed.) (2012), *Conversations with William Maxwell*. Jackson: University Press of Mississippi

Cahill, C., Flanagan, T. and Heaney, S. (eds) (2004), *There You Are: Writings on Irish and American Literature and History,* New York: New York Review of Books

Calisher, H. and Ravenel, S. (eds) (1981), *The Best American Short Stories 1981*, Boston: Houghton Mifflin

Capote, T. (1958), *Breakfast at Tiffany's*, New York: Random House

Carduff, C. (2008), *William Maxwell: Early Novels and Stories*, New York: Library of America

Carpenter, A. and Fallon, P. (eds) (1980), *The Writers: A Sense of Ireland*, Dublin: The O'Brien Press

Cheever, J. (1961), *Some People, Places, and Things That Will Not Appear in My Next Novel*, New York: Harper & Brothers

—. (1964), *The Wapshot Scandal*, New York: Harper & Row

Cheever, S. (1984), *Home Before Dark: A Personal Memoir of John Cheever by His Daughter*, Boston: Houghton Mifflin

Child. J. (1961), *Mastering the Art of French Cooking*, New York: Alfred A. Knopf

Clarke, A. (1974), 'The Paper Curtain', *The Collected Poems of Austin Clarke*, Dublin: Dolmen Press

Clarke, G. (1988), *Capote: A Biography*, New York: Carroll & Graf Publishers

Collins, J. (1957), *Please Don't Eat the Daisies*, New York: Doubleday

Corey, M. F. (1999), *The World Through a Monocle: The New Yorker at Midcentury*, Cambridge, MA: Harvard University Press

Crowther, G. and Steinberg, P. K. (2017), 'These Ghostly Archives 4: Looking for New England', *These Ghostly Archives: The Unearthing of Sylvia Plath*, Stroud: Fonthill Media

Cullinan, E. (1970), *House of Gold*, Boston: Houghton Mifflin

—. (1971), *The Time of Adam*, Boston: Houghton Mifflin

—. (1977), *Yellow Roses*, New York: Viking Press

—. (1982), *A Change of Scene*, New York: W. W. Norton & Co.

D'hoker, E. (2016), *Irish Women Writers and the Modern Short Story*, New York: Palgrave Macmillan

—. (ed.) (2013), *Mary Lavin*. Kildare: Irish Academic Press

Davis, L. H. (1987), *Onward and Upward: A Biography of Katharine S. White*, New York: Harper & Row

Deane, S. (2021), *Small World: Ireland, 1798–2018*, Cambridge: Cambridge University Press

Dickey, J. (1970), *Deliverance*, Boston: Houghton Mifflin

Dickson, L. (1959), *The Ante-Room*, London: Macmillan

Donaldson, S. (1988), *John Cheever: A Biography*, New York: Random House

Donnelly, M. E. (1997) in A. G. Gonzalez (ed.), 'Mary Lavin', *Modern Irish Writers: A Bio-Critical Sourcebook*, Westport, CT: Greenwood Press

Dunleavy, J. E. (1984), 'Mary Lavin, Elizabeth Bowen and a New Generation: The Irish Short Story at Midcentury' in J. F. Kilroy (ed.), *The Irish Short Story: A Critical History*, Boston: Twayne

Ellison, R. (1952), *The Invisible Man*, New York: Random House

Enright, A. (2010), *The Granta Book of the Irish Short Story*, London: Granta

Evans, R. C. and Harp, R. (eds) (1998), *Frank O'Connor: New Perspectives*, West Cornwall, CT: Locust Hill Press

Fanning, C. (1999), *The Irish Voice in America: 250 Years of Irish-American Fiction.* Lexington: University Press of Kentucky

Farrell, J. T. (1946), *The Fate of Writing in America*, New York: New Directions

Faulkner, W. (1954). *A Fable*, New York: Random House

—. (1962), *The Reivers*, New York: Random House

Fleming, I. (1964), *Chitty Chitty Bang Bang: The Magical Car*, London: Jonathan Cape

Fogarty, A. and O'Brien. E. (eds) (2025), *The Routledge Companion to Twenty-First-Century Irish Writing*, London: Routledge

Foley, M. (ed) (1942), *The Best American Short Stories 1942*, Boston: Houghton Mifflin

—. (1965), *The Best American Short Stories 1965*, Boston: Houghton Mifflin

—. (1974), *The Best American Short Stories 1974*, Boston: Houghton Mifflin

—. and Burnett, D. (eds) (1961), *The Best American Short Stories 1961,* Boston: Houghton Mifflin

—. (1966), *The Best American Short Stories 1966*, Boston: Houghton Mifflin

—. (1969), *The Best American Short Stories 1969*, Boston: Houghton Mifflin

Garvin, T. (2016), *The Lives of Daniel Binchy: Irish Scholar; Diplomat, Public Intellectual*, Kildare: Irish Academic Press

Gill, B. (1975), *Here at The New Yorker*, New York: Random House

Ginsberg, A. (1956), 'Howl', *Howl and Other Poems*, San Francisco: City Lights

—. (1961), *Kaddish and Other Poems 1958–1960*, San Francisco: City Lights

—. (1961), *Empty Mirror: Early Poems*, New York: Totem Press

Gottlieb, R. (2016), *Avid Reader: A Life*, New York: Farrar, Straus and Giroux

Grant, J. (1968), *Ross, The New Yorker and Me*, New York: Reynal & Co.

Hamilton, I. (1988), *In Search of J. D. Salinger*, London: Heinemann

Hansberry, L. (1959), *A Raisin in the Sun,* New York: Random House

Harpur, S. and Maxwell, A. (2011), *Jammet's of Dublin: 1901 to 1967*, Dublin: The Lilliput Press

Hazzard, S. (1963), *Cliffs of Fall and Other Stories*, New York: Alfred A. Knopf

Hofer, E. (2018), *New York*, Göttingen: Steidl

Howard, J. (1994), 'Can a Nice Novelist Finish First?' in J. Plath (ed.), *Conversations with John Updike*, Jackson: University Press of Mississippi

Hughes, L. (1951), 'Harlem', *Montage of a Dream Deferred*, New York: Henry Holt and Company

Hulme, K. (1956), *The Nun's Story*, Boston: Little, Brown and Co.

Ingman, H. (2009), *A History of the Irish Short Story*, Cambridge: Cambridge University Press

—. (2013) *Irish Women's Fiction: From Edgeworth to Enright*, Kildare: Irish Academic Press

Jeffares, N. A. (1972), in J. Vinson (ed.), 'Mary Lavin', *Contemporary Novelists*, New York: St Martin's Press

Jordan, N. (1980), *The Past*, London: Jonathan Cape

Joyce, J. (1914), 'The Encounter', *Dubliners*, London: Grant Richards

—. (1922), *Ulysses*, Paris: Shakespeare & Company

Kahn, E. J. (1979), *About The New Yorker and Me: A Sentimental Journey*, New York: G. P. Putnam's Sons

—. (1988), *At Seventy: More about The New Yorker and Me*. New York: Viking Press

Katz, L. S. and W. A. (eds) (1983), *Writer's Choice: A Library of Rediscoveries*, Reston, Virginia: Reston Publishing Company

Keller, H. (1903), *The Story of My Life*, New York: Doubleday

Kellogg, M. (1968), *Tell Me That You Love Me, Junie Moon*, New York: Farrar, Straus and Giroux

Kelly, A. A. (1980), *Mary Lavin: Quiet Rebel*, Dublin: Wolfhound Press

Kerouac, J. (1957), *On the Road*, New York: Viking Press

Kiely, B. (1960), *The Captain with the Whiskers*, London: Methuen

—. (1968), *Dogs Enjoy the Morning*, London: Gollancz

—. (1999), *A Raid into Dark Corners and Other Stories*, Cork: Cork University Press

Killen, J. (ed.) (2006), *Dear Mr McLaverty: The Literary Correspondence of John McGahern and Michael McLaverty 1959–1980*, Belfast: The Linen Hall Library

Kilroy, J. F. (ed.) (1984), *The Irish Short Story: A Critical History*, Boston: Twayne

Kramer, D. (1951), *Ross and The New Yorker*, New York: Doubleday

Kreyling, M. (1990), *Author and Agent: Eudora Welty and Diarmuid Russell*, New York: Farrar, Straus and Giroux

Kunkel, T. (1997), *Genius in Disguise: Harold Ross of The New Yorker*. New York: Random House

—. (ed.) (2000), *Letters from the Editor: The New Yorker's Harold Ross*, New York: The Modern Library

Lavin, M. (1942), *Tales from Bective Bridge*, Boston: Little, Brown and Co. (1943), London: Michael Joseph (1945), London: Readers Union (1952), Dublin: Poolbeg Press (1978) (revised version), Dublin: Town House (1996), London: Faber & Faber (2012)

—. (1944), *The Long Ago and Other Stories*, London: Michael Joseph

—. (1945), *The House in Clewe Street*, London: Michael Joseph, London: Virago Press (1987)

—. (1946), *The Becker Wives and Other Stories*, London: Michael Joseph (1971), New York: New American Library (2018), Dublin: New Island Books (2018)

—. (1947), *At Sallygap and Other Stories*, Boston: Little, Brown and Co.

—. (1950), *Mary O'Grady*, London: Michael Joseph, Boston: Little, Brown and Co. (1950), London: Virago Press (1986)

—. (1951), *A Single Lady and Other Stories*, London: Michael Joseph
—. (1956), *The Patriot Son and Other Stories*, London: Michael Joseph
—. (1957), *A Likely Story*, New York: Macmillan (1967), Dublin: Dolmen Press (1990), Dublin: Poolbeg Press (1990)
—. (1959), *Selected Stories*, New York: Macmillan
—. (1961), *The Great Wave and Other Stories*, London: Macmillan, New York: Macmillan (1961)
—. (1964), *The Stories of Mary Lavin, Vol. I*, London: Constable
—. (1967), *In the Middle of the Fields and Other Stories*, London: Constable, New York: Macmillan (1969), Dublin: New Island Books (2016)
—. (1969), *Happiness and Other Stories.* London: Constable, Boston: Houghton Mifflin (1970), Dublin: New Island Books (2011)
—. (1971), *Collected Stories*, Boston: Houghton Mifflin
—. (1972), *A Memory and Other Stories*, London: Constable, Boston: Houghton Mifflin (1973)
—. (1972), *The Second-Best Children in the World*, London: Longman, Boston: Houghton Mifflin
— (1974), *The Stories of Mary Lavin, Vol. II*, London: Constable
—. (1977), *The Shrine and Other Stories*, London: Constable
—. (1985), *A Family Likeness and Other Stories*, London: Constable
—. (1985), *The Stories of Mary Lavin, Vol. III*, London: Constable
—. (1995), *In a Café*, Dublin: Town House
Leblanc, M. (1934), *L'image de la femme nue*, Paris: Flammarion
Lee, H. (2009), *Biography: A Very Short Introduction*, Oxford: Oxford University Press
—. (2005), *Body Parts: Essays on Life-writing*, London: Chatto & Windus
Lee, J.Y. (2000), *Defining New Yorker Humor*, Jackson, Mississippi: University Press of Mississippi
Levenson, L. (1998), *The Four Seasons of Mary Lavin*, Dublin: Marino Books
Levy, A. (1993), *The Culture and Commerce of the American Short Story*, Cambridge: Cambridge University Press
Luthin, H.W. (ed.) (1960), *The Abbott Christmas Book*, New York: Doubleday
Logan, A. (1965), *The Man who Robbed the Robber Barons*, New York: W.W. Norton & Co.
—. (1970), *Against the Evidence: The Becker-Rosenthal Affair*, New York: McCall Pub. Co.
Luther King, M. (1958), *Stride Toward Freedom*, New York: Harper & Brothers
Lynch, B. (2007), *Parsons Bookstore: At the Heart of Bohemian Dublin, 1949–1989*, Dublin: The Liffey Press
—. (2011), *Prodigals and Geniuses, The Writers and Artists of Dublin's Baggotonia*, Dublin: The Liffey Press

MacDonald, J. D. (1957), *The Executioners*, New York: Simon & Schuster
—. (1960), *Slam the Big Door*, Greenwich, CT: Fawcett/Gold Medal
MacInerney, J. (1984), *Bright Lights, Big City*, New York: Vintage
MacKenzie, R. (1974), *The Wine of Astonishment*, New York: Viking Press
McCarthy, M. (1963), *The Group*, New York: Harcourt, Brace
McGahern, J. (1963), *The Barracks*, London: Faber & Faber
—. (1965), *The Dark*, London: Faber & Faber
—. (1970), *Nightlines*, London: Faber & Faber
McLaverty, M. 1945, *In This Day*, New York: Macmillan
—. (1947), *The Game Cock and Other Stories*, New York: Devin-Adair Co.
—. (1951), *Truth in the Night*, New York: Macmillan
—. (1965), *The Brightening Day*, New York: Macmillan
—. (1989) (ed.), Hillan King, S. *In Quiet Places: The Uncollected Stories, Letters and Critical Prose of Michael McLaverty*, Dublin: Poolbeg Press
Maclean, A. D. (1963), *Winter's Tales 9*, London: Macmillan
Mahon, G. (1989), *The Last Days of The New Yorker*, New York: Plume
Malcolm, D. (2012), *The British and Irish Short Story Handbook*, Chichester: Wiley-Blackwell
Marrs, S. (2005*), Eudora Welty: A Biography*, Harcourt, Brace
—. (2011), *What There Is to Say We Have Said: The Correspondence of Eudora Welty and William Maxwell*, Boston: Houghton Mifflin
Martin, A. (ed.) (1970), *Winter's Tales from Ireland I*, Dublin: Gill & Macmillan
Maxwell, W. (1961), *The Château*, New York: Alfred A. Knopf
Mehta, V. (1998), *Remembering Mr. Shawn's New Yorker: The Invisible Art of Editing*, New York: Overlook Press
Merrill, J. (1976), *Divine Comedies*, New York: Atheneum
Molidor, J. (2008), 'Violence, Silence, and Sacrifice: The Mother–daughter Relationship in the Short Fiction of Irish Women Writers, 1890–1980' (PhD, University of Notre Dame)
Moore, M. (1951), *Collected Poems*, New York: Macmillan
—. (1967), *The Complete Poems of Marianne Moore*, New York: Macmillan
Murdoch, I. (1978), *The Sea, The Sea*, London: Chatto & Windus
Nabokov, V. (1955), *Lolita*, Paris: Olympia Press
—. (1962), *Pale Fire*, New York: G. P. Putnam's Sons
O'Brien, E. (1962), *The Lonely Girl*, London: Jonathan Cape
—. (1964), *Girl with Green Eyes*, London: Penguin
—. (1970), *A Pagan Place*, London: Weidenfeld & Nicolson
O'Brien, G. (ed.) (1962), *A Harbour Green: Celebrating Benedict Kiely*, Kildare: Irish Academic Press
O'Connor, F. (1951), 'The First Confession', *Traveller's Samples*, London: Macmillan, New York: Alfred A. Knopf

—. (1954), *More Stories*, New York: Alfred A. Knopf
—. (1961), *An Only Child*, New York: Alfred A. Knopf
—. (1962), *The Lonely Voice: A Study of the Short Story*, Cleveland: World Publishing Co.
—. (1969), *A Set of Variations*, New York: Alfred A. Knopf
O'Hara, J. (1935), *Butterfield 8*, New York: Harcourt, Brace
—. (1940), *Pal Joey*, New York: Duell, Sloan and Pearce
Olubas, B. (2022), *Shirley Hazzard: A Writing Life*, London: Little, Brown and Co.
Owens Weekes, A. (1990), 'Mary Lavin: Textual Gardens', *Irish Women Writers: An Uncharted Tradition*. Lexington, KY: University Press of Kentucky
Parker, H. (1984), *Flawed Texts and Verbal Icons: Literary Authority in American Fiction*, Evanston: Northwestern University Press
Peterson, T. (1956), *Magazines in the Twentieth Century*, Urbana: The University of Illinois Press
Plath, S. (1963), *The Bell Jar*, London: Heinemann (published under the pseudonym Victoria Lucas)
Porter, K. A. (1962), *Ship of Fools*, Boston: Little, Brown and Co.
Power, R. (1966), *The Land of Youth*, London: Secker & Warburg
Pritchett, V. S., (1965), *New York Proclaimed*, New York: Harcourt, Brace
—. (1967), *Dublin: A Portrait*, New York: Harper & Row
Pudsey, J. (1959), *Pick of Today's Short Stories 10*, London: G. P. Putnam's Sons
Quinn, J. (ed.) (1986), *A Portrait of the Artist as a Young Girl*, London: Methuen
Remnick, D. (2000), *Life Stories: Profiles from The New Yorker*. New York: Random House
—. (2016), Introduction in H. Finder (ed.), *The 50s: The Story of a Decade by The New Yorker*, New York: Modern Library
Roethke, T. (1953), *The Waking*, New York: Doubleday
Ross, L. (1998), *Here But Not Here: My Life with William Shawn and The New Yorker*, New York: Random House
Ross, P. (1929), *Black Bread*, Oxford: Basil Blackwell, Boston: Houghton Mifflin
—. (1930), *The Glass Rose*, Oxford: Basil Blackwell
—. (1935), *Wanton Venus*, New York: The Macaulay Company
—. (1959), *Goodbye, Columbus*, Boston: Houghton Mifflin
Rubens, B. (1969), *The Elected Member*, London: Eyre & Spottiswoode
Ryan, B. (2001), *With a Tap on the Knee: Memoirs of a Reluctant Banker*, Dun Laoghaire: MIS Books
Salinger, J. D. (1951), *The Catcher in the Rye*, Boston: Little, Brown and Co.
—. (1953), *Nine Stories*, Boston: Little, Brown and Co.
—. (1961), *Franny and Zooey*, Boston: Little, Brown and Co.
—. (1963), *Raise High the Roof Beam, Carpenters and Seymour: An Introduction*, Boston: Little, Brown and Co.
Salinger, M. A. (2000), *Dream Catcher. A Memoir*, New York: Washington Square Press

Sexton, A. (1966), 'Sylvia's Death', 'The Bar Fly Ought to Sing', *TriQuarterly Magazine*, Evanston: Northwestern University

—. (1966), *Live or Die*, Boston: Houghton Mifflin

—. (1971), *Transformations*, Boston: Houghton Mifflin

Sharp, M. (1959), *The Rescuers*, Boston: Little, Brown and Co.

Shaw, I. (1960), *Two Weeks in Another Town*, New York: Random House

Shivel, G. (2000), *New Yorker Profiles 1925–1992: A Bibliography*, Lanham, MD: University Press of America

Short Stories from The New Yorker 1925–1940, New York: Simon & Schuster

Shovlin, F. (ed.) (2023), *The Letters of John McGahern*, London: Faber & Faber

Singer, I. B. (1982), *Collected Stories*, New York: Farrar, Straus & Giroux

Snodgrass, W. D. (1959), *Heart's Needle*, New York: Alfred A. Knopf

Spark, M. (1959), *Memento Mori*, London: Macmillan

—. (1961), *The Prime of Miss Jean Brodie*, London: Macmillan

—. (1992), *Curriculum Vitae: Autobiography*, London: Constable

Stafford, J. (1970), *The Collected Stories of Jean Stafford*, New York: Farrar, Straus and Giroux

Stannard, M. (2010), *Muriel Spark: The Biography*. New York: W. W. Norton & Co.

Steig, W. (1990), *Shrek!*, New York: Farrar, Straus and Giroux

Steinman, M. (1996), *The Happiness of Getting It Down Right: Letters of Frank O'Connor and William Maxwell, 1945–1966*, New York: Alfred A. Knopf

—. (2001) (ed.), *The Element of Lavishness: Letters of Sylvia Townsend Warner and William Maxwell, 1938–1978*, Washington DC: Counterpoint

Stories from The New Yorker 1950–1960, New York: Simon & Schuster

Stories from The New Yorker: A thirty-fifth anniversary volume of stories that have appeared in the magazine during the past decade 1950–1960 (1960), New York: Simon & Schuster

55 Stories from The New Yorker 1940–1949 (1949), New York: Simon & Schuster

Sullivan, W. (2006), *Gold Can Stay: A Memoir*, Columbia: University of Missouri Press

Taylor, P. (1986), *A Summons to Memphis*, New York, Alfred A. Knopf

Thomas, D. (1954), *Under Milk Wood*, London: Dent

Thurber, J. (1958), *The Years with Ross*, Boston: Little, Brown and Co.

Townsend Warner, S. (1962), *A Spirt Rises*, New York: Viking

Travers, P. L. (1934), *Mary Poppins*, London: Gerald Howe

Val Baker, D. (ed.) (1947), *Modern British Writing*, New York: The Vanguard Press

Walsh, C. (2008), 'Mary Lavin – A Personal Perspective', Trevor/Bowen Summer School 2008, Mitchelstown Literary Society

Walshe, E. (2020), *The Last Day at Bowen's Court: A Novel*, Cork: Somerville Press

Weeks, E. (1981), *Writers and Friends*, Boston: Little, Brown and Co.

Welty, E. (1964), *The Shoe Bird*, New York: Harcourt, Brace

—. (1970), *Losing Battles*, London: Random House
—. (1972), *The Optimist's Daughter*, London: Random House
White, E. B. (1945), *Stuart Little*, New York: Harper & Brothers
—. (1952), *Charlotte's Web*, New York: Harper & Brothers
White, T. H. (1961), *The Making of a President*, New York: Atheneum
Williams, T. (1955), *Cat on a Hot Tin Roof*, New York: New Directions
Wilson, E. (1941), *The Wound and the Bow*, Boston: Houghton Mifflin
Wolfe, T. (2000), *Hooking Up*. New York: Farrar, Straus and Giroux
Yagoda, Ben (2001), *About Town: The New Yorker and the World It Made*, Boston: Da Capo Press
Yeats, W. B. (1908), *The Collected Works in Verse and Prose of William Butler Yeats, II*, London: Chapman & Hall
—. (1933), *The Winding Stair and Other Poems*, London: Macmillan

Newspaper Articles

Arnold, B. (1996), 'Queen of Palace of Delight', *Irish Independent*, 26 March
Battersby, E. (1996), 'Short Story Writer Mary Lavin dies at 83', *The Irish Times*, 26 March
Binchy, M. (1996), 'A Special Lesson', *The Irish Times*, 30 March
Brentin, M. (2011), 'Manhattan Revised: Jackie Kennedy's Manhattan in 1967', *Saturday Evening Post*, 23 September
Broyard, A. (1977), 'Gallic Chic and Irish Pique', *The New York Times*, 30 October
—. (1971), 'The Odds Are 100% or Zero, Books of the Times', *The New York Times*, 7 May
Burgess, A. (1977), 'What Literature is About', *The Irish Press,* 2 June
Carmody, D. (1992), 'Tina Brown to Take Over at The New Yorker', *The New York Times*, 1 July
Carr, D. and Kirkpatrick, D. D. (2002), 'The Gatekeeper for Literature Is Changing At New Yorker', *The New York Times*, 21 October
The Catholic Times (1960), 'Catholic Book Week Reading Lists 1960', 19 February
De Vere White, T. (1964), 'The Better Half', *The Irish Times*, 8 August
—. (1966), 'Frank O'Connor Dies in Dublin, An Appreciation', *The Irish Times*, 11 March
—. (1967), 'The Art of Mary Lavin', *The Irish Times*, 28 January
Dever, J. (1966), 'Burying Frank O'Connor: Some Dublin Talk over a Jar', *The National Catholic Reporter*, 30 March
Donnelly, B. (1974), 'Michael McLaverty: An Appraisal', *The Irish Press*, 2 March
Drogheda Independent (1962), 'Focus on Mid-Meath Topics, Won French Story Prize', 3 November
The Evening Herald (1970), 'For "Irish Week" in Cologne', 20 May

Farren, R. (1967), 'New Stories by Mary Lavin', *Irish Independent*, 11 February

Fox, G. (1968), 'My Royal Meath Album', *The Meath Chronicle,* 8 April

Gilroy, H. (1966), 'Bellow Assails Literary "Elite"; "Intellectuals" Pose Threat to Literature, P.E.N. Told', *The New York Times*, 14 June

Gough, M.V. (1962), 'Save Those Books by Irish Authors', *Sunday Independent*, 30 December

Gould, J. (1964), 'Four Residents Discuss Life in Irish Capital in C.B.S, "One of a Kind"', *The New York Times*, 24 February

Harmon, M. (1991), 'An Appreciation', *The Irish Times*, 15 January

—. (1996), 'Courageous Chronicler of the Vagaries of the Human Heart', *The Irish Times*, 26 March

The Heights, Boston College Student Newspaper (1963), vol. 40, no. 20, 5 April

Hennigan, T. (1964), 'Going Places', *The Evening Herald*, 13 November

Houlihan, B. (2023), 'John McGahern's The Barracks at 60: Clues to a Classic', *The Irish Times*, 2 March

Hughes, P. T. (1964), 'From the Village Homes of Ireland', *Sunday Independent*, 4 October

Irish Examiner (1964), 'S.S. America Lands 208 Passengers at Cobh', 24 May

—. (1964), 'London Letter', 28 December

Irish Independent (1963), 'Fierce Storm Damage', 12 June

—. (1982), 'On the Instructions of Miss Mary Lavin', 12 May

—. *The Irish Press* (1962) 'New Story', 11 December

—. (1964), 'Literature Deplored', 13 November

—. (1966), Frank O'Connor Dies Suddenly', 11 March

—. (1966), 'P.E.N. Protests at New Tax on Books', 20 July

—. (1966), 'Protest at Tax on Periodicals', 28 September

—. (1967), 'For Benefit of Writers', 29 May

—. (1969), 'Irish Writer Married to Ex-Jesuit', 19 March

—. (1969), 'Want Constant Watch on RTE: 20 Sign a Letter', 6 June

—. (1970), 'Our Culture the Theme in Cologne', 29 May

The Irish Times (1968), '£1,700 Award to Woman Writer', 1 August

J. B. R. (1964), 'The Quiet Voice That Says So Much So Well', *Belfast News Letter*, 10 October

Jordan, T. (2022), 'What Were People Reading in the Summer of 1972', *The New York Times*, 14 July

Kelleher, M. (2022), 'Mary Lavin Papers Cast Fresh Light on the Writing Life', *The Irish Times*, 11 January

Kennedy, M. (1976), 'The Saturday Interview: Maev Kennedy Talked to Mary Lavin', *The Irish Times*, 13 March

—. (1980), 'Past Tense', *The Irish Times*, 8 November

Kiely, B. (1969), 'A Set of Variations', *The New York Times*, 4 May

—. (1972), 'The Greatness of Mary Lavin', *The Irish Times*, 21 October
—. (1977), 'Mary Lavin's New Collection', *The Irish Times*, 28 May
Lavin, M. (1969), 'The Book Page', 'Evaluations', *The Irish Press*, 1 February
—. (1969) 'The Sisters', 'New Irish Writing', *The Irish Press*, 8 November
—. (1985). 'The First Snow', *The Irish Times*, 23 August
The Leader (1952), 'Profile: Mr. Patrick Kavanagh', 11 October
Mac Aonghusa, C. (1964), 'Bean a Bhuil Saothar Álainn Déanta Aici' ('A Woman Who Has Done a Beautiful Job'), *The Irish Press*, 25 August 1964
MacKenzie, R. (1976), 'Concerning Pain and Beauty', *The New York Times*, 25 January
MacMahon, K. (2020). 'Irish Women Writing Fiction Were Dismissed as "Quiet". Ireland Wasn't Listening', *The Guardian*, 30 July
—. (2021), 'Commemorative Essay on Mary Lavin', *The Irish Times*, 27 March
MacMahon, V. (1996), 'Cemetery Sunday in Navan', *The Meath Chronicle*, 20 July
McCullough, D. (1984), 'Historian, Novelist and Much, Much More', *The New York Times*, 8 April
McDowell, E. (1987), '154 at *The New Yorker* Protest Choice of Editor', *The New York Times*, 15 January
McGrath, C. (2003) 'Redeeming John O'Hara', *The New York Times*, 24 August
—. (2009), 'The First Suburbanite', *The New York Times*, 27 February
—. (2010), 'Muriel Spark: Playing God', *The New York Times*, 25 April
—. (2010), 'J. D. Salinger, Literary Recluse, Dies at 91', *The New York Times*, 28 January
McGrory, M. (1961), 'Stories of Erin, A Deep Look into the Irish Heart', *The Evening Star*, 6 August
—. (1961), 'The Literary Scene in 1961', *The Sunday Star,* 10 December
McLaverty, M. (1955), 'A Note on Katherine Mansfield', *The Belfast Telegraph*, 15 January
Marlowe, L. (2012), 'An Arrow Still in Flight', *The Irish Times*, 30 April
Martin, A. (1967), 'Love's Painful Mystery', *The Irish Press*, 28 January
—. (1967), 'The Great O'Faolain', 'Books on Saturday', *Irish Press*, 2 September
The Meath Chronicle (1962), 'Local Snapshots', 5 May
—. (1975), 'Writer Mary Lavin Chosen "Meath Personality of the Year"', 22 March
Mercier, V. (1971), 'A Queer Place Surely', *The Nation*, 8 November
The New York Times (1950), 'Best Sellers List', 19 February
—. (1959), 'Books of the Times', 15 June
—. (1960), 'City is Preparing for Gales Today: L. I. Cleared', 12 September
—.(1962), 'Stewardess is Swept Through Plane Door', 20 October
—.(1966), 'Miller Lauds P.E.N. as Congress Closes', 19 June
—.(1968), 'John Beary, Theater Director, Marries Susan Cora Stevens', 11 November

—.(1971), 'Et Al', 'Risk', 16 May
—.(1976), '60 Was the Last Bad One', 10 August
—.(1977), 'Phyllis Jackson, 69, Agent for Many Major Writers at Two Talent Companies', 22 March
—. (1987), 'Elizabeth Kray, Patron and Friend of Poets and their Art, Dies at 71', 24 November
The Northern Standard (1967), 'Death of Patrick Kavanagh, Famed Monaghan Poet', 8 December
Oates, J. C. (1973), 'Written as if by People from Different Planets', *The New York Times*, 25 November
O'Neill-Barna, A. (1970), 'The Subject is the Struggle of Happiness', *The New York Times*, 24 May
O'Regan, M. (2014), 'English aristocrat Valerie Goulding was Founder and Driving Force Behind Clinic', *The Irish Times*, 20 January
The Ohio Times-Gazette (1968), 'Writer Mary Lavin to Speak at AC', 5 January
Pace, E. (1992), 'William Shawn, 85, Is Dead; New Yorker's Gentle Despot', *The New York Times*, 9 December
—. (1993), 'Jeremiah Kaplan, Veteran Executive in Publishing 67,' *The New York Times*, 11 August
Perlmutter, E. (1968), 'Shots Are Fired in Refuse Strike', *The New York Times*, 5 February
Prescott, O. (1959), 'Books of the Times', *The New York Times*, 15 June
—. (1961), 'Books of the Times', *The New York Times*, 2 August
Siegel, B. (1987), 'Breach of Tradition: *New Yorker* Shake-up Is the Talk of the Town', *The Los Angeles Times*, 12 February
Snoddy, O. (1970), 'Book Review', 'The Phoenix', *Nationalist and Leinster Times*, 11 September
Spark, M. (1961), *The Observer*, 17 December
Stern, J. (1951), 'Aw, the World's a Crumby Place', *The New York Times*, 15 July
—. (1978), 'Home Thoughts', *The Irish Press*, 5 October
Sunday Independent (1962), 'O-oops … and a President Almost Lost a Mortar Board', 'Picture Special', 17 June
—. (1964), 'Honour for Frank O'Connor', 16 August
—. (1965), 'Concrete to Cover Literary Part of Dublin', 17 October
Tóibín, C. (1992), 'In Honour of Mary', *Sunday Independent*, 14 June
—. (2014), 'The Literature of Grief', *The Guardian*, 2 October
Trevor, W. (1969), 'The Lonely Voices', 'The Book Page', *The Irish Press*, 8 November
—. (1996), Mary Lavin Obituary, *The Guardian*, 26 March
Walsh Peavoy, E. (1995), 'Voyage Round My Mother', *Sunday Independent*, 28 May

Winfrey, C. (1980), 'Rachel MacKenzie Is Dead at 70; A Fiction Editor for New Yorker', *The New York Times*, 30 March

Woodworth, P. (1992), 'Lavin and Le Brocquy Honoured', *The Irish Times*, 24 February

Wright, F. (1959), 'Mary Lavin Sails Abroad with Three Daughters and a Baby Car', *Sunday Independent*, 13 September

—. (1962), 'Frank O'Connor Gets a Plea for Books', *Sunday Independent*, 2 December

Magazine Publications & Journals

Aaron, J. (1971), 'Consequences of a Dime', *The New Yorker*, 11 December

Allen, W. (1973), 'The Early Essays', *The New Yorker*, 20 January

The Almanac (1965), University of Pennsylvania, vol. 11, no. 5, 12 January

Angell, R. (1944), 'Three Ladies in the Morning', *The New Yorker*, 18 March

—. (1976), 'Obituary of Frank Sullivan', 8 March

—. (2020), 'The Children's Hour', *The New Yorker*, 30 September

Asprey, R. (1957), 'Rough Shoot', *The New Yorker*, 16 November

Auden, W. H. (1970), 'The Aliens', *The New Yorker*, 21 November

Ayer, E. (1966), *The New Yorker*, 'The Promise of Heat', 3 September

—. (1967), 'The Treasure Dream', *The New Yorker*, 11 March

Balliet, W. (1998), 'Postscript', 'Edith Oliver: One on the Aisle', *The New Yorker*, 9 March

Barthelme, D. (1971), 'Perpetua', *The New Yorker*, 12 June

Behrman, S. N. (1951), 'The Vision of the Innocent, J. D. Salinger's "The Catcher in the Rye", *The New Yorker*, 11 August

Bell, M. S. (1986), 'Less is Less: The Dwindling American Short Story', *Harper's Magazine*, April

Bellow, S. (1952), 'Interval in a Lifeboat', *The New Yorker*, 27 December

Benson, S. (1941), '5135 Kensington', *The New* Yorker, 14 June

Blum, R. (1961), 'The Day of the Lion', *The New Yorker*, 14 January

Boland, E. (1987), 'The Black Lace Fan My Mother Gave Me', *The New Yorker*, 19 October

Botsford, G. (1997), 'The Victorian Game', 'The Talk of the Town', *The New Yorker*, 10 February

Bowen, E. (1941), 'Everything's Frightfully Interesting', *The New Yorker*, 11 October

Bowen, Z. (2001), 'The New York James Joyce Society', *Joyce Studies Annual*, vol. 12 (Summer)

Boyle, K. (1925), 'Summer', in E. Walsh (ed.), *This Quarter*, vol. 1, no. 1, Paris: Herbert Clarke

Brennan, M. (1952), 'The Joker', *The New Yorker,* 27 December
—. (1970), 'Through a Lace Curtain, Darkly', 'Books', *The New Yorker,* 14 February
—. (1973), 'Notes and Comments', 'The Talk of the Town', *The New Yorker,* 20 January
Brock, V. K. (1973), 'Rouault', *The New Yorker,* 20 January
Capote, T. (1965) 'In Cold Blood—I: The Last to See Them Alive', 'Annals of Crime', *The New Yorker,* 25 September; 'In Cold Blood—II: Persons Unknown', 'Annals of Crime', *The New Yorker,* 2 October; 'In Cold Blood—III: Answers', 'Annals of Crime', *The New Yorker,* 9 October; 'In Cold Blood—IV: The Corner', 'Annals of Crime', *The New Yorker,* 16 October
Caswell, R. (1965), 'The Human Hears Vagaries', *Kilkenny Magazine,* nos. 12–13 (Spring)
—. (1968), 'Irish Political Reality and Mary Lavin's Tales from Bective Bridge', *Éire Ireland* 3 (Spring)
—. (1967), 'Mary Lavin: Breaking a Pathway', *Dublin Magazine* 6 (Summer)
Cavanaugh, A. F. (1996), 'Remembering Mary', 'A Bouquet for Mary', *Irish Literary Supplement* vol. 15, no. 2 (Fall)
Cheever, J. (1960), 'Some People, Places, and Things That Will Not Appear in My Novel', *The New Yorker,* 12 November
Cloke, H. (1965), 'Freya Observed', *The New* Yorker, 11 September
Cohen, R. D. (1964), 'Song for My First Child, Noah', *The New Yorker,* 27 June
Colum, P. (1961), 'A Turn to Enchantment', *The Saturday Review* 44, 12 August
Connolly, M. (1983), *Irish Literary Supplement,* vol. 2, no. 1, 1 March
Crow, C. P. (2000), 'Postscript: Remembering Andy Logan', 'The Talk of the Town', *The New Yorker,* 4 December
The Crumb (1954), Bread Loaf Writers' Conference, vol. 29, no. 1
Cullinan, E. (1960), 'The Ablutions', *The New Yorker,* 6 February
—. (1960), 'The Voices of the Dead', *The New Yorker,* 16 April
—. (1960), 'Le Petit Déjeuner', *The New Yorker,* 13 August
—. (1965), 'A Swim', *The New Yorker,* 5 June
—. (1965), 'The Old Priest', *The New Yorker,* 18 December
—. (1967), 'A Sunday like the Others', *The New Yorker,* 26 August
—. (1970), 'Norah's Friends', *The New Yorker,* 29 August
—. (1976), 'Life After Death', *The New Yorker,* 26 January
—. (1976), 'Estelle', *The New Yorker,* 19 April
—. (1977), 'A Good Loser', *The New Yorker,* 15 August
—. (1981), 'Echoes', *The New Yorker,* 15 June
—. (1996), 'Remembering Mary', 'A Bouquet for Mary', *Irish Literary Supplement,* vol. 15, no. 2 (Fall)
Dana, R. (1970), 'The Woman on the Mall', *The New Yorker,* 21 November

Davie, D. (1961), 'The Life of Service', *The New Yorker*, 3 June

DeVries, P. (1962), 'Nobody's Fool', *The New Yorker*, 16 June

D'hoker, E. (ed.) (2008), 'Beyond the Stereotypes: Mary Lavin's Irish Women', *Irish Studies Review*, 16 November

Dickey, J. (1967), 'Falling', *The New Yorker*, 11 February

Dublin Magazine 19 (1944), Jan–March

Dunleavy, J. E. (1979), 'The Making of Mary Lavin's "Happiness"', *Irish University Review* 9, no. 2 (Autumn)

Dufault, P. K. (1960), 'Possibilities', *The New Yorker*, 12 November

Fadiman, C. (1942), 'Books', *The New Yorker*, 30 May

Franklin, N. (1996), 'Lady with a Pencil, *The New Yorker*, 26 February

Fremantle, A. (1959), 'A Certain Craft', *Commonweal*, 70, 18 September

Friel, B. (1959), 'The Skelper', *The New Yorker*, 1 August

Ginsberg, A. (1968), 'Wales Visitation', *The New Yorker*, 11 May

Gordon, M. (2013), 'Mary Lavin and Writing Women', *American Journal of Irish Studies* 10

Gottlieb, R. (2003), 'The Years with Thurber: The Man and his Letters', *The New Yorker*, 8 September

Grant, A. (1976), 'John Cheever, The Art of Fiction, No. 62', *The Paris Review* (Fall)

Guadagnino, K. (2017), 'So Long, Farewell', *The Paris Review*, 20 January

Harmon, M. (1997), 'Conversations with Mary Lavin.' *Irish University Review* 27.2 (Autumn–Winter)

—. (ed.) (1979), 'Mary Lavin Special Issue.' *Irish University Review* 9.2, Autumn

Harrison, L. (2008), '"The Magazine that is Considered the Best in the World": Muriel Spark and *The New Yorker*', *Modern Fiction Studies* 54.3 (Fall)

Hartnett, M., Liddy, J. and O'Connor, L. (eds) (1963), *Arena* no. 1 (Spring)

Hazzard, S. (1961), 'Woollahra Road', *The New Yorker*, 8 April

—. (1965), 'The Evening of the Holiday', *The New Yorker*, 17 April

Hemingway, E. (1927), 'My Own Life', *The New Yorker*, 12 February

—. (1999), 'Miss Mary's Sorrow', *The New Yorker*, 24 May

Hersey, J. (1946), 'Hiroshima', *The New Yorker*, 31 August

Irish Mountaineering Club Newsletter (1969), Dublin Section, no. 2, May

Iyer, P. (2014), '"I Told You When I Came I Was a Stranger": Leonard Cohen's first public musical performance', *Harper's Magazine*, 14 February

Jones, E. P. (2006), 'Bad Neighbors', *The New Yorker*, 7 August

Kiely, B. (1958), 'The White Wild Bronco', *The New Yorker*, 20 December

—. (1960), 'The Wild Boy', *The New Yorker*, 30 January

—. (1970), 'Green Island, Red South', *Kilkenny Magazine*, no. 18

Kosac, H. (1979), 'Mary Lavin: A Bibliography', *Irish University Review* 9 (Autumn)

Kuzma, G. (1971), 'The Fish', *The New Yorker*, 11 December

Lahr, J. (1993), 'Light Fantastic', *The New Yorker,* 31 May

Lavin, M. 'Gabriel Galloway', *Atlantic Monthly,* November 1944, January 1945, February 1945, March 1945, April 1945, May 1945

—. (1962), 'The Fields Will Never Leave You', *Country Beautiful* 2, no. 1, September

—. (1978), 'The First Snow', *CARA* magazine

Lavin, M. and Murphy, C. (1979), 'An Interview.' *Irish University Review* 9.2 (Autumn)

Lavin, T. (1944), 'The Race at Aintree', *The Atlantic,* December

Licht, F. (1962), 'Visit the Sick', *The New Yorker,* 28 April

Londe, G. (2013), 'Mary Lavin's Memory of 1972', *American Journal of Irish Studies* 10, New York: Glucksman Ireland House, New York University

MacDonald, J. D. (1960), 'The Tug of Evil', *Cosmopolitan* 149, January

—. (1962), 'Where the Body Lies', *Cosmopolitan,* August, vol. 153, no. 2

MacKenzie, R. (1938), 'Pattern', *Good Housekeeping,* April

—. (1947), 'The Thread', *Harper's Magazine,* 1 September

—. (1948), 'The Funeral of Sandra Cunningham', *The New Yorker,* 6 March

—. (1970), 'Risk', *The New Yorker,* 21 November

McGahern, J. (1963), 'Summer at Strandhill', *The New Yorker,* 21 September

McGrath, C. (1974), 'The Worst', *The New Yorker,* 14 October

—. (2022), 'The Summer Friend', *The New Yorker,* 27 May

McNulty, J. (1949), 'Back Where I had Never Been', 'Reporter at Large', *The New Yorker,* 2 September

McPhee, J. (2012), 'Editor & Publisher: The Name of the Subject Shall Not Be the Title', *The New Yorker,* 25 June

Martin, A. (1963), 'A Skeleton Key to the Stories of Mary Lavin', *Irish Quarterly Review,* vol. 52, no. 208 (Winter)

Maxwell, W. (1965), 'Further Tales about Men and Women', *The New Yorker,* 7 August

Menand, L. (2001), 'Holden at Fifty: *The Catcher in the Rye* and what it spawned', *The New Yorker,* 1 October

Merrill, J. (1960), 'The World and the Child', *The New Yorker,* 13 February

Middlebury College, *Bread Loaf Writers' Conference Catalogue 1954*

Moore, M. (1960), 'St Valentine', *The New Yorker,* 13 February

Morgan, D. (1980), 'Rachel MacKenzie' (obituary), *The New Yorker,* 14 April

Nash, O. (1959), 'Sticks And Stones May Break My Bones, But Names Will Break My Heart', *The New* Yorker, 13 June

—. (1959), 'Brief Lives In Not So Brief-1', *The New Yorker,* 31 October

The New Yorker (1950), 'Books: Briefly Noted', 28 January

—. (1958), 'Wolcott Gibbs' (obituary,), 30 August

O'Brien, E. (1967), 'The Love Object', *The New Yorker,* 13 May

—. (1981), 'Sister Imelda', *The New Yorker,* 9 November

O'Connor, F. (1949), 'Ireland', *Holiday*, December
—. (1960), 'The Girl at the Gaol Gate', *Review of English Literature*, vol. 1, no. 2, April
—. (1966), 'The Corkerys', *The New Yorker,* 30 April
—. (1966), 'The School for Wives', *The New Yorker,* 5 November
—. (1967), 'An Act of Charity', *The New Yorker,* 6 May
—. (1967), 'Bring in the Whiskey Now, Mary', *The New Yorker,* 12 August
O'Hara, J. (1964), 'All Tied Up', *The New Yorker,* 3 October
O'Neill, E. (2011), *The New Yorker,* 'Exorcism', 17 October
Panter-Downes, M. (1941), 'Letter from Dublin', *The New Yorker,* 11 October
—. (1946), 'Letter from Dublin', *The New Yorker,* 24 August
—. (1970), 'Letter from Dublin', *The New Yorker,* 25 July
Perelman, S. J. (1962), 'If It Please Your Honour', *The New Yorker,* April 28
Perlberg, M. M. (1962), 'Hiroshige', *The New Yorker,* 28 April
Phelan, F. J. (1958), 'Story of My Life', *The New Yorker,* 2 August
Plath, S. (1960), 'The Net Menders; Benidorm, Spain', *The New Yorker,* 20 August
—. (1970), 'Gigolo', *The New Yorker,* 21 November
Pritchett, V. S. (1947), 'The Collection', *Harper's Magazine*, September
Roth, P. (1958), 'The Kind of Person I Am', *The New Yorker,* 29 November
—. (1959), 'Defender of the Faith', *The New Yorker,* 14 March
Russell, G. (Æ) (1930), 'Enchantment', *The New Yorker,* 5 April
Salinger, J. D. (1946), 'Slight Rebellion Off Madison', *The New Yorker,* 21 December
—. (1955), 'Franny', *The New Yorker,* 29 January
—. (1955), 'Raise High the Roof Beam, Carpenters', *The New Yorker,* 19 November
—. (1957), 'Zooey', *The New Yorker,* 4 May
—. (1959), 'Seymour: An Introduction', *The New Yorker,* 6 June
—. (1965), 'Hapworth 16, 1924', *The New Yorker,* 19 June
Schiff, S. (1993), 'Muriel Spark Between the Lines', *The New Yorker,* 24 May
Schwartz, D. (1959), 'A Little Morning Music', *The New Yorker,* 18 April
Seabrook, J. (1982), 'William Maxwell, The Art of Fiction, 71', Interview with William Maxwell, *Paris Review*, no. 85 (Fall)
Sexton, A. (1959), 'Sunbathers', *The New Yorker,* 13 June
Sharp, M. 'The Creative Urge', *Cosmopolitan*, vol. 153, no. 2, August
Shawn, W. (1936), 'The Catastrophe.' *The New Yorker,* 14 November
Shorer, M. (1945) 'A Masque of Reason', *The Atlantic Monthly*, March
Skow, J. (1961), 'Sonny: An Introduction', *Time*, 15 September
Snodgrass, W. D. (1959), 'Lying Awake', *The New Yorker,* 13 June
Spark, M. (1960), 'The Ormolu Clock', *The New Yorker,* 17 September 1960
—. (1961), 'The Prime of Miss Jean Brodie', *The New Yorker,* 14 October
—. (1963), 'The Gentile Jewesses', *The New Yorker,* 22 June

Stafford, J. (1948), 'Children are Bored on Sunday', *The New Yorker*, 21 February
Stevens, R. L. and S. (1997), 'An Interview with Mary Lavin', *Irish Quarterly Review* (Spring)
Stevenson, J. (1967), 'Ned O'Gorman', 'Talk of the Town', *The New Yorker*, 2 December
Stuart, F. (1961), 'Mary Lavin's Short Stories', *The Irish Times*, 3 June
Sundgaard, A. (1959), 'Ken', *The New Yorker*, 19 September
Thurber, J. (1939), 'The Secret Life of Walter Mitty', *The New Yorker*, 18 March
—. (1942), 'The Catbird Seat', *The New Yorker*, 14 November
Tóibín, C. (1995), 'Dublin's Epiphany', *The New Yorker*, 3 April
—. (2013), 'Mary Lavin: Context and Character', *American Journal of Irish Studies*, vol. 10
Townsend Warner, S. (1963), 'Their Quiet Lives', *The New* Yorker, 11 May
—. (1961), 'A Spirt Rises', *The New Yorker*, 8 July
Trillin, C. (1993), 'Culture Shopping', *The New Yorker*, 15 February
Updike, J. (1955), 'Youth's Progress', *The New Yorker*, 26 February
—. (1956), 'Toward Evening', *The New* Yorker, 11 February
—. (1959), 'Should Wizard Hit Mommy?', *The New Yorker*, 13 June
—. (1959) 'Dear Alexandros', *The New Yorker*, 31 October
—. (1961), 'Telephone Poles', *The New Yorker*, 21 January
—. (1961), 'The Astronomer', *The New Yorker*, 1 April
—. (1962), 'The High-Hearts', *The New Yorker*, 24 February
Walden, W. (1962), 'Folk Songs from the Oblivion', *The New Yorker*, 28 April
Weeks, E. (1959), 'The Peripatetic Review', *The Atlantic Monthly*, August
Wells College Cardinal, 1930, Aurora, New York: Wells College
Welty, E. (1946), 'Delta Wedding', *The Atlantic Monthly*, February
—. (1951), 'The Bride of Innisfallen', *The New Yorker*, 1 December
—. (1963), 'Where Is the Voice Coming from?', *The New Yorker*, 6 July
White, E. B. (1969), 'The Art of the Essay No. 1', *The Paris Review*, no. 48 (Fall)
Wilbur, R. (1968), 'Thyme Flowering Among Rocks', *The New Yorker*, 14 December
Williams, T. (1952), 'Three Players of a Summer Game', *The New Yorker*, 1 November
Wilson, E. (1945), 'Briefly Noted', *The New Yorker*, 26 May
—. (1947), 'Books', *The New Yorker*, 8 February
Wray, T. and Lavin, M. (2015), '"Any Story I Would Ever Tell, I Would Certainly Never Write": An Interview with Mary Lavin', *New Hibernia Review*, 19
Wright, J. (1970), 'Echo for the Promise of Georg Trakl's Life', *The New Yorker*, 21 November
Yeats, W. B. (1927), 'Death', *The New Yorker*, 27 April

Index